Axel Busch

Quality-driven Reuse of Model-based Software Architecture Elements

The Karlsruhe Series on Software Design and Quality
Volume 29

Chair Software Design and Quality
Faculty of Computer Science
Karlsruhe Institute of Technology

and

Software Engineering Division
Research Center for Information Technology (FZI), Karlsruhe

Editor: Prof. Dr. Ralf Reussner

Quality-driven Reuse of Model-based Software Architecture Elements

by
Axel Busch

KIT Scientific Publishing

Karlsruher Institut für Technologie
Institut für Programmstrukturen und Datenorganisation

Quality-driven Reuse of Model-based Software Architecture Elements

Zur Erlangung des akademischen Grades eines Doktors der Ingenieurwissenschaften von der KIT-Fakultät für Informatik des Karlsruher Instituts für Technologie (KIT) genehmigte Dissertation

von Axel Busch aus Pirmasens

Tag der mündlichen Prüfung: 13. Juni 2019
Erster Gutachter: Prof. Dr.-Ing. Anne Koziolek
Zweiter Gutachter: Prof. Dr. Sebastian Abeck

Impressum

KIT Scientific Publishing

Karlsruher Institut für Technologie (KIT)
KIT Scientific Publishing
Straße am Forum 2
D-76131 Karlsruhe

KIT Scientific Publishing is a registered trademark
of Karlsruhe Institute of Technology.
Reprint using the book cover is not allowed.

www.ksp.kit.edu

Print on Demand 2019 – Gedruckt auf FSC-zertifiziertem Papier

ISSN 1867-0067
ISBN 978-3-7315-0951-6
DOI: 10.5445/KSP/1000097163

Abstract

In modern software development processes, existing components or libraries are increasingly being used for the implementation of standard functionalities. Functionalities that can be widely used in different systems do not have to be re-developed from scratch. Reuse of functionalities through software components or even complex partial systems, i.e. subsystems, leads to efficient development and higher-quality software.

Due to a multitude of similar solutions for the same functionality, however, software architects often have to decide which solutions they should select and how the configuration in the architecture to be designed best fits the requirements of the whole software system. Subsystems often provide a multitude of higher level functions, i.e. the software features that lead to unclear effects on the quality attributes (e.g. performance) of the target software architecture. Particularly at design time or when new functionality is required, it is unclear whether the quality requirements of the overall system can be met by using a certain feature.

Quality requirements are often operationalized by functions aiming at improving quality. Such operationalized requirements usually have the goal of improving one or more quality attributes, such as security or usability. These quality attributes, however, are often in conflict or influence each other, such as performance and security. At the same time, however, some of these quality attributes are difficult to quantify because suitable functions are often not sufficiently scientifically researched, e.g. security. For others, the evaluation would be too time-consuming or costly, such as for usability user studies. In practice, quality requirements that are difficult to quantify are often neglected or only insufficiently systematically taken into account in the planning of the software system.

Software models can be used to weigh design alternatives at an early stage of the software design process in order to analyse and evaluate the expected quality properties in the software development process. When software architects want to evaluate the effects on the quality attributes of their software architecture due to the use of complex subsystems, many architecture candidates must be evaluated. Through a multitude of combinations and configurations in practice, several thousand architecture candidates have to be evaluated, due to naturally given degrees of freedom in component-based software architectures. A single evaluation of such an amount of candidates is usually not possible due to time and cost constraints. Thus, reusing complex subsystems during software architecture design requires automatic decision support to optimize the quality attributes of the software architecture. In addition, many quality attributes cannot be taken into account in existing automatic decision support processes due to missing quantitative evaluation functions. Thus, by the use of existing approaches questions on quality attributes without quantitative evaluation functions cannot be meaningfully studied. The approach presented in this dissertation, *CompARE*, enables software architects to automatically evaluate effects on the quality attributes of a software architecture resulting from the reuse of models. The approach supports optimization of quality attributes without a quantitative evaluation function by modelling existing informal knowledge by using a qualitative representation. This knowledge can then be used to optimize software architectures together with existing quantitative evaluation functions. Such a method helps software architects to decide i) whether the use of certain features justifies the effects on quality attributes and which interactions are to be expected, ii) which of the possible subsystems and its configuration represents the best choice and iii) whether the given technical implementations fulfils the project requirements.

This dissertation presents the following contributions: First, we present a preliminary study that shows how to develop a quantitative evaluation functions using the example of the quality attribute security in component-based software architectures and discuss required effort. Second, we design a meta model that enables to model subsystems for later reuse. Further, this can be used for automatic model integration. Software architects can then integrate models of subsystems automatically so that they can be evaluated and optimized automatically. Using this method, software architects can automatically reuse desired features in various target architecture models with comparatively low modelling effort. Finally, we show how informal knowledge can be modelled to be analysed and evaluated together with quantitative evaluation functions.

The evaluation is carried out on the basis of two classes of subsystems, each with two different concrete solutions. Each solution provides its own set of features. Further, each solution has its own software architecture and thus influences the quality attributes of the target architecture in which the subsystem will be used. We reuse the subsystems in three target systems to show how architecture design decisions can be optimized by the use of *CompARE*. Two of the target models represent real-world systems that are used in industry, while the other is a community case study that is considered representative in the component-based software architecture modelling community. On the basis of these systems, 11 scenarios are used to demonstrate the analysis of relevant questions regarding software architecture design, decisions on software quality attributes, and software requirement prioritization through a structured process. The evaluation shows the applicability and benefits of *CompARE* and discusses conclusions to be drawn from the results.

Zusammenfassung

In modernen Software-Entwicklungsprozessen werden, insbesondere zur Implementierung von Standardfunktionalitäten, immer häufiger bestehende Komponenten oder Bibliotheken wiederverwendet. So müssen Funktionalitäten, die breite Anwendung in unterschiedlichen Systemen finden können, nicht für jede Verwendung von Grund auf neuentwickelt werden. Wiederverwendung von Funktionalitäten durch Software-Komponenten oder gar von komplexen Teilsystemen, den Subsystemen, die höherwertige Funktionalitäten, die Features, anbieten, führt so zu kosteneffizienterer Entwicklung und qualitativ hochwertigerer Software.

Durch eine Vielzahl ähnlicher Lösungen für die gleiche Standardfunktionalität stehen Software-Architekten allerdings häufig vor der Frage, welche Lösungen sie auswählen sollten und wie deren Konfiguration in der Zielarchitektur optimal zu den Anforderungen an das Software-System passen. Subsysteme bieten häufig eine Vielzahl an Features an, die zu unklaren Effekten auf die Qualitätsattribute der Software-Architektur, wie z.B. auf die Performance, führt. Insbesondere zur Entwurfszeit oder wenn Software-Systeme um Funktionalität erweitert werden soll ist unklar, ob durch die Verwendung eines bestimmten Features eines bestimmten Subsystems die Qualitätsanforderungen an das Gesamtsystem haltbar sind. Neue Qualitätsanforderungen werden zumeist durch Funktionen operationalisiert. Operationalisierte Qualitätsanforderungen haben meist zum Ziel eine oder mehrere Qualitätsattribute, wie z.B. Sicherheit oder Bedienbarkeit, zu verbessern. Gerade diese Qualitätsattribute stehen jedoch häufig gegenseitig oder mit anderen Qualitätsattributen, wie z.B. Performance, in Konflikt oder beeinflussen sich gegenseitig. Gleichzeitig sind diese allerdings schwierig quantifizierbar, weil Funktionen zur quantitativen Evaluation dieser Qualitätsattribute häufig nicht ausreichend wissenschaftlich erforscht sind, wie beispielsweise für das Qualitätsattribut Sicherheit. Die Evaluation selbst kann auch einen zu großen zeitlichen und finanziellen Aufwand erfordern, wie dies beispielsweise bei Nutzerstudien zur Evaluation der Bedienbarkeit der Fall wäre. In der Praxis werden entsprechend schwierig quantifizierbare Qualitätsanforderungen nicht oder nur unzureichend systematisch in der Planung des Software-Systems berücksichtigt.

Zur Analyse von Entwurfsalternativen können Software-Modelle genutzt werden, um möglichst früh im Software-Entwicklungsprozess die zu erwartende Qualität zu analysieren und zu evaluieren. Möchten Software-Architekten die Auswirkungen auf die Qualitätsattribute ihrer Software-Architektur durch die Verwendung von Features realisiert durch komplexe Subsysteme evaluieren, müssen, durch eine Vielzahl an Kombinationen und Konfigurationen, schnell sehr viele Architekturkandidaten evaluiert werden. In der Praxis können, durch natürlich gegebene Freiheitsgrade komponentenbasierter Software-Architekturen, schnell mehrere tausend Architekturkandidaten entstehen. Eine einzelne und manuelle Evaluation einer solch großen Anzahl an Kandidaten ist durch die damit entstehenden Zeit- und somit Kostenaufwände meist nicht möglich. Neben einer Vielzahl an zu evaluierenden Architekturkandidaten können, aufgrund fehlender quantitativer Evaluationsfunktionen, viele Qualitätsattribute nicht in bestehenden automatischen Entscheidungsunterstützungsverfahren berücksichtigt werden. Dadurch zeichnet sich entsprechend ein unvollständiges Bild bei der Suche nach den optimalen Architekturkandidaten. Der in dieser Dissertation vorgestellte Ansatz *CompARE* ermöglicht Software-Architekten, Effekte auf die Qualitätsattribute einer Software-Architektur, die durch die Verwendung von Features entstehen, automatisch zu evaluieren. Auch die Optimierung von Qualitätsanforderungen ohne quantitative Evaluationsfunktion wird unterstützt, indem bestehendes informell vorliegendes Wissen über Architekturentscheidungen modelliert und dadurch zusammen mit bestehenden quantitativen Evaluationsfunktionen optimiert wird. Das Ergebnis soll Software-Architekten dabei unterstützen, zu entscheiden, i) inwiefern die Verwendung von bestimmten Features auf Qualitätsattribute Auswirkungen hat und welche Wechselwirkungen untereinander zu erwarten sind, ii) welches der möglichen Subsysteme und seiner Konfiguration die beste Wahl darstellt und iii) ob die gegebenen technischen Umsetzungen mit den Projektanforderungen vereinbart werden können.

Daraus ergeben sich folgende Beiträge der Arbeit: Zunächst wird eine Vorstudie vorgestellt, die den Aufwand der Erstellung von quantitativen Evaluationsfunktionen, am Beispiel des Qualitätsattributs Sicherheit in komponentenbasierten Software-Architekturen, zeigt. Die Modellierung von wiederverwendbaren Subsystemen zur Verwendung in automatischen Entscheidungsunterstützungsprozessen stellt den ersten Beitrag des *CompARE* Ansatzes dar. Es wird ein Meta-Modell entworfen, das die Modellierung von Subsystemen zur einfachen Wiederverwendung unterstützt und dadurch zur automatischen Modellintegration verwendbar macht. Die automatische Modellintegration von Teilmodellen ist der nächste Beitrag der Arbeit. Hierbei werden Teilmodelle automatisch integriert, so dass diese automatisch evaluiert und optimiert werden können. Durch diese Methode können Software-Architekten Features mit vergleichsweise geringem Modellierungsaufwand automatisiert in die Zielarchitektur einbauen. Schließlich zeigt die Arbeit wie informelles Wissen modelliert werden kann, um es gemeinsam mit quantitativen Funktionen zur Bestimmung von Qualitätseigenschaften zu analysieren und zu evaluieren.

Die Evaluation wird anhand zweier Klassen von Subsystemen mit jeweils zwei unterschiedlich modellierten Lösungen durchgeführt. Jede Lösung bietet verschiedene Features. Dabei hält jede Lösung seine eigene Software-Architektur und beeinflusst dadurch individuell die Qualitätsattribute der Zielarchitektur, in der das Subsystem zum Einsatz gebracht werden wird. Die Wiederverwendung der Subsysteme und die aus dem vorgestellten Ansatz resultierende Architekturoptimierung wird anhand dreier Zielsysteme durchgeführt. Bei diesen Zielsystemen handelt es sich um zwei Realweltsysteme, die in der Industrie zur Anwendung kommen und um eine Community Fallstudie, die in der Community der komponentenbasierten Software-Architekturmodellierung als repräsentativ gilt. Anhand dieser Systeme werden insgesamt 11 Szenarien durchgeführt, die die Analyse relevanter Fragestellungen zu den Themen Software-Architekturentwurf, Entscheidungen mit Bezug auf Software-Qualitätsattribute und Software-Anforderungspriorisierung durch einen strukturierten Prozess analysierbar machen. Dabei wird die Anwendbarkeit und der Nutzen von *CompARE* gezeigt und die aus den Ergebnissen ableitbaren Schlussfolgerungen diskutiert.

Danksagungen

Viele Menschen haben mich inspiriert und unterstützt diese Dissertation zu schreiben. Ihnen möchte ich an dieser Stelle danken.

Zuerst möchte ich meiner Doktormutter Frau Professorin Anne Koziolek danken. In unzähligen Gesprächen hat sie mich stets durch Ihre Ideen und fachlichen Input hervorragend unterstützt und gefördert. Außerdem möchte ich sehr herzlich Herrn Professor Ralf Reussner danken, der schon in meiner Studienzeit mein Interesse für die Wissenschaft geweckt hat. Auch auf sein wertvolles Feedback in Diskussionsrunden konnte ich stets zählen, das mir immer einen wertvollen zweiten Blick auf meine Forschung und Ergebnisse gegeben hat. Weiter möchte ich mich sehr herzlich bei beiden bedanken, dass sie lehrstuhlübergreifend eine tolle Arbeitsatmosphäre schaffen und stets ihre Mitarbeiter unterstützen. Bei Herrn Professor Sebastian Abeck möchte ich mich herzlich bedanken für die übernahme meines Zweitgutachtens und das tolle, informative Gespräch zu meiner Arbeit. Ich möchte mich auch bei den Professoren Oberweis, Böhm und Beckert bedanken, die Interesse für mein Thema gezeigt und mich zum Professorengespräch eingeladen haben.

Ein ganz besonderer und herzlicher Dank geht an meine beste Freundin und Ehefrau Kiana, auf die ich mich immer verlassen kann. Sie hat mich unzählige Male motiviert, unterstützt und mir die Kraft gegeben dieses Werk zu schreiben und schließlich zu vollenden. Von den unzähligen Diskussionen über unsere Forschung konnte ich viel lernen und neue Ideen einbringen. Ebenfalls ein ganz besonderer und herzlicher Dank geht an meine liebe Familie, insbesondere an meine Eltern Vera und Gerhard Busch. Ich kann mich wirklich glücklich schätzen auf ihre Unterstützung mein Leben lang zählen zu dürfen. Sowohl emotional, als auch finanziell konnte und kann ich mich immer auf sie verlassen. Ich empfinde dies als großes Glück.

Weiter möchte ich mich bei meinen lieben Kollegen der beiden Lehrstühle ARE und SDQ bedanken, ihren fachlichen Input bei Gesprächen, für ihre Freundlichkeit, Ihr Verständnis und ihr freundschaftliches Miteinander.

Ein besonderer Dank geht ebenfalls an Maximilian Eckert, Dominik Fuchß, Jan Keim, Max Scheerer, Yves Schneider und Dominik Werle. Ich möchte mich sehr herzlich für die tolle Zusammenarbeit bei Abschlussarbeiten, Forschung, Implementierungstätigkeiten und Publikationsprojekten bedanken. Es freut mich zu sehen, dass ich bei Yves Schneider, Max Scheerer und Jan Keim das Interesse an der Wissenschaft wecken und sie für eine Promotion begeistern konnte. Ebenfalls herzlich bedanken möchte ich mich bei Professor Jörg Hettel, der mich gerade in den Anfängen als Informatikstudent besonders unterstützt hat und motiviert hat den höchsten akademischen Grad anzustreben.

Solche Eltern, Freunde und Kollegen zu haben macht mich stolz und glücklich.

Preliminary remark

Use of "we"

In this dissertation, for a better flow of reading I use the term “we” instead of the use of “I”. However, I would like to emphasize that the work is my own contribution and any parts that have been created in cooperation with third parties have been explicitly marked.

Contents

1. Introduction

1.1. Motivation

In the recent years, it has been shown that software systems has become more and more complex. Software systems take over tasks which have previously been taken over by human actors. As a result, software systems are given real responsibilities, such as processing payments, surveillance of critical infrastructures, or handling claims in insurance companies. Such kinds of responsibilities are no longer tasks that play any subordinate role. Rather, these are critical activities that can be crucial for the success of modern business models. Although the success of modern business models depends on the functionality of the software system, non-functional attributes are no less important. However, designing a system with many features satisfying high quality and cost constraints is often challenging, since achieving higher quality often requires more resources. In modern software development approaches reuse has been established as common practice. To avoid errors and build software more cost-efficiently software architects reuse (third-party) libraries or use repositories containing ready to be used COTS-components (Commercial Off The Self).

Today, software architects have to cope with highly complex software systems, high demands on functionality, quality and cost boundaries. To meet the requirements on functionality, high quality, and costs, more and more solutions for functions or even solutions for whole subsystems are taken from COTS-repositories and integrated in the system under development.

1.2. Challenges

When reusing functions or subsystems, there are often many solutions on the market that fulfil a similar set of functionalities but have different quality and costs. A growing market of COTS components leads to many products that are potentially suitable for the implementation of requirements [Com+02]. The high number of different similar solutions makes the product selection complex, time-consuming, costly and increases the risk of selecting the wrong product. In order to evaluate possible solutions, they must usually be purchased, installed, and executed using typical scenarios. The high effort of such evaluations often leads to the fact that possible solutions are not carried out or carried out only to a limited extent. This makes a software development process less efficient and increases the risk to not achieve the necessary quality and cost compliance.

Using model-driven techniques helps to predict quality and costs for a given software architecture at design time and provide the (Pareto-)optimal solutions as feedback. However, previously existing solutions only provide support if the product to be used has already been selected, but lack the support for selecting the best matching product from all products on the market. Even if software architects are already familiar with the class of products, they still have to integrate all models of the products on the market into their existing software architecture models. With many solutions and many variation possibilities, this is a time-consuming and possibly error-prone task.

Subsystems for monitoring system services rather contribute to the actual business requirements. They often belong to the class of quality improvement activities. In existing decision support processes it is often only possible to either evaluate quantified knowledge or qualitatively modelled knowledge.

However, many quality attributes cannot be modelled quantitatively, e.g. due to non existing quantitative functions or too high quantitative modelling effort. They are often too time-consuming and cost-intensive, e.g. for studies on the usability of graphical user interfaces. Usability tests that have to be performed with many participants can quickly result in high costs, starting at under 10.000 $ up to more than 100.000 $ [Jef; Nie97]. Budget constraints often make it difficult to conduct such investigations systematically. However, experienced software architects often have an implicit understanding of the quality properties of software architectures. The implicit understanding often cannot be represented by quantitative functions. On the basis of their implicit understanding they can reason on quality attributes of a given software architecture. Such reasoning remains unconsidered in previous model-driven approaches.

In this work, we develop novel approaches to improve the software development process in order to cope with complex software systems. In particular, the approaches provide automated decision support for software architects at design time and functional extension scenarios whenever complex subsystems are subject to reuse and the resulting quality plays an important role.

To this end, we formulated three main challenges for supporting the decision support process that are considered in this dissertation. In the following, we describe challenges and solution ideas in more detail:

1. **Reusing Models of Subsystems:** Software architecture models represent an abstraction of the software architecture of a particular software system. Such models are essential artefacts in model-driven prediction approaches. Reusing models of subsystems for typical problem domains, e.g. intrusion detection, and data logging is often hard. Often, functional similar solutions of the subsystem have inhomogeneous software architectures and several degrees of freedom manually. The inhomogeneous architecture comes from different design decisions and different levels of abstraction that were made by different architects. For example, a database management system and the corresponding data access interface may be modelled by one or several components. Both results may be well-designed models – depending on the pragmatism of the model. Different degrees of freedom come from their provided functionalities and possibilities to be integrated in another software architecture. Reusing such complex models in automated decision support processes cannot be carried out by related approaches.

   To reuse models of different subsystem solution alternatives in different contexts in automated decision support approaches, a formalism is required to unification. As a result, such a uniform formalism can be applied to several subsystem solution alternatives and can finally be used in systematic processes for automated analysis.

2. **Model Weaving:** Reusing features of a subsystem in a base architecture model requires integration of the software components of the particular subsystem solution. Automated decision support for different solutions of a subsystem needs automatic integration of the software components of a subsystem solution in the base architecture. Otherwise, software architects may have to integrate each subsystem solution into the base software architecture and their individual degrees of freedom manually. Manual generation of many model candidates can be very time-consuming and error prone. Therefore, a mechanism is required to automatically integrate models of subsystem solutions into the base software architecture model. This would allow comparing the effects on quality attributes when reusing features broken down according to the different subsystem solutions on the market automatically.

   Supporting architects at making design decisions without the need of manual application requires an approach for automated model weaving according to a formal description.

3. **Quality Reasoning:** Subsystems are often reused in another system, i.e. base systems, to fulfil functional or quality requirements and the base system's quality attributes. Often, they influence quality attributes that cannot be evaluated model-based by quantitative functions, due to a lack of suitable functions. Let us assume we reuse the subsystem *intrusion detection system* that allows detecting attacks on system components, and the subsystem solution *OWASP AppSensor* [Mel15]. Software architects may include such a system to fulfil or improve security attributes of the system. Even though, there is no quantitative function to assess the security quality properties. Also, other important quality attributes like usability cannot be evaluated by functions. Nevertheless, software architects may have an experience based reasoning on the security and usability. In typical quantitative decision support approaches such knowledge cannot be adequately analysed and

therefore remains unconsidered. The experience and implicit knowledge of developers, however, affects the design decisions they make. Omitting such knowledge from decision support processes would degrade the results due to a lack of information.

To support software architects in the quality reasoning process requires representations and analysis techniques for such informal knowledge and a method for evaluating them together with quantitative functions.

1.3. Approach & Contributions

The contributions of this dissertation extend automatic methods for the improvement of component-based software architectures based on model-based quality predictions. The proposed methods focus on reuse of complex models of third-party solutions considering recurring problems, such as payment processing, logging, intrusion detection, or access control. The developed approach allows optimization methods to apply and evaluate new degrees of freedom during the software architecture design. Software architects should be able to create the configuration of the models to be evaluated with comparatively low effort.

The method automatically explores solutions of the same interest, e.g. Logging, and evaluates them on the basis of the configured quality attributes. The method extends the set of usually (quantitatively determined) quality attributes, such as performance, reliability and costs, by any (not quantitatively determined) quality attributes, such as security and usability. The result is a set of optimal architecture candidates, i.e. the Pareto-optimal architecture candidates, that have been determined based on several quality criteria within the design space. On the basis of these criteria, software architects get i) the optimal selection of functionalities to reuse in their base system, ii) which concrete solution is optimal from the large number of products, and iii) how the selected features influence the quality attributes of the overall system. These results can be used to select the optimal software architecture and can be used as basis to discuss the requirements together with stakeholders on a well-founded data basis. Thus, software requirements can be iteratively improved and prioritized. The contribution considers the following four major aspects:

- We analyze the effort required to design a quantitative method for evaluating quality attributes using the example of the quality attribute security in component-based software architectures. We show how such a method can be developed to analyse the required effort for its development.
- We extend a process model for the design of component-based systems by a new method presented to evaluate the effects on quality attributes when reusing models of complex subsystems. In addition, we examine further scenarios in which our method can be applied and discuss its possible benefits.
- We describe a meta model that structures models of complex systems despite inhomogeneous software architecture to automatically integrate into a base system. In addition, our meta models abstract from the particular implementations of the subsystem solutions. Thus, their reuse in any base system becomes possible without knowledge of the architecture of each individual subsystem solution.
- We design a method for modelling and analysing non-quantitative quality attributes based on qualitative reasoning. We combine this method with quantitative evaluation methods. Finally, we use the combination to extend trade-off analysis between quality attributes, optimization of software architectures, and requirements prioritization.

1.4. Motivating Scenario

Reuse of functionality encapsulated in software components has long been common practice in component-based software development processes. When user traffic should be recorded in a web shop scenario in order to improve the customer experience and thus increase the number of sales, experienced software architects use existing solutions.

Software architects rely on their experience to select the best solution for the given scenario. They are familiar with the existing products, that we call solutions in the following, on the market in the system's domain. They select a suitable solution based on both functional requirements and quality requirements and integrate this solution at the appropriate positions in the base system.

However, this requires in-depth expertise in various areas: Software architects must have expert knowledge in the system's domain and be familiar with the relevant functionalities and quality attributes and solutions on the market. Without the support of model-based simulations they can often only estimate the impact of the solution on quality attributes such as performance, reliability or other quality attributes. In addition, they must have detailed knowledge of the internal architecture and functionalities of both the architecture of the target system and the subsystem to be integrated.

In order to include solutions in the base system properly, software architects often first have to learn about the domains. However, this is a very lengthy, time-consuming and therefore costly process. Only a subset of the different solutions on the market can usually be evaluated. Promising solutions may therefore be missed through time and cost constraints.

In addition to selecting the appropriate solution, the best possible placement in the base architecture is unclear. In the scenario previously outlined, the naive assessment of the best possible placement of sensors to capture user traffic would be simple: at all points in the software architecture user traffic should be recorded. Such a realization would have the assumption in mind collecting as many data as possible has a positive effect on the correct evaluation of user traffic. However, frequently capturing data causes a correspondingly frequent call to the routine responsible for recording data. The more data is recorded, the better is the results of the analysis. At the same time, however, the latency of the actual user request increases due to higher resource utilization of CPU, HDD, and LAN. Further, it worsens the maintainability of the software code parts that implement the actual business requirements. Amazon has found that 100 ms longer response time leads to approximately 1 % less successful purchases in its web shop [Nat19]. In 2006, Marissa Mayer, then vice president of Google, reported a 20 % reduction in search queries if the search engine's response time was extended by 0.5 seconds [Mar06; Gre06]. Considering that response time has a direct impact, for example, on purchases in an online store, a negative impact on system performance is a critical quality attribute. Such critical quality attributes, having direct impact on the company's sales, performance and competitiveness, must be evaluated at design time for each design decisions.

In this case, the relentless record of user traffic would harm two other requirements, namely ensuring high performance of the overall system and good maintainability for later extension of business requirements. Finding good trade-off decisions when reusing features with higher complexity, such as *record user traffic* is the challenge supported by the *CompARE* approach.

CompARE should enable software architects making good decisions considering functional requirements and quality requirements of the software project. In-depth knowledge of the requirement's domain, solutions and knowledge about potential effects of different placement positions in the software architecture is not required for automated analysis on the quality attributes of the whole software system. This allows critical wrong decisions on software architecture or requirements to be identified before the actual implementation. Boehm and Basili estimated [BB01] every phase of the software development process that has to be repeated due to errors causing an increase in costs by a factor of 10. Early avoidance of wrong decisions, especially errors in the early phases, is therefore particularly important.

1.5. Outline

The overview of this work can be described as follows:

Chapter 1 introduces and motivates this dissertation. Section 1.1 introduces a general motivation. Section 1.2 starts with the introduction of challenges. In Section 1.3, we briefly introduce the approach and contributions of this work. Finally, in Section 1.4, we introduce a motivating scenario that briefly introduces problems and typical cases this work considers.

Chapter 2 introduces our example systems. In Section 2.1, we briefly describe the requirements for example systems and then introduce use cases, and their software architectures. Altogether in section 2.2 we introduce two systems, while the first system represents the base system, and in Section 2.3 the second system represents a subsystem to be built into the base system. Based on these two systems, the concepts introduced in the following chapters will be explained and applied to several examples.

Part I comprises basic concepts, related work, and introduces our preliminary study on modelling a quantitative function to evaluate the quality attribute security. Chapter 3 introduces foundation this dissertation is basing on. Section 3.1 introduces software architectures and software architecture models. Section 3.2 introduces the terminology about software quality, quality attributes, and basic knowledge on modelling architecture knowledge. In Section 3.3, we introduce basic concepts about the optimization of software architecture models. This is followed by an introduction to component-based software development and model-based software development in Section 3.4

Chapter 4 describes related work. Section 4.1 introduces approaches considering modelling knowledge and the use of such models in decision-making approaches. Section 4.2 provides an overview of approaches for automatic model generation and variability modelling. Finally, Section 4.3 we give an overview of automatic, semi-automatic, and manual approaches to optimize or improve software architectures regarding quality attributes.

Chapter 5 introduces our preliminary study on quantitative modelling of quality attributes. This chapter shows required steps to develop such an evaluation function for quality attributes and to evaluate the effort we used for the development. We conduct this preliminary study developing an evaluation function for security in component-based software architecture models. After the motivation in Section 5.1, in Section 5.2 we introduce the overview of the approach for quantifying security in component-based software architectures. In Section 5.3, we describe the basic concepts and then formalize in Section 5.4 the concepts using a Semi-Markov process. We then evaluate the approach in Section 5.5 using an example system. Section 5.6 applies the approach to a component-based software architecture model, the Palladio Component Model (PCM). In Section 5.7, we briefly discuss related approaches, while Section 5.8 describes limitations of the approach. Section 5.9 discusses the effort that is required to develop the approach. Finally, we summarize the approach in Section 5.10.

Part II of this dissertation considers the quality-driven reuse of software architecture models. **Chapter 6** describes our approach, namely the Component-based Architecture and Requirements Evaluation (CompARE) approach. Section 6.1 introduces terms, definitions and roles in the context of *CompARE*. In Section 6.2, we introduce prerequisites for the approach, while in Section 6.3 we introduce the goals of *CompARE*. Section 6.4 introduces the big picture of *CompARE*. In Section 6.5 we introduce the integration of *CompARE* into the Component-Based Software Engineering process (CBSE). Finally, in Section 6.6, we introduce possible scenarios in which the CBSE extended by *CompARE* can be used, discuss in Section 6.7 assumptions and limitations, and close in Section 6.8 with a summary.

Chapter 7 describes all entities that are necessary for reusing subsystems and the solution of subsystems. In Section 7.1, we introduce relevant roles and requirements for the entities. In Section 7.2, we explain the formalization of the entities with regard to modelling, use, and automatic weaving of models. In Section 7.3, we briefly introduce how the formalized entities could be applied to software architecture models. Subsequently, in Section 7.4, we structure all formalisms in a hierarchical model to separate the concerns according to role and process of use, discuss in Section 7.5 assumptions and limitations, and close in Section 7.6 with a summary.

Chapter 8 introduces formalisms and mechanisms of weaving sub model and introduces new degrees of freedom resulting from the previous formalisms. We introduce the chapter in Section 8.1 with a brief discussion how to extend software architecture models. Afterwards, in Section 8.2 we describe the model synchronization and change propagation in order to extend software architecture models. Section 8.3 and Section 8.4 describes how to extend software architecture models using adapters and the abstract behaviour respectively. In Section 8.5, we demonstrate the concepts and mechanisms using the Palladio Component Model as an example. Several concepts of architecture constraints are proposed in Section 8.6. Section 8.7 introduces software architecture degrees of freedom arising from adapter extension and abstract behaviour extension, discuss in Section 8.8 assumptions and limitations, and close in Section 8.9 with a summary.

Chapter 9 introduces the modelling and analysis of architectural knowledge. First, in Section 9.1, we extend existing mechanisms and thus make it possible to model informal knowledge qualitatively. In Section 9.2, we then use these model concepts to carry out analyses using qualitative reasoning. In Section 9.3, we then describe how the newly defined models can then be used to evaluate qualitative knowledge together with quantitatively modelled knowledge, discuss in Section 9.4 assumptions and limitations, and close in Section 9.5 with a summary.

Part III of this dissertation considers the evaluation of the *CompARE* approach and discusses findings from the results.

Chapter 10 introduces the evaluation and the case study systems. Section 10.1 introduces validation levels and evaluation questions relevant for the evaluation, while Section 10.2 describes our evaluation concept. Section 10.3 introduces how *CompARE* has been integrated into a tool, namely the design decision support tool PerOpteryx, to evaluate *CompARE*. For the evaluation we use two subsystems, each with two subsystem solutions, and three base systems. We introduce the subsystem solutions in Section 10.4, the alignment to our meta model in Section 10.5 and the base systems in Section 10.6 in detail.

Chapter 11 introduces the first part of our evaluation, regarding the model inclusion of features into software architectures. Six scenarios and several sub scenarios demonstrate how models of software systems can be extended by subsystems.

Chapter 12 introduces the second part of our evaluation, the combination of qualitative and quantitative knowledge. Using four scenarios, we provide insights on the modelling of quantitative knowledge and the evaluation in combination with quantitative modelled knowledge. Overall, we show the applicability and possible benefits of model weaving for the component-based software engineering process on the example of several scenarios related on real-world decisions. In addition, we discuss possible benefits of the combination of qualitative and quantified knowledge in automated decision support processes.

Chapter 13 introduces an additional scenario showing how requirements and quality attributes can be systematically evaluated. The scenario considers subsystem positions and subsystem solutions in a setting that is related to realistic environments and design questions, while **Chapter 14** gives a summary of the scenarios and further concludes the evaluation.

Chapter 15 discusses future work in Section 15.1 and gives final conclusions in Section 15.2.

2. Example Systems

This chapter is intentionally used to introduce the concepts of the approach discussed in this thesis using example systems. On the basis of the running example, the concepts of this dissertation are motivated and applied in the following chapters. We use a UML-like representation to make it easier to understand. Our approach aims at evaluating design decisions that introduces new functionality by features within the design of an application. Several design entities should already exist so that they can be used as a basis. However, this existing software architecture can also be in an early design phase and does not have to be completed yet. Existing systems and systems extending others by functionalities are defined as follows:

- *Base system:* The base system is a software system fulfilling several functionalities. The system should be open for extensions by additional functionalities, as provided by subsystems. We call the software architecture of the base system the base (software) architecture.
- *Extending system:* An extending system fulfils functionalities that are usually used as service providers, such as subsystems, for other systems. They intent to be used in a broader context, but not as stand-alone systems.

2.1. Prerequisites for the Example Systems

This section describes the prerequisites of all example systems for the applicability of all concept presented in this dissertation.

2.1.1. Base System

In this subsection, we will introduce the prerequisites for the system used as base system in order apply the concepts and mechanisms of *CompARE.*

- *Type of system:* The kind of systems must be information-processing. The system should not initiate an action for itself, but should be dependent on being activated by a human actor or another external system.
- *Component-based system:* The example systems used as base system must have a component-based structure, or it must be possible to identify individual concerns in the system. In other words, the system must not be constructed monolithically. A reasonable separation of interests must be given in the architecture model.
- *Task distribution concept:* Highly scalable, modern systems are designed to allow distributed processing of data. The use of this work focuses on this type of distributed systems. The running example systems should therefore also allow distributed processing of the tasks.
- *Quality concerns:* Modern software systems often consist of different requirements from different stakeholders involved in the project. Often, many quality attributes have to be taken into account in order to meet the requirements of the stakeholders. However, often not all quality attributes can be improved by an optimization at the same time, i.e. the improvement of one quality attribute results in a degradation of another quality attribute. Therefore, trade-off decisions often have to be made between several quality attributes. In particular, functionality can be reused for the purpose of improving one or more quality attributes of the base system: for example, the use of an access control system has the purpose of increasing the overall security of the system by restricting access to certain groups of people. At the same time, this decision has an impact on other quality attributes such as the maintainability of the system. Since the optimization of software architectures regarding its quality attributes is the focus of this

work, the model of the running example must support several quality attributes, such as performance, costs, security and usability.

- *Degrees of freedom:* The optimization of software architecture models requires several possibilities to (automatically) adapt the architecture model to improve the software architecture (according to the requirements). In this work, current degrees of freedom such as component exchange, allocation configuration and hardware selection described in the foundations are extended by further degrees of freedom. We focus on optimizing the software architecture when reusing functionality represented by features and their different possibilities of integration into the existing base software architecture. Simultaneously we consider their effects on the quality attributes (such as performance). The current example must therefore contain possibilities for exchanging components, allocation configuration and hardware selection. It must support extensions for additional degrees of freedom coming from automated feature-driven extension of the software architecture models.
- *Extendability:* In order to realize the additional degree of freedom, it must be possible to extend an existing software architecture with additional components and their interdependencies. The base system must be open for extending the corresponding software architecture model with new components and thus new functionality.

2.1.2. Extending system

In this subsection, we introduce the prerequisites of the system, which we use to extend the base system by additional features to demonstrate the concepts and mechanisms of *CompARE*.
Several requirements of the extending system correspond as far as possible to those of the base system:

- *Type of system:* The system must process information to allow the integration into the base system.

- *Task distribution concept:* The system must be able to be distributed among several resource containers to span degrees of freedom.
- *Quality concerns:* To evaluate quality attributes, the system must have appropriate quality annotations. As before, these are quality annotations for performance and cost.

In addition to the prerequisites that correspond to the prerequisites of the application context, the design decision objective must fulfil the following prerequisites:

- *Realization of requirements:* The system must implement requirements driven by reusable features and worth to be integrated into the base system.
- *Separated concerns:* The software architecture of the system must comprise several concerns. These concerns must be possible to divide in separated parts.

2.2. Base system: Media Store

The Media Store system is introduced in [Reu+16; SK16]. The main concepts presented here are based on this design. We have extended the original PCM software architecture of the Media Store to better demonstrate several concepts of our approaches.

The Media Store system implements a system to store audio files. Users can upload audio files to make them available to other users and also download audio files for their own use. Before uploading, a user can specify the metadata of an audio file. To make it easier to find files, there is a catalogue that lists all available audio files. The user can then select the audio file for download. Before downloading the audio files, users can configure their preferred bit rate. A user can also select multiple audio files for simultaneous downloads. For easier download, all selected files are bundled in one download archive.

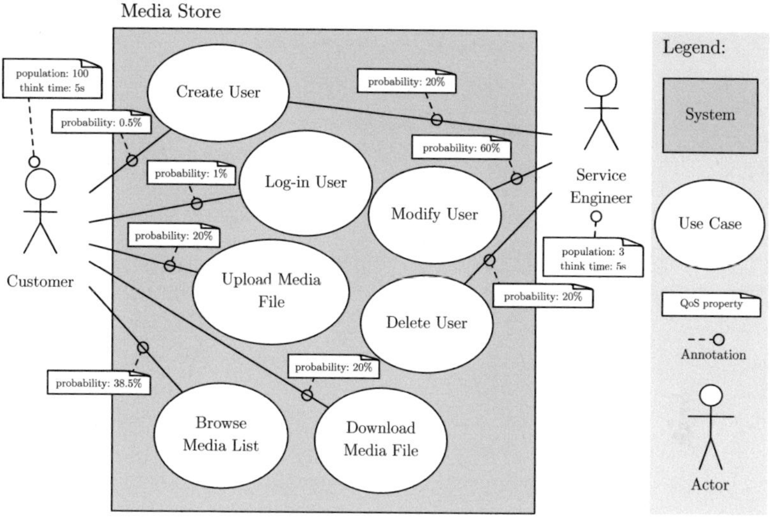

Figure 2.1.: Use-case diagram of the Media Store system enriched with a usage scenario.

2.2.1. Media Store's Use Cases

The Media Store system supports use cases considered by two actors namely the *customer* and the *service engineer.* Customers represent the primary actors, while service engineers represents the secondary actors. Customer use the business functions of the system while service engineers processes service functions such as processing incorrect entries in the user database. All users of the system call functions with certain probabilities. Figure 2.1 illustrates the use cases of Media Store.

Customers create new user accounts for 0.5 % and logs on the system in 1 % of all cases. In 38.5 %, they search the media library while uploading or downloading media files for 20 % of all cases each.

Service employees create a new user in 20 % of all cases. In 60 % of all cases they modify user data, while they delete a user in 20 % of the cases.

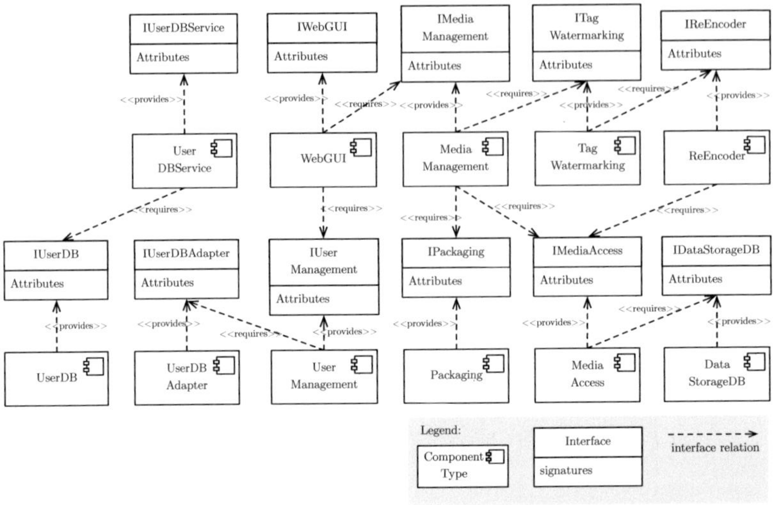

Figure 2.2.: Illustration of the Media Store system repository model.

The definition of our business scenario workload is 100 concurrent users in the system at the same time. In addition to the users, three service engineers are simultaneously using the system.

The main task of the system is therefore to transfer information. The system can represent a typical business information system.

2.2.2. System components

Media Store is internally designed as a component-based software architecture. Components and interfaces are represented in the repository. Figure 2.2 illustrates the repository and the provided and required interfaces of the components. The Media Store comprises eleven components:

The `WebGUI` component delivers the user interface (web page) to the user and handles session management. The `MediaManagement` component coordinates the communication between the WebGUI and other components of the system. Its main task is to process the individual steps required for downloading and uploading audio files in the correct order. The `TagWatermarking` component encodes a digital watermark on top of the actual audio file. The watermark allows to uniquely associate a downloaded audio file with a user. The `ReEncoder` component is responsible for decoding an audio file at a user defined bit rate. The `Packaging` component bundles several user-selected audio files into a single archive. The `MediaAccess` component coordinates access to audio files, such as downloading or uploading a file when a user is searching for a file in the audio catalogue or when a user requests a download or upload of a file. In addition, the component supports to edit metadata. The `DataStorage` component contains the metadata for existing audio files. The raw data is stored directly in the file system of the operating system and can be accessed using the metadata. The `UserManagement` component handles requests for the initial user registration and authentication. It forwards the requests to the database using the `UserDBAdapter`. The authentication data is salted and hashed by the user management component. The `UserDBAdapter` receives requests from the UserManagement component and generates JDBC statements for user data requests in the database with the user data database. User data for user authentication is stored in the `UserDB` component. This component answers queries from the UserDBAadapter. Finally, for maintenance purposes, the `UserDBService` can be used to manage the users in the UserDB.

2.2.3. System Architecture

As the client-server architecture of the Media Store system, we use a three-tier architecture that comprise presentation, application and data management functions. We have decided to model a three-tier architecture for a realistic scenario that is a common pattern of multi-tier architectures [Fow02]. Often, three tier-architectures comprises three layers, namely presentation, domain, and data source layer. A graphical illustration of the system architecture is shown in Figure 2.3.

The Media Store system is distributed across three server systems: the frontend server, the middleware server and the back end server. The WebGUI component is deployed on the frontend server, while the two database components and DataStorage are deployed on the back end server. Further,

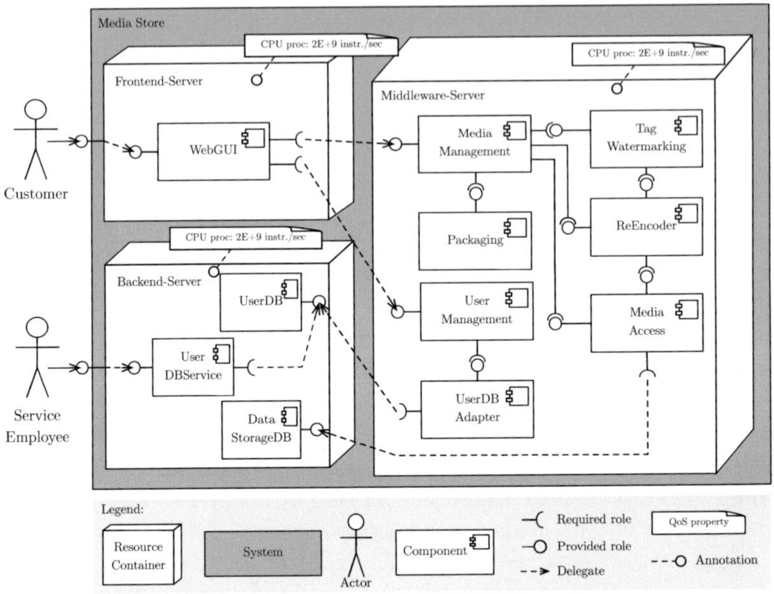

Figure 2.3.: Component-based software architecture and example deployment of the Media Store system.

the service interface UserDBService that is used to manage user data is deployed on the back-end server. All other components of the business logic are deployed on the middleware server. An overview of the distribution of the components among the resources is shown in Table 2.1.

In addition, the resource containers are annotated with QoS annotations that represent the performance of the hardware. The Media Store System focuses on modelling CPU resource requirements. Therefore, the resource containers are only annotated with the CPU hardware configuration. Each of the three resource containers is equipped with a 2 GHz processor.

The system architecture of the components can be divided into two areas for easier comprehensibility: Access to media files and access to user data. Each customer demands the Media Store system's service by the WebGUI component. The WebGUI component requires two other components to provide its service: The MediaManagement component, which is responsible for

Layer	Resource Container	Component	System provides interfaces
Presentation	Frontend	WebGUI	IWebGUI
Application	Middleware	MediaManagement TagWatermarking ReEncoder Packaging MediaAccess UserManagement UserDBAdapter	
Data Management	Backend	UserDB UserDBService DataStorageDB	IUserDBService

Table 2.1.: Allocation of Media Store components to architecture layers, resource containers, and system provides interfaces.

accessing media files, and the UserManagement component, which provides user login and session handling. Access to media files works as follows: For media management purposes, the MediaManagement component accesses services of the TagWatermarking component, the MediaAccess component and the Packaging component. The TagWatermarking component must re-encode the video stream using the ReEncoder to add a watermark. The ReEncoder requires corresponding access to the raw data, which it also receives from the MediaAccess component. The Media access component finally obtains the raw data by accessing the DataStorageDB component.

The second area, namely access to user data, is provided by the UserManagement component: It first calls the UserDBAdapter, which can query the corresponding user data from the UserDB. Alternatively, the service engineer can directly access the data of the UserDB by bypassing the UserManagament with the help of the UserDBService component.

On the basis of the previously introduced system architecture two external system interfaces can be derived that the actors can use to demand the system services. The customer demands the services via the IWebGUI interface while the service engineer uses the IUserDBService interface for managing user data (see section 2.2.1).

2.2.4. Internal Process

Representing the internal processes of the Media Store system, we show a concrete process, namely the process of the processFile service of the MediaManagement component. Figure 2.4 shows the internal process. The process begins with an internal action that causes a CPU resource demand of 40.000 units. Then the control flow is distributed, depending on the state of the file: If the file is not encoded yet, an external action is called, where the file is encoded (namely by the service *encode* of the component ReEncoder). This encoding process depends on the bit rate passed by an InputVariableUsage. If the file is already encoded, it is decoded. This is done via an external call action to the service *decode* of the ReEncoder component.

2.2.5. Quality of Service Attributes

The models of the hardware and software components of the Media Store system come with different QoS annotations, that model different quality properties and can be used to evaluate different quality attributes by using objective functions. Three types of annotations are used: annotations for performance, modelling the Service Effect Specification (SEFFs) and the cost of the system. To explain the concepts of *CompARE*, presented in this dissertation, we focus on the performance annotations.

To model the QoS annotations for performance, the PCM uses an abstract description of the behaviour of the internal processes of system components, the (resource demanding) Service Effect Specification (RD-SEFF). For introducing the example, the concepts of SEFF and RD-SEFF is only briefly introduced. Section 3.1.2.1 and Section 3.2.4 introduce the concepts in detail. The component developer models the behaviour of the components and between the components using the SEFF. Internal actions abstract from instructions executed within the component. Internal actions therefore represent code blocks or calls of further methods. If components require

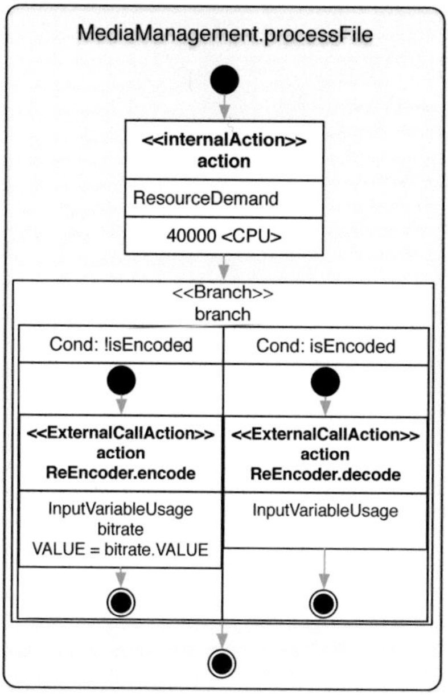

Figure 2.4.: Internal process (SEFF) of the service processFile of the MediaManagament component.

additional services of other components to provide its own service, the external call actions within the SEFF can be used to access the required services of other components.

For a full-featured description of the QoS attribute performance, only modelling the abstract control-flow is not sufficient. In addition, we must model resource demands at hardware level that are caused by internal actions. The resource demand service effect specification (RD-SEFF) extends the SEFF by hardware resource demands of the components. That could be milliseconds or CPU instructions required per internal action. These values can be derived, for example, from profiling or performance measurement tools.

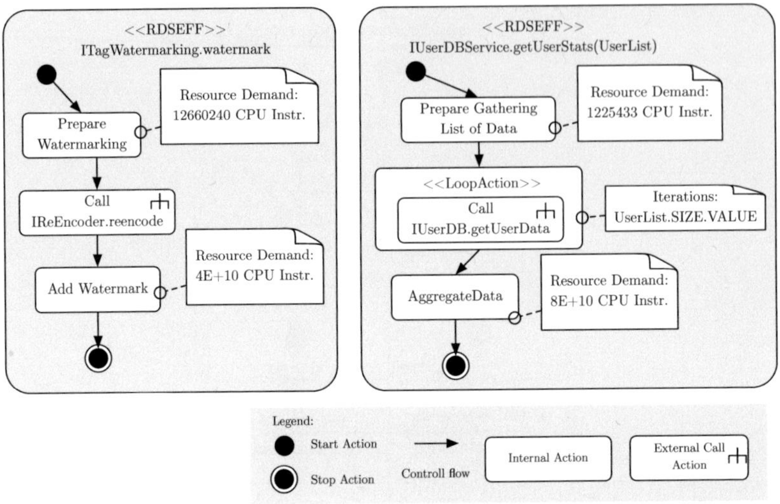

Figure 2.5.: RD-SEFF of the services watermark of the ITagWatermarking interface and getUserStats of the IUserDBService interface of the Media Store PCM model.

Figure 2.5 shows a UML-like representation of the RD-SEFFs for the service `watermark` (left-hand side) of the `ITagWatermarking` interface and the service `getUserStats` (right-hand side) of the `IUserDBService` interface.

The RD-SEFF *watermark* begins with an internal action, namely the preparation of adding the watermark to the video (and audio) stream. This operation results in a resource demand of 12660240 CPU instructions. After the preparation, the re-encoding of the corresponding component is called. The control flow is passed on to the component (not shown in the picture) that actually process the encoding. The watermark RD-SEFF is finally continued with the internal action `Add Watermark`. Add Watermark adds the actual watermark (by an internal action) and thus creates a resource demand of $4 \cdot 10^{10}$ CPU instructions.

The second RD-SEFF, `getUserStats` of the `IUserDBService` interface prepares the request of the list of user data (i.e. `Prepare Gathering List of Data`) by an internal action. This results in a resource demand of 1225433 CPU instructions. In the next step, the RD-SEFF demands the external call action `getUserData` of the `IUserDB` interface within a loop until all users in the *UserList* have been successfully queried. At the end, the user data is aggregated using an internal action. The aggregation function of the internal action requires $8 \cdot 10^{10}$ CPU instructions.

In addition to the two RD-SEFFs described in detail, the Media Store model comprises several other RD-SEFFs. We have, however, omitted them from this example description because their more detailed description is not relevant for the explaining and applying *CompARE*.

2.2.6. Degrees of Freedom

The Media Store has several degrees of freedom given by its component-based structure, namely component exchange, resource scaling and deployment configuration.

- Component exchange: The Media Store comes with interface equivalent alternatives for several components. These components provide the same functionality but differ in quality and thus influence the overall quality of the system. For example, in the Media Store system both watermarking components can be used as alternatives to each other.
- Resource selection: The resources of the three resource containers of the Media Store system can selected. On the basis of 2 GHz clock frequency, the frequency can be adjusted at design time. Higher frequency corresponds to higher costs and vice versa.
- Allocation configuration: The allocation configuration shown in Figure 2.3 and summarized in Table 2.1 can be changed. The components defined in the system can be distributed over the three available resource containers. If the resource demand is low to use less than three servers would make the system cheaper. In each case, differences in the overall performance of the services can be expected.

2.2.7. Expanding Points

Due to its component-based structure, the Media Store system offers expanding points on every component of the system. All provided and required interfaces can be expanded with additional features or functionality (e.g. by adding additional components). This results in a total of 13 possible expansion points in the media store system.

2.3. Extending system: Logging System log4j

Log4j version 2.0[1](in the following referred to as log4jv2) is a system widely used. Log4jv2 is a java-based[2] framework for logging data. log4jv2 is a system that can be reused in any application, is complex in its architecture due to its 6 components, and is always used in the context of other systems. It provides several services in the area of logging, that can be reused in base systems. Log4jv2 is flexibly configurable and supports different modes for formatting the recorded data. In addition, log4jv2 offers various options for storing the data, such as saving it in a database, outputting the data to the console or to a file.

2.3.1. log4jv2 Use Cases

A extending system is usually not accessed by human actors, as shown in the Media Store system example. Its provided services are used by delegation triggered by other systems, such as the base system Media Store. Accordingly, there is only one actor, namely the base system. Therefore, the Media Store would demand the services of log4j. For the running example we have selected and modelled a subset of the implemented features, which are representative for log4j on the one hand and are suitable for explaining the mechanisms of the presented approach on the other hand.

[1] https://logging.apache.org/log4j/2.x/

[2] There are already ports to various other programming languages, such as C, C++, C#, Python, etc.

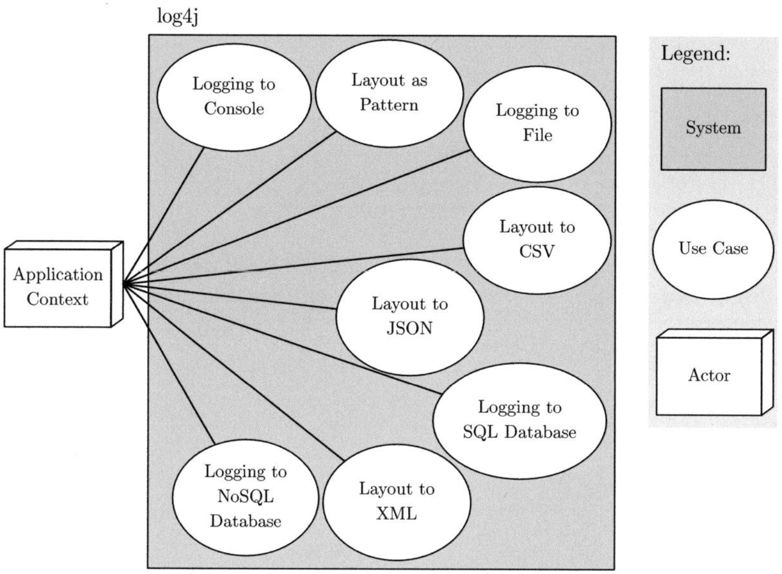

Figure 2.6.: Use case diagram of the log4jv2 system.

Log4j supports two categories of use cases: It supports functions for logging data and persisting them at a selected destination and to select a certain logging format.

In the first category, the logging of data can be configured as follows: Logging to the console, logging to a file, logging to an SQL database, and logging to a NoSQL database. In the second category different types of layouts can be selected. We can select the types CSV, JSON format, XML and formatting according to a certain pattern. In contrast to the base system, it does not make sense to build a usage model for the extending system. In this context the user profile depends in particular on the execution profile of the base system.

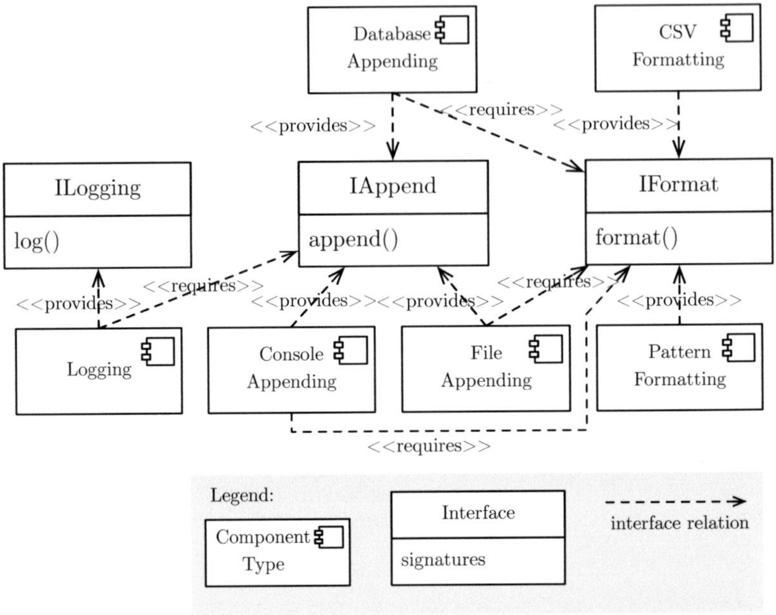

Figure 2.7.: Simplified repository diagram of the extending system log4j 2.0.

2.3.2. System components

Like the Media Store system, log4jv2 comes with a component-based software architecture. Thus, both systems are compatible with each other at model level. As before, the components and interfaces are organized in the repository model. Figure 2.7 shows the provided and required interfaces of log4j as well as the corresponding components.

For the running example, we have chosen an abstraction of the log4jv2 system that is mainly comprising 6 components: The `Logging` component is the main access point of log4jv2. With the associated interface it provides methods for logging data. Additional components are required to process and write back the data: `ConsoleApplication` is responsible for data output on the system console, while `FileAppending` and `DatabaseAppending` are responsible for writing data back to a file or database system. The appender

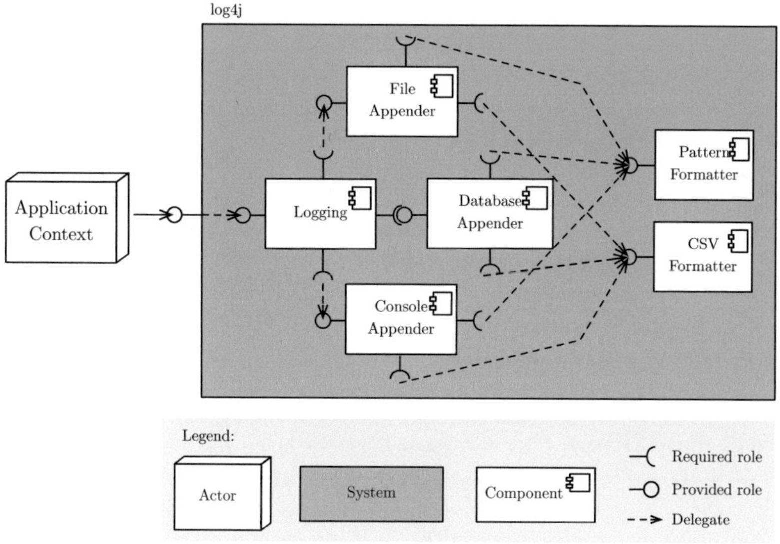

Figure 2.8.: System model of log4jv2.

components require some other components. The data can be converted into different formats, for which the formatter components provide their services. `CSVFormatting` formats the data into CSV format, while the component `PatternFormatting` is responsible for the conversion according to a certain pattern.

2.3.3. System Architecture

Since log4jv2 always run in the context of another system, there is no need for modelling a resource environment. Therefore, we concentrate on the description of the interaction of the components. Figure 2.8 shows a model of the log4jv2 system. The logger component provides the external provided interface that can be used by the application context to demand the logger services. The logger itself demands the three appender components, which then call the corresponding formatter that depends on the service that the application context actually demanded. However, the components of log4jv2 can be distributed to all resource containers.

2.3.4. Quality of Service Attributes

The log4jv2 architecture model provides QoS annotations for performance and cost. The RD-SEFFs are modelled similarly as the RD-SEFFs of the Media Store system.

2.3.5. Realization of Requirements

A logger provides functionalities that aim at improving the quality attributes of the base system. The recorded data could be used, for example, to long term performance bottleneck identification by recording the average number of accesses. Such data could also be used to improve the user interface to increase the usability by the analysis of the number of cancelled purchases. Usually, however, no business requirements are achieved by the logging functionality. However, logging also influences other quality attributes, such as performance or maintainability. Usually, performance decreases due to calculation overhead. Maintainability might also decrease, due to additional components in the system that do not support the actual business requirements.

2.3.6. Concerns

We identified three functional concerns in the architecture of logging systems and log4jv2 particularly:

- Collector
- Appender
- Formatter

The `Collector` realizes the access point of the incoming data to the logging engine, while the components of the `Appender` write the data back to the corresponding interface (console, database,...). Components of the `Formatter` format the data into the corresponding output format.

A more detailed introduction to the concerns, that we call a reference architecture for a certain subsystem and its concepts can be found in Section 7.2.5.1.

Part I.

Foundations, Related Work and Preliminary Study

3. Foundations

This chapter presents the concepts this dissertation bases on. We first start in Section 3.1 with the concepts of the field of mode-driven software development. Then, we introduce in Section 3.2 concepts and terms about software quality and knowledge modelling. In Section 3.3, we introduce basics on the optimization of software architecture models. Finally, in Section 3.4, we introduce the component-based software engineering process.

3.1. Software-Architecture and Software Architecture Models

3.1.1. Model-driven Software Development

There are several definitions in the area of model-driven approaches in the field of software architecture models. Brambilla et al. categorize them in [BCW12] as follows [Kla14]:

- **Model-driven Architecture (MDA):** MDA defines models and languages for modelling software architectures.
- **Model-driven Development (MDD):** MDD is on top of the definition of models and languages to automatically generate software models that can be used to implement the system.
- **Model-based Engineering (MBE):** MBE uses models to plan and design the software system. However, the implementation itself is not supported and is implemented later or in parallel.
- **Model-driven Engineering (MDE):** MDE uses models for design, planning, analysis and implementation of the software system.

The approach presented in this dissertation uses models for design, planning and analysis. Later, the models support the implementation process. Therefore, the approach presented in this dissertation can be attributed to the field of Model-driven Engineering.

3.1.1.1. Models and Model Levels

According to Becker [Bec08] (based on the definition of Stachowiak [Sta73]), a formal model can be defined as a formal representation of entities and relationships in the real world (abstraction) with a certain correspondence (isomorphism) for a certain purpose (pragmatics). On the basis of the concept of a model, Koziolek [Koz11] (based on Stahl and Völter [SV06]) derives the concept of the meta model, which defines the set of all models of a certain domain.

Definition 3.1.1 *Meta model (from Koziolek [Koz11, p. 24] , based on Stahl and Völter [SV06]):*
A meta model is a formal model that describes the possible models for a domain by defining the constructs of a modelling language and their relationships (abstract syntax) as well as constraints and modelling rules (static semantics).

A meta model therefore describes all entities and their (structural) relationships to represent all possible models of its domain. Models are therefore instances of their corresponding meta models. Figure 3.1 shows the relations between the modelling concepts according to [SV06]. The meta model describes relevant concepts of the domain. Entities and structure are defined by the abstract syntax and concrete syntax. The static syntax is based on the abstract syntax and the concrete syntax is itself an abstract syntax. Semantics is finally realized by the domain-specific language (DSL) for a certain meta model and its associated concrete syntax.

The Object Management Group (OMG) defined the Meta Object Facility (MOF) that specifies several modelling concepts at different abstraction levels [Man17]. Figure 3.2 shows the individual levels of the levels by Völter et al.[SV06] Level M0 corresponds to data objects in run times of programs, such as runtime objects of classes. Analogously to objects, level M1 describes the classes the runtime objects from level M0. Level M0

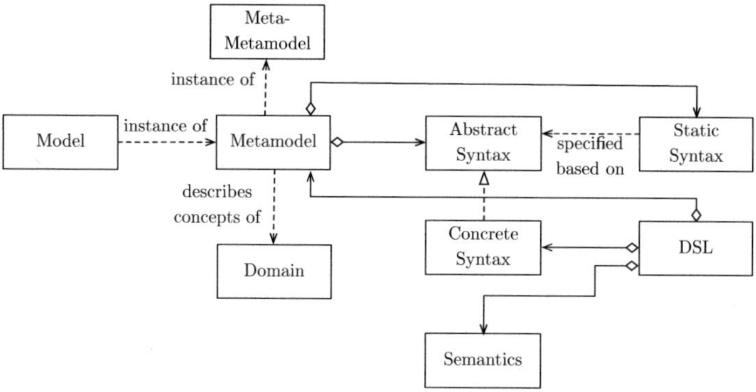

Figure 3.1.: Modelling concepts and their relation [SV06].

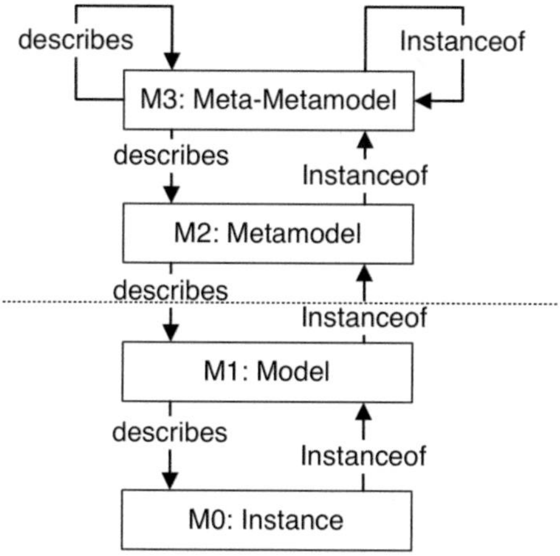

Figure 3.2.: Levels of abstraction in models [SV06]. Graphic from [Kla14].

and M1 correspond to the models that software developers usually use in object-oriented programming languages. All higher abstraction levels are usually not covered by standard programming languages. The next higher level M2 describes meta models used to describe models. In software architecture design, software architects often come into contact with the

Unified Modelling Language (UML), which is very often used to specify models in level M1. Accordingly, the UML is based on the meta model level M2. The level with the largest abstraction M3 defines meta meta models, which allow defining new modelling languages and meta models. Concepts on this level describe themselves and can therefore be used universally.

3.1.1.2. (Essential) Meta Object Facility

Component-based software architectures often use the Essential Meta Object Facility (EMOF). It is based on the MOF, but is specifically designed for modelling object-oriented systems. For example, classes, attributes, data types, references between classes, enumerations and operations are defined. In analogy to programming languages, each class is of a certain type. A class contains a set of properties that are also typed elements. Each property is described either by data types, such as primitive data types, or by abstract data types, such as classes.

3.1.1.3. Eclipse Modeling Framework

The Eclipse Modeling Framework (EMF) [Ecl19a] allows designing and editing structured data models and meta models. EMF is fully integrated with Eclipse and provides the ecore notation for modelling meta models. In addition to the meta model, EMF provides generators that allow modelling entities to be used as runtime objects in Java. On the basis of EMF, Xtext [Ecl19c] was developed, which allows creating DSLs with textual syntax. Xtext provides a grammar whose syntax is similar to the extended Backus-Naur-Form (EBNF). It also comes with generators that allow to automatically transfer the textually defined models into runtime object models.

3.1.1.4. Model Transformation using Triple-Graph-Grammars

In this section, we describe model transformation using triple-graph-grammars (TGG). We use graphs as formalism to represent meta models and TGGs as formalism for graph transformations. The model transformation transforms a source model S according to a set of rules to a target model T. Both models share a corresponding structure.

Hermann et al. define in [Her+11] forward and backward operations for model transformation based on graph modifications. Let us define a triple graph G. TG is a typed triple graph, following the graph morphism $type_G : G \rightarrow TG$. TG is the typed triple graph of G. Let us denote a typed triple graph $TG := (TG^S \leftarrow TG^C \rightarrow TG^T)$, while TG_S is the source typed triple graph, i.e. the source model, TG_C is triple graph of the correspondence structure G^C, and TG_T is the target typed triple graph. The *CompARE* approach relies on additive operations. Thus, we focus on forward-propagating operations, hereinafter defined as f_{fw}.

The function $\delta : G \rightarrow G'$ can be defined by a graph modification. In more precise terms, $\delta : G \overset{i_1}{\leftarrow} I \overset{i_2}{\rightarrow} G'$ can be derived, where i_1 and i_2 are two graph morphisms, i.e. mapping between two graphs according to their structure, while I contains the elements that are preserved during model transformation. The graph morphism $i_1 : I \rightarrow G$ enables to derive the elements in G that are deleted, while the elements that are added to the model are defined with $i_2 : I \rightarrow G'$. Based on the model transformation δ, Hermann [Her+11] enables to derive the forward propagation operation as follows:

$$
\begin{aligned}
f_{fw} &: (R \otimes \Delta_S) \rightarrow (R \times \Delta_T) \\
\Delta_S &:= \{\delta_S : G^S \rightarrow G'^S | G^S, G'^S \in VL(TG^S)\} \\
\Delta_T &:= \{\delta_T : G^T \rightarrow G'^T | G^T, G'^T \in VL(TG^T)\} \\
(R \otimes \Delta_S) &:= \{(r \times \delta_S) \in (R \times \Delta_S) | r : G^S \longleftrightarrow G^T, \\
&\qquad \delta_S : G^S \rightarrow G'^S\}, \delta_S \text{ and } r \text{ coincide with } G^S,
\end{aligned}
$$

while R is the set of correspondence relations, Δ_S the set of graph modifications of the source graph G^S and Δ_T the set of graph modifications of the target graph G^T. More precisely, a forward propagation contains a specific correspondence relation $r_1 \in R$ and a graph modification δ_S. $VL(M)$ determines all model instances from a meta model M (formulated as a graph).

The result is the correspondence relation $r_2 \in R$ and the graph modification δ_T, which enables to derive the target model G'^T.

$$\begin{array}{ccc} G^S & \overset{r_1}{\longleftrightarrow} & G^T \\ \delta_S \Big\downarrow & \searrow f_{fw} & \delta_T \Big\downarrow \\ G'^S & \overset{r_2}{\longleftrightarrow} & G'^T \end{array}$$

δ_S and r coincide with G^S restricts the set of rules that correspond to the same source model. Otherwise, all correspondence rules would be considered due to the Cartesian product of correspondence relations and source graphs.

3.1.2. (Component-based) Software Architecture

According to Reussner et al. [Reu+16], architecture decisions that are made when designing a software architecture play a particularly critical role.

Definition 3.1.2 *Software Architecture (from Reussner [Reu+16, p. 37]):*
A software architecture is the result of a set of design decisions relating to the structure of a system with components and their relationships as well as their mapping to execution environment.

However, design decisions that influence the software architecture are made not only in the design phase, but also in the development or evolution process, and in the process of reusing systems. This is because each building block, the software component, that is reused, each relation between elements changes the structure of the architecture. In later phases of the design process, design decisions are being changed, removed, or added due to new or changed requirements. However, design decisions are made not only during design, but also when deploying the implemented system to hardware resources: The hardware environment influences the architecture due to the hardware configuration. Relevant factors are CPU, disk, and network resources. All these structural properties ultimately influence the software architecture.

Reussner et al. describes in [Reu+16] the previously mentioned software components, which are essential parts of component-based software architectures, as follows:

Definition 3.1.3 *Software Component (from Reussner [Reu+16, p. 47]):*
A software component is a contractually specified building block for software, which can be composed, deployed, and adapted without understanding its internals.

Contractually specified means that preconditions and subsequent conditions are specified. If the software architecture in which the software component is used complies with the precondition, the software component fulfils its specified postcondition. The contractual specification enables reuse of software components in any component-based software architecture without having any knowledge of the internals of the component. Software components comply with the contractual specifications by means of interfaces.

Definition 3.1.4 *Interface (from Reussner [Reu+16, p. 45]):*
Interfaces are abstract descriptions of units of software. They can be used as points of interaction between components.

The contract consists of two types of interfaces, the roles, namely the provided and required roles. The interaction between components is done by a pair of two compatible required and provided roles. Interfaces with provided roles are often called provided interfaces. This applies analogously to interfaces with required roles. Provided interfaces define the services provided by a component, while required interfaces define services a component requires for realizing the provided services.

3.1.2.1. Palladio Component Model

The Palladio Component Model (PCM) is part of the Palladio approach [Reu+16] from Reussner et al. PCM is a domain-specific modelling language for software architectures that focusses on modelling and analysis of software quality. Palladio and the PCM support the software architect in designing component-based software architectures. Palladio implements and extends the component-based software engineering process by Cheesman and Daniels [CD00].

The PCM is based on the previously introduced concepts of component-based software architectures, such as contractually specified components, interfaces, and roles. It refines interfaces internally with a list of signatures that corresponds to the provided and required services of a component using the interface. A signature corresponds to an operation, a name, a parameter list, and a return parameter. This corresponds to concepts of methods in programming languages. PCM also uses the concept of roles for the two types of interfaces mentioned above, the providing and requiring roles. The interface itself is defined neutrally. A specific role is assigned when assigned to a component. The role determines whether the component provides (providing role) the services specified in the role itself or requires (requiring role) them to realize its services.

The PCM divides the various requirements of a software architecture into different parts, namely the architecture view type, as defined in the ISO 42010 standard.

Definition 3.1.5 *View type (from Reussner [Reu+16, p. 42]):*
A view-type defines the set of meta-classes whose instances a view can display and comprises a definition of a concrete syntax plus a mapping to the abstract meta model syntax.

View-types divide the meta classes of a meta model (such as the PCM) into different parts in order to reduce the complexity of use.

The PCM defines three viewpoints representing classes of view-types, namely the structural viewpoint, the behavioural viewpoint, and the deployment viewpoint.

Structural Viewpoint

The structural viewpoint represents the dependency structure and the components, interfaces, etc. of systems. It comprises two view-types, namely the repository view-type and the assembly view-type.

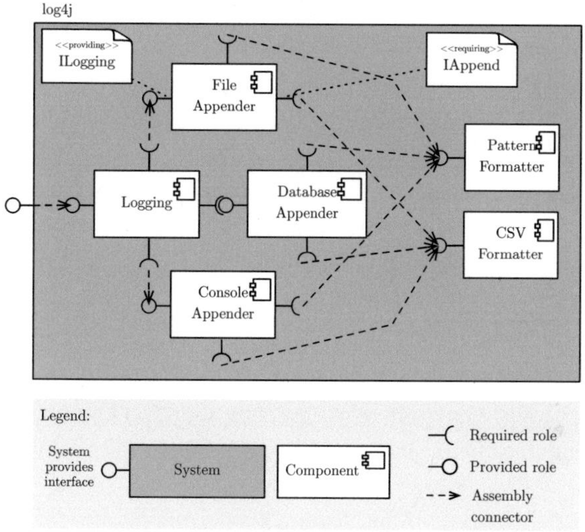

Figure 3.3.: Assembly view type of log4jv2.

PCM components and interfaces are stored in a repository. The repository contains further elements that are not central for the concepts of this dissertation and are therefore not considered further. An example of a repository is shown in Figure 2.7. It shows the components and interfaces of our running example, the log4jv2 system. The repository is the central base used by component developers to make new components available for (re-)use, as well as by software architects that can use the available components to design their software architecture. The design of the software architecture is carried out by assemble components to composites.

The assembly is represented by the assembly view type. Assembly contexts connect components with interfaces using the two types of roles. Let us take the `FileAppender` component shown in Figure 3.3 as an example. `FileAppender` provides the `IAppend` interface, while it requires the `IFormat` interface to provide the services from `IAppend`.

The connection between two corresponding roles (requiring role and corresponding providing role) and thus between two assembly contexts is realized via the assembly connector `PCM::AssemblyConnector`. In Figure 3.3, assembly connectors are graphically illustrated by the dashed arrows between matching interface roles. Assembly connectors themselves do not provide any functionality, but merely serve as connecting entities between interfaces.

In addition to assembly connectors, systems have system provides interfaces. They are used to providing services of the system to users or other systems. Analogously there can be system requiring interfaces.

Behavioural Viewpoint

The behavioural viewpoint focussed on the behaviour of the internals of components and behaviour between components. The main concept of internal behaviour is the service effect specification (SEFF).

Definition 3.1.6 *Service Effect Specification (from Reussner [Reu+16, p. 53]):* *A service effect specification (SEFF) describes the intracomponent behaviour of a component operation on a highly abstract level by specifying the relationship between provided and required services of a component.*

SEFFs abstract from the individual program statements of components. Code is reduced to control structures such as branches, loops or forks (and several others). Statements are abstracted with internal actions. The call of external methods is abstracted with external call actions. Internal actions represent one or more program statements, such as variable assignments, or complex algorithmic calculations. This depends on the degree of abstraction of the model.

The intercomponent behaviour (via interfaces and connectors) is done by the SEFF of a component via the external call action. The external call action creates links to services of other components in the system. If an external service must be called to fulfil the component's own service, this is realized via this link. If an external call action is required by a SEFF of a component, this implies an additional interface in the requiring role with which the component must be associated.

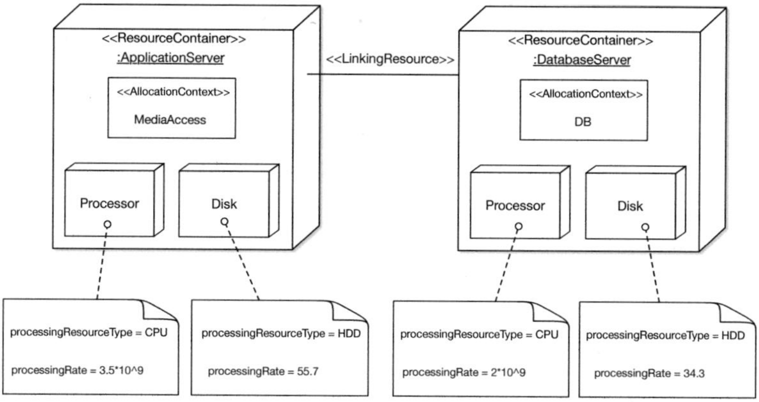

Figure 3.4.: Example of a resource environment and component allocation [Reu+16].

Deployment Viewpoint

In the resource environment the physical or virtual nodes are defined, as well as their resources regarding CPU and hardware equipment, the processing resource types. For example, the clock rate of the processor or the I/O throughput of hard disks can be defined. Networks between nodes and their throughput can also be defined. The allocation to resources is finally done in the allocation view type. The previously modelled assembly contexts are assigned to the hardware resources modelled in the resource environment view type. Figure 3.4 shows both resource environment and component allocation.

Usage Profile

The usage profile defines the protocol of typical actors accessing the system. For this purpose, externally exposed services of the system (provided interfaces of the system) can be used. The usage profile is modelled using an activity diagram, which can be enhanced with information on parameters or input data. Similar to SEFFs, loops or control structures for modelling alternative paths can also be defined in the usage profile.

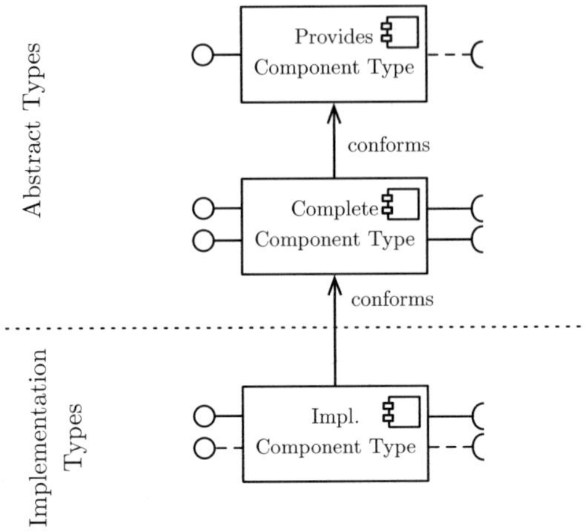

Figure 3.5.: Component type hierarchy [Reu+16].

3.1.3. Component Type Hierarchy

PCM defines a type hierarchy [Reu+16] for components that abstracts components to different levels. Thus, they limit the information content required for the respective development stage or usage process to reduce complexity. The different levels of abstraction and the information displayed in each case are chosen such that the necessary information is available in the current process as precisely as possible in order to keep complexity as low as possible. Figure 3.5 shows the component type hierarchy. The hierarchy is divided into two parts: abstract types and implementation types. The most abstract type is the *Provided Component Type.* Whenever software architects need new components, they specify them using the provided interfaces with the services required for their system. Optionally, they can also define required services. However, this can often not yet be specified at this design level, which is why required interfaces are only modelled optionally. These components specified on the provided type can now be submitted to the component developer for implementation.

The `Complete Component Type` is still abstract, but enriched with additional information. At this level, the component developer defines (if necessary) or refines further provided interfaces and adds the necessary required interfaces. The specification can now be used by the software architect to extend his system.

The abstract behaviour is introduced in the `Implementation Component Type`. At this level the internal behaviour of components is specified using the SEFF. Several components usually exist, with the same interfaces, but different internal behaviour that does not affect functionality. That is, all components with the same interface specifications are treated as functionally equivalent. However, they differ in the resulting quality attributes (as introduced in more detail below).

3.1.4. Reference Architecture

Complex systems often contain many software components including the appropriate interfaces. These are in relations to each other to fulfil the function of the system. Due to this high number of components and relationships between the components, the complexity of the overall system easily increases and quickly becomes difficult to manage. In particular, reusing such systems as subsystems in a base system becomes more difficult due to this complexity.

Definition 3.1.7 *Reference Architecture (from Reussner [Reu+16, p. 85], inspired by [TMD09]):*
A reference architecture is the set of principal design decisions that are simultaneously applicable to multiple related systems, typical within a single application domain, with implicitly defined points of variation, such as the presence or absence of a component.

A reference architecture helps to make this growing complexity of systems more manageable and to simplify reuse. They contain architecture knowledge of the domain and the experts who designed this system and allow this architecture knowledge to be reused when reusing these systems. This easier reuse can be achieved by grouping software components from software architectures and standardizing them for a specific domain. The result is a template that is made available for the design of other systems and determines the main design of the systems. Structural elements, types

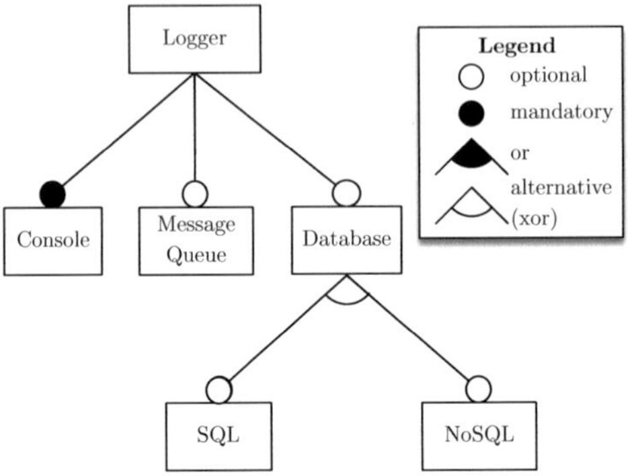

Figure 3.6.: Simplified feature model of the logging system log4jv2.

and their relationships to each other are modelled in such a template. Such a template is designed that many similar systems of the same domain can be applied [Reu+16].

3.1.5. Feature Models

Feature Models are a graphical notation to represent hierarchical structures of parent and child features according to Kang et al. [Kan+90]. In this dissertation, we use features as defined in Definition 3.1.8.

Definition 3.1.8 *Feature (from Bosch [Bos00, p. 194]):*
Features are logical units of behaviour specified by a set of functional and quality requirements.

Feature models are often associated with variability within models, but can also be used to represent complex functionalities. Child features usually complement the parent feature or each serves as an alternative to other child features. There are different types of variability. For example, it is possible to define features as exclusive alternatives to each other (XOR), as an alternative (OR) or in combination (and).

The types differ in the graphical notation. An OR relation is modelled with a filled circle, while XOR is modelled with an unfilled circle. It is also possible to model different features either as optional (marked by an unfilled circle) or as mandatory (represented by a filled circle). This is also illustrated by the feature model of the log4jv2[1] logging framework Figure 3.6.

For this dissertation we use the EMF feature model [Ecl19b] from EMF. This ecore-based specification implements the feature model, together with a graphical editor according to Czarnecki and Eisenacker [CE00]. Figure 3.7 shows the meta model graphically. In the following, we will introduce the main classes and properties of the meta model. `FeatureObjective`, `Feature`, `FeatureGroup`, and `Constraint` are the main classes of the meta model. `FeatureObjective` is the container of the features. `Feature` defines if a feature is a mandatory feature, an optional feature. A feature can have sub features by the `ChildRelation`. Children can be mandatory or optional child features. Child features are contained in a feature group. On features and feature groups constraints can be defined by the `Constraint` class. Features can either exclude other features (`ProhibitsConstraint`) or require other features (`RequiredConstraint`).

3.2. Software Quality and Modelling Knowledge

3.2.1. Software Quality and Quality Attributes

Definition 3.2.1 *Software Quality (from ISO/IEC 25030:2007(E) [Int07]): Software quality is the capability of software product to satisfy stated and implied needs when used under specified conditions.*

According to Definition 3.2.1, software quality depends on the requirements of the software system and its environment (such as the usage profile).

Requirements can be distinguished by two terms, namely functional requirements and quality requirements.

Definition 3.2.2 *Quality Attribute (from ISO/IEC 25030:2007(E) [Int07]): A quality attribute is an inherent property or characteristic of an entity that*

[1] `https://logging.apache.org/log4j/2.x/`

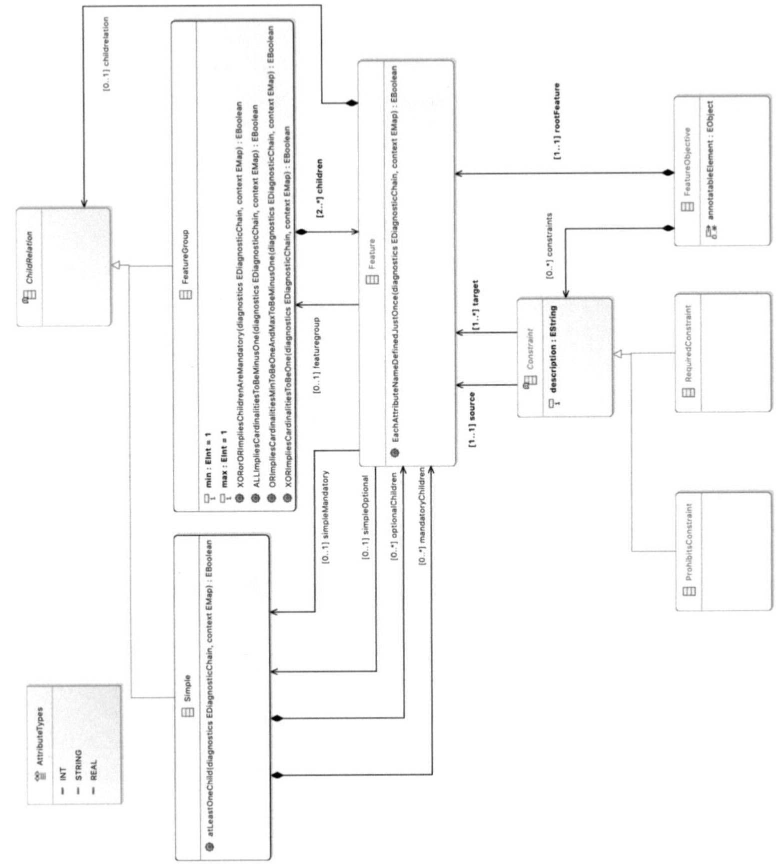

Figure 3.7.: Graphic showing the meta classes of the ecore-based meta model for defining features.

can be distinguished quantitatively or qualitatively by human or automated means.

Therefore, quality attributes can be either quantitative or qualitative. The type depends on the formulation of the appertaining requirement. For

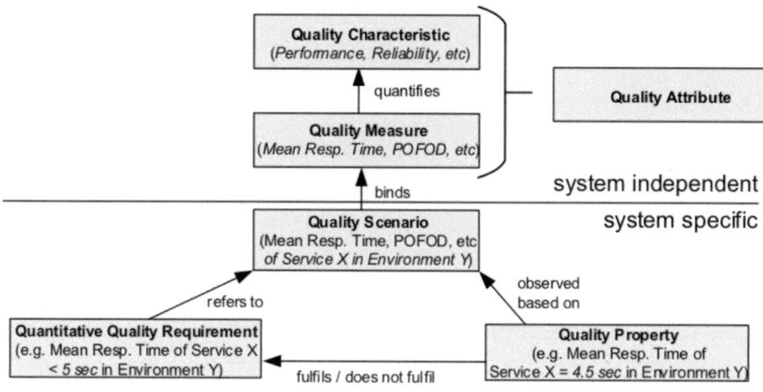

Figure 3.8.: Terms in the field of quantitative quality requirements [Reu+16; Koz11].

quantitatively described quality requirements, various further terms can be derived. Figure 3.8 shows relevant terms regarding quantitative quality requirements. The term *quality attributes* can be divided into two parts, namely *quality characteristics* and *quality measures.* For example, quality characteristics can be instantiated by the term performance, reliability, and safety. Quality measures, on the other hand, are the dimensions of these characteristics, such as mean response time (for performance), probability of failure (for reliability), or mean time to security failure (for security). both quality attributes are system independent.

In contrast, the quality scenario, the quality property, and the quality requirement are dependent on the system under study. The quality scenario defines a particular service and environment for a particular quality measure. This means, that the quality scenario specifies the average response time for a particular service provided by the system and a particular hardware context. In turn, a quality property represents the observed value for the quality scenario, such as the mean response time of 4.5 seconds. The (quantitative) quality requirements, on the other hand, finally determine whether the observed quality characteristic within the scenario meets the required quality requirements. An upper limit for the response time can be defined, for example an average response time of less than 5 seconds (for the given scenario).

3.2.1.1. Performance

Performance is one of the critical quality attributes of software systems. In the case of web shops, performance can even have a direct impact on a company's sales if, for example, purchases cannot be finished due to poor performance or if purchases can be made particularly quickly due to good performance. Another aspect of performance is real-time systems, which must have completed their function by a certain deadline in order to ensure their required usefulness. Quantitative metrics can be used deriving the three quality measures [Reu+16]:

- **Response Time:** Response time is the time a system requires to perform the service, from receiving the user request to sending the final response to the user.
- **Throughput:** Throughput can be measured by the number of requests the system can process within a given time unit.
- **Utilization:** Utilization describes the resource utilization of hardware resources in percent within a given time period.

3.2.1.2. Cost

Costs can also be regarded as a quality attribute. They usually depend directly on other quality attributes, such as higher performance or higher security, which are usually associated with higher costs. Different types of costs can be distinguished, such as the following three types (adapted from [Reu+16]):

- **Component costs:** Component costs describe the costs of components within their life-cycle for in-house developed or licenced components. These costs include requirements engineering, development process, customization, evolution, testing, maintenance and care. Licensing costs may also arise.

- **Hardware costs:** Hardware costs arise from the processing of software components on hardware. These costs are subdivided into acquisition costs for hardware, such as server systems or networks, and also into run time costs, such as the costs arising from the use of cloud services.
- **System costs:** System costs refer to costs of the overall system that cannot be attributed to individual components. Such costs are usually incurred through the use of middleware systems, such as application servers, operating systems or load balancers.

3.2.1.3. Security

There are different definitions for security in software systems. This work focuses on information security, which can be represented by the CIA-triad of confidentiality, integrity and availability.

Definition 3.2.3 *Information Security (from Cherdantseva & Hilton [CH15]): Information Security is a multidisciplinary area of study and professional activity which is concerned with the development and implementation of security mechanisms of all available types (technical, organizational, human-oriented and legal) in order to keep information in all its locations (within and outside the organization's perimeter) and, consequently, information systems, where information is created, processed, stored, transmitted and destroyed, free from threats.[..]*

CIA represents the core of information security, which can be defined as follows:

- **Confidentiality:** Confidentiality *is the property, that information is not made available or disclosed to unauthorized individuals, entities, or processes [Bec15].* Confidentiality guarantees that sensitive information is only accessible by authorized persons or systems.
- **Integrity:** Integrity guarantees that transmitted information is unchanged during transmission. This means that the information that arrives at the receiver equals to the information submitted by the sender.

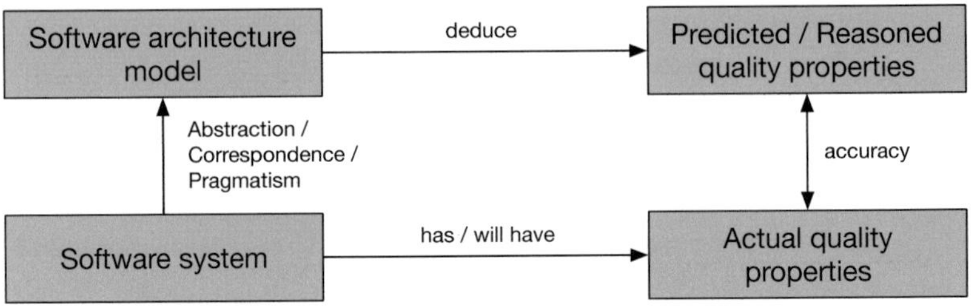

Figure 3.9.: Model-based quality prediction after [Koz11].

- **Availability:** Availability guarantees that (saved) information and resources are available for authorized persons or systems. Their availability should not be restricted by attackers.

3.2.2. Model-based Quality Prediction

Definition 3.2.4 *Quality Models (from ISO/IEC 25030:2007(E) [Int07]):*
Quality models define a set of characteristics, and of relationships between them, which provides a framework for specifying quality requirements and evaluating quality.

With this definition, together with the definition of software models, the core of the model-based quality prediction can be described:

We show an overview in Figure 3.9. A given software system has (or will have), due to its given design, certain quality properties. A software architecture model in turn is an abstraction of this software system. Various quality attributes can be predicted on its basis. Which quality attributes and in which level of detail can be predicted depend on the attributes of the model, i.e. on the abstraction, the correspondence, and the pragmatism of the model. If software performance should be predicted, information on the quality properties for the quality attribute performance must be included, so that performance can be predicted on the basis of this model. The capability and accuracy to predict the performance of the software system depends on the software architecture's meta model. These predicted quality characteristics then have a certain accuracy compared to the actual (or future) quality characteristics of the software system.

Furthermore, the accuracy also depends on the type of modelling. Quantitatively modelled quality attributes tend to achieve higher accuracies than qualitatively modelled quality attributes. Which type is used depends on two factors: importance of the quality attribute for project success and available budget. Generally, quantitative models are more complex and thus more time-consuming in development than qualitative estimates.

3.2.3. Quality of Service Modelling Language

The Quality of Service Modelling Language (QML) allows modelling quality attributes, quality dimensions and quality requirements. QML has been defined by [FK98] in the EBNF and extended by Noorshams et al. [NMR10]. The extension defines the language as a meta model and enables use in automatic analysis procedures based on software architecture models. The language itself consists of three parts, namely the *Contract Type*, the *Contract* and the *Profile*.

- **Contract type:** The contract type defines quality attributes such as performance, reliability, security, and refines these quality attributes with dimensions, as introduced in Section 3.2.1.1. For the performance quality attribute, possible dimensions might be mean response time and throughput. The contract type defines a name, a domain, and the semantics of ascending and descending values for each dimension. In the case of response time, ascending values mean worse quality, while in the case of throughput, this corresponds to an improvement in quality. Each dimension has a corresponding numeric domain, which values are defined in the contract type. For example, an interval is possible in which possible values can range. Alternatively, we can define individual (single) values on which an order relation is defined.
- **Contract:** The contract is derived from the contract type and can be seen as an instance of the contract type. While the contract type determines which quality dimensions are possible for a particular quality attribute and which values are valid within the dimension,

the contract specifies which quality attribute is to be examined and which quality dimension is to be examined. Quality requirements can also be defined here. From the set of all possible values of the contract type, a subset of valid values is defined that are derived directly from the requirements. In the case of performance, for example, a response time from zero to infinite is possible. Realistic values from a requirement could be in the range of 200 - 1000 ms, for example. All resulting quality properties that do not lie within the defined range would be invalid.

- **Profile:** The profile assigns elements of the software architecture, such as components or services, to the defined contract. Using this information, an automatic analysis approach can determine which quality attributes and dimensions are to be analysed for a particular service and in which range the resulting values must lie in order to be valid.

We use QML as a basis for modelling and analysis of qualitative quality attributes, for later common analysis with quantitative modelled quality attributes.

3.2.4. Modelling Quality in Palladio

Palladio is an approach for modelling software architectures, and enables the evaluation of quality attributes at design time. Palladio focuses mainly on the evaluation of the quality attribute performance, but can also analyse reliability, cost and maintainability of software architectures. Thus, it enables predictions of quality attributes long before the actual implementation. Thus, already during the software design phase, the modelled software architecture regarding its quality attributes. Palladio combines model-driven software architecture design techniques with quality modelling, including the simulation of quality attributes based on these models.

To model and later analyse performance, Palladio uses the SEFF concept shown in Definition 3.1.6 and extends it to include resource demands, the resource demanding SEFFs (RD-SEFF). An active resource, such as a component running on hardware, naturally consumes a certain amount of processing resources on that hardware. These processing resources can be, for example, clock cycles of the CPU or input/output operations of a hard disk. A SEFF models the abstract behaviour of the processing steps within a component. As mentioned earlier, these processing steps are the internal actions. In an implementation, these internal actions correspond, for example, to a specific calculation step that requires hardware resources. This set of hardware resources is modelled using the resource demands.

Together with the modelled processor clock rate or throughput of a hard disk and the underlying usage profile, the resulting response time can be calculated for a specific service. As with software models in general, RD-SEFFs can be modelled with different levels of granularity. A constant value up to parametrized probability density functions can be modelled. Thus, complex modelling possibilities are given, which enable a higher accuracy of the predicted response times with the corresponding additional modelling cost.

3.2.5. Qualitative Reasoning

Qualitative reasoning comes from the field of artificial intelligence and allows the expression of conceptual knowledge. We use its concepts for modellig architecture knowledge such as defined in Definition 3.2.5.

Definition 3.2.5 *Architecture Knowledge (derived from Kruchten [KLV06]): Architecture knowledge is the result of architecture design decisions and the design of a software architecture.*

Qualitative reasoning is often used to describe physical relationships such as quantity, space and time. It supports reasoning about these continuous aspects, even if only little information is contained. Qualitative reasoning is also used to model and simulate knowledge in industry or science and other engineering domains. Simulations based on models are also possible. Continuous aspects describing the dynamic characteristics of a system are qualitatively modelled. For example, the mapping consists of the current size of a characteristic and the direction of possible changes (such as increase or decrease). In most cases, an ordinal scale is used as a basis on which an order relation is defined. All values within this scale are characteristic values that a system can assume. This is also referred to as *quantity space.*

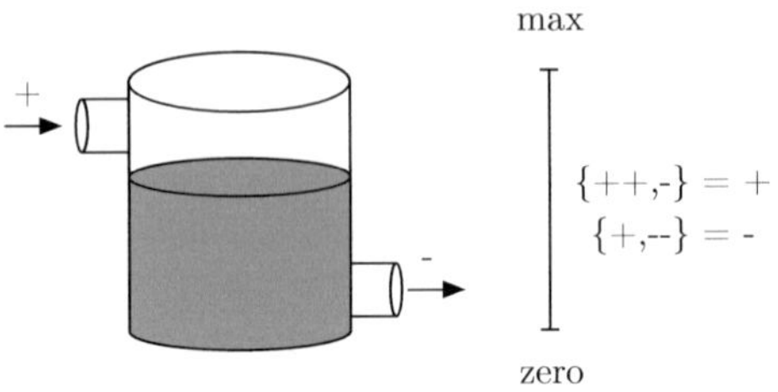

Figure 3.10.: Vessel example for qualitative reasoning: water flowing in is marked with + sign, while water flowing off is marked with -. {++,-} = {+} means more water flowing in than out, what means vessel overflows, while {+, --} = {-} means the opposite.

Another property of qualitative reasoning is that it becomes possible to model coarse granular or very fine granular. This enables trade-off decisions regarding the effort required to represent knowledge and the accuracy of the achievable results. Of course, it also plays a role whether sufficient information is available to model the desired granularity.

Central to qualitative reasoning is the way in which a system is described, e.g. when the state changes over time. Although the system changes in reality, this change does not necessarily have to be reflected in the model. This is because an objective change in the state of the system does not necessarily have to be relevant to modelling the behaviour of the system. An example of this is a water vessel, as shown in Figure 3.10. The water vessel has an inflow and an outflow and according to the strength of the inflow and the amount of water flowing out a certain water level results. When designing a system that describes the state water empty, contains water and vessel at the overflow, then the intermediate change of state (for example litre amount of water) is not relevant. Rather, the future state of the vessel is determined by whether the quantity of water flowing off is greater than the quantity of water flowing in, is exactly the same, or whether the quantity of water flowing in is greater than the quantity of water flowing off. All states in between remain unknown. Therefore, no statement can be made about the quantity of water at a certain point in time, but only about the state that will arise in the future when behaviour remains constant. However, no physical connections between inflow and outflow velocity, size of the vessel, gravity, etc. need to be known in order to determine the future state. This is related to the trade-off decisions aforementioned. Not all correlations need not be known, but can be derived by mere observation and this observed knowledge can be captured in a structured process and formal model. Thus, observed knowledge or informally available knowledge can be formally modelled and, for example, made machine-processable. On the other hand, the recorded knowledge and the possibilities of analysis are limited and the state cannot be determined by a quantitative objective function at any given point in time [Bre+09].

The water level of the vessel can therefore be defined by the amount of water flowing in and out. Water level and quantity change can be described for example by the quantity space {++,+,0,-,--}. Whereby *0* means no change and +,++ as well as -,-- a corresponding positive change or negative change. If a larger amount of water flows into the vessel (++) than out (-), the total amount of water in the vessel (+) increases. If as much water flows into the vessel (+) as out (-), the resulting total change is *0*.

With this method, architecture knowledge and informal knowledge can be formally modelled, automatically processed and therefore automatically analysed.

3.3. Optimizing Software-Architecture Models

Optimization determines the best solution in a given context. The available solutions correspond to a set of decisions that include a set of possible alternative choices. The better solution can be determined by an *objective function* that must either be minimized or maximized. An example of such a function is the performance analysis of a software architecture model. When analysing the response time of a service, the associated objective function must be minimized. If throughput should be analysed, the objective function must be maximized.

Every possible decision is contained within a design space that must be searched for optimization. Searching the design space for the optimal solution is also called *design space exploration.*

If several objectives are considered simultaneously, i.e. several objective functions that must be minimized or maximized at the same time, a *multi-objective optimization* must be carried out [Koz11].

3.3.1. Multiple Criteria

In real-world scenarios it is often necessary to consider several quality criteria at the same time. For example, the response time and also the reliability of a given software service can be simultaneously relevant for optimization. Multiple criteria and articulation for preferences can be treated in three ways: a Priori, a Posteriori and interactive (cf. [VL00; Bra+08]).

3.3.1.1. Preference Articulations

For a priori preference articulation, all criteria are first reduced to one objective function. This objective function can be examined individually after evaluation (a priori).

The a Posteriori preference articulation first determines the optimal solutions based on all relevant objective functions. The search for optimal solutions on the basis of several objective functions results in several trade-off solutions (Pareto-optimal solutions), which, based on the available information, are in themselves all optimal solutions. Compares two solutions with each other, one solution is only objectively better if it outperforms (or is equal to) the other solution in all the considered objectives. If one of the considered objectives is better in the first solution and another objective is better in the second solution, then both solutions are not directly comparable. Both solutions are then treated as Pareto-optimal solutions. Decisions on the optimal solution is made later (a posteriori) for example due to analysing the requirements or reasoning of software architects.

The interactive preference articulation allows decision makers to adjust their preferences interactively during the search process. Usually, this method iteratively processes a posteriori methods. After each iteration the decision makers review the resulting solution and adapts their preferences. The adapted preferences are then used for further iterations.

This dissertation focuses on a posteriori preference articulation. An a posteriori analysis of the Pareto-optimal solutions allows decisions on alternatives and prioritization of the requirements regarding the results of the objective functions. No preferences have to be defined in advance. The preferences can be weighted against each other on the basis of reviewing the set of Pareto-optimal solutions. [Koz11]

3.3.1.2. Pareto-Optimality

A multi-objective optimization problem is described by a vector comprising *n* objective functions to be optimized. Each function in this vector results in a property for an objective. Each vector describes the specific properties of a solution. Objectively optimal, a solution is exactly when each property is greater or equals of another solution, i.e. *Pareto-dominance*. If solutions are not comparable, neither dominates the other, they are *Pareto-non-dominance*. If one solution is greater or equal in all properties of the vectors of all other solutions in the search space, the solution is globally Pareto-optimal. The set of Pareto-optimal solutions comprises all globally Pareto-optimal solutions of the search space that are non-dominated [Koz11].

Figure 3.11 shows an example of Pareto-optimal solutions (green) and dominated solutions (red). The plot shows two objective functions, response time and cost. Both functions must be minimized to find the optimal solutions. A pair consisting of a response time and a cost amount, such as (0.25 ms, 2000 monetary units), characterizes a solution. The green Pareto-optimal candidates form the Pareto-front. From these candidates, decision makers will then select a solution. The red solutions are rejected and not pursued further.

3.3.2. Software-Architecture Optimization

The PerOpteryx approach proposed by A. Koziolek [Koz11] optimizes software architectures on the basis of software architecture models. The optimization requires a design space describing all possible architecture candidates. The design space is described by software architecture degrees of freedom (DoF). They are part of the basis for the automated generation of alternative architecture candidates. Architecture candidates are

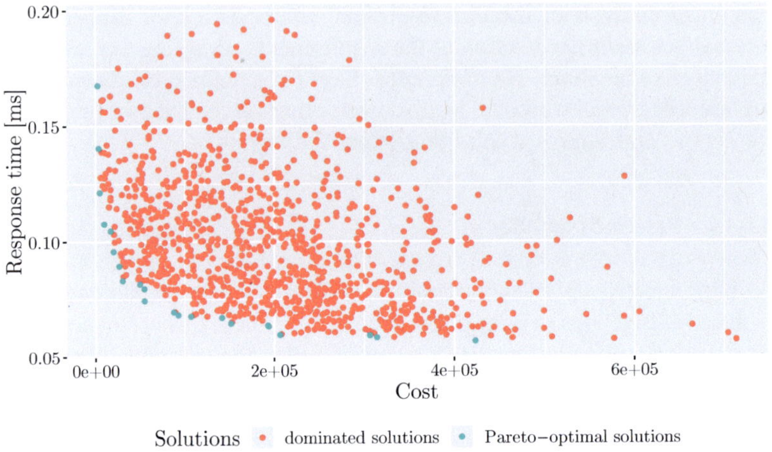

Figure 3.11.: Example showing Pareto-optimal and dominated solutions.

automatically generated using an evolutionary algorithm. The generated architecture candidates serve as input for the objective functions, such as the performance analysis or cost evaluation of Palladio. Their results are used to generate new, improved candidates and to find the Pareto-optimal architecture candidates in the search space. The Pareto-optimal candidates can then be used as a basis for implementing the software system.

3.3.2.1. Evolutionary Algorithms

Evolutionary algorithms originate from the field of biological processes of evolution and were originally introduced by Holland [Hol92]. They belong to the class of meta heuristics, i.e. approximate search-based optimization strategies independent of the search problem. The principle of evolutionary algorithms is based on creating new offspring from an existing population. Survivable offspring of each population are selected by natural selection.

Each offspring is described by its genotype and its phenotype. The genotype describes possible properties, the alleles. In organisms, an allele determines

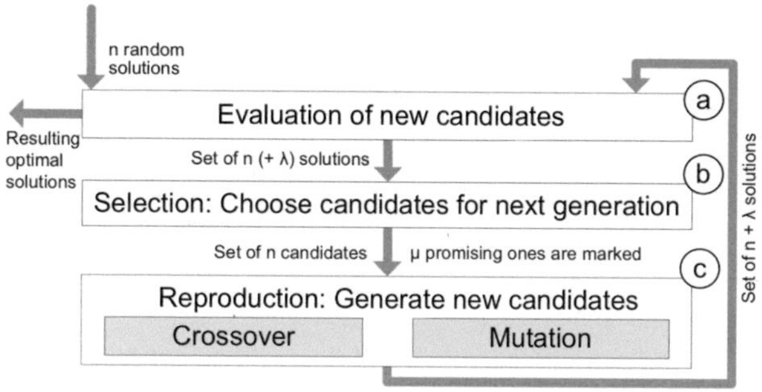

Figure 3.12.: Basic Evolutionary Process [Koz11].

possible manifestations during reproduction, such as hair colour, e.g. brown hair or blonde hair. The genotype encodes genetic dispositions for all possible hair colours of the organism. One of the allele is the one that prevails in reproduction, such as brown hair and determines the phenotype.

PerOpteryx uses evolutionary algorithms creating new, promising architecture candidates. We introduce the basic algorithm of this class of algorithms in the following.

Figure 3.12 shows the basic algorithm. The basic algorithm consists of three parts, namely evaluation of the new candidates, i.e. new solutions of the population, selection of candidates, i.e. solutions for the next generation, and generation of new candidates, i.e. solutions of the population. To generate a new population, the population size n is required as input. Another input parameter is the number of parents of each generation μ, as well as the number of offspring λ in each iteration. The initial input consists of a number of random candidates.

In step *a*, the evaluation step, all unevaluated solutions are evaluated. The evaluation of the solutions is calculated using the objective functions. All evaluated and survivable solutions, i.e. the initial solutions and the surviving new solutions, are used in the next step.

In step *b*, the candidate selection step, the population is first reduced to n solutions. The weakest candidates, according to results of the objective function, are removed. In addition, a set of solutions μ is defined which represent the parents for the next iteration.

In step *c*, the reproduction step, new candidates are generated with the help of cross-over and mutation operations. The parents from the previous step are used as a basis. The set of solutions from the previous step and the newly created candidates are finally passed back to step *a*. This process continues until a defined stop criterion is reached. The result is a set of optimal solutions.

The two operations cross-over and mutation are used for reproduction. Cross-over generates new solutions from the characteristics of two or more parents. All parents come from the set of promising solutions. The assumption here is that by combining their beneficial properties, these are propagated to their offspring. The genotypes of two promising solutions are merged into one new solution.

The mutation operator searches for new candidates in the neighbourhood of given, promising input candidates. This is based on the assumption that good or better candidates can be found in the neighbourhood of good candidates. The basis for the mutation operator is one promising parent candidate. To generate candidates by mutation, a number of genes from the parent candidate are selected and mutated. All other genes are inherited unchanged.

3.3.2.2. Design Space of Software-Architecture Models

The design space of software architecture models describes the set of all possible valid architecture candidates. The meta model used for defining the software architecture models and the meta model's DoFs define the set of architecture candidates. Several DoFs can be identified for the PCM: Component selection, component allocation and resource selection [Koz11].

The *component selection* DoF can be spanned due to the component-based nature of PCM. Software components encapsulate the implementation of functions. Interfaces are decoupled from software components. If several components exist with the same interfaces, these components are interchangeable. Functionally, the software architecture remains equivalent, but will differ in the quality attributes. These differences can be evaluated by the objective function for performance.

The *component allocation* DoF can be spanned when the software architecture model provides choices for allocating software components. Several options are available in multi-tier systems, where software components are distributed on several server systems. In a three-tier server system, each component can be distributed on each server. Due to different hardware configuration and network latency, the type of allocation influences the objective function for determining performance.

Possible hardware configurations of each server system span another DoF, namely the *hardware selection* DoF. Processing resources in Palladio are described by the CPU clock rate and hard disk throughput. The resource selection DoF span the configured values of clock rate and hard disk throughput. For example, the design space can span clock rate values from 1 to 3 GHz. In general, DoFs can span continuous values, such as values in intervals, or by discrete values.

Let us consider the Media Store example to demonstrate the concepts: Media Store consists of eleven software components and three hardware resources. For each of the three hardware resources, the clock rate can be selected between one and three GHz. Figure 2.3 shows schematically several degree of freedom instances for each of the three DoFs. One instance of the DoF allocation determines the allocation of the WebGUI component on the frontend server. An instance of resource selection defines the clock rate of 2 GHz for the frontend server. The allocation DoF spans discrete values, while resource selection spans continuous values.

3.3.2.3. Software Architecture Optimization Process

The PerOpteryx approach supports software architects at improving component-based software architectures by searching the design space using the evolutionary algorithm NSGA-II [Deb+02] and several objective functions for quality attribute evaluation. Figure 3.13 shows the software architecture optimization process that is based on the evolutionary process introduced in Section 3.3.2.1.

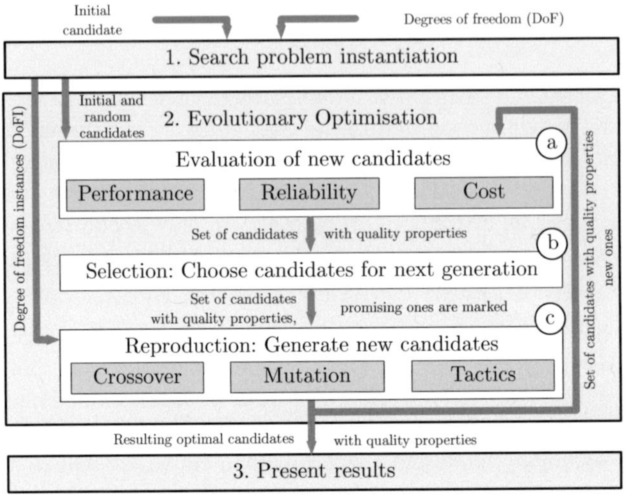

Figure 3.13.: Software Architecture Optimization Process (based on [Koz11]).

PerOpteryx uses the three steps of the evolutionary algorithm as a basis to generate, select and evaluate new software architecture candidates. One of the input parameters for evolutionary algorithms is the base population. Usually, however, software architects only model one initial candidate that serves as the basis. Therefore, PerOpteryx instantiates in step 1 random, new candidates to set up the base population. The base population is created on the basis of the initial candidate and the configured degrees of freedom. It is later used in the evolutionary optimization process.

PerOpteryx evaluates (step 2.a) the candidates with the help of a set of objective functions. The objective functions correspond to the quality attributes to be evaluated, such as performance. Their results are the basis for selecting promising candidates.

The evaluated architecture candidates are then passed into the selection step (step 2.b): the weakest candidates are removed from the population. For example, weak candidates are Pareto-dominated candidates. The Pareto-optimal candidates are kept in the base populations for the reproduction step.

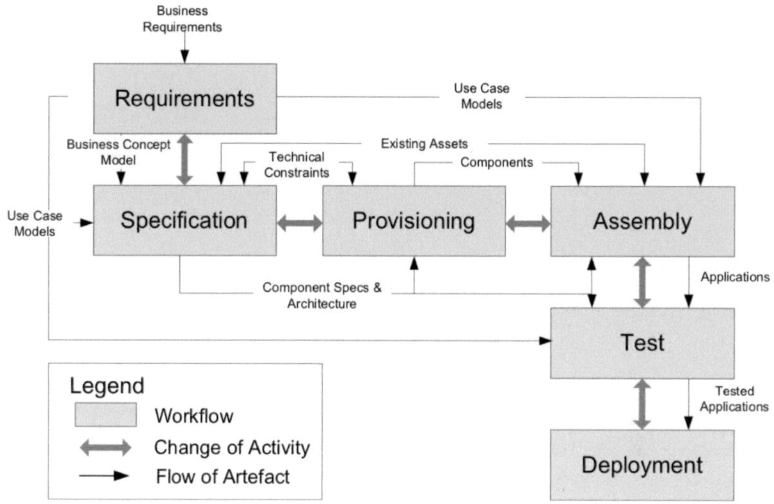

Figure 3.14.: Component-based Development Process after Cheesman and Daniels, 2000 [CD00]. Graphic from [KH06b].

In the reproduction step (step 2.c), the promising candidates are used as a basis for the generation of new candidates with the help of cross-over or mutation operators. In addition, PerOpteryx introduces the *tactics* operator. The tactics operator has been optimized for software architecture models and models architecture knowledge to improve the performance of newly generated candidates.

PerOpteryx repeats the three steps until the stop criterion is reached. This is for example a configured number of iterations or a convergence criterion of the Pareto-front. After the stop criterion has been reached, the Pareto-optimal candidates are returned (step 3). Based on the results, decision makers can select the best suitable architecture candidate.

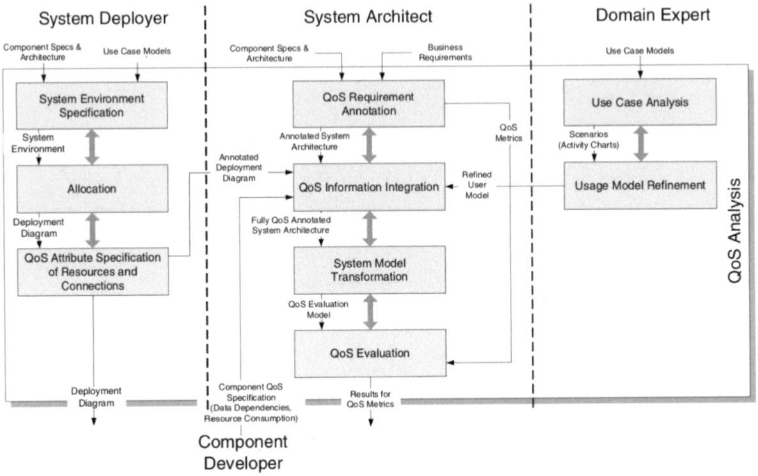

Figure 3.15.: Quality analysis workflow of extended CBSE after Koziolek and Happe, 2006 [KH06b].

3.4. Component-based Software Development Process (CBSE)

The component-based software development process (CBSE) by Cheesman and Daniels is based on the object-oriented design of classical software engineering. CBSE divides individual work steps according to different roles of a structured development process. During the process, the phases (workflows) are carried out known from the Rational Unified Process (RUP). The process starts with the collection of requirements, specification, provisioning, assembly, test and finally deployment. Each phase can be repeated such as in the RUP and thus requirements and system can be improved step by step. The tasks of the individual workflows are as follows:

- **Requirements:** In the first step, the main task is to determine the business requirements of the system. The result is a business concept model with use cases that play an important role in the business model. In addition, a concept model of the business domain and a shared understanding of the vocabulary used between all stakeholders involved is created.

- **Specification:** The software architecture is designed in the specification. The business concept model and the use cases defined in the previous workflow are used as the basis. If technical restrictions exist, they are also defined in the specification. The system architect first identifies components and defines their interaction with each other. This specification of the software components is then passed on to the component developer for implementation. Finally, the system architect performs an interoperability check on the components.
- **Provisioning:** In this workflow, either components are selected from existing repositories or 3rd party components are purchased. The repository also contains components that were designed in the previous workflow and passed on to the component developer. If necessary, these components are implemented. Technical restrictions are also analysed and applied.
- **Assembly:** In this step, the components provisioned in the previous step are assembled to the system. The component architecture and the use cases defined in the requirements workflow serve as the basis.
- **Test:** In the test workflow, the application created in the previous workflow is tested by using the use case model. Test development also takes place in this workflow.
- **Deployment:** In the deployment workflow, the application is installed on the physical hardware resources. The hardware environment may also have to be adapted and employee training carried out.

3.4.1. Quality Analysis in the CBSE

The component-based software development process was revised and extended by H. Koziolek and J. Happe [KH06b] to enable the prediction of quantitative quality properties using software architecture models. For this reason, they introduce a new workflow into the process, namely the *Quality Analysis* workflow. It is arranged between specification and provisioning. The quality analysis is performed on the basis of the component specification and software architecture, as well as the use case models and technical constraints. The resulting (predicted) quality properties are fed back into the specification and validated. If they do not meet the requirements, the specification is adapted accordingly.

The quality analysis workflow internally consists of three parts, which are carried out by three different roles. Domain expert analyse use cases and extract relevant properties for the quality prediction. On their basis, they adapt the usage model so that quality predictions become possible. Deployers provide the system architect additional information about the resource environment of the system. System architects finally integrate all information, execute the *system model transformation* workflow that automatically generates the integrated models. Finally, they perform the quality prediction in the *QoS Evaluation* workflow based on the integrated models.

3.4.2. Quality Exploration in the CBSE

Based on the quality prediction of the quality analysis, software architectures can be optimized.

Quality analysis inputs are requirements, represented by use cases, the software architecture, represented by software components and their relationships to each other. Further, it uses information about the resource environment describing the intended hardware specification, and the usage context of the system. At this point, however, it is unclear whether the existing specification works together, i.e. the hardware environment, selected components and usage profile can meet the business requirements. The quality analysis itself provides information at the end whether requirements are being met or whether they need to be adapted. However, it remains unclear whether, for example, hardware resources or components and their allocation to the resources must be changed. System architects would now use either their existing domain knowledge or their experience to adapt the aforementioned parameters until they fit the requirements. In such cases, it would remain unclear whether the configuration found matches

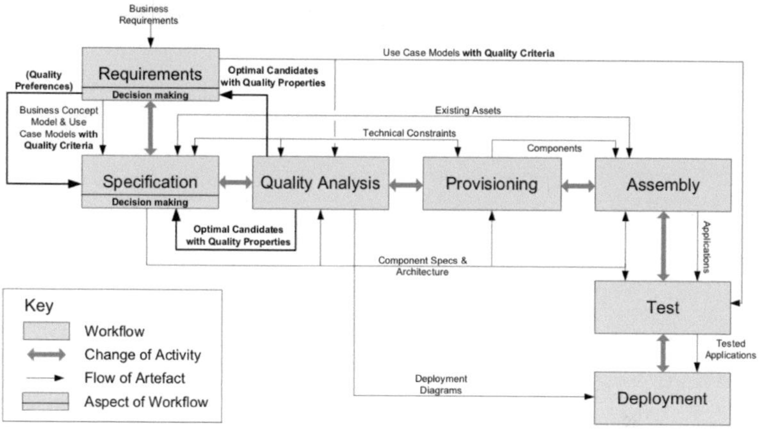

Figure 3.16.: Component-based Development Process with quality exploration after A. Koziolek, 2011 [Koz11].

the requirements optimally. In addition, manual adaptation of the models and evaluation of the quality properties is time-consuming. Therefore, the quality exploration extension by A. Koziolek replaces the system model transformation workflow and the QoS evaluation workflow with the architecture exploration workflow. This allows to automatically optimize software architectures according to its quality attributes.

Figure 3.17 illustrates the automated exploration workflow replacing the QoS evaluation. The workflow for automated architecture exploration uses the software architecture with all quality-relevant information as input. The information depends on the quality attribute that is to be examined. Based on the system architecture, degrees of freedom can be identified automatically. Degrees of freedom correspond to the parameters that had to be manually adjusted in the original QoS evaluation workflow, namely allocation of components, hardware selection, and selection of software components. The automatically derived degrees of freedom can be revised by the software architect. For example, additional hardware resources can be made available that cannot be automatically derived from the existing software architecture models. In addition, exploration restrictions can be defined, such as restrictions for certain hardware configurations. Finally,

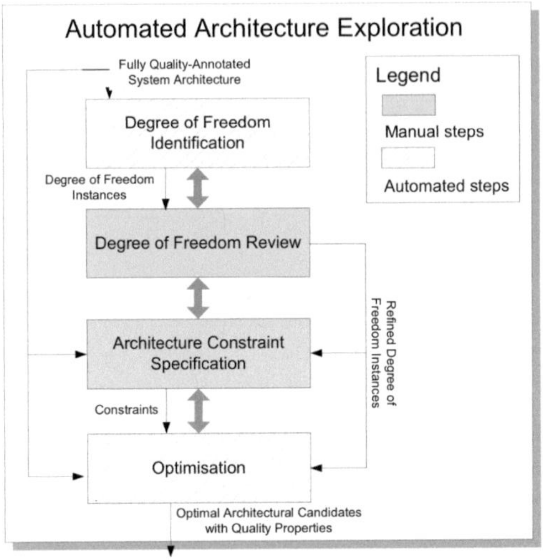

Figure 3.17.: Automated exploration workflow after A. Koziolek, 2011 [Koz11].

the architecture is automatically optimized with the revised degrees of freedom and the Pareto-optimal architecture candidates with the quality properties can be used in the decision-making step.

The result of the exploration can be used in the two workflows *requirements* and *specifications* for the *decision making*. The Pareto-optimal architecture candidates obtained from the quality analysis serve as the basis for further decisions. Now, costs for quality attributes, such as increasing or decreasing performance or reliability are known. On this basis, requirements engineers and system architects together with other stakeholders can now decide on the individual quality attributes and weight them against each other. A suitable candidate can now be selected on the basis of quantitative data. If none of the candidates matches the requirements, requirements can be prioritized or revised.

4. Related Work

This chapter presents related work to the *CompARE* approach. We discuss related work and approaches that are relevant to the challenges of automatic optimization of software architecture models when reusing complex subsystems and are within the scope of the contributions of this dissertation. All discussed approaches in the foundations from the previous chapters will not be discussed again.

Figure 4.1 illustrates the main groups of related work that correspond to the main phases of the *CompARE* approach: The first part considers modelling and evaluation of knowledge for the optimization of software architectures. The second part is about automated model generation, variability and automated reuse of software architecture models and software artefacts. Finally, the third part considers supporting software architects in the design of component-based software architectures.

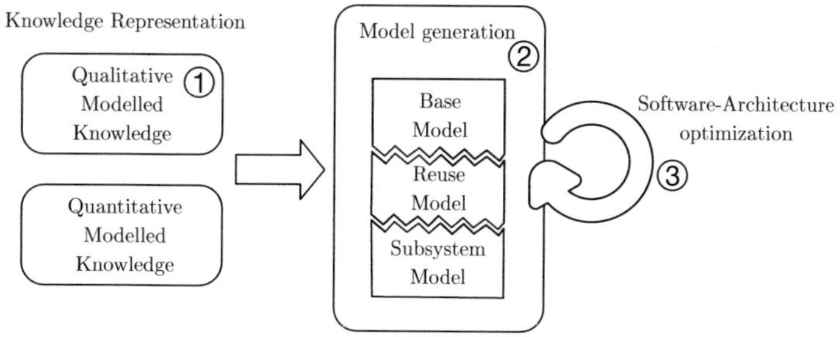

Figure 4.1.: Groups of related work in context of the *CompARE* approach.

4.1. Modelling and Representing Knowledge

Related work in this category is divided into knowledge modelling for decision-making and general knowledge representation. However, both categories are not selective, but overlap in each case.

4.1.1. Knowledge for Decision Making

Gordon et al. present in [GKN15] their QuABaseBD approach, a knowledge base containing the major architecture characteristics of distributed databases. The knowledge base is enriched by semantics such that analysis by queries can be carried out. The approach aims at the high challenges of software architects whenever they design distributed systems and need to make decisions on the database technology. Often, challenges arise in terms of quality attributes and architecture design since the database technology chosen has direct influences on the software architecture and the quality attributes. QuABAseBD should help software architects in that decisions by using the knowledge base. They use a feature based taxonomy modelling software and data architectures. On the basis of the taxonomy knowledge about database systems can be captured, queried and visualized. The knowledge model comprises two parts: The first part considers concepts related to quality attributes, quality attribute scenarios, and architecture tactics. They support the significant architecture requirements, helping to identify the architecture trade-off. The second part represents a feature taxonomy: For the feature taxonomy, they introduce three categories considering the data architecture, namely data model, query languages, and consistency. Further, they introduce three categories considering the software architecture:

- **Scalability:** The architecture design of a database influences the overall performance and scalability of the application. Replication, load balancing or locking strategies can have major influence on the performance.
- **Data Distribution:** Strategies about the distribution of data has influences on the software architecture and by this on the quality attributes. In case of higher data distribution on several nodes, the

data management overhead increases, can have a positive influence on performance, but the data reliability may decrease.

- **Data Replication:** Replicating data on different nodes influences the software architecture. Replication could be achieved for instance by physical replication. However, the replication and consistency overhead increases, performance may be influenced negatively, but the data availability may increase.
- **Security:** The main consideration of security is data integrity and preventing unauthorized access. Features such as client authentication, database encryption, and logging increase the quality attribute security, influence the software architecture and by this other quality attributes.

These two sections are linked to each other. By this relationship, software architects can reason about architecture qualities resulting from architecture decisions considering distributed databases.

Liu et al. present in [LG03] the i-Mate process that is similar to QuABaseBD. In contrast, they focus on COTS-middleware components providing core software infrastructure. They argue, that due to a growing COTS market, the product selection became complex what increases the risk of selecting the wrong product that does not fit the requirements. Middleware products become increasingly complex, larger, and offer thousands of features that strongly affect the behaviour in the user application. In addition, many competing middleware products appear to contain similar or identical features, but differ in quality attributes, prices, and their actual implementation. Thus, i-Mate defines a knowledge base containing data on middleware systems. As in QuABaseBD, i-Mate's knowledge base includes categories containing the products. It also includes evaluations of middleware products on a scale from one to five.

The i-Mate selection process is shown in Figure 4.2. The selection process for the appropriate middleware component requires information about the stakeholders' requirements as input. These are first formalized and initially prioritized. The resulting ranking is then used for product evaluation (using the i-Mate knowledge base). If the identified product meets the requirements, it is used, for example, to develop a prototype; if not, requirements are re-prioritized.

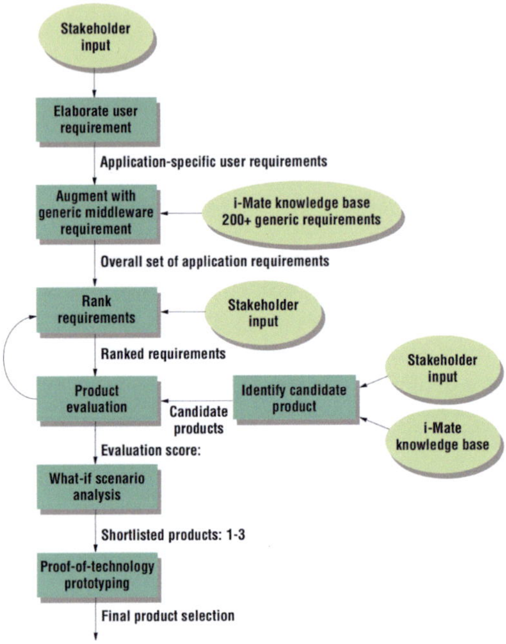

Figure 4.2.: The i-Mate middleware selection process [LG03].

Both approaches are similar to the approach presented in this dissertation. It is about supporting architecture decisions regarding quality attributes when using features. In contrast to the approaches from Gorton and Liu, the *CompARE* follows a generalized method of subsystem reuse (such as the database and middleware systems). In addition, *CompARE* supports the optimization of software architectures and is based on software architecture models.

4.1.1.1. Knowledge Representation

Glinz demonstrates in [Gli08] a risk-based, value-oriented approach to represent knowledge instead of the quantification of quality attributes. He focuses on the representation of quality requirements so that they deliver the greatest benefit. In other words, this means identifying the risk of developing the wrong system and reducing those risks with countermeasures. To achieve this, different risk assessments, namely stakeholder importance and impact must be performed for all requirements. He also assesses whether a requirement is difficult to quantify or easy to quantify. The result is a table showing the importance, risk and quantifiability of each requirement. In case of an easy quantifiable requirement with high risk, the requirement should be quantified. If a quality requirement is not quantifiable or difficult to quantify but has high risk and importance, countermeasures are operationalised.

The value-oriented approach of Glinz is similar to the modelling approach of informal knowledge introduced in this dissertation. However, in this dissertation, the formally represented knowledge (by a formalized meta model) can be evaluated automatically. Furthermore, the knowledge can be used together with quantitative methods for automatic evaluation and optimization.

Lenhard and Wirtz combine in [LW13] quantified knowledge with quality-valued knowledge to model the portability of executable service-oriented processes. They reuse process definitions in an XML based format and define metrics that consider characteristics of process-oriented programs. They enrich the metrics with domain knowledge of the languages and environments of the programs. Further, they use empirical data on language support in current run times. Portability of a program depends on the runtime of each program. Each runtime has its own supported set of language elements. For their analysis they define a degree of portability for each language element. The fewer languages support a particular element, the lower is the degree of portability for the particular element.

Lenhard and Wirtz combine quantified and qualitative modelling techniques to evaluate the portability of service-oriented processes. The approach results in a value that gives an initial assessment of portability. However, the procedure is strongly tailored to the quality attribute portability and incorporates platform-specific characteristics. For software models, we abstract from the platform and the available language constructs.

Bredeweg et al. describe in [Bre+09] the Garp3 workbench allowing modelling, simulation, and analysis of qualitative models of system behaviour. Garp3 is based on qualitative reasoning. Since qualitative reasoning is a powerful approach that can be quite complex to use, they limit the method enabling domain experts a user-friendly approach to represent their conceptual knowledge. Garp3 comprises two parts, namely the knowledge representation model, and the reasoning engine.

The knowledge representation model is divided into two parts. It consists of the basic model ingredients and aggregates. Aggregates internally consists of basic model ingredients. The aggregates consist of two parts, the scenarios and the model fragments. Scenarios are the input elements of the qualitative reasoning simulator. The simulator generates initial states from the scenario, which are used as a basis for generating the remaining behaviour graph. The behaviour graph represents the possible behaviour of systems. Model fragments model the architecture and behaviour of systems. Internally, model fragments consist either of conditions or consequences. Conditions define when fragments can be applied, while consequences define the knowledge that is introduced when a condition applies. Therefore, they can be understood as a kind of rules. They are stored in a library, which are used by the scenario, to perform the simulation. Further, proportionalities, i.e. direct relations between quantities, can be modelled.

Garp3 has similarities with the analysis of quality-valued quality attributes of the approach presented in this dissertation. We also use scenarios, such as the evaluation of a specific service with respect to specific quality attributes. We also define conditions and consequences in the form of quality values of individual quality attributes per component and effects across the boundaries of multiple quality attributes. In contrast, we developed the approach specifically for evaluating quality attributes in component-based software architecture models. Furthermore, the result of the analysis can be used to automatically optimize software architectures. A common consideration of the results from the qualitative reasoning analysis and the result of quantitative objective functions by this becomes possible.

Chung, Mylopoulos et al. present in [Chu+12; MCN92] their NFR framework for representing non-functional requirements. The framework consists of five components: namely goals, link types, goal refinement methods, correlation rules, and labelling positions.

- **Goals:** A set of goals defines the non-functional requirements, design decisions, and arguments that support or oppose goals. NFR defines different classes of goals. These goals are later organized in a graph structure.
- **Link Types:** Link types allow linking of goals to each other. For example parent goals can be defined together with a set of sub goals.
- **Goal refinement methods:** Goal refinement methods can be used by the designer to refine goals in one or more offspring or satisfying goals.
- **Correlation Rules:** Correlation rules define possible conflicting interactions across goal boundaries.
- **Labelling Procedure:** Labelling positions model the degree of fulfilment of a design decision with respect to non-functional requirements.

Similar to the approach described here, the NFR framework defines elements for modelling informal knowledge. Our form of knowledge representation allows performing qualitative reasoning analysis and automatically evaluate and optimize software architectures according to its results.

Supakkul et al. describe in [SC12] the RE-tools. The basis of the RE tools is StarUML[1], a UML modelling tool. The RE tools extend StarUML by a UML profile that allows annotating values to UML entities using stereotypes. The RE tools are based on the qualitative reasoning of the NFR framework, but extend it with quantitative, weight-based trade-off analysis. This annotates weights to entities, such as 1.0 for high, 0.5 for medium, or 0.2 for low. By mapping them to weights, further analyses can be performed on the basis of the values.

The approach presented in this dissertation also uses stereotypes to annotate values or multi-value functions to UML entities. However, we do not annotate numerical values, but remain in a qualitative notation as long as possible and run aggregation analyses directly on these qualitative values.

1 http://staruml.sourceforge.net

4.2. Automated Model Generation and Model Variability

Related work in this category is divided into reusing model artefacts by completions and modelling variability in software architecture models. Related work in both categories is described in detail in the following.

4.2.1. Reuse model artefacts by completions

Lehrig et al. present in [LHB18] the architecture templates. Architecture templates can be used to reuse architecture styles and architecture patterns in component-based software architectures and to apply them to a base software architecture model. The approach defines a formal language for modelling architecture styles on Palladio's software component model. They use model transformations in the QVT-O transformation language to incorporate architecture elements into the PCM model. The approach provides templates to automatically implement architecture styles, such as multi-tier architectures. Each template also contains a set of quality annotations that can be evaluated after the model transformation with the other quality properties of the software architecture.

However, Lehrig's approach does not allow new functionality to be introduced into the architecture in the form of subsystems. It is limited to the implementation of architecture styles. Furthermore, it is not possible to evaluate qualitative modelled quality attributes.

Kienzle et al. present in [Kie+16b] their approach to Concern Oriented Reuse (CORE). It is based on aspect oriented extension techniques and has been adapted for software architecture models and software product lines. The goal of CORE is to extend software architecture models and code through functionalities as well as to evaluate the expected quality attributes [AKM13]. The reuse unit is represented by the *Concern*, which provides multiple interfaces to reuse, adapt, and model variations [Kie+16c]. The reusable aspect model [KAK09] can be used for modelling variants as aspects. By using this model, architects can define the architecture and the behaviour. Variability is modelled by using feature models. Effects of the functionalities on the quality requirements of the overall system

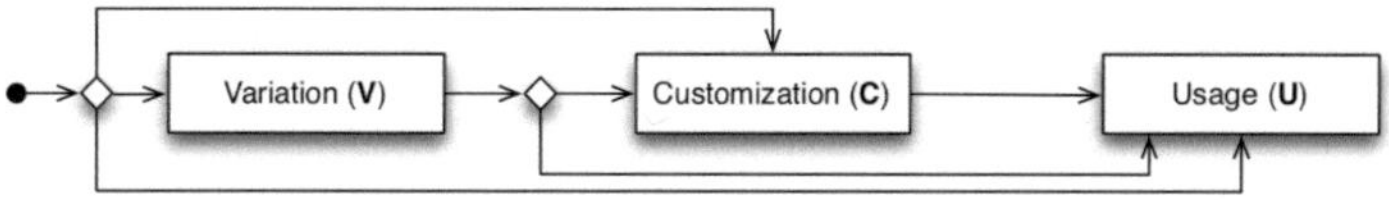

Figure 4.3.: The variation, customization and usage interface reuse approach [Kie+16c].

are modelled by using goal models. CORE defines three interfaces (see Figure 4.3) mentioned above:

- **Usage:** The usage interface defines how to use the concern from outside and what functionality is provided by the concern.
- **Customization:** The customization interface is related to the software product line paradigm. Customization is achieved by leaving elements open at the design time of the concern needed to be complemented later. Software architects must complement the models in the reuse process.
- **Variation:** The variation interface is responsible for the variants provided by the concern. Functionality is described by feature models, while effects on quality are described by goal models.

Although CORE has similarities to the presented approach, especially in the representation of the interfaces, with CORE it is not possible to integrate variable functionalities of subsystems. Further, no implementation alternatives of subsystems in a base system can be automatically exchanged, evaluated and optimized. The description of the quality requirements with the help of goal models further represents a comparatively coarse granular estimation of the quality attributes than a simulation with subsequent software architecture optimization.

J. Happe [Hap09] and L. Happe [Hap11] introduce configurable completion, which complements software architecture models (more precisely Palladio software architecture models) on the infrastructure layer. The goal is to explicitly represent performance effects of middleware systems, such as the Java Messaging Service, in models. L.Happe extended the middleware approach by architecture patterns, such as concurrency patterns, thread pools, and pipe and filter architectures.

Becker also concentrates in [Bec08] on middleware completions, which for example integrate the overhead of different protocols into software architecture models by annotations. The approach extends software architecture models to refine performance-relevant information for design time predictions. Becker also uses the concept of completion components, which, however, introduces quality effects at the infrastructure layer.

The mentioned approaches focus on the extension of software architecture models regarding lower-level infrastructure services, whose main purpose is the refinement of the performance model. We focus on the introduction of new functionality, e.g. to implement or refine requirements.

4.2.2. Variability Models

Beuche et al. describe in [BPS04] how feature models can be used for managing variability in software development processes by using CONSUL. CONSUL uses feature models from Kang et al. [Kan+90] to describe the modelled external functionalities. The feature models are then refined by the family model. The family model defines a kind of architecture for a family of components and links it to the parts model. In the case of C/C++, for example, the parts model consist of header files or C++ source code files. However, build instructions can also be included. In total, a part contains all instructions and artefacts that are necessary to generate executable code.

CONSUL comprises two languages: Prolog is used to model the relations between different features. The selection of components and their adaptation is also modelled with Prolog. The XML-based language XMLTrans is used to describe the transformation to code. XMLTrans is used to model all the steps necessary to transform from feature selection to executable code. Information about the platform itself is also contained, for example whether file links are available on the target platform.

CompARE also uses feature models to describe the externally visible functionalities. However, we concentrate on the assembly of software models and their variability of features within the base architecture in which the feature functionality is to be integrated. In addition, another main feature of *CompARE* is that design decisions of the software architecture regarding the expected quality can be evaluated before implementation.

Deursen and Klint introduce in [DK01] their Feature Description Language (FDL), a domain-specific language to describe features formally. The FDL expresses all relationships between features, as is also possible in graphical notation. The advantage of the FDL, however, is its formal definition, on which automatic analyses can then be performed: On the FDL, analyses can be performed on the FDL using a feature diagram algebra. For example, it is possible to query whether the feature model contains a configuration to meet a specific requirement. Such queries are not possible on pure graphically represented feature models. The FDL can also be used to automatically build UML diagrams or Java code skeletons that match the design of the feature model. Such a process potentially increases the efficiency of the software development process by transforming models into code artefacts.

Krueger present in [Kru02; Kru08] the GEARS approach, a commercial tool, allowing managing variability. They use feature models to define product line feature diversity for the software product life cycle. By using the product configurator, software architects configure the product line and its instances by selecting features from the feature model. The product configuration is then used as a basis to instantiate all products with its individual features.

In contrast, *CompARE* combines features from feature models with software architecture models that can be used for further analysis. The purpose of this combination is that the analysis and knowledge representation is not bundled in the features, but is contained in the linked software architecture models. This has the advantage that any knowledge can be mapped and analysed later. In other words, features are used to define variability points in the base architecture and to generate different model instances at these variability points that can be used for further analysis.

4.3. Support for Software-Architecture optimization

In this section, we introduce several automatic, semi-automatic and manual approaches to optimize or improve software architectures regarding quality attributes.

Falessi et al. survey in [Fal+11] decision-making techniques for software architecture design. They compare 15 decision-making techniques considering 4 categories, namely solution selection, stakeholder disagreement, attribute meaning and solution property. They find that no decision-making technique is best, but all have their strength and weaknesses.

None of the approaches considers a combination of quantitative and qualitative evaluated quality attributes or allows to automatically include new requirements by integrating subsystems into a base software architecture, to evaluate different solutions and to automatically analyze their effects on the quality attributes.

4.3.1. Automatic and semi-automatic approaches

Aleti et al. describe in [Ale+09] their ArcheOpteryx approach, a framework implementing evaluation techniques and optimization heuristics for software architecture models. They base on the architecture analysis and description language (AADL) MetaH [Bin+96]. It represents an automated approach for software architecture optimization considering quality attributes. ArcheOpteryx comprises three major modules as illustrated in Figure 4.4:

- **AADL model parser:** The AADL model parser reads the models specified in MetaH into ArcheOpteryx for further processing. The software architecture is built with respect to processors, processes, networks, etc. This input model is the basis for the architecture analysis module.
- **Architecture analysis module:** In the architecture analysis module, the parameters of the model and the application domain are stored in an abstract representation. On this basis, the quality

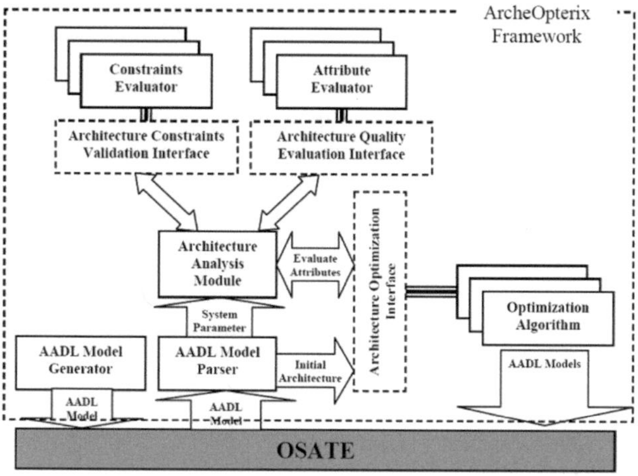

Figure 4.4.: Illustration of the ArcheOpteryx architecture [Ale+09].

evaluation of an architecture is carried out using different evaluation techniques. The evaluation itself is analyzed by the attribute evaluators. In addition, constraints are checked on the software architecture models. For this purpose there is a set of constraint evaluators.

- **Architecture optimization interface:** The architecture optimization interface uses the results of the architecture evaluation and the architecture constraint checker. From these results, Pareto-optimal or almost Pareto-optimal architecture candidates are derived and used for later analysis or for further iterations. The architecture candidates resulting as Pareto-optimal can then be transformed back into MetaH. ArcheOpteryx uses evolutionary algorithms for the generation of new architecture candidates. These can be fed back to the attribute evaluators and constraint checkers for re-evaluation.

ArcheOpteryx enables varying the deployment of components and allows to evaluate the quality attributes data transmission reliability and communication overhead. However, it can be extended by other quality attributes. ArcheOpteryx focused on constraints within software architecture models.

Quality attributes, such as performance, can be analyzed, but in a much more limited scope than is possible with the method used in *CompARE*. In addition, no arbitrary quality attributes can be considered, for example by a qualitative evaluation on the basis of qualitative reasoning. An evaluation of the use of complex subsystems and the comparison of implementation alternatives is also not possible.

In [Wal+13], Walker et al. describe their automatic, multi-objective approach for optimization of system architectures. They base on EAST-ADL, an architecture description language in the automotive domain. Their approach allows optimizing software architectures according to several quality attributes, such as dependability, timing/performance and cost. They use the NSGA-II genetic algorithms to explore the design space of software architecture models. They use a variability model to define variability in the automotive domain, such as the optional inclusion of a rain sensor. The variability is then used as degree of freedom. In total, the approach can optimize architecture candidates using substitution of components, functions or subsystems for others with different quality properties, replication of components to improve reliability, and allocation to balance load.

The approach has similarities to the *CompARE* approach with regard to the variability of software models. Walker's approach, however, is limited to the exchange of already integrated components, whereby either single components or entire subsystems can be exchanged. However, it is not possible to automatically integrate functionalities that do not exist in the architecture, to evaluate different positions of the subsystem and to analyze their effects on the quality attributes. Furthermore, the possibility of evaluating quality attributes is limited. A detailed performance evaluation or an examination of any quality attributes is not possible.

Abdeen et al. present in [Abd+14] a rule based optimization approach. They use the NSGA-II evolutionary algorithm to process the rule-based design space exploration. The basis is an initial model on which they apply a sequence of rules to find alternative candidate models. To make sure generating valid models, they apply a set of constraints. The rules are represented by graph transformation rules, coming with input and output parameters to pass information between rules when processing rules in a sequence. As quality attributes, the approach considers server utilization and cost.

Abdeen's rule-based approach to optimizing software architectures calculates comparatively simple quality attributes. Furthermore, the initial candidate is particularly important, since it is used as the basis for the application of the rules. If the initial candidate is chosen suboptimally, the optimal candidates are not necessarily found, depending on the rule set.

With ArcheE, Bachman et al. describe in [Bac+05] their approach for supporting software architects to weight against quality requirements in the design phase. It supports the architect in creating the software architecture model and collecting suitable requirements. The optimization of the software architecture is carried out based on rules. Rules are provided for the modifiability of the system. In addition to the modifiability, the performance analysis is supported as a further quality attribute to be analyzed. The modifiability is analyzed based on the model from Bohner and Arnold [BA96], while for performance analysis the rate monotonic analysis method from Klein et al. [Kle+93] is used.

ArcheE is a semi-automated approach to improve software architectures. The approach requires the interaction with the user and consultation with the stakeholders. This interaction implies that search space cannot be searched automatically, but is derived from the interactions with the user and the rules.

Xu introduced in [Xu12; Xu08] Performance Booster, a rule-based approach for automatic software performance diagnosis and improvement. Performance Booster focuses on improving the performance of software architectures. Performance data is obtained from annotated UML models and evaluated using layered queuing networks (LQN). The approach can identify performance bottlenecks or long execution paths. If found, rules can be applied to improve the response time or throughput of the service. Performance Booster provides rules for redistributing components, reduction of component resource demands, or introduction of asynchronous processing. This results in recommendations for software architectures that do not necessarily have to be functionally equivalent to the base architecture.

Performance Booster is limited to improving performance and cannot analyze any other quality attributes. As with the rule-based approach of Abdeen, the selection of the initial candidate is important. In addition, bottlenecks can only be recognized if the performance properties are modelled in detail. The *CompARE* approach has similarities in that functionally

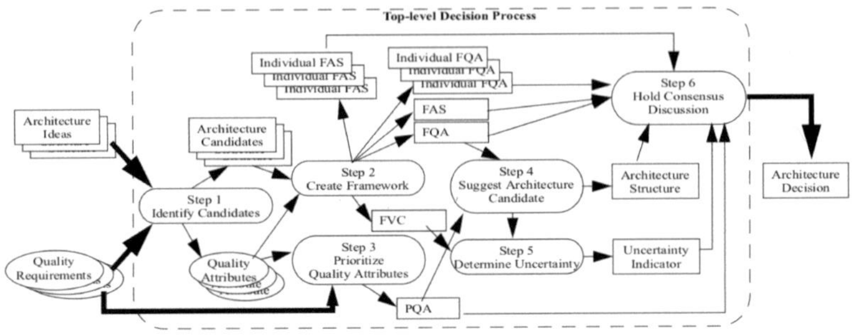

Figure 4.5.: Illustration of the decision support process from Svahnberg et al. [Sva+03].

equivalent software architectures do not necessarily result after optimization. However, the software architect explicitly chooses to use certain functionalities that result directly from the requirements.

4.3.2. Manual approaches

Svahnberg et al. showed in [SW05; Sva+03] a method basing on an analytical hierarchy process (AHP) enabling the (pair-wise) evaluation of software architecture candidates considering quality attributes. They use a multi-criteria decision method. Their approach comprises six steps (as shown in Figure 4.5) to identify the best architecture candidate according to the considered requirements:

- **Identify candidates and quality attributes:** In the first step, potentially fruitful architecture candidates and relevant quality attributes are selected. Architecture candidates can, for example, be created using various design methods such as the unified software development process by Jacobson et al. [JBR99]. Standard requirements engineering methods such as the NFR framework [Chu+12] can be used to collect the relevant quality attributes. Depending on the importance of the individual aspects of the architecture candidate, these are modelled in different modelling granularity. The resulting model of the architecture candidates and the selection of relevant quality attributes serve as input parameters for the process.

- **Framework:** During the use of the framework, architecture candidates are compared in pairs. It aims at getting the understanding on the degree of fulfilment of a software architecture candidate regarding quality attributes. For the pairwise comparison, they use the AHP method from Saaty and Vargas [SV12]. The result of the analysis is two vectors: A vector describes the relative support of the quality attributes between architecture candidates. The second vector describes the reverse case, namely a comparison of different quality attributes for each of the considered software architecture candidates.
- **Prioritize quality attributes:** In the third step, quality attributes are prioritized according to the system requirements. The approach is based on the AHP process. As a result, the prioritized quality attributes are mapped in a vector.
- **Suggest architecture candidate:** This step analyses the most suitable software architecture candidate. The best candidate is determined with the help of the vectors from the second step. The analysis is carried out with the help of value comparisons between vectors. The architecture candidate with the values closest to the expectation vector dominates the comparison.
- **Determine uncertainty:** In step five, the degree of uncertainty is determined. For this, the variance of the architecture candidates is determined. If the uncertainty is high, this means that the quality attributes of the architecture candidate are not sufficiently well understood or investigated and deeper analyses are necessary.
- **Consensus discussion:** In the discussion, the selected architecture candidate and various possible architecture alternatives with their respective quality attributes are discussed. The main goal is to work out disagreements between the participants of the discussion. These will then be discussed and problems worked out. The result is a list of problems that need to be analysed in more detail and a solution worked out so that the project can be carried out successfully.

The process of Svahnberg et al. is based on AHP and is therefore a manual process that requires strong interaction between stakeholders to lead to promising results. Only comparatively few architecture candidates can be evaluated. This is because AHP requires pairwise comparisons. The number of comparisons increases exponentially with the increase in the number of architecture candidates considered. Therefore, in practice only few architecture candidates can be considered and the initially selected architecture candidates, which are to be analysed, are particularly important. Promising candidates that have not been considered in this phase are not considered. The approach presented in this dissertation is based on the search for promising architecture candidates using evolutionary algorithms. It allows many candidates to be automatically generated, evaluated and dominant candidates selected without manual effort.

Regnell et al. propose in [RSO08] their QUPER approach that analyses software architecture trade-off decisions regarding quality attributes, such as performance and cost. They developed QUPER to be robust to uncertainties, easy to use and domain relevant. QUPER's main concept is the relation between benefit and quality level. Therefore, the authors define four levels, namely useless, useful, competitive and excessive. Additionally, they define breakpoints between these levels, namely the utility breakpoint, differentiation breakpoint and saturation breakpoint. Depending on the market position and budget, it has to be decided which breakpoint should be reached. Further, each quality level has cost barriers. The application of QUPER requires four main steps: First, the quality indicators are determined. Second, for each quality indicator users of QUPER must determine breakpoints and barriers. Third, users of QUPER must determine the current quality of the product. Fourth, users of QUPER must estimate current targets and candidate targets considering quality attributes and costs.

Kazman et al. propose in [Kaz+98] their architecture trade-off analysis method (ATAM). They build on the Software Architecture Analysis Method (SAAM) [Kaz+96]. Similar to approaches described before, ATAM analyses software architectures with respect to quality attributes. ATAM is a system design and analysis method that introduces technical aspects considering collecting and the analysis of relevant data, as well as social aspects considering the communication between stakeholders. The method is designed as a spiral model, where each iteration aims at improving understanding,

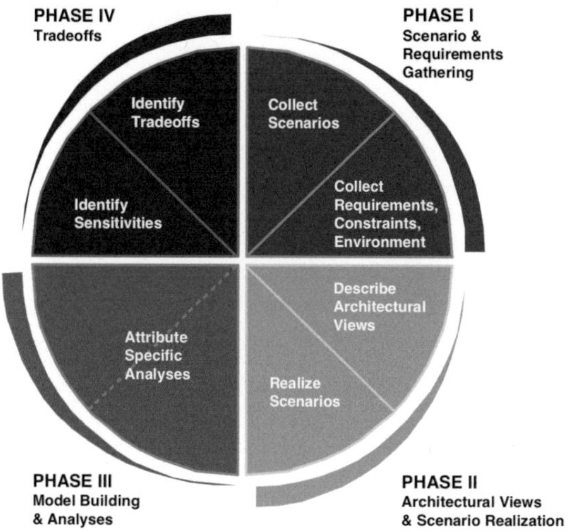

Figure 4.6.: Process phases of the Architecture Trade-off Analysis Method (ATAM) [Kaz+98].

design, and reducing risks. The process is divided in four major parts with 6 steps as shown in Figure 4.6.

The first step and the second step of ATAM collects usage scenarios and requirements as well as constraints and environment details. The purpose of this part is to operationalize functional and quality requirements. This collection facilitates communication between stakeholders. The third step describes the architecture candidates. This includes the software architecture and its entities, as well as properties of the relevant quality attributes. Mostly, several architecture candidates are created that can be compared with each other. After the specification of scenarios, requirements and an initial set of architecture candidates, the quality attributes of each individual architecture candidate are evaluated in step four. This results in quantitative values, such as response times for the performance quality attribute in milliseconds or the average failure rate in days. In step five, a sensitivity analysis of a given software architecture is performed. If the software architecture is changed, the resulting quality characteristics changes. The sensitivity analysis determines which changes to the architecture result in the largest changes in quality. Step six evaluates the previously created architecture models. Trade-off points in the architecture are evaluated using the previously identified sensitivity points. The results of the six phases are then compared with the requirements. If the results do not match the requirements, the phases can be repeated until convergence. Each iteration takes the result of the last iteration as input.

Like the process by Svahnberg, the QUPER approach and the ATAM are manual processes. Architecture candidates cannot be found, evaluated and optimized by automatic support.

5. Quantifying the Quality Attribute Security

Many approaches to design time prediction of quality attributes rely objective functions resulting in quantitative values. Such an objective function is the basis of Palladio's performance evaluation. The throughput and response time of a software model service is calculated by functions that provide quantitative results. While quantitative objective functions for predicting performance, reliability and costs have already been scientifically considered, there are no objective functions for many other quality attributes. One example is the quality attribute security in component-based software architectures.

However, creating a quantitative objective function according to scientific criteria requires a high degree of domain knowledge, is time-consuming and often has many limitations. In this chapter, we create a quantitative objective function for the quality attribute security. We discuss the approach, apply it to an example system, discuss its limitations and the time required for its development.

In the following sections, we show how an objective function and a meta model for the analysis of the quality attribute security can be defined in the context of component-based software architectures. For demonstration purposes, we combine several aspects that are typical for security estimation approaches (cf. [Mad+04]): i) the skill of attackers or groups of attackers, ii) a specific target of the attack, iii) security properties of the components of the system and iv) mutual security influences between components. We divide the evaluation problem into several sub-models to keep the approach open for extensions.

We combine the resulting sub-models and represent them in a mathematical model using a semi-Markov process. This results in an integrated model that offers a metric, namely the mean time to security failure (MTTSF). The metric allows comparing different architecture candidates of component-based software architectures with respect to security quality attributes, but keeps the model sufficiently modular for extensions. To apply the approach to an already existing approach, we extend the PCM by security annotations. For the integration into Palladio and its component model, we create a transformation that transforms the annotated architecture model into a semi-Markov process. As a result, our objective function represents a stochastic model for estimating the security quality attribute of component-based systems.

5.1. Motivation

Security is becoming increasingly important due to the increasing network-demand of services. Attacks on such services are becoming more likely due to a growing variety of highly connected services and increasing expected profits. In the years 2010 - 2013, the number of incidents involving personal data theft has increased by more than 40% [Ver13]. It is therefore necessary to consider security attributes in software architectures.

Especially for the design of component-based software architectures, it seems appropriate to use the quality of the individual components as a basis for estimating the security quality of the overall system. The quality properties of the individual components then allow conclusions to be drawn about the quality properties of the overall system.

Our approach assesses the security by systematically evaluating security attributes of software systems in component-based systems. The objective function helps to systematically compare different software architecture candidates and to support trade-off decisions on other quality attributes.

To assess the security performance of software systems, we take into account a number of factors that influence security. Typical attacks involves i) an attacker with specific attacker skills, ii) a possible start and target (component) in the system, iii) the component design itself, iv) the effort that was spent in security considerations, v) the deployment of software

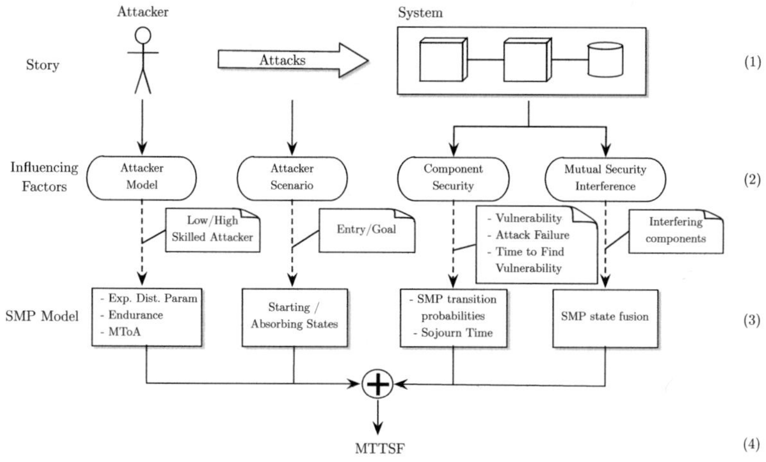

Figure 5.1.: Overview of the software architecture security evaluation approach.

components to hardware, and finally vi) possible mutual influences between components with respect to their security strength.

For this purpose, we have developed a hierarchical model that takes into account the aforementioned security factors. The main concepts and results of this chapter appeared in our publication Busch et al. , [BSK15].

5.2. Quantification Approach

Figure 5.1 shows an overview of the approach. Our model takes into account four influencing factors: the attacker, the attack scenario, security attributes of system components and mutual influences of the system components. For a formalized representation of the aforementioned factors, we use a semi-Markov process (SMP) model. The SMP provides appropriate mechanisms, such as states, transitions and sojourn times. This allows modelling different phases of an attack, the probability of success of an attack and the time required to execute the attack itself. The SMP model results in the Mean Time to Security Failure (MTTSF), which represents the system's security of the overall system. The MTTSF metric was introduced by Madan et al. in [Mad+04; Mad+02; GMT05]. In our approach, we consider system components, their attributes and deployment configurations.

The *story* (Figure 5.1: (1)) of a system attack involves several entities. The attacker who attacks the system and the system under attack. These entities are influenced by several influencing factors (Figure 5.1: (2)):

The first factor that determines the *attacker's skill* models the general knowledge of an attacker about how to attack systems. The *target* represents the current purpose of the attack (for example, obtaining data access). The third factor is *component security*, which represents the probability of observing hidden vulnerabilities to certain components. Further, it describes the time required to observe this vulnerability. Mutual security interference affects possible security interferences between components that can potentially be exploited by attackers. We use the SMP (Figure 5.1: (2)) to mathematically represent the aforementioned factors.

As before, the mathematical SMP model represents the four parts that model the four influencing factors: the attacker's skill is modelled by an exponential density function (as suggested by [JO97]) and the Mean Time of Attack (MToA). The second part defines the starting points and the end points of the Markov process. Related to the Markov process, the starting point defines the entry states, while the end point is represented by the absorbing state. The third part defines the transition probabilities of certain states and the effort that was spent on security considerations (by the software architects and developers) for each component. In the SMP model, this is represented by the sojourn time. The fourth part combines states that allow a simple state transition according to the architecture's component interferences. Finally, the model results in the MTTSF (Figure 5.1: (4)), which should represent the degree of security of a software architecture. This value can be used to compare different architecture alternatives on a particular hardware configuration at an ordinal scale level.

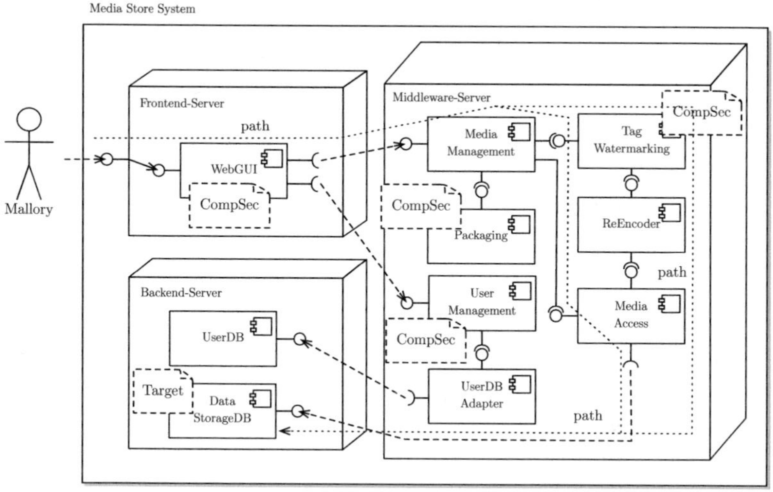

Figure 5.2.: Architecture overview of the running example Media Store with schematic illustration of security annotations.

5.3. Definition of Security Relevant Properties

Each of the influencing factors is represented by a sub-model, which is introduced in the following from a high-level perspective. For the introduction of the models we use our running example, for a better understanding of the model and its sub-models.

5.3.1. Application Example

For the introduction and exemplary application of the model elements, we use the architecture of our running example from Section 2.2.

The 3-tier system is structured as follows: the frontend server is physically connected to the middleware server (through a LAN). The middleware server is physically connected to the back-end server. The frontend server is *not* physically connected to the back-end server. In order to get to the

UserDB, the attacker must in any case take the path from the frontend server via the middleware server to the back-end server.

Figure 5.2 shows an abstract depiction of the model elements of the security assessment approach applied to our running example.

5.3.1.1. Attacker

Different classes of attackers are represented by different attacker models. Usually, a system is subject to different classes of attackers. The effort attackers spend on the attack depend on the expected profit attackers expect from a successful attack. To demonstrate attacker models, we define two types of models, namely the model of a comparatively weak and the model of a comparatively high-skilled attacker.

5.3.1.2. Scenario

We simplify uur running example to provide one entry point: The WebGUI component. Usually, the user would demand the system to upload and download music files. However, this component is also available to an attacker to gain access to the system's internal architecture via its external interfaces.

As a target for the scenario, we define the access to the data of the DataStorageDB component as the target of the attacker.

5.3.1.3. Control flow

The control flow depends on the attacker scenario. In the previous section, we have defined the DataStorage component as the target of the scenario. This results in the following control flow:

An attacker must access from the external interface of the WebGUI component. From the WebGUI, the only possible way is the transition to the MediaManagement component. Then, there are two possible paths: The first path leads via the TagWatermarking component, and via the ReEncoder component, to the MediaAccess component. The second possibility is to get access to the MediaAccess component directly from the MediaManagement component. From the MediaAccess component the attacker finally reaches its destination, namely the DataStorageDB.

5.3.2. Attacker Model

5.3.2.1. Rationale

The attacker model represents the behaviour of different attackers. Verizon's data breach investigations report [Ver13] reports that intrusions into systems are mainly committed by parties outside the company. In 2013, approximately 92% of all security breaches were caused by this group. For this reason, we focus on attacks from outside.

Attackers have a certain probability of success, which depends on their skill. During the attack on a system, attackers pass through three phases: First, they learn about the architecture of the system. Then they start attacking the system with their standard repertoire of attacks. If this fails, they try finding new methods to successfully attack the system. In addition, each attacker has a certain degree of tenacity that measures how much effort he invests in attacking the system. We represent this value by the average time the attacker tries to successfully attack the system.

The result of the model is the average probability of an attacker to detect a potentially exploitable system vulnerability within a certain time.

5.3.2.2. Model

The attacker model comprises two parts: the phase of carrying out an attack and the attacker's skill.

An attack typically consists of three phases: the learning phase, the standard attack phase and the innovative attack phase. Several of the following terms are derived from [JO97]:

- *Learning phase:* The attacker learns strategies to attack the system and learns about the system itself to increase the probability of successful attacks. In this phase, the number of successful attacks is comparatively low due to a lack of experience with the system and possible attacks. An attacker with low skill would need more time than an attacker with higher skill.
- *Standard Attack Phase:* In the standard attack phase, the attacker uses his knowledge and repertoire of attack techniques to attack the system. In this phase, most successful attacks are expected.
- *Innovative Attack Phase:* In the innovative attack phase, the repertoire of possible attacks by the attackers is exhausted. They must develop new methods and strategies to successfully attack the system. In comparison to the standard attack phase, the execution of a successful attack typically takes longer.
- *Skill:* The ability to detect a potential vulnerability of the system within a certain period.
- *Endurance:* Endurance is the average time an attacker spends on searching for vulnerabilities of the system.

We define a modified cumulative density function of the exponential distribution, which models the phase of an attack as well as the attacker's skill and his specific endurance:

$$\phi_{\lambda,\Delta}(x) = \begin{cases} 1 - exp(-\lambda \cdot (x - \Delta)), & 0 \leq x - \Delta \\ 0 & x - \Delta < 0, \end{cases} \tag{5.1}$$

where λ is the parameter that models the attacker's ability in the standard attack phase and the innovative attack phase. Δ represents the duration of the learning phase. In our attack model, x is the input that represents the average time an attacker with a certain skill requires to attack the system. Accordingly, the attacker model will be parametrized by the parameters (λ, Δ). The skill of certain attackers is described by a random variable. For all parameters of the models, we assume that the values can be estimated or determined by the domain expert.

5.3.2.3. Example

Figure 5.3 shows two examples of parametrized attacker models. In both examples we parametrize the attacker models to get a lower skilled and a higher skilled attacker. For the attacker with lower skill, we use ($\lambda = 0.007$, $\Delta = 150$), while the higher skilled attacker is represented by the following values ($\lambda = 0.01$, $\Delta = 100$). Both parameters, lambda and delta, could be extracted from log files.

5.3.3. Attacker & Scenarios

5.3.3.1. Rationale

An attacker typically has a specific target when attacking a system. The system includes a starting point and the actual destination: the exit point or goal point. Depending on the target, the attacker takes various actions that are helpful in achieving the target. In our approach, we focus on component access to copy or modify data in order to gain higher system privileges. Another possible target would be an attack on the availability of the system. The attacker may have the goal of making the system unavailable. Our model focuses on the goal of obtaining higher privileges, whereby the scenario of unavailability could potentially also be covered.

5.3.3.2. Model

We use a semi-Markov process to model the attacker scenario. The entities of the attacker are shown in Figure 5.4. It comprises the attacker's entry point and goal point:

- *Entry point:* The entry points, i.e. interfaces in component-based systems, are the first entities that get in contact with the attacker during an attack. Here the attacker tries to access the system. In practice an entry point is an open port or certain web interfaces that can be accessed from outside. In component-based systems, these correspond to the external interfaces of systems.

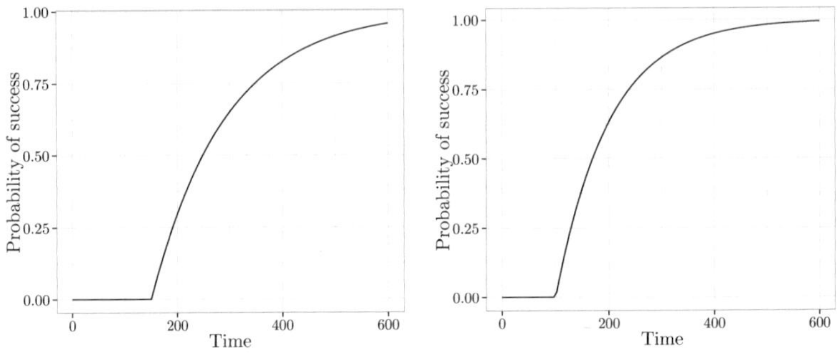

Figure 5.3.: Lower skilled (left) and higher skilled (right) attacker model.

- *Exit/Goal Point*: The goal point is the component an attacker in the system architecture attacks. This corresponds to the state of the Semi-Markov process. We focus on exactly one exit/goal point.

In our SMP model, we map the entry point and exit/goal points to the starting state and the absorbing state of the SMP. The SMP achieves a data breach in the target component by reaching the absorbing state.

Our approach focuses on attacks that lead into the system architecture via the external provided interfaces of systems. The path through the system is determined by the external provided interfaces, the attacker's goal point, and the inner architecture of the system. Attacking a specific component forces the attacker to follow the control flow defined by the architecture. We assume that an attacker cannot take abbreviations within the architecture to change or shorten the control flow. Further, we assume the attacker accesses the system via the defined interfaces. More precisely, he cannot enter via any component, but must begin the attack with the external provided interfaces of systems.

The SMP model can be flexibly adapted to support other objectives besides data breaches. Scenarios that can be modelled with the help of sojourn times, state transitions and certain probabilities can thus become potentially modelled by the SMP process.

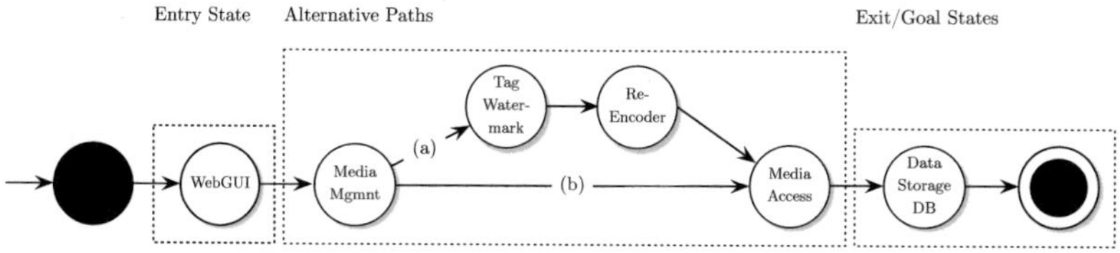

Figure 5.4.: Attacker Scenario: Entry states, alternative paths and goal state.

5.3.3.3. Example

Figure 5.4 shows the states and possible state transitions according to the control flow, which is determined by the component-based software architecture of our running example. The architecture of the running example provides access to the system architecture via one component. Therefore, we define the WebGUI component as the entry point which is represented as a state in the SMP. As the goal scenario, we define a data breach in the DataStorageDB component. Therefore, we define the `DataStorageDB` component as the goal point and introduce the `DataStorageDB` state in the SMP model accordingly.

The DataStorageDB component is only accessible by two paths: First, either the control flow WebGUI-MediaManagement-TagWatermarking-ReEncoder-MediaAccess-DataStorageDB or second, WebGUI-MediaManagement-MediaAccess-DataStorageDB is taken by the attacker. We assume that the attacker has no specific knowledge of the internal system architecture. Thus, both possible ways are equally taken by attackers.

5.3.4. Component Security

5.3.4.1. Rationale

The *component security* considers the specific security of a component in the system architecture. For our model we adapt several concepts from [Mad+04].

Depending on the effort invested in security considerations by the developers, the likelihood of hidden vulnerability in a particular component is

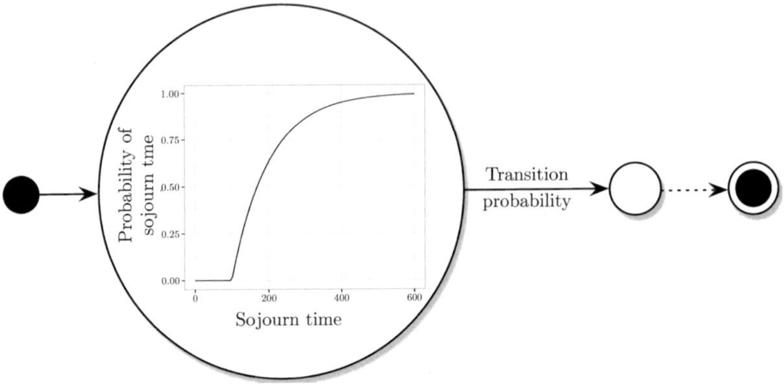

Figure 5.5.: Schematic figure of the component security model.

affected. We assume that the more effort invested in security considerations, the lower the probability of hidden vulnerability and vice versa. In addition to probability, we introduce the aspect time: revealing a vulnerability requires a certain amount of effort. This effort is incurred, although a vulnerability can be found, and even if this was not successfully. The probability of finding a vulnerability and the time needed to find the vulnerability is based on the following rationale:

Developers invest a certain amount of time and use common quality assurance techniques while testing and fixing issues in components. This influences the number of hidden vulnerabilities of a component that are easy to obtain in a positive sense. Nevertheless, it is possible that the internal architecture of the system may make it easily possible to find remaining vulnerabilities. The time to find a possible vulnerability would therefore be comparatively short. If no time aspect would be taken into account, this would put other components at a disadvantage whose number of hidden vulnerabilities is higher, but more difficult to discover.

5.3.4.2. Model

The model for the component security is schematically depicted in Figure 5.5. It can be represented by the following pair:

$$CompSec(c) = (TTDV,\ PoCoB), \tag{5.2}$$

while TTDV is the *Time to Discover a Vulnerability*, while PoCoB is the *Probability of Component Breakability*:

- *TTDV:* The *Time to Discover a Vulnerability* is the average time required to discover a potential vulnerability of a particular component. The TTDV does not make a statement about whether the observed vulnerability can actually be exploited for the execution of an attack. The unit of the metric is time units.
- *PoCoB:* The *Probability of Component Breakability* is represented by the probability of actually use a potentially exploitable vulnerability in the component for performing an attack successfully. The metrics therefore represent the probability that an attacker can actually exploit the vulnerability to attack a component to gain higher privileges on the system.

The model results in the *Mean Time to Break Component* (MTTBC) of a given component c. This value represents the time an attacker requires to successfully attack the component c. MTTBC is calculated as follows:

$$MTTBC_c = \frac{TTDV_c}{PoCoB_c} \tag{5.3}$$

An attacker needs a mean time, denoted by TTDV, to discover a component's vulnerability. The probability of successfully exploiting this vulnerability for breaking the component is represented by PoCoB. This means that the higher the values for TTDV and PoCoB, the longer the mean time for a component to be broken successfully.

5.3.4.3. Example

Let us assume that the components `MediaManagement` and `MediaManagement'` have the following security properties:

$$CompSec(MediaManagement) = (20,\ 0.25) \tag{5.4}$$

$$CompSec(MediaManagement') = (30,\ 0.3) \tag{5.5}$$

Therefore, the following MTTBC values result:

$$MTTBC_{MediaManagement} = \frac{20}{0.25}[time\ units] = 80\ [time\ units] \tag{5.6}$$

$$MTTBC_{MediaManagement'} = \frac{30}{0.3}[time\ units] = 100\ [time\ units] \tag{5.7}$$

In other words, an average skilled attacker for the component MediaManagement would require 20 time units to find a vulnerability in the component that is potentially harmful. The probability that the discovered vulnerability is actually harmful is 25%. Component MediaManagement', on the other hand, has slightly weaker values, namely a TTDV of 30 and a PoCoB of 30%. According to formula 5.3, the $MTTBC_{MediaManagement} = 80$ time units. The alternative component MediaManagement', has $MTTBC_{MediaManagement'} = 100$ time units. Component security can be derived, for example, from the experience of developers, the development process, the technology and platform used, the source code size of the component and its maturity.

5.3.5. Mutual Security Interference

5.3.5.1. Rationale

Mutual security interference describes the security effects of several components that influence each other. A possible scenario is shown in Figure 5.6. Such mutual influences exist if, for example, resources or permissions are shared across several components. A shared resource is, for example, when access to the same data is shared (e.g. reading from or writing to a shared file) or exchanging information about shared memory accesses. Other reasons can be shared access permissions across multiple components. Two components that work with shared user permissions would potentially

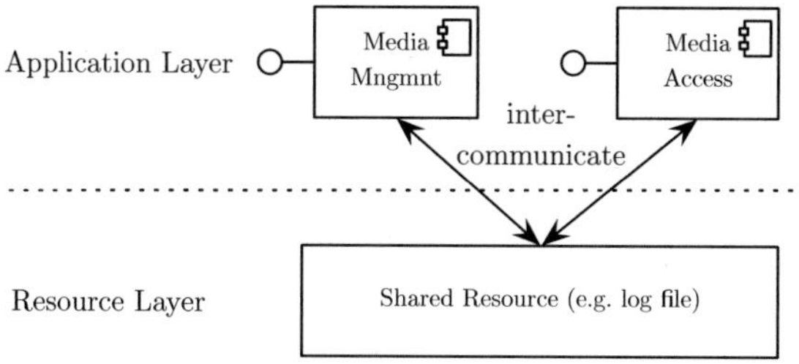

Figure 5.6.: Mutual Security Interference illustration.

interfere with each other. In the worst case, all components that share the same privileges could be compromised by successfully attacking only one single component (from the set of components that share the same privilege).

5.3.5.2. Model

Mutual security interferences create additional paths and possible transitions, in addition to the paths already defined by the architecture. These can potentially be used by an attacker to move through the architecture of the system. Figure 5.6 shows an example in which component `MediaManagement` communicates with component `MediaAccess`, while both use a shared resource, namely a log file. When an attacker would have successfully compromised the component `MediaManagement`, the attacker may be able to use the shared resource to compromise component `MediaAccess`.

To include the mutual security interference in our model, additional transitions and transition probabilities are added to the associated SMP model. To do so, we use a transformation described in Section 5.6.2.

5.3.5.3. Example

Figure 5.7 shows an application of the mutual security interference on our running example. We assume that component `ReEncoder` and component `MediaAccess` run in a shared memory environment. This means that a security breach of one component can potentially lead to a security breach of

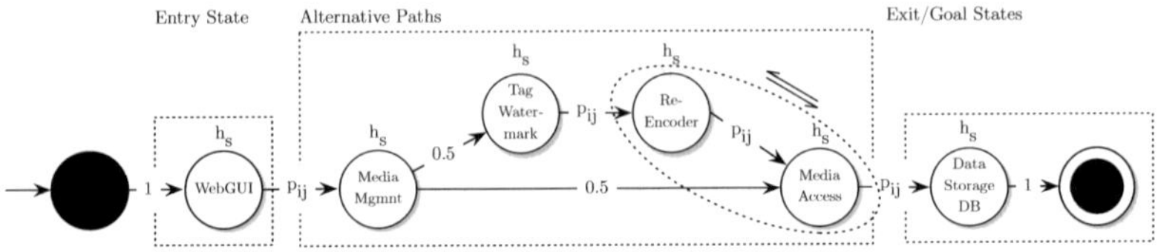

Figure 5.7.: SMP model representation with sojourn times, transition probabilities, alternative paths, and mutual security interference applied to the example scenario for the Media Store system.

the other component. For a worst case estimation it is therefore necessary to assume that there exists a mutual security interference between components `ReEncoder` and `MediaAccess`.

5.4. Security Modelling using SMP

In order to represent our hierarchical model mathematically we use a semi-Markov process. The SMP process is suitable to represent our sub-models with their model elements. In the following, we describe the requirements for our mathematical representation:

- An attacker must be able to be modelled separately from the other model elements. However, component security should not be mixed with attacker properties. Furthermore, the mathematical models require a mechanism to represent the attacker's skills.
- An attacker must access the system via defined interfaces and adhere to defined paths. Furthermore, a state must be selectable as target point.
- In a component-based software architecture, the software components are interconnected via their interfaces and interact with each other. Each differs in security properties. These connections, interactions and properties must be represented in mathematical models.

- A particular service is realized by a certain combination of software components and their corresponding control flow.
- Software components influence each other in terms of security. This influence must be modelled in the mathematical representation.

An SMP comes with elements to model all the aforementioned security modelling requirements of a component-based software architecture.

The states and transitions of an SMP's embedded discrete time Markov chain (DTMC) allow modelling attackers and its control flow in a software architecture. The sojourn time of the SMP in each state represents the temporal aspect of the component security of each component (see Section 5.3.4). An overview of the model elements is shown in Figure 5.7.

5.4.1. Base Model

Let us define the underlying stochastic process as

$$\{X(t) : t \geq 0, t \in \mathbb{N}_0^+\}. \tag{5.8}$$

Let us consider a system that contains k components. If each component is represented by an individual state, then $S_k, k \in \mathbb{N}_0^+$ is defined as the set of all k states representing the presence of an attack within a given component, in the considered system. In addition, a Ω success state is added. The discrete state space of the stochastic model is represented by S. The transition probabilities p_{ij} are determined by the control flow of the system and the selected attack scenario. The sojourn time of the DTMC is defined as h_k.

5.4.2. Component Security

Our *CompSec* component security model from Section 5.3.4 has been designed to be easily mapped to an SMP representation. We define

$$p_{ij} = PoCoB_i \tag{5.9}$$
$$h_i = TTDV_i, \tag{5.10}$$

while $i, j \in X_t$.

5.4.3. Composing Component and Attacker Model

Combining the component security model and attacker model together requires several extensions of the previously introduced mapping of the component security model to the SMP. The attacker model affects two parts of the SMP:

1. It influences the probability of the state transition probability p_{ij} of the embedded DTMC. In other words, it influences the probability of a successful attack (PoCoB) of a given component depending on the skill of a particular group of attackers.
2. It affects the average time an attacker spends on attacking a particular component.

Both the aforementioned properties lead to an adaptation of the basic models as follows:

$$PoCoB_i^{\phi} = \phi_{\lambda,\Delta}(x) \cdot PoCoB_i \tag{5.11}$$

$$MTTBC_i^{\phi} = \frac{TTDV_i}{PoCoB_i^{\phi}}, \tag{5.12}$$

while $i \in I := \{0, \ldots, k-1\}$. $PoCoB^{\phi}$. $PoCoB^{\phi}$ represents the adapted PoCoB, which includes the skill of the attacker group and the adapted MTTBC namely $MTTBC^{\phi}$, which contains the resulting mean time to break component for a particular attacker group.

5.4.4. Attacker Scenario

The attacker scenario defines the entry points and exit/goal points of the attack. This results in entry states and absorbing states of the embedded DTMC. $S_e \subseteq S$ represents the set of all input states and $S_a \subseteq S$ represents the absorbing state of the attacker model. In addition to the input states and the initial states of the attack scenario, we define the control flow of the software architecture. Let Θ be an $S \times S$ array:

$$\Theta := \begin{pmatrix} \theta_{00} & \theta_{01} & \dots & \theta_{0k} \\ \theta_{10} & \theta_{11} & \dots & \theta_{1k} \\ \vdots & \vdots & \ddots & \vdots \\ \theta_{k0} & \theta_{k1} & \dots & \theta_{kk} \end{pmatrix} = (\theta_{ij}), \tag{5.13}$$

while $(\theta_{ij}) \in \mathbb{N}_0^+$ depends on the probabilities of changing from state i to state j (while $i, j \in X_t$). The values also depend on the number of possible visits resulting from the control flow of the architecture: If a transition between two states (i.e. components) is possible, it applies $\theta_{ij} > 0$, if not $\theta_{ij} = 0$ is used. Using Θ, the number of relevant requested services of a component can be calculated:

$$\Xi = (\xi_i)_{i \in I} = \sum_{l \in \{j \in J | \theta_{ij} > 0\}} 1, \tag{5.14}$$

while $j \in J := \{0, \dots, k\}$.

5.4.5. Combining the Sub-Models

The assembling of our sub-models to a hierarchical model enables estimating the overall security of a software system. The inclusion of the attacker model, which represents the attacker's skill, is optional. Therefore, we start by combining the component security model with the attack scenario model:

$$MTTSF = \sum_{i-1} \frac{1}{\xi_i \cdot (\theta_{ij} + 1) - \xi_i \cdot \theta_{ij}} \sum_j \frac{TTDV_i}{PoCoB_i} \cdot \theta_{ij} \tag{5.15}$$

$$= \sum_{i-1} \frac{1}{\xi_i \cdot (\theta_{ij} + 1) - \xi_i \cdot \theta_{ij}} \sum_j MTTBC_i \cdot \theta_{ij} \tag{5.16}$$

while $i, j \in X_t$. Similarly, we include the skill of the attacker group (if desired) to calculate the MTTSF:

$$MTTSF^{\phi} = \sum_{i-1} \frac{1}{\xi_i \cdot (\theta_{ij} + 1) - \xi_i \cdot \theta_{ij}} \sum_{j} \frac{TTDV_i}{PoCoB_i \cdot \phi_{\lambda,\Delta}(x)} \cdot \theta_{ij} \tag{5.17}$$

$$= \sum_{i-1} \frac{1}{\xi_i \cdot (\theta_{ij} + 1) - \xi_i \cdot \theta_{ij}} \sum_{j} MTTBC_i^{\phi} \cdot \theta_{ij} \tag{5.18}$$

The resulting $MTTSF^{\phi}$ value represents the result of the model. The value can now be used to compare two or more software architecture alternatives. This can be used as an objective function in automatic design decision support process when automatically selecting subsystems (as illustrated in this thesis) to include security properties in the decision process.

5.5. Evaluation

To demonstrate the application of the approach, we use a software architecture model from a real-world software system, the Remote Diagnostic Solutions (RDS) that was used in [Goo+12]. The system is used in an industrial context and receives status data from power plants, processes them, stores it and displays aggregated data. The software architecture of the system is shown in Figure 5.8. A detailed description of the system can be found in Section 10.6.2. We apply our approach to three different scenarios in the context of the RDS system. First, we demonstrate the security assessment on the original software architecture model, our original architecture, that was defined in [Goo+12]. The second scenario shows how the model behaves in a components exchange scenario. In the third scenario, we change the configuration of the architecture, i.e. we remove components, change the hardware configuration and introduce mutual security interferences between components.

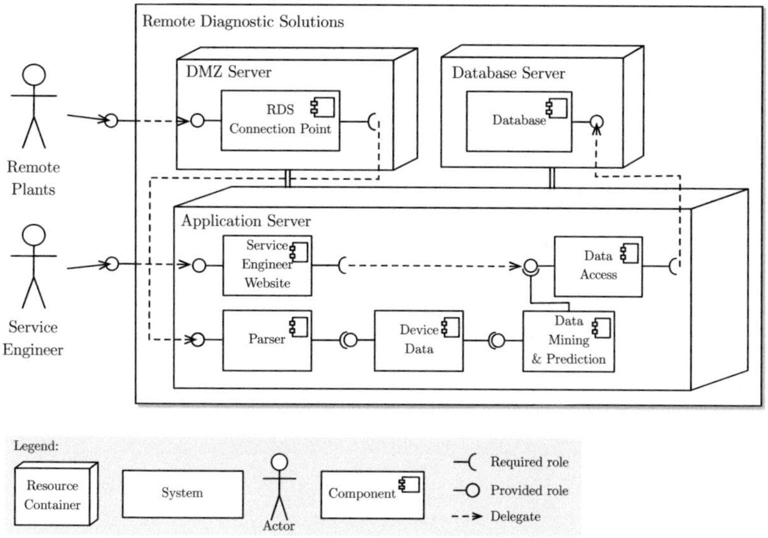

Figure 5.8.: System model of the Remote Diagnostic Solutions (after [BK16]).

5.5.1. Reference Scenario

The software system of the first scenario contains 5 software components. This results in the following system topology:

$$RDS = (Access, Web, Pars, DA, DB)$$

Based on this system topology, we define the security properties according to our security model for each of the architecture elements. In the example, we assume that the components are well tested and that several security mechanisms have been applied. For the `Access`, `DA` and `DB` components we set the PoCoB value for a medium skilled attacker to 20%[1]. We consider the components `Web` and `Parser` to be less mature and less secure, which is why their PoCoBs were given higher values of 30 % and 40 %, respectively. We

[1] Note that the architecture model was originally created for performance assessment and does not necessarily reflect the actual security attributes of this system. In fact, most security-related design decisions of this system are unknown to us. We only use the information published in [Goo+12] here and add our own assumptions where needed

set the TTDV of the access component to 200, since historical data might show that the selected architecture structure of this component has resulted in an average retention time of 200 time units for attackers. We define the TTDV of the web component to 250, pars to 125, DA to150 and DB to 300 time units.

This results in the following values:

$$CompSec(RDS) = ((200, 0.2), (250, 0.3), (125, 0.4), (150, 0.2), (300, 0.2))$$

We define the states for the SMP model together with the final state Ω:

$$S(RDS) = \{Access, Web, Pars, DA, DB, \Omega\}$$

The system contains two interfaces that are available as entry points for accessing the software architecture. We define an attack on the DB component as our attack scenario. This results in the DB component as the target point:

$$S_e(RDS) = \{Access, Web\}$$
$$S_a(RDS) = DB$$

The control flow of the system is defined by the following SxS matrix:

$$\Theta = \begin{pmatrix} 0 & 0 & 1 & 0 & 0 & 0 \\ 0 & 0 & 0 & 1 & 0 & 0 \\ 0 & 0 & 0 & 1 & 0 & 0 \\ 0 & 0 & 0 & 0 & 2 & 0 \\ 0 & 0 & 0 & 0 & 0 & 2 \\ 0 & 0 & 0 & 0 & 0 & 0 \end{pmatrix}$$

We use Formula 5.14 to calculate Ξ:

$$\Xi = \{1, 1, 1, 1, 1, 0\}$$

Finally we define an attacker. We use the attacker with higher knowledge from Section 5.3.3:

$$att_{high} = (\lambda = 0.01, \Delta = 100) \Rightarrow$$
$$\phi_{\lambda=0.01,\Delta=100}(200) \approx 0.632$$

We combine the previously defined sub-models to calculate the MTTSF of the architecture with the previously defined attacker model:

$$MTTSF_{\phi} \approx 4070.29 \; [time\ units]$$

5.5.2. Component Variation Scenario

In the component variation scenario, components from a system architecture are replaced by alternative, functionally equivalent components. Interchangeable components provide the same functionalities as the components already in use. They provide and require the same interfaces, but differ in their implementation in particular. This difference is reflected in the security properties.

In the example scenario, we replace the `Access` component with an implementation with improved security properties and the `DA` component with a weaker implementation (for example, due to performance aspects):

$$\begin{aligned} CompSec(Access') &= (150, 0.15) \\ CompSec(DA') &= (50, 0.4) \\ S'(RDS) &= \{Access', Web, Pars, DA', DB, \Omega\} \end{aligned}$$

The MTTSF metric results as follows:

$$MTTSF'_{\phi} \approx 3608.88 \; [time\ units]$$

We replace the `Access` component with a slightly more secure implementation compared to the original component. At the same time, we replace a comparably secure `BA` component with a component of lower security quality. The overall quality of the modified architecture should be intuitively lowered in terms of security. This assumption is supported by the MTTSF's results. Comparing the original architecture with the architecture of this scenario, the comparison is in favour of the original architecture.

5.5.3. Deployment Variation Scenario

We change the configuration of our original architecture again and introduce a mutual security influence between components. First, we remove the DMZ server and deploy the `Access` component on the application server. Secondly, we introduce a mutual security influence between `Access` and the `DA` component: as described in Section 5.3.5, the mutual security interference changes the security attributes of the overall system. This applies if the interfering components are deployed on the same hardware container.

The introduced influence results in an additional path through the software architecture. This results in a modified Θ and Ξ:

$$\Theta'' = \begin{pmatrix} 0 & 0 & 1 & 1 & 0 & 0 \\ 0 & 0 & 0 & 1 & 0 & 0 \\ 0 & 0 & 0 & 0 & 1 & 0 \\ 0 & 0 & 0 & 0 & 3 & 0 \\ 0 & 0 & 0 & 0 & 0 & 3 \\ 0 & 0 & 0 & 0 & 0 & 0 \end{pmatrix}$$

We use Θ'' to calculate Ξ'':

$$\Xi'' = \{2, 1, 1, 1, 1, 0\}$$

Based on our adapted models, we calculate the result of the metric as follows:

$$MTTSF''_{\phi} \approx 3707.76 \ [time\ units]$$

Intuitively, a mutual security influence of components has a negative impact on the software architecture in terms of security. This enables additional paths to be chosen by the attacker on the way to his target. These paths may be shorter than the paths defined by the system architecture. In addition, security mechanisms could be circumvented.

This expectation is supported by the results of MTTSF. In a comparison with the original architecture, the choice of MTTSF is in favour of the original architecture.

5.6. Applying the approach to the Palladio Component Model

Based on the security properties of the elements of a component-based software architecture, we design a function in our approach to compare architecture candidates with each other. This procedure is applied to the Palladio Component Model (PCM). We extend the PCM so that we can annotate security properties to the model elements (i.e. the components) already defined in PCM. Annotated PCM model instances can then be transformed into our SMP model to perform the security analysis. In combination with decision-making tools, such as PerOpteryx that was intruduced in Section 4.3, trade-off decisions can be made between security and other quality attributes such as performance, and cost. However, the approach is not limited to PCM, but can be applied to other component-based software architecture models.

5.6.1. PCM Security Extension

To use PCM models as input for our analysis, we extend the meta model of the PCM to include several new attributes. Relevant for the security extension is the `Repository` view-type and the `Resource Environment`.

We extend the components in the repository by adding two attributes: *the time to discover a vulnerability* and *the probability of component breakability*. When a component is used in the system, all its instances inherit the values of these attributes. In addition, the mutual security interference must be introduced by introducing new relations between components.

In addition, we need two new meta-models, namely the attacker model and the attacker scenario. Both models are modelled separately to allow the attacker model to be used optionally. Furthermore, the separation of concerns makes the models better to be extended.

5.6.2. Transformation to SMP

We transform the architecture model, which has been extended by security annotations, into an SMP model, which is further analysed in a subsequent step. This transformation is specified in pseudo code, as shown in Algorithmic 1.

The resulting model contains a start state and a target state. A separate state is generated for each component in the architecture. The `getComp` helper function receives the component to which an external provided interface of the system is connected through a delegation connector. The MTTBC is then calculated according to Formula 5.3. Then, we create the transitions from the start state to the state of the components connected to the external provided interfaces of the system. In the SMP representation, the state representing the target component finally transits to the final target state. Transitions are also added for each state representing the assembly connector. The `toTrans` helper function generates a transition between the states of the connected components connected.

Mutual security interference is only relevant for components that are deployed on the same resource containers. The `onSameContainer` helper function checks that condition. It returns true if two affected components are deployed on the same resource container. Within a resource container, a mutual security interference leads to merging several states in the SMP. This, in the case of components are directly connected to each other. The `unifyStates` helper function modifies the states and transition quantities. One of the two affected states is first marked for deletion (m). All incoming and outgoing transitions are transferred to other states affected by m. At the end the marked state is removed.

Algorithm 1 Transformation from software architecture model to SMP representation.

```
Input:
K ← Component instances
g ← Goal components (g ∈ K)
C ← Connectors
I ← System interfaces
M ← Mutual security interference
Output:
C                                              ▷ States
T ⊆ C × C                                      ▷ Transitions

Algorithm:
C ← {start, end}                               ▷ (1)
C ← C ∪ K                                      ▷ (2)
for i ∈ I do
    T ← T ∪ {(start, getComp(i))}              ▷ (3)
end for
T ← T ∪ {(g, end)}                             ▷ (4)
for c ∈ C do
    T ← T ∪ {toTrans(c)}                       ▷ (5)
end for
for m ∈ M do
    if onSameContainer(m) then                 ▷ (6)
        (C, T) ← unifyStates(m, C, T)          ▷ (7)
    end if
end for
```

5.7. Related Approaches

There are several approaches for estimating security properties: Sharma et al. show in [ST07] a hierarchical model for the estimation of several quality attributes, such as security, in component-based software architectures. They also use discrete time Markov chains to model the software architecture of the system. The model is based on the assumption that the security of the system depends on the number of accesses to components. We do not take into account the number of accesses that occur, for example, as a result of loops in a component. Further, the system is considered to have been successfully broken once a vulnerability has been discovered in a component. We decided against this assumption because modern systems typically run on several machines and a breakdown of a single component often does not gain access to the entire system. Consequently, we use the control flow of the system as a basis.

Madan et al. developed in [Mad+04] a model for the quantification of security properties of intrusion tolerant systems using a semi-Markov process. They defined two different state transition models that models the scenario of denial-of-service attacks with the goal of compromising the system. Both models describe the behaviour of such a system during an ongoing attack. The models describe a DTMC steady-state probability using state transition probabilities. Finally, they calculate the mean time to security failure, which allows to quantify the security of the system as a whole. By contrast, our approach allows the evaluation of security properties in component-based architectures and is not limited to monolithic systems. For this purpose, we assign states to each component to estimate the properties in component-based systems. In addition, we consider the skills of attackers.

Jonsson uses in [JO97] empirical data to develop an attacker model that represents the process of an attack. The approach comprises three phases: learning phase, standard attack phase and the innovative attack phase. This behaviour is approximated using an exponential distribution function. In our approach, we use a similar model for the attacker behaviour. We use the cumulative density function of an exponential distribution and the probability of a particular group of attackers to successfully model a component's vulnerability within a given time to discover.

Several other related approaches consider the quantification of security or the development of security models: Wang et al. show in [WSJ07] a framework for the measurement of security properties to estimate security aspects in networks using attack graphs.

Dacier et al. use in [DDK02] Markov chains to model attacker scenarios. The model takes into account the time and effort required by an attacker to attack a system successfully. For this purpose they use privilege graphs.

For larger systems, such a graph can quickly contain many elements and is therefore complex to understand. Furthermore, this requires vulnerability models at a very high level of detail.

Schechter showed in [Sch02] the cost to break metric to estimate the costs required for a successful attack. From a cost point of view, the metric is supposed to provide a first idea of the difficulty of attacking a monolithic system.

McQueen et al. show in [McQ+06] a model for estimating the time that is required to attack a certain externally visible system component.

5.8. Limitations

5.8.1. Data Streams

The model focuses mainly on the control flow of the software architecture and the assumption of its compliance. It remains unclear how data flows would affect the quality of security properties. It might be possible that data could pass unhindered through components (without the need to break them) and cause damage only in a component later in the control flow. In such cases, attackers would no longer have to follow a specified control flow (and thus break each component on that control flow).

5.8.2. Getting the Data

To use the approach in practice, it is necessary to estimate for the DTMC quite a lot of values, namely the transition probabilities between the states and the sojourn times in the states. Three different approaches to the collection of data are discussed in the following:

- *The experience of developers:* Component developers could determine the values on the basis of their experience about the development process of the component. Accurate values, however, are difficult to deduce from the developer's experience.

- *Log-files:* Log-files are probably the most reliable type of the presented data sources. Log files are a verifiable source and a human independent source. However, data from logs is only a fragment and depends on the type of system (and its value for attackers). Furthermore, it is unclear how to distinguish between regular access by users and attacks.
- *Historical data:* Historical data from comparable attacks and systems is often sparse. Historical data has similar problems than log files: Many attacks tend to be classified incorrectly (e.g. as regular behaviour) and vice versa.

A further difficulty for all those three data sources in general is that the boundary between transition probability and sojourn time is difficult to deduce from the data source.

5.8.3. Meaningful values

The validity of the results remains unclear. It is also not clear whether a comparatively simple estimation of the security quality properties (based on architecture knowledge) with subsequent qualitative modelling would lead to comparable results. It should therefore first be shown whether quantitative modelling would have advantages over qualitative modelling and would not lead to similar results, for example in the analysis of trade-off decisions between the quality attribute safety and other quality attributes.

5.9. Cost Analysis

This section provides an overview of the costs used for the development of the method presented here for the quantitative evaluation of the quality attribute security in component-based software architectures. From the first considerations, elaboration of the method, implementation, evaluation and scientific publication we spend about 7.5 man-months of a post graduate. This time span includes familiarization with the topic, literature research and identification of state-of-the-art, first drafts for a modular model, concept discussions in scientific exchange meetings, discussions in pairs with individual security specialists, implementation, scientific elaboration, publication at the international conference for quality, reliability, and security (QRS) and presentation to an international audience.

With appropriate domain knowledge of the quality attribute to be developed, the time required for the development could certainly be shortened. However, our result serves as an upper barrier to the cost of developing an objective function for a previously unquantifiable quality attribute. However, as the detailed description of the method shows, it can only be seen as a basis for further refinements and does not claim to be a scientifically fully reliable method for quantifying security properties.

5.10. Discussion

In this chapter we show how to model the quality attribute security in component-based software architectures and how to develop a quantitative objective function. We have oriented to state-of-the-art research in this area and refined the models and analyses so that they can be applied to component-based software models. The model is hierarchically and can therefore be parametrized in its use. Therefore, it is also possible to add new modules or exchange modules to change or refine the analysis.

The procedure of developing the procedure has taken a total of 7.5 man-months of post graduates and still has many assumptions and limitations that limit its practical applicability. This means for practice, quantitative objective functions can neither be created for general cases nor for special cases with low effort. When applying the model to a scenario many values (in this case probabilities) must be determined (as in the model presented here) requiring a non-negligible effort. In particular, if values must be estimated fine-granularly, the application of the procedure becomes quickly complex. The more complex the procedure, the more critical the analysed quality attribute must be for the project success, so that the effort is justified. However, this is often the problem: due to time and cost constraints, quality attributes are not or only insufficiently considered and therefore risks are accepted. Therefore, there is a need to include already existing (informal) knowledge in the evaluation of other quantitatively determined quality attributes to have a simple procedure for analysing such quality attributes.

Part II.

Quality-driven reuse of software models

6. Automated Feature-Driven Extension of Software Architectures

This chapter introduces the *CompARE* approach. *CompARE* is a structured process focussing on feature-driven reuse of software models of complex subsystems and to evaluate different implementations, i.e. different subsystem solutions. By using *CompARE*, features, and thus complex functionality can be rapidly included in a base software architecture model. *CompARE* focuses on reusing models of complex subsystems such as libraries, packages or frameworks that can be used in many application contexts.

Using *CompARE*, software architects do not require domain knowledge of the subsystems to be reused nor any need to review the software architectures of the solutions realizing the subsystems. Reusing models often requires adaptations due to incompatible interfaces. *CompARE* abstracts from component interfaces so that software architects do not need to consider interface compatibility. By using *CompARE*, software architects select features from a repository and annotate them to possible desired positions in the base software architecture. Afterwards, *CompARE* automatically generates the extended software architecture models and evaluates the desired positions of the features according to their impact on the quality attributes of the software architecture automatically. As a result, software architects could evaluate design-decisions regarding the use of features on the quality attributes of the software system without knowledge about the underlying software architecture of the subsystem and its solutions. In summary, *CompARE* provides the following advantages to software architects:

- *CompARE* automatically evaluates how the use of features of complex subsystems affects the quality attributes of the overall software architecture.
- *CompARE* automatically evaluates subsystem solution alternatives in the context of the base system.
- *CompARE* supports software architects to find optimal positions for including features in the base software architecture according to quality attributes, such as performance and costs.

Section 6.1 introduces terms, definitions and roles in the context of the *CompARE* approach. In Section 6.2, we introduce prerequisites required for the use of *CompARE*. In Section 6.3, we present goals and requirements for an automatic feature-driven extension of component-based software architectures. Section 6.4 presents the big picture of *CompARE*. Section 6.5 describes how *CompARE* can be integrated into the CBSE process of Cheesman and Daniels [CD00] and the extensions considering quality attribute evaluation and optimization by Heiko Koziolek, Jens Happe [KH06a], and Anne Koziolek [Koz11]. Section 6.6 presents scenarios, *CompARE* supports software architects in the software architecture design. Section 6.7 presents assumptions and limitations of the approach. Finally, in Section 6.8, we conclude with a summary.

6.1. Terms, Definitions and Roles

In this section, we introduce terms and definitions in the context of *CompARE*. We introduce the concept of features, subsystems and subsystem solutions. Further, we introduce several roles involved when using *CompARE* as software development process. In the selection and description of roles, we base on the roles of the component-based software engineering approach.

6.1.1. Features

According to the definition for features by Bosch (see Definition 3.1.8) and the definition by Svahnberg [SGB05] is "features [...] may be implemented as a set of collaborating components", features represent units of logical behaviour that are realized by several software components. Each function block fulfils a functional requirement or quality requirement of a software system. Requirements and features are therefore linked to each other. For example, the requirement with the concern *data logging* can be implemented by the feature *log to file system* of a logging system. Due to its high level of abstraction, a feature can also be realized through various implementations.

6.1.2. Subsystem

Definition 6.1.1 *Subsystem (from Melvin Conway [Con68]):*
Any system of consequence is structured from smaller subsystems which are interconnected. A description of a system, if it is to describe what goes on inside that system, must describe the system's connections to the outside world, and it must delineate each of the subsystems and how they are interconnected. Dropping down one level, we can say the same for each of the subsystems, viewing it as a system.[..]]

In Definition 6.1.1, Conway describes subsystems as entities that build systems as building blocks. They describe their internal architecture, and the connection to the system in which the subsystem takes part. From a higher level view, subsystems can be used as systems.

Due to the higher level abstraction, subsystems provide higher level functions to the outside world, that we describe and formalize by features. They abstract from concrete functions such as sorting or other calculations, that are often represented by software components. In contrast to software components, subsystems are more coarse-grain entities.

The subsystem's internal architecture can be partitioned into several functional concerns. Each functional concern describes functions at a higher level such as data persistence or intrusion detection. Subsystems define an internal architecture comprising several functional concerns and relationships between them, i.e. the subsystem architecture. Subsystems therefore define a reference architecture for a certain class of systems to be reused. Therefore, we use the term *subsystem* as defined in Definition 6.1.2.

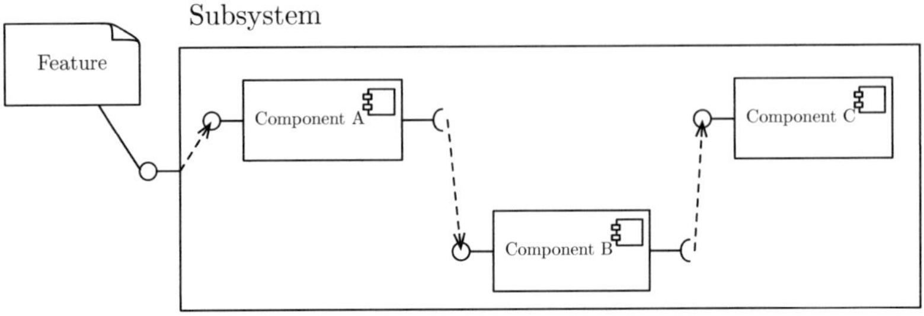

Figure 6.1.: Schematic illustration of a subsystem.

Definition 6.1.2 *Subsystem: A subsystem is a self-contained entity and abstracts functions by features. Internally, they define an architecture comprising functional concerns and their relationship to each other. Each subsystem represents its own class of software systems. The internal functional concerns and their relationships define a reference architecture for the domain of the subsystem.*

Examples of subsystems are loggers, intrusion detection systems, authentication systems, and database systems.

An illustration of a subsystem is shown in Figure 6.1. A subsystem fulfils one or more functional or operationalized quality requirements. Subsystems are self-contained entities. The self-contained nature of subsystems means that they do not require further external services to fulfil its inherent function. However, they can access the infrastructure of the base system by requiring components for instance to get access to a common database system or other operating system infrastructure. Subsystems therefore provide one or more features at their system boundaries, and can also require external (infrastructure) services.

Let us consider a vendor specific implementation of a logging subsystem as the logger from the running example. A logger monitors systems or single components of a system in order to store interesting or important data for later analysis. Its major components are shown in Figure 6.2 together with the example feature *Console Logging*. In this simplified description, the logger fulfils one feature namely the monitoring of various data for console

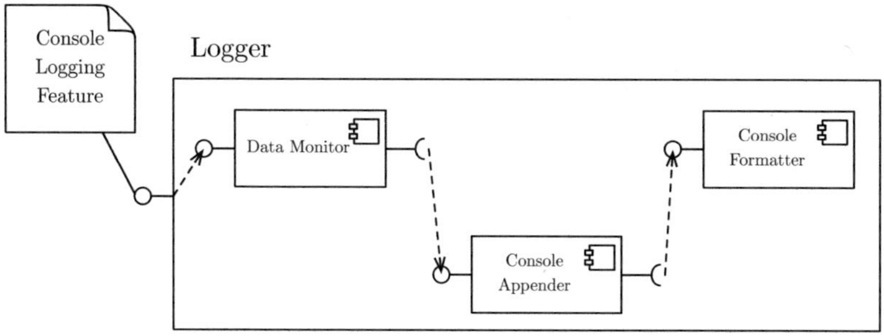

Figure 6.2.: Simplified representation of a Logger subsystem with feature *Console Logging*.

analysis. Internally, the logger comprises three concerns, namely gathering data, persisting data and formatting data to the required format.

There are different logger realizations from different vendors at the market, while they often fulfil a similar set of features. Due to different architecture decisions and other factors such as Conway's law [Con68] of different software architects and company structures, each logger realization and internal architecture differs to a certain extent. The reference architecture of subsystems defines the basic structure and the interrelationships of the internals of each vendor specific solution on the market. The reference architecture later enables automatic evaluation of all vendor specific solutions that apply to the reference architecture. This without the need to review and adapt the models' architecture of the vendor specific solutions.

6.1.3. Subsystem Solution

A subsystem solution is a vendor specific software architecture model that applies to the domain of a subsystem. It fulfils the features of the subsystem, or at least a subset (the core features) of a subsystem. Furthermore, the software architecture of the solution applies to the reference architecture of the subsystem. A subsystem solution usually represents the model of an implementation of a library or a framework.

6.2. CompARE Prerequisites

In this section, we describe several prerequisites that are necessary for the application of *CompARE*.

As prerequisites, several basic project-relevant quality attributes must be known beforehand and a certain base software architecture model must exist. *CompARE* allows the analysis of quantitative or qualitative modelled quality attributes. Although the approach supports qualitatively modelled quality attributes in isolation, these should be analysed together with quantitatively modelled quality attributes, such as performance. Qualitatively determined quality attributes are usually based on estimations or experience of software architects and therefore tend to be inaccurate compared to quantitative determined values.

In addition to the base software architecture model, quality annotations, and a pre-selection of architecture degrees of freedom is necessary. Component selection, allocation configuration, or resource selection (see Section 3.3.2.2) are common degrees of freedom in component-based software architecture models. In addition to these degrees of freedom, *CompARE* provides additional degrees of freedom, such as required or optional features and dimensions, with feature configuration options.

6.3. Goal of Feature-Driven Software Architecture Extension

The goal of *CompARE* is to support software architects in optimizing architecture decisions when using software features and analysing their impact on the quality attributes of the software architecture. The approach can be used in new design scenarios, as well as evolutionary scenarios.

Using *CompARE*, software architects could evaluate design decisions regarding the implementation of features during the design phases, before the actual implementation. Software architects only need to select possible, meaningful target positions of the feature implementing the requirements in the base software architecture model. No in-depth knowledge of the architecture or implementation of the features, nor the effects on the quality attributes of the base software architecture is required. Lightweight reuse could enable a more cost-efficient evaluation of design decisions in early phases of development. There is no need for an initial review of documentations or code artefacts of many solutions or technologies that implement the required features. In addition, barriers could be reduced to evaluate a larger number of design decisions and thus potentially makes it easier to find better candidates.

In addition to select a solution, the approach should also support software architects in applying the feature in the base architecture and keeping critical quality requirements in mind. In a logging scenario, for example, the trade-off between the number of data collected (measurement points) and the resulting effects on other quality attributes (such as performance) must be met. In component-based architectures with a variety of components, interfaces and abstract control flows, there are thousands of combinations how features could be applied. Each instance of these combinations corresponds to an architecture candidate, all of which have different and, without analysis, unclear effects on the quality attributes of the overall system. The result of the analysis could help software architects to make decisions on favourable positions and number of positions having certain features in consideration of the resulting quality properties of the project-relevant quality attributes, supported by a systematic and automatic process.

In early design phases, the effects of design decisions could by this been evaluated at design time. Effects of the feature selection on project-relevant quality attributes could be evaluated automatically. Costs could thus be displayed on non-monetary metrics, such as the cost of a feature on performance or other quality attributes. Such results could be used as a basis for discussions with stakeholders on the effects of features on quality attributes of the system and prioritization of requirements. Using *CompARE* enables a sound basis for discussions with stakeholders that are not familiar with architecture design. In addition, requirements could be reassessed: If the implementation of requirement desired by the stakeholders not only causes monetary costs but also a visible influence on quality attributes, such as security or usability, the priority of the requirement could be reassessed on the basis of these results. In a data-supported analysis of the effects on quality requirements, priorities could be re-evaluated on a solid basis.

CompARE could also contribute in evolutionary scenarios: When new functionalities should be integrated in the software architecture this could be implemented by using features of third-party subsystems. Another interesting evolution scenario might be when software architects have to decide between different versions of the same solution. When a new version of a product is released it is unclear what effects on the quality attributes come from the evolved software architecture of the product and its new features. Software architects could be interested in, whether the migration to the newer version with its changed set of features fulfils the project's needs in terms of functionality and the quality attributes. Without automatic analysis, the software architecture models must be adapted and evaluated manually. The automatic analysis of *CompARE* could automatically re-evaluate of subsystem's alternative solutions when new alternatives become available.

6.4. CompARE in a Nutshell

Figure 6.3 gives an overview of the phases of *CompARE*. *CompARE* essentially consists of two main phases: The modelling phase and the model reuse phase. The result of the modelling phase are models of the subsystem, comprising features and reference architecture, as well as solutions that are annotated to the reference architecture. Creating the models can be a time-consuming task. However, model creation is only carried out once. They can then be reused in any context.

The model creation phase consists of two parts: The first part considers the analysis of the subsystem's domain. During the domain analysis, subsystem domain experts define the reference architecture to structure the subsystem. Further, they define the set of quality attributes the subsystem potentially affects. The reference architecture models the structure each subsystem solution applies to. The structure abstracts the internal architecture of the vendor specific solutions. Further, they abstract from provided services by features, dependencies between the individual functional concerns and dependencies of the subsystem to the base system. Such a structure is required to enable an automated exchange of different solutions realizing the same subsystem and features. In addition to the structure, domain

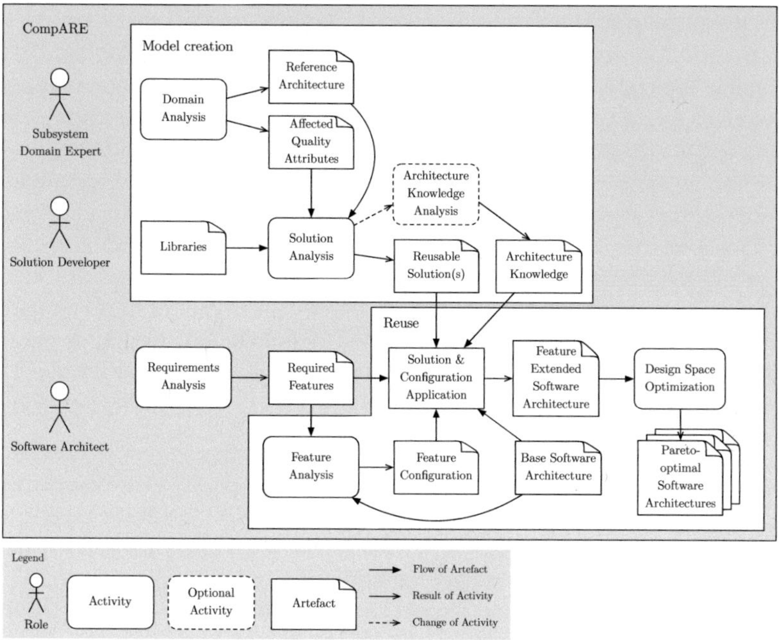

Figure 6.3.: Overview of the *CompARE* approach showing the roles, phases, process steps and artefacts.

experts define the quality attributes affected by the subsystem and their related dimensions.

In the second part, solution developers use the reference architecture and the predefined affected quality attributes to apply them to the subsystem solutions. In addition, they analyse and model architecture knowledge for each subsystem solution on the basis of qualitative reasoning. They consider the affected quality attributes that have been modelled by the subsystem domain expert. This step allows software architects in reuse scenarios to automatically analyse the effects of the subsystem and the solutions on the quality attributes of the system. Qualitative reasoning annotations allow considering quality attributes without quantitative objective functions.

In the reuse phase, software architects reuse the models that have been created by the subsystem domain expert and the solution developers. They review the features required for the base system that should be realized by reusing subsystems. Later, they define the feature configuration. In the feature configuration, they first select desired features. Then, they define possible positions of the features in the base architecture model. Features can be set to be included mandatory or optional. Selecting optional spans a degree of freedom of including the feature or not including the feature in the base software architecture. The configurations are then used to automatically extend the base architecture. The result is software architecture models of the base software architecture extended by features. These models are the basis for an automatic analysis of the resulting quality properties.

Using the models, *CompARE* explores the design space and evaluates and optimizes the quality attributes. The result of the process is Pareto-optimal software architecture models. On the basis of the results, software architects evaluate the design alternatives for the software architecture and use the results as a basis for improving their design decisions. Further, the results can be used to discuss requirements with the stakeholders. If the result is a software architecture that meets all requirements, the system can be implemented.

6.4.1. Domain Analysis

The reference architecture and the influenced quality attributes depends on the domain of the subsystem. Subsystem domain experts analyse the domain and model the reference architecture and the affected quality attributes.

6.4.1.1. Reference Architecture

The reference architecture defines a uniform structure for all subsystem solutions. Such a uniform structure allows to automatically apply and exchange different subsystem solutions in the base software architecture. Although each subsystem solution differs in their software architecture and implementation, the internal functional concerns remain the same. We use these similarities to include and exchange different subsystem solutions automatically. Software architects do not require detailed knowledge of the software architecture or even implementation of the subsystem solutions. By abstracting from the complex internal architecture, modelling effort should be reduced and the reuse process made more efficient. Without such a reference architecture that allows generating models automatically, many models including the desired features on all optional positions in the base architecture model software architects would have to create manually.

6.4.1.2. Affected Quality Attributes

Adding new functionality affects the software architecture and thus, the quality attributes of the system. They influence for example the response time, reliability, security and other quality attributes of the system.

Let us take our running examples for a more detailed explanation, namely the Media Store system and the reuse of a subsystem that monitors user activity to increase customer satisfaction. The software architect might estimate that the user satisfaction correlates positively with the number of successful business transactions, e.g. successfully concluded purchases in online shops. High user satisfaction therefore supports the business requirement aiming at improving the relationship between users who add items to the shopping cart and successfully complete the purchase. At the same time, however, the implementation of this requirement can have negative effects on other quality attributes, such as the performance and maintainability of the system. The performance of the entire system is influenced, since the same resource configuration, i.e. same CPU, same network throughput and same read and write throughput of the HDD, must now process the additional effort of the function for monitoring the user traffic. The overall performance of the system would therefore tend to be negatively affected by the implementation of this requirement. Logging user traffic is no necessary function that ensures the business operation of the online shop. However, the implementation of the function in both the software architecture and the subsequent program code causes additional routines that increase the resource demand.

The affected quality attributes depend on the domain. During domain analysis, the subsystem domain expert models the affected quality attributes.

This set of affected quality attributes is used as basis for a later solution-specific refinement during the architecture knowledge analysis. In the optimization step, the refined affected quality attributes are used to evaluate and optimize the quality of the architecture decision, regarding selection of the solution and configuration. Due to qualitative modelled architecture knowledge, the analysis is not limited to quality attributes with quantitative objective functions.

6.4.2. Solution Analysis

Solution developers analyse solutions and applies them to the reference architecture of the subsystem. They are the functional and technical experts for a certain subsystem solution. They apply the reference architecture, that has been defined in the domain analysis, to the solution. They determine the solution specific extension mechanism and refine the affected quality attributes. The extension mechanism automatically includes architecture models of subsystem solutions into the base architecture. Applying the reference architecture to solutions and the selection of the extension mechanism is done in the structuring solution phase. Refining the affected quality attributes is done in the architecture knowledge analysis phase.

6.4.2.1. Application to the Reference Architecture

Solution developers apply the reference architecture to the subsystem solutions. Each solution might differ in their internal architecture and the implemented features. The solution developers first identify the functional concerns of the reference architecture and aligns them to the software components of the subsystem solutions.

Each subsystem defines a set of features to be fulfilled by the solutions. The solution developer identifies the component interfaces responsible for fulfilling the features. In addition, they model dependencies of the subsystem solution to the base system, such as a common database. The dependencies to the base architecture is modelled by abstract entities that are substituted by concrete interfaces when reusing the subsystem models.

CompARE is based on the assumption that the individual solutions have already been modelled component-based. The model requires components that abstract from meaningful classes of the implementation and make them available or use the services by explicit interfaces. These tasks require experts who are familiar with the architecture and its degree of abstraction, the implementation and the actually implemented features of the subsystem solutions. This has the advantage that every model already created does not require any detailed knowledge at the time of use.

6.4.2.2. Extension mechanism

When selecting the extension mechanism, the solution developer determines for each solution individually, how the solution should be (automatically) integrated into the base architecture. *CompARE* supports two different strategies. The selection of the right strategy depends on the internal software architecture of the subsystem solution. The solution developer must have detailed architecture knowledge of the solution to select the appropriate extension mechanism. *CompARE* supports the following two extension strategies: Non-intrusive extension by adaptation of interfaces and intrusive extension of the abstract control flow of components.

6.4.2.3. Architecture Knowledge Analysis

Qualitative modelling has advantages if either no quantitative objective function exists, if it has not yet been well researched scientifically or if modelling would be too complex or time-consuming. For component-based software architectures the quality attribute security is an example, which has not yet been sufficiently researched scientifically to quantify security of a component-based software architecture. Usability can be measured quantitatively but requires a high amount of time and money due to necessary user studies. Nevertheless, experienced architects can often estimate trends in the quality properties of software architectures or parts of the software architecture due to their experience.

Such informal knowledge and architecture reasoning initially is modelled by solution developers. Thus, architecture knowledge can be reused later and optimized together with quantified quality attributes. Solution developers concentrate on modelling knowledge that is reusable in general. An example for general reusable knowledge could be effects on the general influence on the overall data backup usability of a system affected by the reliability of the backup process of a certain database management system.

CompARE uses the method of qualitative reasoning, which we have extended to model and analyse mutual effects between components and their quality attributes. The result of the analysis is an architecture knowledge model that can be reused together with the previously modelled reference architecture and software architecture of the subsystem solutions.

6.4.3. Reuse Process

In the reuse process, software architects use the models previously created by the subsystem domain expert and solution developers to evaluate the effect on quality attributes of the system by using features. For this purpose, during the requirement analysis software architects analyse the requirements of the software system in advance. Using the requirements as a basis, the software architect derives required features. Finally, the software architects review the provided features for the subsystems and select a suitable subsystem fulfilling the requirements.

6.4.3.1. Feature Analysis

In the requirement analysis phase, software architects create the feature configuration based on the required features and the base software architecture in which the features should be integrated. The feature configuration must be created or adapted individually for each base software architecture.

In the feature configuration, software architects determine which features are intended for use in the base software architecture and defines their application in detail. Features can either be selected as mandatory or optional. In addition to the selection of features, the feature configuration is used to model the later positions of the features in the base architecture. The software architect can either select the exact (mandatory or optional) positions in the software architecture or define classes of required positions. Optional features and positions can later be used as a degree of freedom to allow *CompARE* to automatically optimize the given set of desired features. Modelling them as degrees of freedom the optimal set of features and positions considering the quality attributes of the software architecture can be analysed.

6.4.3.2. Subsystem Application

In a first step, *CompARE* generates degrees of freedom, consisting of base architecture, features and their configuration. The subsystem solution architecture model and configuration application is an automatic step. *CompARE* analyses the subsystem and its solutions together with the optionally modelled architecture knowledge and the feature configuration modelled in the previous step. On their basis, *CompARE* generates the architecture model comprising the base software architecture and the software architecture elements of the extending system at the desired positions in the base architecture. The result is software models of the base software architecture with features.

6.4.4. Design Space Optimization

The design space optimization process is based on the PerOpteryx approach introduced in Section 4.3. *CompARE* extends the design space exploration and design space analysis of PerOpteryx by additional subsystem related degrees of freedom, as well as a joint analysis of qualitative and quantitative modelled knowledge.

The result of the optimization is a set of Pareto-optimal architecture candidates from which the software architect can select the most suitable candidate according to his requirements for the base system. In comparison to the PerOpteryx approach, the software architect can also use *CompARE* to decide more easily whether i) the use of a particular feature is worth the impact on the quality attributes of the base software architecture, i.e. requirements prioritization, ii) which subsystem solution would be most suitable and iii) how its placement in the base software architecture should be used to best meet the requirements of the overall system. The process allows trade-off decisions to be made on the basis of analysis results.

6.5. CompARE in the Component-based Software Engineering Process

This section introduces how *CompARE* can be integrated to the quality-driven component-based software engineering (CBSE) process.

The CBSE was originally introduced by Cheesman and Daniels [CD00], extended by Heiko Koziolek and Jens Happe [KH06a] to evaluate quality attributes, and finally refined by Anne Koziolek to optimize software architectures to automatically improve their quality attributes [Koz11]. The activities of the approach introduced in Section 6.4 are adapted and included into the CBSE process and in its workflows.

This section is organized as follows: Section 6.5.1 shows the extension of the process for quality-driven optimization of component-based software architectures. Section 6.5.2 introduces roles involved in the CBSE. Section 6.5.3 shows the extension of the requirement elicitation workflow, while Section 6.5.4 describes the extension of the (model) specification workflow. Section 6.5.5 describes our extension of the quality analysis workflow. Section 6.5.6 finally describes the decision making process that bases on the results of the workflows.

6.5.1. Component-based Development Process

The process refined by Anne Koziolek to automatically optimize quality-driven component-based software architectures supports the automatic exploration of software architectures according to several architecture degrees of freedom. The main degrees of freedom enable software architects to exchange components, change the allocation of components to hardware resources and change the setup of hardware resources. In principle, however, further degrees of freedom can be included. The process uses the results of the evaluation of the architecture models, which are automatically created on the basis of these degrees of freedoms. The iterative process improves the software architecture to achieve better quality attributes.

In this process, however, software architects have already pre-selected software components to be used in the software architecture. They are already

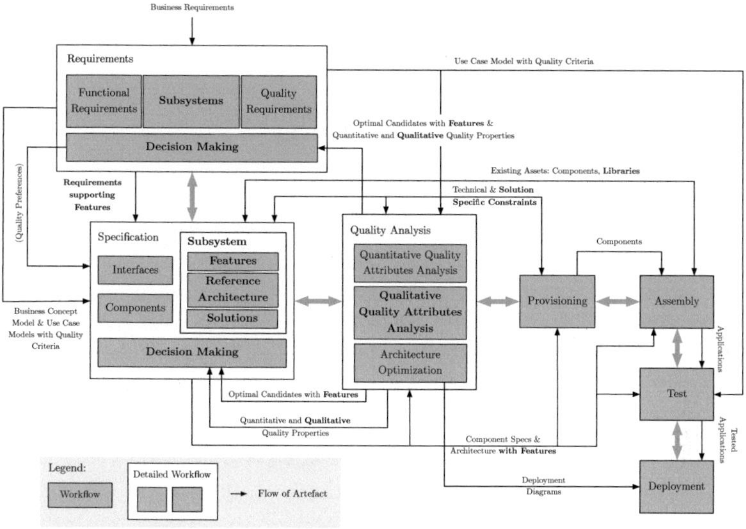

Figure 6.4.: Component-based software development process with feature-driven integration of subsystems and quality optimization of software architectures (based on ([KH06b; Koz11])). Bold terms/workflows were introduced by *CompARE*.

familiar with functionality implemented by the software components and have learned how these individual components can be integrated into the software architecture. The assembly itself must be carried out manually. In addition, software components whose interfaces are not compatible or even require additional services for their function cannot be exchanged automatically.

Figure 6.4 shows the extended process that enables feature-driven integration of subsystems into software architectures without pre-selection and manual assembly of software components and optimization by the use of subsystem solutions and their configuration in the base software architecture. The extension of the process contributes the process of building a software architecture from components by the selection of features. Features are higher level abstraction of functionality, compared to component interfaces. This reduces the complexity when reusing complex subsystem models.

CompARE extends the CBSE process mainly within the three workflows *Requirements, Specification* and *Quality Analysis.* The *CompARE* extensions are bold marked.

The initial *requirements* workflow consists of transforming business requirements to functions. Based on the results of the quality analysis, these functional business requirements can then be improved by refining them in the decision-making workflow. We initially extend the workflow to include the process of selecting subsystems that support the business requirements , i.e. supports the functional requirements and the quality requirements. In this step, the requirements engineers decide whether a requirement should be implemented by the reuse of software components, subsystems or whether the requirements should be realized by an individual implementation. This results in a set of requirements supporting features.

In the initial specification workflow, the focus is on the definition of component interfaces, system interfaces and associated components. The workflow returns the Pareto-optimal architecture candidates supporting the requirements on the basis of the decision-making workflow.

Based on the set of features supporting the requirements, subsystem solutions can now be pre-selected. All pre-selected solutions are used in the optimization process as a degree of freedom. Each feature is fulfilled by several (but not necessarily every) subsystem solutions. For each feature, there is a configuration determining desired positions in the base software architecture model. Based on the selected features, subsystem solutions, and feature configuration, the decision-making workflow is extended to allow subsystem solutions to be used as a degree of freedom for automatic exploration in addition to the definition of degrees of freedom based on interfaces and components.

The quality analysis workflow initially consists of the quantitative analysis of the software architecture's quality attributes. We extend the workflow by the exploration of qualitatively modelled informal architecture knowledge, together with quantitative knowledge. The combination allows trade-off decisions with a broader data basis.

6.5.2. Roles of the extended CBSE

In the extended CBSE, three main roles are involved in creating the models: the subsystem domain expert, the solution developer and the software architect. When additional subsystem solutions are required, the role of the component developer is also involved. The activities of the roles can be described as follows.

6.5.2.1. Subsystem Domain Expert

Subsystem domain experts are familiar with the domain of the subsystem. They have a broad overview of the subsystem solutions available on the market and have knowledge on features that these solutions must realise in order to meet the requirements of the domain. In addition, they identify the functional concerns in the software architecture of subsystem solutions and analyse their relationships. They use the functional concerns and relationships as basis for creating the reference architecture of the subsystem. Additionally, the subsystem domain experts model the dependencies of the subsystems to the base architecture. In the case of affected quality attributes, they make suggestions for the affected quality attributes and dimensions.

6.5.2.2. Solution Developer

Solution developers use the models created by the subsystem domain experts. They are the technical experts for the subsystem solutions. They are familiar with the solution in detail, i.e. its architecture, the provided features and the services required by the solution (from the base system later including the subsystem solution). They create the relations between the features and the component interfaces or signatures of the solutions. In addition, solution developers optionally model their informal knowledge for automatic quality attribute reasoning.

6.5.2.3. Software Architect

Software architects reuse the models created by subsystem domain experts and the solution developers. Together with requirements engineers, they decide whether software components should be used to implement the requirements, should be implemented from scratch, or whether subsystems should be reused. When deciding on subsystems, software architects determine the features and potentially suitable positions in the base system.

6.5.3. Requirements Workflow

In the *requirements* workflow, stakeholders first define relevant functional and quality requirements. A software architect or a requirements engineer can provide assistance.

When requirements should be implemented by subsystems, a suitable subsystem is selected. Let us consider our running example, the logging system, for demonstration:

> *Improving the user experience of the media store, visitor's movements in the systems shall be recorded. For further processing with analysis software, it is important to store the data of the movements in a database management system.*

This requirement as a basis, features can be derived which could be realized using the subsystem *logging* and for instance the subsystem solution *log4jv2*.

6.5.4. Specification Workflow

Three roles are involved in the specification workflow: The software architect, solution developer and subsystem domain expert. Figure 6.5 shows the workflow from the software architect point of view and the input artefacts of the workflow. We show also the interaction to the component developer. The artefacts modelled by the component developer are particularly important for the workflows of the solution developer. Figure 6.6 shows workflow and artefacts for the roles of the solution developer and subsystem domain

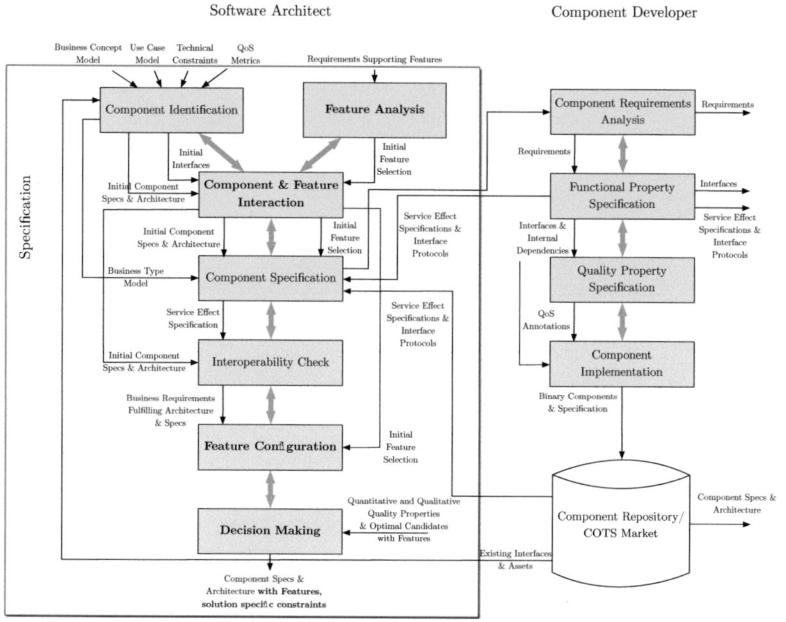

Figure 6.5.: Specification workflow from the software architect's and the component developer's perspective (based on ([KH06a])). Bold terms/workflows were introduced by *CompARE*.

expert. Software architects first *analyse features* to preselect the suitable subsystem solutions. Several solutions could be excluded in advance. In our running example and according to the requirement of Section 6.5.3, the *database logging* feature of the subsystem logging, together with the subsystem solution log4jv2 could be preselected.

In the second step, the interaction between components and features in the next workflow, the *Components & Feature Interaction* workflow, together with the initial interfaces of the software components and the initial component specification and component architecture. This interaction includes dependencies of the features to and from the software components of the base system. Based on this interaction model, software architects configure the positions of the features in the *Feature Configuration* workflow. Alternatively they configure a set of (optional) positions that can be used by the optimization as a degree of freedom. In the Media Store system, three assembly connectors with the *database logging* feature could be selected as optional. This would result in a combination of all possibilities corresponding to $2^4 = 16$ architecture candidates.

The models are then evaluated and optimized in the *decision making* workflow. The specification workflow results in the component specification and software architecture with features. Each subsystem solution has its own constraints that are also contained in the model. As in the original CBSE process, missing components can be sent to the developer component for commission.

Figure 6.6 shows workflow and artefacts for the roles of the solution developer and subsystem domain expert. The subsystem domain experts analyse the domain of the requirement for the definition of the subsystem and its reference architecture (see Section 6.4.1). In the *Domain Analysis* workflow, they first analyse the domain of the requirement to model the subsystem, its reference architecture and features. On the basis of the domain analysis, the domain experts model in the *Feature Specification* workflow features of a subsystem for a certain domain. Applied to the running example, for the subsystem logging subsystem domain experts could define the features, namely *database logging* and *file logging*.

The workflow *Reference Architecture Specification* considers modelling the reference architecture of the subsystem. They model the functional concerns of a subsystem and create the relationship between them, i.e. dependencies between the functional concerns. The resulting functional concerns, internal dependencies and solution constraints are then addressed in the next workflow, the *Interaction and Dependency Specification.* In the logger example, the functional concerns correspond to the three functions *Collector, Appender* and *Formatter.* They have several dependencies to each other, namely that Collector requires Appender and Appender requires Formatter. Collector realizes both features, namely database logging and file logging. Further, Appender requires a database system of the base architecture to store the data.

The previously defined reference architecture is then used in the next workflow to define the *Interaction and Dependencies Specification* used to get the relation to the base architecture the subsystems should be later integrated.

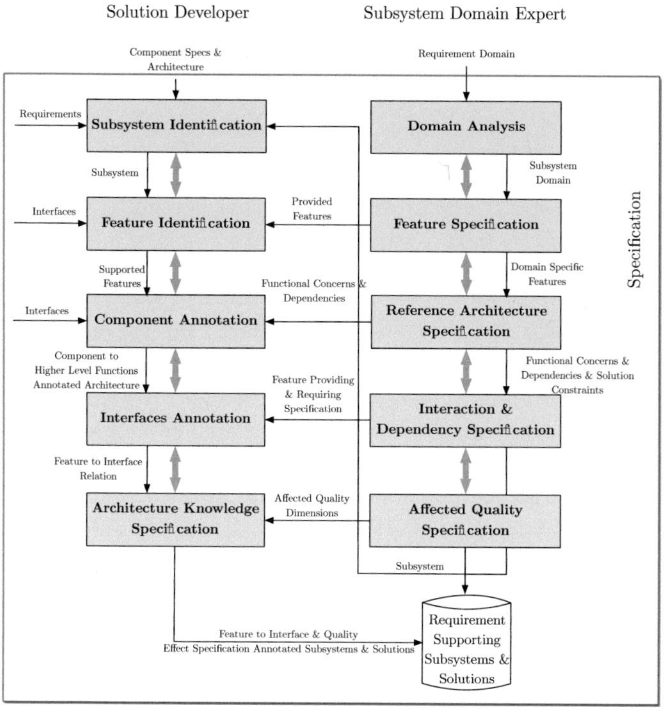

Figure 6.6.: Specification workflow from solution developer's and subsystem domain expert's perspective (based on ([KH06a])). Bold terms/workflows were introduced by *CompARE.*

The following shows an example of the interaction and dependencies: The *database logging* feature is provided by *Collector*. In addition, *Appender* is dependent on the base architecture, since the recorded data must be written to the database management system. This database management system provides services required by the logger.

Finally, the subsystem domain experts model the quality attributes involved in the *Affected Quality Specification* workflow, which are influenced by the use of the subsystem. For example, the subsystem domain expert could define influences on the quality attribute usability and maintainability of the software architecture since the first tends to be increased, while the other would be decreased at the same time.

The resulting subsystem is stored in the repository and can then be used by software architects for reuse to build their software architectures containing the subsystem.

Before software architects can use the subsystem like software components, subsystem solutions must be applied to the subsystem and its reference architecture. This step is carried out by solution developers (see section Section 6.4.2). In the first workflow, the *Subsystem Identification*, the solution developer selects the subsystem for applying the solution. In addition, solution developers use the component specification and component architecture of the solution, as well as the requirements from the *Component Requirements Analysis* workflow of the component developer. The solution developer can then select each feature that fulfils the requirements and interfaces of the solution components. These features then correspond to the provided features of the subsystem defined in the feature specification workflow. In the *Components Annotation* workflow, solution developers annotate the software components of the subsystem solution with the functional concerns of the subsystem. Then, they model the abstract dependencies to the base architecture from a component interface point of view. As a basis they use the required interfaces of the solution's software architecture. The result of this workflow is a model of the relation between abstractly modelled functional concerns and concrete software components. In the *Interface Annotations* workflow, this model is finally complemented by a relation between the provided features, required services (of the base system) and the concrete software interfaces of the software components of the subsystem solutions implementing these features. Both dependencies must be resolved by the software architect when the subsystem is reused. In the workflow *Architecture Knowledge Specification*, the solution developer refines the affected quality dimensions defined by the subsystem domain expert. If the dimension should be modelled quantitatively, quantitative functions can be used to evaluate the quality attribute. In case of qualitative modelling, the quality properties and other effects between quality attributes can be determined using qualitative reasoning annotations. Therefore, the solution developer analyzes artefacts of the solution, such as program code, documentation, but also postings in discussion groups, bug trackers or other sources. This is used as basis to model properties

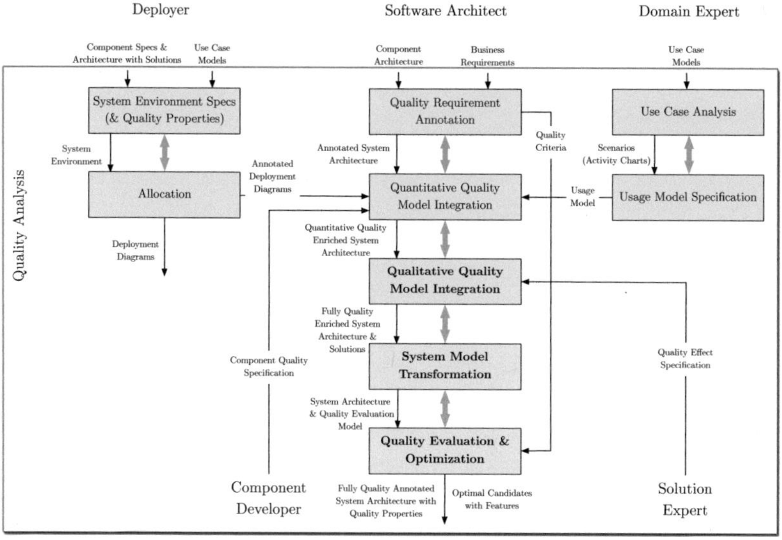

Figure 6.7.: Quality Analysis workflow from deployer's, software architect's, and domain expert's perspective (based on ([Koz11; Reu+16]). Bold terms/workflows were introduced by *CompARE* into the process.

related to the affected quality attributes of the individual components and, through their interaction, to other components. This model is then reused by the software architect and can be annotated together with quantitatively modelled quality attributes to the corresponding software components. As mentioned before, in this step only effects on quality attributes that affects quality attributes in general can be modelled to be reused.

6.5.5. Quality Analysis Workflow

The *Quality Analysis* workflow evaluates the quality of the software architecture and optimizes the software architecture according to the results. In Figure 6.7, we show the workflow in detail.

We split the quality analysis workflow into three parts: *quantitative quality model integration* workflow, *qualitative quality model integration* and *architecture optimization.* In the first workflow, software architects use the component quality specification modelled by the component developer and integrate them into the system architecture. In the qualitative quality model integration, they use the system architecture model with quantitative model entities. The model can be refined by the software architect to increase the precision due to effects that are specific for the base software architecture. In practice, this is done in one step when annotating the features to the desired positions of the base architecture. In the *System Transformation* workflow, the resulting annotated software architecture model with the annotated features is transformed automatically in a component-based software architecture model. During the transformation, the degrees of freedom are instantiated and the annotated features are resolved and replaced by software components. The transformation result in a software architecture model including the software components implementing the required features. Finally, in the *Quality Evaluation & Optimization* workflow, the software architecture model and the quality evaluation models are analysed and the resulting quality properties of the quality attributes are determined. *CompARE* uses analysis engines to determine the quality properties, such as described in Section 3.2.4. The optimization of the software architecture according to the considered quality attributes is automatically carried out by the evolutionary algorithm NSGA-II. We reuse the concepts introduced in Section 3.3. The resulting quality properties and optimized software architecture candidates are then fed back into the requirements and specification workflow in order to refine decisions and prioritize requirements.

6.5.6. Decision Making

The decision-making workflow considers both workflows, the requirements workflow, and the specification workflow. From the overall process, the decision makers select the optimal candidates from the results of the quality analysis workflow to select the optimal architecture candidate. This step is not always straightforward or clear, as requirements can conflict with each other.

Let us consider the quality attribute security and usability. Higher security properties could be achieved by querying authentication credentials more

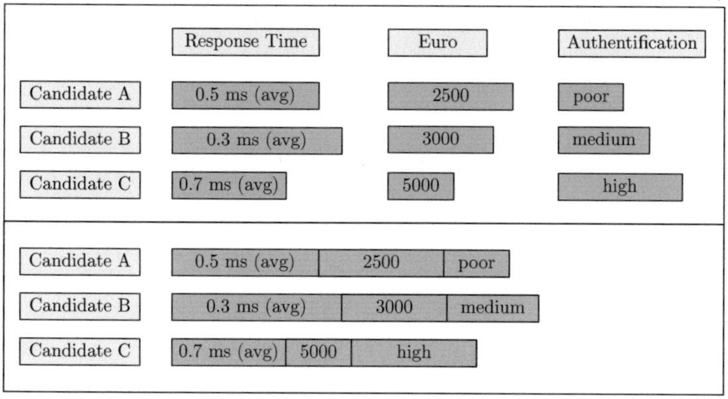

Figure 6.8.: Modified value chart example based on Rohrberg showing results of the decision making workflow. The chart considers quantified quality attributes such as the performance dimension *response time* and the cost dimension *euro*, and the qualitative values quality attribute of the security dimension *authentification* (based on ([Koz11])). The width of a box represents the utility of a quality property.

frequently. However, the usability decreases due to additional queries. Therefore, often trade-off decisions are necessary, which, at least on the basis of quantitative quality attributes, can already be made with the CBSE process extended by Anne Koziolek [Koz11].

Security properties of software architectures cannot yet be calculated using quantitative functions. Nevertheless, experienced software architects can qualitatively assess the security properties of different components. With our extension, decisions can now be made which also include qualitative knowledge. For example, stakeholders can consider whether the project requires features improving security by reducing the performance. Figure 6.8 shows an example of trade-off decisions between dimensions of three quality attributes: *Response time* for performance, *Euro* for costs and *authentication* for security using a value chart. The value chart contains the aforementioned three dimensions, as well as three architecture candidates with different resulting quality properties. All three candidates are Pareto-optimal candidates. From the resulting response time, the resulting costs and the resulting level of authentication, we can determine which candidate is optimal for the project according to the requirements. The width of a

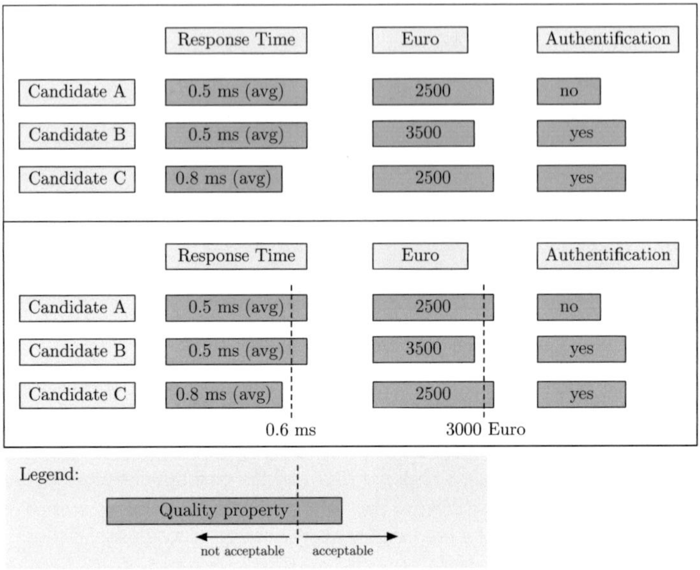

Figure 6.9.: In the upper part of the picture, we show the quality influence of the *authentification* feature on response time and cost (Euro). In the lower part of the picture we show the acceptable and not acceptable properties of quality attributes. If a property is in an unacceptable range, requirements must be prioritized.

box represents the utility of a quality property. The weight can be adjusted to correspond to the priorities of the requirements. We have also assigned a weight of the qualitatively determined quality attribute security. The second part of the graphic shows the resulting ranking of the individual candidates. In the example, Candidate B would be selected and used for the next step in the CBSE process. The value chart represents one example of many possible weights and thus resulting charts. The weights of the quality attributes in the value chart in practice depend on the requirements and how stakeholders set the priorities.

Decisions that influence the requirements workflow can also be analysed: We can analyse the degree of requirements fulfilment by using the features and how their use would affect the quality attributes of the software architecture. In other words, effects of individual features on the quality attributes of the software architecture could be estimated at design time. The upper area of Figure 6.9 shows this in an example. The *authentication* feature either increases the response time by an average of 0.3 ms or leads to higher costs of 1000 Euros. Based on this data, stakeholders could now decide whether the feature justifies reducing the properties of these quality attributes.

In addition, requirement prioritization becomes possible: Based on the results, stakeholders can decide whether a feature can implement the desired requirements at all in the available environment or whether individual quality requirements would no longer be feasible if they were applied. Adjustment or prioritization of the requirements (both functional and quality requirements) would be necessary. This is shown in the lower part of Figure 6.9. The average response time must be 0.6 ms or lower (less is better) and the costs must be 3000 euros or lower (less is better). However, the *authentication* feature affects both quality attributes. The results show, fulfilling both requirements would no longer be possible by using the feature. Requirements must therefore be prioritized: Either the requirements must be adjusted to the average response time or costs. Alternatively, the desired feature could be removed.

The decision-making workflow can also support the specification workflow. It helps to determine the specification of the final software architecture model: due to several subsystem solutions the same feature can be realized by different solutions. To find the optimal solution implementing the feature is a challenging process without a systematic and automatic process. The automatic process helps to find the best subsystem solution in the specific usage context. This considerably simplifies the model creation for later evaluation and finally the optimal selection of the subsystem solution.

In summary, the decision-making workflow supports the following areas:

- *Requirements prioritization:* Prioritization of requirements on the basis of analysing quantitative and qualitative modelled quality attributes.
- *Specification of software design:* Selection of the optimal software architecture candidate to realize the business requirements and analysing effects of features by reusing subsystems and subsystem solutions.

6.6. Further Scenarios

There are several further scenarios for which *CompARE* can be used. When new solutions realizing an already designed subsystem appear on the market, *CompARE* can be used to re-evaluate design decisions. Additionally, the effect on the quality attributes by migration from one subsystem solution to another can be evaluated upfront. *CompARE* therefore can evaluate scenarios at the design time as well as to quickly evaluate new requirements in later phases of the design process or to learn about benefits of releases of new solutions.

New Alternative Solutions Over Time

Over time, new solutions with similar features may appear on the market. New solutions could support quality requirements better or may provide new features that better support the business requirements. It may therefore be worth to re-evaluate new releases. It may be possible to find solutions that did not yet exist and could have the potential to further improve quality attributes.

Evolving Solutions

If a later version of the solution used, such as log4j version 3, instead of version 2, is available and should be used, potential effects on the quality attributes can be quickly evaluated by using *CompARE*. To do this, software architects could re-evaluate the new set of subsystem solutions by applying them to the initial architecture. If all models are already available, the exploration can be repeated without additional effort. While the selected features remain unchanged, changes in quality requirements may become visible. This makes it clear even before the actual implementation of the evolution whether the expected quality requirements can be fulfilled or whether individual quality requirements will be improved or worsened.

Trade-off decisions using Qualitative Knowledge

Even without reusing solutions, *CompARE* supports trade-off decisions between quality attributes of quantified modelled quality attributes and qualitative modelled quality attributes. To do so, software components can be annotated by qualitative knowledge and then evaluated and optimized together with quantitatively modelled quality attributes. This allows *CompARE* to evaluate and optimize design decisions considering a combination of quantitative and qualitative knowledge without the need of using subsystems.

6.7. Assumptions & Limitations

We make the following assumptions for applying *CompARE*:

- *Relevant quality attributes:* We assume the relevant quality attributes have already been identified by the stakeholders. In addition, there must be an idea about required quality properties. However, due to the evolutionary search and the a posteriori evaluation of architecture candidates determining quality bounds before analysis is not required.
- *Quality annotated models:* We assume component-based architecture models are already annotated with the quality attributes that should be quantitatively evaluated. This applies to both reused subsystem and software components of the base system.
- *Recurring nature of subsystems: CompARE* focusses on reuse of subsystems that realize features that could potentially used in a wide range of applications. Individual solutions such as GUIs or special algorithms should be modelled as standard software component models. They are often solutions tailored to one system and their utility to reuse is limited.
- *Qualitative modelled knowledge:* We assume that the evaluation of the qualitatively modelled knowledge should not be explored alone, but in combination with quantified quality attributes for the analysis of trade-off decisions between the relevant quality

attributes. It is unclear what significance and reliability the resulting values of the analysis would have when relying on qualitative modelled quality attributes alone. This is, because the values are often determined by the reasoning of architects or developers.

We identified the following limitations of CompARE:

- *Reference architecture: CompARE* relies on the solutions of a subsystem sharing the same reference architecture: All solutions used as alternative solution of the subsystem apply to the reference architecture and support a similar set of features. If the software architecture of a solution does not apply to the reference architecture, the solution cannot be used in the automatic exploration.
- *Additive extension of software architectures: CompARE* enables the additive extension of architecture elements. *CompARE* does not support removing components or functions from the system model or to perform modifications to the architecture in the sense of subtracting a set of components with subsequent addition. The application of architecture patterns, such layering, pipes-and-filters, etc. is not possible by the use of *CompARE.*

In addition to the assumptions and limitations, all assumptions and limitations of the method on which *CompARE* is based are inherited, namely PerOpteryx (see [Koz11]) and the underlying quality analysis methods, as for instance Palladio for performance quality (see [Reu+16]).

6.8. Summary

In this chapter, we showed how requirements could be implemented by reusing subsystems and the software architecture could be optimized. We showed how qualitative knowledge and quantitative knowledge could be used in combination to make trade-off decisions between quality attributes. Further, we showed how *CompARE* could help to support the software design process. We showed how our extensions could be applied to the CBSE process that was initially designed by Cheesman and Daniels, and refined by Heiko Koziolek, Jens Happe and Anne Koziolek.

By the extended process, when reusing features by subsystems, architecture decisions could be evaluated and optimized with comparatively low modelling effort. Software architects should require less effort and knowledge when reusing the features, while they do not require deep insight into the software architecture of the individual subsystem solutions.

7. Formalising the Entities of Reuse

This chapter formalizes the entities that are necessary for reusing subsystems and the solution of subsystems in automatic analysis approaches. In Section 7.1, we introduce relevant roles and requirements for the meta model. In Section 7.2, we explain the formalization of the entities with regard to modelling, use, and automatic weaving of models. In Section 7.3, we briefly introduce how the formalized entities could be applied to software architecture models. Subsequently, in Section 7.4, we structure all formalisms in a hierarchical model to separate the concerns according to role and phase of use.

The formalization presented in this chapter describes meta models to define subsystems and subsystem solutions to be reused by software architects. Reuse is done by selecting features supporting the requirements. Such a formalization allows to automatically compare several solutions and configurations in terms of placement and selection of features according to the requirements. At the end, software architects should be able to choose the optimal software architecture candidate that best fulfils the requirements. However, often the solutions are complex in their internal architecture what makes it complex for the software architect to evaluate different solutions by hand. Thus, by using our formalization abstracts from the internal complexity of different solutions and allows them to be evaluated and optimized automatically.

The basis for an automated decision support of subsystem solutions is a formalized representation, i.e. a meta model that formalizes the entities, relationships and the architecture of such entities of reuse.

We propose a meta model defining all required entities for an automated decision support for architecture design decisions with the focus on reuse of complex models such as models of subsystems. The meta model requires entities that allows a software architect to reuse architecture elements in a context that is open at their design time. To design the models the meta model follows a process that is aligned to component-based software development processes and therefore supports to separate the process of model design over different roles. Thus, we formulate the leading question for this chapter:

> Which entities, relations between the entities, and reference architecture a formalization requires modelling different non-uniform solutions of one class of subsystems in order to optimize design decision automatically?

In this chapter, we define the formalized model that contains the information about architecture, relations, and solution specific information of several non-uniform solutions of subsystems such that it can be used to support the software architect to evaluate the best solution and its configuration automatically. We call such entities *feature completions.*

The remainder of this chapter is organized as follows: Section 7.1 introduces roles involved in the design process and requirements on a model to make entities reusable and to be used in automated decision support processes. In Section 7.2, we introduce the meta model of the entities of reuse. Section 7.3 introduces how to apply the meta model to subsystem solutions. Section 7.4 introduces the multi-level structure of our formalization. We discuss in Section 7.5 assumptions and limitations, and close in Section 7.6 with a summary.

7.1. Roles and Requirements

7.1.1. Roles

Our approach is designed to support developers in different roles and phases the development. We define three different roles.

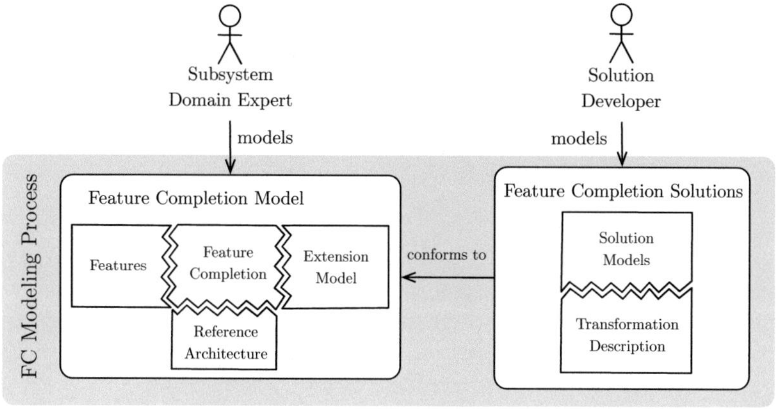

Figure 7.1.: High level description of roles and their tasks for defining feature completions and their solutions

7.1.1.1. Subsystem Domain Expert

Subsystem domain experts are responsible for the analysis of the domain of the subsystem. They model the features (cf. Section 6.1.1), the functional concerns, the internal architecture, interactions to the base system, as well as for defining the affected quality dimensions.

Overall, subsystem domain experts are considered with three processes:

- *Feature modelling:* Modelling the features of a subsystem requires deep knowledge about required, domain specific functionality. The set of features of a subsystem could be the union of the features provided by the subsystem solutions on the market.
- *Reference Architecture:* Domain experts model the reference architecture of subsystem, namely the functional concerns and their relationships to each other. The functional concerns define functional parts to be found in each subsystem solution. They assign the provided features to each of these functional concerns. In addition, they model internal dependencies between the functions and functional dependencies, e.g. shared resources, to the base system in which the subsystem is to be used later.

- *Affected Quality Attributes:* Subsystems can support functional requirements and quality requirements. While functional requirements are implemented through features, the quality attributes of the overall system depend on the quality attributes and its dimensions influenced by the subsystem. The subsystem domain expert therefore defines the influenced quality dimensions on an abstract level. These are later refined by the solution developer.

In practice, for defining that models, subsystem domain experts rely on their knowledge about the domain and public knowledge databases, such as manuals, discussions, or other databases for knowledge management, to extract the features of subsystems. Additionally, they review implementations or architecture models to extract the reference architectures.

7.1.1.2. Solution Developer

For each class of subsystems there are several possible subsystem solutions. Internally, each subsystem solution comprises software components and corresponding provided/required interfaces. All solutions realize a similar set of features that is a subset of the features of the subsystem. Further, the subsystem solutions differ in their software architecture, but comply to the reference architecture of the subsystem.

Solution developers are experts for a certain subsystem solution. They are familiar with features that can be used by its provided interfaces and its internal software architecture. They have deep insight into the technical realization of a solution and therefore define all models and description that are specific for a solution. Further, they align the software components to the functional concerns of the subsystem. Overall, they are considered with three processes:

- *Annotating reference architecture:* Solution developers align the reference architecture of the subsystem to the subsystem solution. Therefore, they identify the functional concerns of the subsystem in the subsystem solution and annotate them to the software components of the solution.
- *Annotating features:* They identify features provided by the solution and annotate them to the corresponding interfaces of the subsystem

solution. In addition, they resolve dependencies to services of the base system and annotate them to the required interfaces of the solution.

- *Modelling Quality Effects:* They model architecture knowledge regarding quality effects on the solution, i.e. they model effects on the overall quality attributes on the base architecture by the use of the subsystem (solution).

7.1.1.3. Software Architect

From the set of available subsystems, software architects select the suitable subsystem. The procedure is based on the features: They concentrate on the features provided by the subsystem. Further, they select possible positions in the base architecture that might be suitable positions for including the feature. Overall, the software architect uses the defined subsystems and subsystem solutions in software design and evolution processes.

7.1.2. Requirements for the Reuse and Automated Decision Process

This section defines a meta model that contains all the entities needed to make models of subsystems and subsystem solutions reusable. At design time the context of reuse are not fixed. They are designed to be reused with comparatively low effort by the software architect. At the same time, the resulting models can be used for quality prediction of different quality attributes as well as for optimizing the software architecture in automated decision support processes.

Reusing models allows reuse of design knowledge and design considerations without the need of repeating the whole design process. Such a reuse process requires a formalized model to be used in automated processes such as an automated decision support process.

We assume the need of reusing entities follows a certain requirement in the software design process. The meta model focuses on subsystems that consider functional requirements and quality requirements. We do not consider requirements that necessitate changes affecting the software architecture as a whole, i.e. architecture patterns. This is in contrast to similar approaches such as architecture template method by Lehrig [LHB18]. The functional requirements and quality requirements supported by *CompARE* at least include new functionalities, but never reduce or limit functionality.

The formalization should support different roles and different modelling and usage times. The modelling step should be divided into tasks performed by the subsystem domain expert and tasks performed by the solution developer. The subsystem domain expert has the main overview of the domain and can thus model domain related entities. The solution developer applies this common structure to individual solutions. The software architect finally uses the model in software design or evolution processes.

In addition to different roles, the formalism should be applicable independently of a specific component meta model. The formalism should therefore be flexibly so that it can be applied to existing, component-based meta models.

7.2. Feature Completion Meta Model

In this section, we introduce the formalism for defining and reusing subsystems and subsystem solutions, that we call *feature completions*. We base on the meta model that has been demonstrated in the Bachelor's thesis of Schneider [Sch16], supervised by me. We describe the activities of the different roles and give a detailed description of the models and their meta models.

7.2.1. Feature Completion

In this section, we define the feature completions and its related entities. First, we introduce general terms. Second, we define concepts and terminology that are important for the use of feature completions by the software architect. Due to the feature-driven use of the approach, we describe the structure of the features and their use in reuse processes. In the next step, we describe the actual definition of the feature completions.

7.2.1.1. Definition & Model

A feature completion is an abstract representation of a subsystem, such as a logging system. Subsystem solutions represent vendor specific implementations of subsystems, e.g. logging systems. Reusing a subsystem by the abstract entity feature completion, allows software architects to reuse the features of different implementations of subsystems, i.e. the subsystem solutions, by a uniform interface without coming in touch with the vendor specific internal architecture. To achieve this, the feature completion is designed for the following concerns:

C1a: The feature completion represents a high level abstraction from the implementations of subsystems and subsystem solutions.

C2a: The feature completion models the functionalities as features of a particular subsystem.

C3a: The feature completion determines an extension mechanism that defines how a subsystem solution applies in the base software architecture.

Focus of a feature completion therefore is i) the abstraction from vendor specific characteristics of subsystem solutions, ii) the modelling of the provided features of the subsystem, iii) the selection of the extension strategy of the base software architecture and iv) providing a uniform interface in reuse processes. Therefore, a feature completion comprises three elements, namely the supported features, i.e. feature objectives FO, functional concerns, i.e. the feature completion components FCC, reuse model `Complementum` C, and the architecture constraints AC. We define the feature completion as follows:

Definition 7.2.1 *Feature Completion: A Feature Completion FC is an abstract definition of a subsystem that fulfils certain requirements. Internally, a feature completion comprises feature completion components that correspond to the functional concerns that realize the provided features on an abstract level. For the software architecture while reusing, implementation and the fine-grain architecture is hidden (C1a). The feature completion models solutions for both the functional or quality requirements as features, i.e. the feature objectives (C2a), and instructions to automatically include instances* *of the feature completion, i.e. the subsystem solutions, into a base software architecture model (C3).*

The feature objectives *FO* are comprised of core (required) features *CF* and optional features *OF*. Together with feature completion components *FCC*s, the reuse model *Complementum C* and optional architecture constraints *AC* define the feature completion *FC*. *FO* and *FA* are defined as follows:

$$FO := CF \cup OF \tag{7.1}$$

$$fc := (FCC, FO, C, AC), \tag{7.2}$$

while $CF = \{cf_1, \ldots, cf_a\}$, $OF = \{of_1, \ldots, of_b\}$ and $a, b, c \in \mathbb{N} \geq 1$. Finally, the feature completions are organized in a feature completion repository *FC*:

$$FC = \{fc_1, \ldots, fc_c\} \tag{7.3}$$

7.2.1.2. Feature Completion Abstract Syntax

The feature completion defines the main entity for the reuse of subsystems. We have defined an abstract syntax, defining the language concepts and how they can be combines, covering the following parts:

- Feature objectives, i.e. provided features (see Section 7.2.2)
- Feature completion reuse architecture, i.e. the complementum (see Section 7.2.3)
- Feature completion architecture constraints (see Section 7.2.4)
- Feature completion architecture, i.e. the feature completion components that define the reference architecture (see Section 7.2.5)
- Feature completion extension mechanisms (see Section 7.2.6)
- Feature completion solutions, i.e. the association between abstract feature completions and concrete solutions (see Section 7.2.7)

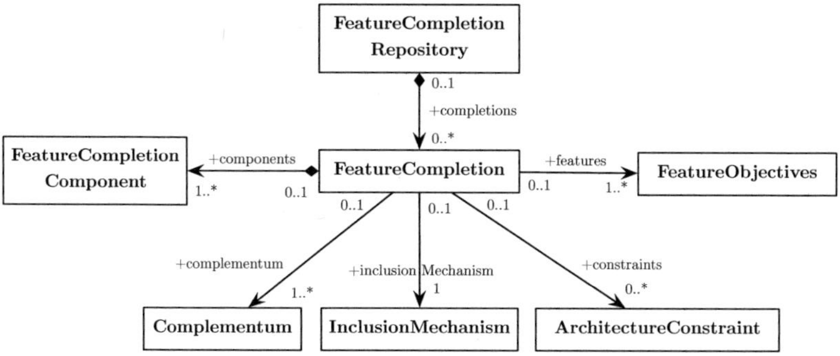

Figure 7.2.: Main entities of the feature completion meta model with the focus on the feature completions and its related entities.

The abstract syntax of the above-mentioned parts are described in detail in the corresponding sections. An overview of the abstract syntax of the feature completion is shown in Figure 7.2.

The feature completions are managed in a repository by using the entity `FeatureCompletionRepository`. The feature completion repository contains the feature completions from which the software architect can choose. It models the fine architecture by an arbitrary number of components representing the functional concerns, that we call the `FeatureCompletion-Components`. Feature completion components are individually designed by the domain expert and therefore assigned to exactly one feature completion.

In addition to the feature completion components, the feature completion contains a description of the realized feature objectives, i.e. the supported features. A feature completion can realize any number of features, whereby a feature is assigned to exactly one feature completion.

The rationale of a feature completion is as follows: a feature completion contains all entities and information for integrating subsystem solution models in a base software architecture model automatically. The entities for integration is modelled by the `Complementum` and the `Complementum Visnetis` entity, that is a sub entity of complementum. The complementum extends the base software architecture so that it can be automatically extended by features. Each complementum is assigned to a particular feature completion.

Finally, a feature completion contains the entity `ArchitectureConstraint`. The architecture constraint models restrictions in the degrees of freedom when extending base software architecture models. Accordingly, each architecture constraint is assigned to exactly one feature completion.

7.2.2. Feature Objectives

As mentioned before, each feature completion has a specific purpose such as logging. The feature completion's features describe the functionalities of the feature completion more formally in comparison to natural language (C2a). The purpose in turn is derived from the requirements that are fulfilled by the feature completion.

7.2.2.1. Feature Objectives Model

The provided features of feature completions are represented by the feature objectives in the meta model. Similar to the interfaces of components, feature completions can be described by their provided features and services required from the base software architecture. In terms of software components, this corresponds to the provided and required interfaces. A feature objective comprises one or more features. The set of all features F of a feature completion corresponds to the union of all features of the feature objectives.

$$F := \bigcup_{i=1}^{n} FO_i, \tag{7.4}$$

while n is the number of all feature objectives. Subsystem domain experts can derive the core features and optional features from the subsystem solutions or rely on their domain knowledge to define the relevant sets of features. Let $FCSol := \{fcsol_1, fcsol_2, \ldots, fcsol_o\}$ be the set of all solutions (hereinafter referred to as *feature completion solutions*) that realize the functionalities of a feature completion $fc \in FC$. o represents the number of possible solutions. We define the *realize* relation on the sets *FCSol* and *FC*.

$$realize : FC_{sol} \rightarrow FC, fc_{sol} \mapsto fc \textit{ iff} \tag{7.5}$$

the solution developer associates the subsystem solution *fcsol* ∈ *FCSol* to the feature completion *fc* ∈ *FC*, if the subsystem solution *fcsol* realizes the feature completion fc. Each *fcsol* ∈ *FCSol* can support a set of features that can be included in different sets of feature objectives.

The features are comprised of two types of features, namely the core features and the optional features:

1. *Core features:* The core features *CF* describe mandatory features that must be fulfilled by a subsystem solution.
2. *Optional features:* The optional features *OF* describe features that are not mandatory for a particular subsystem solution, but extend the feature completion by meaningful features to increase the benefit of a subsystem solution.

Therefore, we define *CF* as the set of core features, and *OF* as the set of optional features. Features can also be assigned to feature groups as sub-features. Sub-features of feature groups are uniquely assigned to a feature group. These sub-features can include core features and optional features. In addition, features can require other features.

7.2.2.2. Constraints Model

Two types of constraints can be defined on a set of features:

- Required constraints: A feature may require one or several other features for its function.
- Exclusion constraint: A feature cannot be implemented with one or several other features at the same time.

We define the $requires\_const$ and $excludes\_const$ relations on the set F. $requires\_const$ associates feature $x \in F$ to feature $y \in F$, if the feature x requires feature y. This relation results in the set of all pairs (x, y) for which the *feature x needs feature y* rule applies. $excludes\_const$ associates feature $x \in F$ to feature $y \in F$, if feature x excludes feature y. Similarly, it results in the set of all pairs (x, y) for which *feature x excludes feature y* to be feasible.

7.2.2.3. Meta Model: Abstract Syntax

The abstract syntax describes the entities for the core features, optional features and their assignment to feature completions. The entities for defining features, their dependencies and constraints are omitted here, but they were introduced in Section 3.1.5.

Our meta model for the description of the abstract syntax mainly consists of three parts:

1. Meta classes that define the superset of features namely the feature objectives of a feature completion.
2. Meta classes that define the core features.
3. Meta classes that define relations between features, such as required relations or exclusion relations.

The configurations model can be automatically derived from the structure of the feature completion meta model.

7.2.2.4. Example

Let us consider the logger subsystem from the running example to reuse the logger in a base software architecture. Such a logger usually provides the features of logging at different points in the base system to record data. In addition, the logger can record data in different formats. Figure 7.3 shows a simplified feature model of a logger with several features.

A typical feature of such a logger would be the output of data on the console. Less common, but possible, would be, the output to different databases or to a message queue. From this, three main features can be derived namely logging to the `Console`, the `Database`, and the `Message Queue`.

The console logging feature is modelled as required, while the database logging is modelled as optional feature group. If SQL database logging is selected, NoSQL cannot be selected and vice versa. Both features are

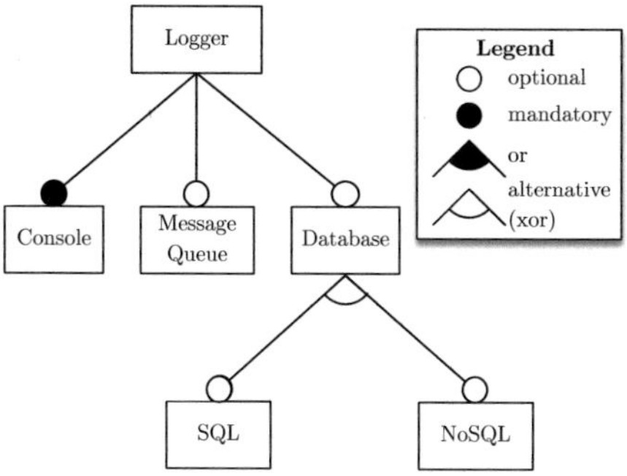

Figure 7.3.: Example feature model for the logging system log4j.

therefore exclude each other (XOR). Message Queue logging is modelled as optional feature. The database logging feature group comprises the feature `SQLDBLogging` that is required, while the other feature `NoSQLDBLogging` is optional. We therefore derive the following sets:

$$CF = \{ConsoleLogging\} \quad (7.6)$$

$$Database = \{SQLDBLogging, NoSQLDBLogging\} \quad (7.7)$$

$$OF = \{Database, MessageQueueLogging\} \quad (7.8)$$

$$\Rightarrow F := \{ConsoleLogging, Database, MessageQueueLogging\} \quad (7.9)$$

In this example, we derive one core feature and three optional features.

7.2.3. Reuse Architecture

The reuse architecture must be designed for the meta model of the base architecture. Individual application is required, because each meta model has individual concepts for the entities to be extended. The following reuse architecture is introduced using the PCM as example.

7.2.3.1. Rationale

Reusing existing subsystems requires changes of the base software architecture (C3a). How exactly this changes must be made depends on the subsystem to be integrated, on the base architecture, and on the meta model used by the base architecture. In addition, it may be necessary for the subsystem to access services or infrastructure of the base architecture.

This information is modelled by our reuse model *Complementum*. The subsystem domain expert define the models, while the software architect reuses the models. We first introduce how a software architect reuses the models, while we will later introduce, in Section 7.2.5.1, how the other roles define the models.

The complementum is a concept that allows lightweight reuse of models or model elements in component-based software architectures. We have defined the complementum using UML profiles that leave the original meta models and its instances untouched, but offer additional model entities that enriches them with additional entities. UML profiles are a generic extension mechanism that adds entities to meta models. The standard semantic of the meta model is not contradicted.

In reuse processes, a complementum extends a model (of the base architecture) by two elements. The kind of extension is dependent on two different processes:

- Feature application: In the feature application, the software architect defines the positions in the base architecture that should be extended by the features. This part is applied by the complementum visnetis part of the reuse model. The complementum visnetis defines the positions in the base system where the feature $f \in F$ of the subsystem could apply.
- Dependency resolution: All services the subsystem requires from the base architecture are annotated by the complementum entity.

In component-based software architectures different annotation positions become possible to be annotated in the base architecture:

- Assembly Connector
- Signature
- Interface
- Component

When applying a complementum using `Signature` means the subsystem requires a certain signature of an interface of the base architecture so that the subsystem solution can realize its function. Similarly, `Interface` means that a component interface of the base architecture is required. If `Component` is defined, all interfaces provided by a component of the base architecture are required.

In this step, when *modelling* subsystems, the complementum visnetis can only be applied to assembly connectors. This selects the position for a corresponding feature in the system view-type of the base software architecture model. This selection is used later in the weaving step to include the subsystem at the desired positions.

To reuse features, the software architect preselects the relevant positions in the software architecture using the complementum visnetis. When *reusing* the modelled subsystem, a complementum visnetis can be applied to signature, interface, and component. This determines To define a feature as optional or mandatory, software architectures can configure the complementum visnetis accordingly. Optional later span a degree of freedom. The feature later can apply in the architecture optionally.

A complementum visnetis can introduce dependencies from services of the base software architecture. The software architects resolve these dependencies by selecting the required entities with the complementum. However, the concrete entities that correspond to that four different annotation positions depend on the meta model in which the mechanism should be applied. For each meta model to which *CompARE* should be applied, other relations between the concept assembly connector, signature, interface and component must therefore be created.

7.2.3.2. Meta Model: Abstract Syntax

The abstract syntax of the reuse meta model consists of two parts. The first part consists of the definition of the model entities. The second part consists of the UML profile, the non-intrusive extension of the meta model of the component-based software architecture, which is to be extended by the model entities. The first part is used by the subsystem domain expert. The profile is used by the software architect in reuse scenarios.

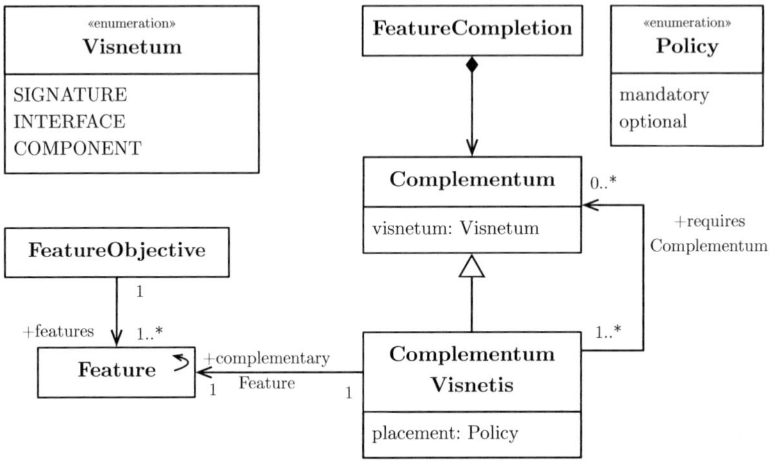

Figure 7.4.: Overview of the Complementum meta model *FC*. The arrow links of another meta model (not shown).

Meta Model

Figure 7.4 shows the meta model and the elements of the complementum meta model. The abstract syntax of the meta model required for the automated extension of software architectures by a subsystem, comprises the `Complementum` and the `ComplementumVisnetis` entities.

At the meta model level, complementum and complementum visnetis are related since the complementum is the super class of the complementum visnetis. The complementum visnetis combines the desired feature from the set of possible feature objectives, the desired later positions of the feature in the base architecture and the required services and infrastructure provided by the base architecture. The complementum visnetis has several attributes in addition to the attributes of the complementum: The feature represented by the complementum visnetis is modelled by the role `complementaryFeature`. Each complementum visnetis refers to exactly one feature from the corresponding feature objective.

The role `requiresComplementum` models the services required by the base architecture. Each complementum visnetis can (optionally) reference any number of required complementum. Instances of the complementum are modelled if the acquired services of the reused features require services of the base architecture in order to provide their service.

The complementum includes the `Visnetis` attribute. The enum `Visnetis` defines the entity on which the complementum should apply. This information is important for the subsequent step namely the automatic inclusion of the subsystem solutions into the base architecture model. The automatic weaving mechanism varies the type of weaving according to the selected Visnetum. There are three different strategies: `signature` applies the complementum visnetis to a specific signature, while `interface` applies to all signatures of the entity to be extended.

The enum `Policy` is used to define a complementum visnetis either as required mandatory or optional.

UML Profile

We use UML profiles for the non-intrusive extension of meta models of component-based software architectures. Figure 7.5 shows the feature completion reuse profile that is used to define the extension of component-based software architectures in a feature completion reuse scenario with the focus on PCM. The `featureTarget` stereotype using the role `extendedBy` aligns the complementum visnetis with the desired position in the base system where the feature should apply. In PCM, the assembly connector `PCM::AssemblyConnector` connects two interfaces with the corresponding provided and required roles. A complementum visnetis applies to the assembly connector to select it as desired position to be extended by the feature. Any number of complementum visnetis can be annotated to an assembly connector.

The second stereotype `complementumTarget` determines services in the base architecture required by the feature. Whether a `complementumTarget` is determined by the selected complementum visnetis. A complementum visnetis contains the information if `complementumTarget` are required for realizing a certain feature. The weaving mechanism later uses this annotation to automatically associate services the feature completion requires from the base architecture.

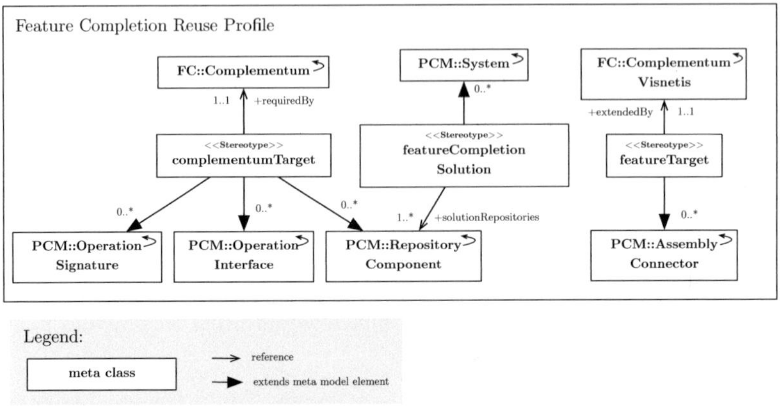

Figure 7.5.: Illustration of the feature completion reuse profile: stereotypes, entities, relations. The arrow links to the System view-type of PCM.

In the context of PCM, there are three possible entities that can be required by the subsystem: `PCM::OperationSignature`, `PCM::OperationInterface`, and `PCM::RepositoryComponent`. The role `requiredBy` allows to annotate each of the three entities a complementum.

By using the stereotype `featureCompletionSolution` software architects can select the solutions to be considered by the design space exploration. By the role `solutionRepositories`, software architects can assign a list of repository components bundling components each representing a subsystem solution to the base system. Later, these solutions will be considered in the design space exploration.

7.2.3.3. Example

Let us consider the logger example again. Figure 7.6 shows four complementum visnetis instances with two corresponding instances of the complementum. Both are derived from the features that we have introduced before. We derived the complementum visnetis `LogToConsole` from the core feature *console logging*. Further, we have derived two complementum visnetis that represent the *database logging* features that depend on both

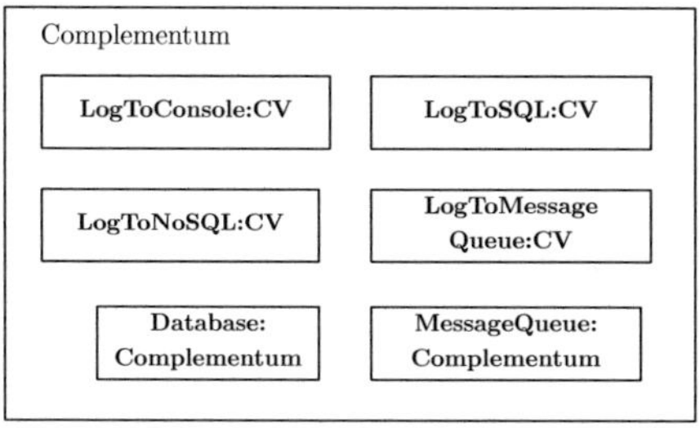

Figure 7.6.: Complementum and complementum visnetis of a logger derived from the logger feature objectives. CV is abbreviation for complementum visnetis.

flavours namely *SQL database logging* (i.e. `LogToSQL`) and *NoSQL database logging* (i.e. `LogToNoSQL`). Both require the `Database` complementum. To allow message queue logging, we have modelled the complementum visnetis `LogToMessageQueue` that requires the complementum `MessageQueue`.

Let us consider the base system from the running example, the Media Store system, in that we want to include the logger. We have simplified the software architecture to demonstrate how to use the reuse model.

Figure 7.7a shows the simplified view on the system model of Media Store's PCM software architecture.

Let us assume the requirements engineering process of developing the Media Store comes up with new requirements namely logging the customer's process of buying media. More precisely, the transition from user management to media management should be recorded. The recorded data should be stored in an existing central SQL database system. Two positions in the software architecture are essential for extending the media store to include the new requirement: The transition from the `UserManagement` component to the MediaManagement component and the *ISQL* interface of the database.

The aforementioned requirement can be satisfied by the feature completion logger. For annotating suitable positions, we use the complementum visnetis mechanism by annotating the stereotypes `featureTarget` and `complementumTarget` to desired positions in the media store architecture model. In practice, both stereotypes must be set by the software architect.

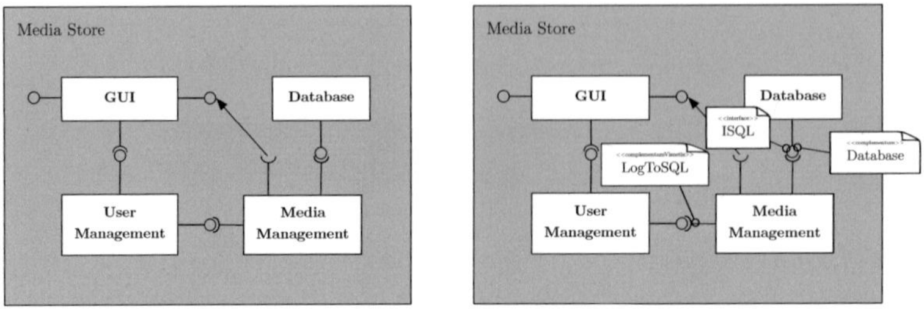

(a) Simplified system model view of Media Store's software architecture model,

(b) Complementum visnetis and corresponding complementum annotated to Media Store system model to fulfil the feature *console logging*

Figure 7.7.: Application of complementum visnetis to Media Store's system view of the software architecture model.

For including the requirement in the Media Store architecture, we use the complementum visnetis `LogToSQL`, that realizes the requirements by the SQL database logging feature. Figure 7.7b shows an example of this step using our running example.

In our Media Store PCM model, we annotate the appropriate assembly connector with the `featureTarget` stereotype to select the SQL database logging feature to be included at the particular position. The conducted complementum visnetis requires additional services from the base architecture to provide its function. More precisely the subsystem requires an SQL database from the base architecture. The required SQL database is therefore annotated by using the corresponding complementum *Database*. For this, we use the `complementumTarget` stereotype to annotate the complementum *Database* to the SQL interface of the database component in the base architecture.

In a later step, the modelled knowledge enables the weaving mechanism to automatically generate software architecture models of the Media Store, extended by the SQL database logging feature.

7.2.4. Architecture Constraints

A feature completion can optionally define architecture constraints. Such mechanisms are important to ensure or support certain quality attributes and architecture restrictions of the solutions. Such constraints can be used, for example, to define security properties for compliance, such as the definition of perimeter networks (also known as DMZ) [Mic09a].

7.2.4.1. Rationale

Architecture constraints are defined if the subsystem to be integrated into the base architecture has requirements on the deployment context. The architecture constraints require entities with specific properties to be defined, the *constrainable elements.* Constrainable elements are feature completion components or complementum visnetis entities. Entities of foreign meta models are excluded, otherwise semantic independence to the meta model would no longer be guaranteed, but could be extended by another stereotype.

We have defined several possible modes for the architecture constraints:

- Indifferent: No constraint defined.
- Together: The constrained elements must be deployed on the same physical container.
- Isolated: The constrained elements must be deployed in isolation from any other components of the system.
- Separated: Each constrained element must be deployed on another physical container.

Several constrainable elements can be selected for modelling the constraints together and separated. Isolation can also be applied to one single entity. On the basis of that constraints the weaving mechanism ensures compliance when generating the resulting feature enriched software architecture.

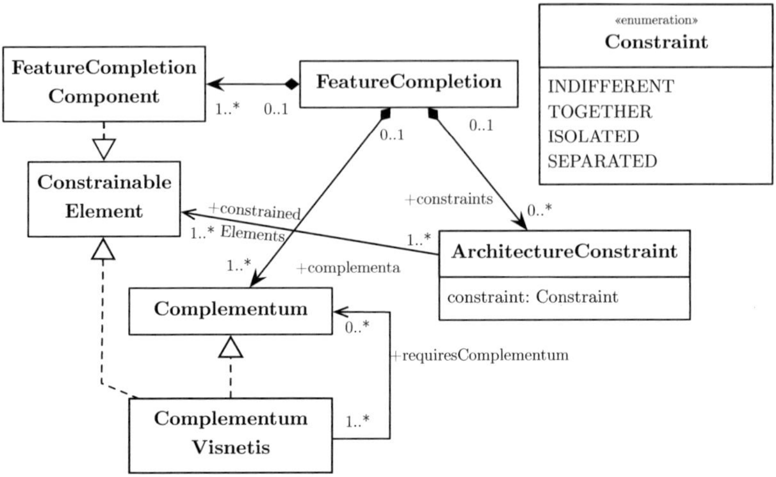

Figure 7.8.: Meta classes and relations for the architecture constraints.

7.2.4.2. Meta Model: Abstract Syntax

Figure 7.8 shows the meta model of our architecture constraints meta classes and its relations. The main relevant meta classes are `ConstrainableElement`, `ArchitectureConstraint` and the enum `Constraint`. For better illustration, we have also shown the related context classes that are influenced by the aforementioned meta classes. Relevant context classes are the `FeatureCompletionComponent`, and the `ComplementumVisnetis` that are both contained by the `FeatureCompletion`.

`ComplementumVisnetis` and `FeatureCompletionComponent` both are `ConstrainableElements`. The meta class `ArchitectureConstraint` serves as a container for constrainable elements and defines the type of constraint. One of the four elements can be selected from the enum `Constraint` that later define the type of constraint. A feature completion can define any number of architecture constraints. The enum contains the four possible constraints, as explained in the previous section, namely indifferent, together, isolated, and separated.

7.2.4.3. Example

Let us consider a perimeter network as an example of an architecture constraint. Basically, a perimeter network is used to protect services from attacks. Technically, an additional hardware layer is inserted between users (and potential attackers) and systems worthy of protection, which is particularly hardened against attacks. Thus, a perimeter network can be simplified by providing additional hardware containers. Critical software components should then be deployed exclusively on that containers. The inclusion of architecture constraints in quality prediction models is important, as many design decisions, especially those with safety relevance, require such restrictions.

Let us again use the Media Store example system, we could define an architecture constraint for the WebGUI with the constraint characteristic *isolated*[1]. This would mean that the WebGUI component would always be allocated on a hardware container alone. Since the WebGUI also offers external interfaces, it would ensure that it always represents the interface between the user and the back end system. A perimeter network would therefore be guaranteed for the external interfaces of the frontend.

Another requirement is the deployment of all database systems together on one hardware container. To achieve this, the architecture constraint `together` can be defined for the two components UserDB and DataStorageDB.

7.2.5. Feature Completion Component

Implemented solutions of complex subsystems (e.g. log4j for the subsystem *logger*) usually have inhomogeneous software architectures. Inhomogeneous architecture means that they differ in components, interfaces and how they are connected to each other. Due to the inhomogeneous architecture, it is very time-consuming to model and analyse architecture candidates by hand. Automatic decision support processes, however, are not fully capable of automatically exchanging complex subsystems with

[1] Note: The component entity of PCM would have to be extended by the class `ConstrainableElement` by another UML profile.

their inhomogeneous architectures using existing formalisms. To overcome that issue, we have introduced the feature completion components.

7.2.5.1. Definition & Model

Each feature completion *FC* comprises a set of feature completion components *FCC*. A set of feature completion components defines the coarse-grain software architecture of a feature completion. They break a complex feature completion down into its elementary components representing the functional concerns of a feature completion. Together with the relationships between the FCCs, they build the reference architecture of a subsystem.

Feature completion components define which other feature completions are required in order to provide their service. Further, they define external services required by feature completions from the base system. These external service definition extends the concepts of the complementum meta model that was introduced in Section 7.2.3. Feature completion components therefore regard the following concerns:

C1b: They define a reference architecture that represents the architecture design of the subsystem solutions.

C2b: They define the functional concerns each concrete instance of a particular feature completion has to fulfil.

C3b: They define a set of perimeter interfaces that define the boundaries, i.e. the external interfaces required by the subsystem solution.

Therefore, a feature completion component is determined by a triple namely the required feature completion components of a feature completion component, and the provided and required perimeter interfaces:

$$FCC := (FC_{req}, Pi_{prov}, Pi_{req}) \tag{7.10}$$

Feature Completion Reference Architecture

The architecture of a feature completion is defined by its feature completion components and their relationships to each other. These feature completion components thus represent the reference architecture and their dependencies of the subsystem solutions of a feature completion (see concern C1b). Further, each feature completion component implements a subset of all features of the feature objectives defined by the feature completion (see concern C2b) and their perimeter interfaces (see concern C3b).

The feature completion reference architecture defines the functional concerns of a subsystem. By the reference architecture the abstract functional concerns are instantiated by a set of software components of subsystem solutions. Feature completion components can have dependencies to each other. This reference architecture ensures that concrete feature completion solutions can be exchanged automatically. Automatic exchange becomes possible, because the analysis engine knows by the use of the reference architecture and its application to the subsystem solutions how to exchange whole solutions.

When modelling the reference architecture of a feature completion by feature completion components, we assume that the feature completion components corresponding to the feature completions have been modelled for the specific purpose of a particular feature completion. Therefore, we assume that feature completion components cannot be used for more than one feature completion and therefore feature completion components are uniquely assigned to one feature completion.

Perimeter Interfaces

The interfaces define transitions at the boundaries of the subsystem to the base system. Subsystem solutions provide their functionalities at their external interfaces and are integrated into the base software architecture at meta level.

As mentioned before, the concept of the feature completion component creates relations to concrete components and their interfaces of the solution. Perimeter interfaces model the relationship between features that a feature completion fulfils and concrete interfaces of solutions that implement these features. In case of provided perimeter interfaces, they connect the concrete interfaces of solutions with the corresponding complementum visnetis. The required perimeter interfaces realize, analogously to the provided

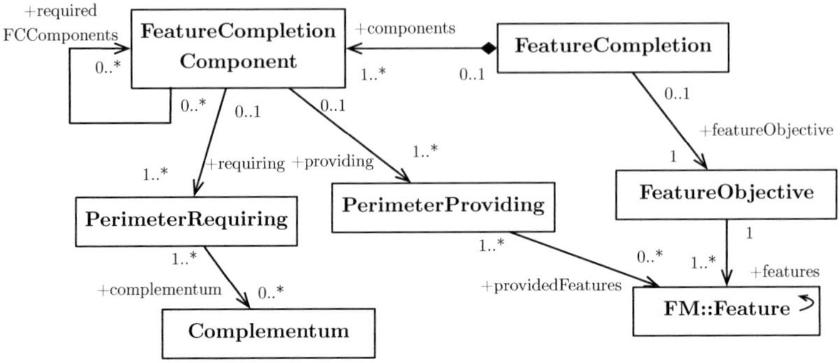

Figure 7.9.: Overview of the feature completion meta model with the focus on the feature completion reference architecture.

perimeter interfaces, the relation between complementum and actually required interfaces of the solution (see concern C3b).

In contrast to software components, not all provided perimeter interfaces or required perimeter interfaces of a feature completion must be integrated into the base architecture. It is sufficient to integrate the corresponding interfaces of the desired features.

7.2.5.2. Feature Completion Meta Model: Abstract Syntax

Figure 7.9 shows the meta model of the feature completion reference architecture to describe the relationships between feature completion, its components, their interrelationship and the relationship to the features of the feature objectives. The feature completion contains all its `components` namely the feature completion components, which are required to fulfil the features defined in the feature objective. Each of the referenced feature completion contains any number of other feature completion components, by the role `requiredFCComponents`. The referenced feature completion components thus define the reference architecture of the feature completion. In addition to the required feature completion components, the perimeter interfaces are defined here. Providing perimeter interfaces reference features from the feature objectives referenced by the feature completion. In

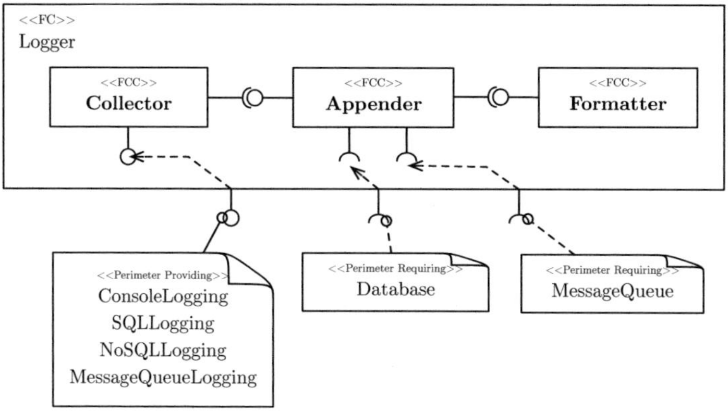

Figure 7.10.: Reference architecture of the feature completion *Logger* derived from the log4j subsystem solution.

other words, provided perimeter interfaces define which signature, interface, or component as a whole, i.e. all provided interfaces of a component, are responsible for a certain feature. Required perimeter interfaces in turn reference instances of the complementum defined by the feature completion. More precisely, we define services of a certain type that are required by the subsystem from the base architecture.

Feature completion components, however, are no entities to be reused in other feature completions. Therefore, explicit interfaces for the definition of required relationships between feature completion components are not necessarily.

Each feature completion component references models of software components of subsystem solutions. The underlying meta model of the referenced software components defines concepts for defining dependencies between its components.

Reference Architecture Example

Let us consider log4jv1 and log4jv2, both solutions for the feature completion *Logger* as described for log4jv2 in the running example section. We use both systems as a basis for building the feature completion that serves the logging feature completion. The reference architecture of the feature completion `Logger` is shown in Figure 7.10.

By analysing the log4j architecture that was introduced in Section 2.3.2, the domain expert can derive three different concerns: log4j contains the logging component that is responsible for capturing and collecting raw data required by the logger. Further, the PatternFormatter and CSVFormatter are responsible for formatting the raw data into the corresponding output format. Finally, there are several components namely the FileAppender, the DatabaseAppender, and the ConsoleAppender that transfer the processed data to the corresponding resources. Let us assume, our domain expert extracts these three feature completion components, the `Collector`, the `Appender`, and the `Formatter`.

In the next step, the domain expert analyses the dependencies between the components: The collector components always demands services from `appender` components, while the `Appender` components always uses logic from the formatter components. This results in an architecture that requires the feature completion component collector to demand services from the appender feature completion component. Meanwhile, `Appender` requires services from the feature completion component*formatter.*

When considering other logging subsystems, such as LogBack [2], an additional feature completion component may be required to process the raw data. For the simplicity of the example, we did not consider this component.

Perimeter Interface Example

To illustrate the perimeter interfaces, we use the *Logger* feature completion. In Figure 7.10, we show an illustration of their perimeter interfaces. We modelled three perimeter interfaces that can be derived from Section 2.3.2 and the software architecture from log4jv2. These include one provided perimeter interface and two required perimeter interfaces. In log4j, the `Logging` component is mainly responsible for realizing the feature completion component `Logger`. The Logging component provides the ILogging

[2] https://logback.qos.ch/

interface, which implements the individual features. The ILogging interface provides the following signatures:

- *consoleOutput():* The consoleOutput signature performs logging of data and subsequent output to the console. It fulfils the feature *console logging.*
- *fileWrite():* The fileWriter signature is responsible for writing the data to the console. It fulfils the feature *file logging.*
- *databaseWrite():* The signature databaseWrite initiates a connection to the database and stores the data in a relational representation. It fulfils the feature *sql database logging.*

The realization of the database logging feature using the databaseWrite() signature requires a connection to a database system. Therefore, this feature uses a required perimeter interface to connect to the database. For this example we omitted how signatures or interfaces are included in the base architecture model.

7.2.6. Feature Completion Extension Mechanism

Basically, there are two possibilities of extending component-based software architecture models by features: The extension by modifying the control flow between components and the extension by changing the abstract control flow, modelling the behaviour (see Section 3.1.2.1). In the following, we will introduce both mechanisms. Further we will introduce the relevant meta model elements and use of the mechanisms.

7.2.6.1. Adapter Extension Mechanism

The adapter extension is, from the component point of view, a non-intrusive extension of base architecture models by new features. It modifies the sequence of calls of the system. We modify the delegation process of calls between components and interfaces by additional functions. At the model level, we connect the functionality provided by the base system and the features of the subsystem through adapters. The adapter is required for the integration at system model level, since the base software architecture and external interfaces of the subsystem usually have incompatible interfaces.

Model

Essentially, the adapter enables incompatible interfaces to be made compatible at the model level. This step is necessary to automatically include of features, implemented by components with various interfaces , as otherwise the creation or adaptation of interfaces would have to be carried out manually or semi-automatically. Considering two compatible interfaces I_{prov} and I_{req}, that are connected by an assembly connector in the base system. The required feature f_{req} is provided by $I_{incomp_{prov}}$ interface, which is incompatible to I_{prov}. To make them compatible, an adapter is created that has the interfaces I'_{prov}, I'_{req}, and $I'_{incomp_{prov}}$ and models the abstract control flow accordingly. Details on the abstract control flow is introduced in Section 8.4.1, but is not relevant for introducing this formalism. The interfaces I_{prov} and I'_{req}, as well as $I'_{incomp_{req}}$ and $I_{incomp_{prov}}$, and finally I'_{prov} and I_{req} are compatible in pairs. This allows new assembly connectors to be created between I'_{prov} and I_{req} ($assembly'$), as well as between $I'_{incomp_{req}}$ and $I_{incomp_{prov}}$) ($assembly''$), and finally I_{prov} and I'_{req} ($assembly'''$). Based on the newly created assembly connectors, the following call sequences are meaningful:

- *Before:* The option *before* calls the feature providing interface $I_{incomp_{prov}}$ *before* I_{prov}. The call sequence of the assembly contexts therefore corresponds to first call to $assembly'$, then to $assembly''$, and finally to $assembly'''$.
- *Afterwards:* The option *afterwards* calls the feature providing interface $I_{incomp_{prov}}$ *after* I_{prov}. The call sequence of the assembly contexts therefore corresponds to $assembly'$, then $assembly'''$ and finally to $assembly''$.
- *Surrounding:* The option *surrounding* calls the feature providing interface $I_{incomp_{prov}}$ *before* and *after* I_{prov}. The call sequence of the assembly contexts therefore corresponds to $assembly'$, than to $assembly'''$, afterwards to $assembly''$, and finally to $assembly'''$.

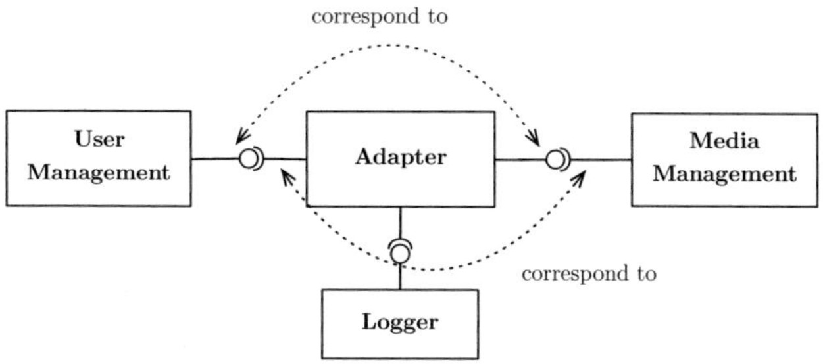

Figure 7.11.: Simplified example of Media Store with logger feature included by an adapter.

To ensure the three call sequences mentioned above, we reduce the transitive closure to the corresponding transitive reduction.

Besides the call sequence, we define how many instances we need of the components implementing the features. Each pair of adapters and adapted components of the feature that affects the abstract control flow can be built into the system model. It can be configured to be instantiated either once or several times (automatically). If it is instantiated once, the same pair is used for each delegation of the requesting components. With multiple instantiation, a separate pair is used for the assembly for each weaving operation. This type of modelling can be relevant to ensure assurances of certain quality attributes, such as safety or reliability.

Example

Figure 7.11 shows schematically how the feature logger can be included in the Media Store system architecture. For simplification of the example, the logger feature is represented as one single component namely `Logger`.

We have chosen the delegation between `UserManagement` component and `MediaManagement` component as the target point in the system model. An adapter connects the three interacting components. Figure 7.12 shows the possible interaction through the three possible call sequences of the abstract control flow. Using *Before*, first calls `UserManagement`. The control flow is

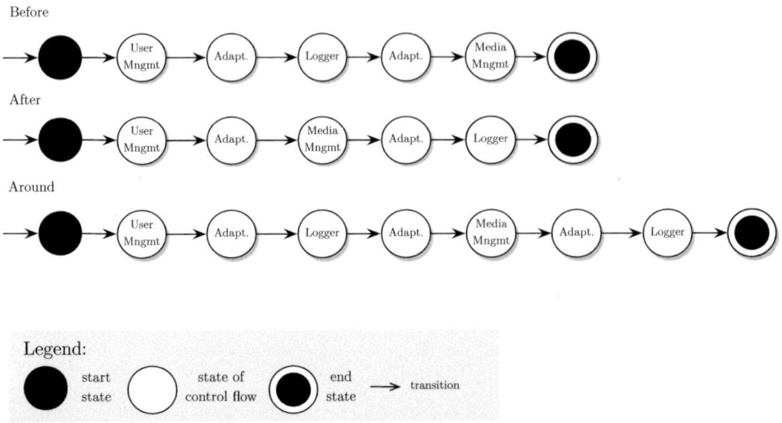

Figure 7.12.: Illustration of before, after, and around call sequences of the logger in context of UserManagement component and MediaManagement component of the Media Store.

then passed on to the adapter, which then calls the logger. The control flow returns to the logger, which then calls `MediaManagement`.

Using *After*, also calls `UserManagement` first. As before, the control flow is passed to the adapter, which calls `MediaManagement` first. Afterwards the adapter calls the `Logger`.

Using *Around*, `UserManagement` is called first. The adapter then calls the `Logger` for the first time. `MediaManagement` is called afterwards. In contrast to *Before* and *After*, the logger is now called a second time.

Please note that the example presented here has been simplified. Instead of components, services are called in the components, since only services can be called by delegation. To simplify the example, we abstracted from the services and their respective abstract control flows.

7.2.6.2. Abstract Control Flow Mechanism

The abstract control flow extension mechanism intercepts the internal sequence of the processes in software components. The mechanism is not dependent on compatible interfaces, but instead extends components by additional interfaces, which generally assume the requiring role. Main concepts have been introduced in the master's thesis by Maximilian Eckert [Eck18], supervised by me.

Abstract Control Flow Language

For better usability and easier design, we have created declarative language constructs within a domain-specific language. This allows software architects to specify a set of weaving positions using domain specific constructs. The description effort should be kept as low as possible. As already introduced in previous sections, the abstract control flow is a sequence of control structures, internal actions, and external calls. These concepts correspond to the concepts of common programming languages: Control structures apply to (e.g. branches or loops), internal actions (e.g. mathematical calculations) and external calls (e.g. method calls). We can extend at the beginning and end of the abstract control flow of a service. Analogous to the appearance definition of the adapter extension, the change can be applied to the three named positions before, after, or both before and after the statement.

- **Internal Action Extension:** the strategy for extending internal actions extends the internal behaviour of components without violating the black box principle. This allows software architects to extend internals of services with features without having concrete insights into the process.
- **Control structure extension:** The control structure extension strategy extends the abstract behaviour of loops and other control structures. With the help of a before/after indicator, the insertion of the new model elements can be configured at the beginning or at the end of the control flow behaviour. The exact process paths do not have to be known by the software architect.
- **External calls extension:** All external calls to a certain interface (or signature/service) can be extended without the software architect necessarily having to know the concrete positions of the calls within the abstract control flows of the entire software architecture.

For all extension strategies, the software architect defines classes of positions to be extended. The grammar of the abstract control flow mechanism can be described by the following formalism:

$$ACFE := (V, T, P, S), \tag{7.11}$$

while V represents the vocabulary of the domain specific language, T is the set of terminal symbols, P the production rules and S the start symbol. The production rules can be divided into the four subsets $P_{ExtensionMechanism}$, $P_{FeatureSelection}$, $P_{PointCut}$, and P_{Advice}. *ExtensionMechanism* corresponds to the start symbol, while terminal symbols are displayed in magenta.

$$
\begin{aligned}
&P_{ExtensionMechanism} = \{\\
&\quad ExtensionMechanism \rightarrow (Imports) * Multiple\ \textbf{ExtensionInclusion}\\
&\qquad\qquad Name\ ID\ Description\ FeatureSelection\\
&\qquad\qquad \textbf{PointCuts}\ (PointCut) *\ \textbf{Advices}\ (Advice)*\\
&\quad Imports \rightarrow \textbf{import}\ (String)*\\
&\quad Multiple \rightarrow [\textbf{multiple}]\\
&\quad Name \rightarrow String\\
&\quad ID \rightarrow String\\
&\quad Description \rightarrow \textbf{Description}\ String\\
&\quad String \rightarrow [\text{a-zA-Z\_.:/}]*\}
\end{aligned}
$$

The P_ExtensionMechanism rule derives a name, ID, description, any number of imports, the multiple inclusion option (see Section 7.2.6.1), the selection of features, point cuts, and advices. Name, ID, description and import are derived to a string, while the multiple option is optional. A string is alphanumeric.

$$
\begin{aligned}
&P_{FeatureSelection} = \{\\
&\quad FeatureSelection \rightarrow FeatureCompletion\ \textbf{FeatureList}\ (FeatureList)*\\
&\quad FeatureList \rightarrow ((\textbf{optional})?\ ComplementumVisnetis)*\\
&\quad ComplementumVisnetis \rightarrow Name\\
&\quad FeatureCompletion \rightarrow \textbf{FeatureCompletion}\ Name\\
&\quad Name \rightarrow String\\
&\quad String \rightarrow [\text{a-zA-Z\_.:/}]*\}
\end{aligned}
$$

The P_FeatureSelection rule defines the selected features. The feature selection defines the feature completion and a list of features to be used. The list of features again refers to complementum visnetis that can be marked as mandatory or as optional. The complementum visnetis and the feature completion are defined as a name that are later translated into a concrete meta model element.

$$
\begin{aligned}
P_{PointCut} = \{ & \\
PointCut &\rightarrow \textbf{PointCut}\ Name\ PlacementStrategy \\
PlacementStrategy &\rightarrow \textbf{PlacementStrategy} \\
& \quad ExternalCallPlacementStrategy\ | \\
& \quad InternalActionPlacementStrategy\ | \\
& \quad ControlFlowPlacementStrategy \\
ExternalCallPlacementStrategy &\rightarrow \textbf{ExternalCallPlacementStrategy} \\
& \quad Signature \\
InternalActionPlacementStrategy &\rightarrow \textbf{InternalCallPlacementStrategy} \\
& \quad Component \\
ControlFlowPlacementStrategy &\rightarrow \textbf{ControlFlowPlacementStrategy} \\
& \quad Component \\
Signature &\rightarrow \textbf{MatchingSignature}\ Name \\
Component &\rightarrow \textbf{MatchingComponent}\ Name \\
Name &\rightarrow String \\
String &\rightarrow \text{[a-zA-Z\_.:/]}*\}
\end{aligned}
$$

The P_PointCut rule shows how software architects describe the actual placement strategy of the feature to be included into the base software architecture model. The placement strategy is selected and the architecture element matching the placement strategy is specified. For external calls, signatures can be defined as application elements, while for internal actions and control structures, control flows of entire components can be defined.

Signature and components are again defined as name and later transformed to meta model elements.

$$
\begin{aligned}
P_{Advice} &= \{ \\
\textbf{Advice}\ \mathit{Advice} &\rightarrow \mathit{Appearance\ PointCut\ PlacementPolicy} \\
\mathit{Appearance} &\rightarrow \textbf{Appearance BEFORE} \mid \textbf{AFTER} \mid \textbf{AROUND} \\
\mathit{PlacementPolicy} &\rightarrow \textbf{PlacementPolicy OPTIONAL} \mid \textbf{MANDATORY}\}
\end{aligned}
$$

Finally, we define the advice. By the advice, software architects can define the previously introduced options (Section 7.2.6.1). Advices are always defined for exactly one PointCut. Additionally, the placement policy can be set, which allows to define an advice and thus the later use in the base software architecture model as optional or mandatory.

Example

Figure 7.13 shows an example instance of the grammar in a derivation tree. First, we define the base system and the feature completion model to be included. In the example, we include the feature completion *Logging*. The alternative features `PatternLayout` and `JSONLayout` are evaluated against each other. The `ConsoleLogging` and `FileLogging` features are declared mandatory and must therefore always be included. The feature JSONLayout was declared as optional, i.e. the feature can, but does not have to be included in the architecture (this remains a degree of freedom). The example also shows the PointCut `allDBCalls`. The grammar allows to reference the signature `getDB` via the external call extension strategy as well as an advice, which processes the desired feature before the call of `allDBCalls` (BEFORE). This advice is declared as optional.

7.2.6.3. Meta Model: Abstract Syntax

Figure 7.14 shows the meta model of the extension mechanism. Each feature completion has an extension mechanism assigned by the role `Extension-Mechanism`. Both extension mechanisms, `AdapterExtensionMechanism` and `FCLExtensionMechanism`, have the same superclass namely the abstract class `ExtensionMechanism`.

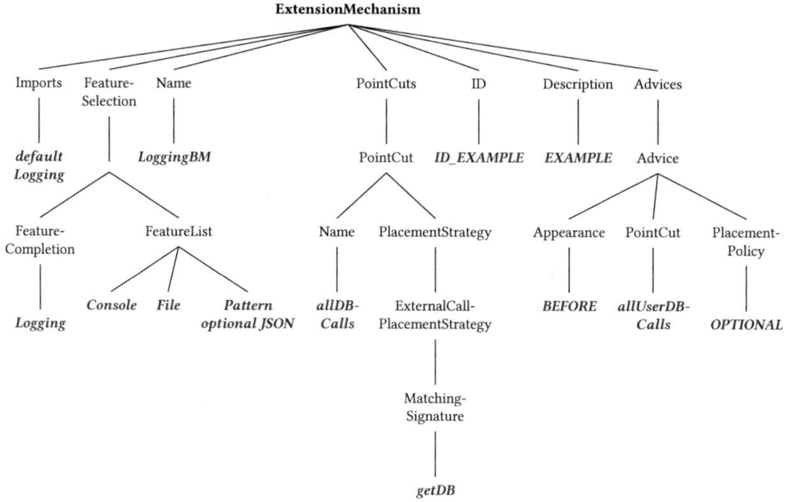

Figure 7.13.: Derivation tree of an example instance of the grammar for defining the abstract control flow extension on the example of the Media Store as base system and logger as feature completion to be included. Purple items have been set by the software architect in a reuse process.

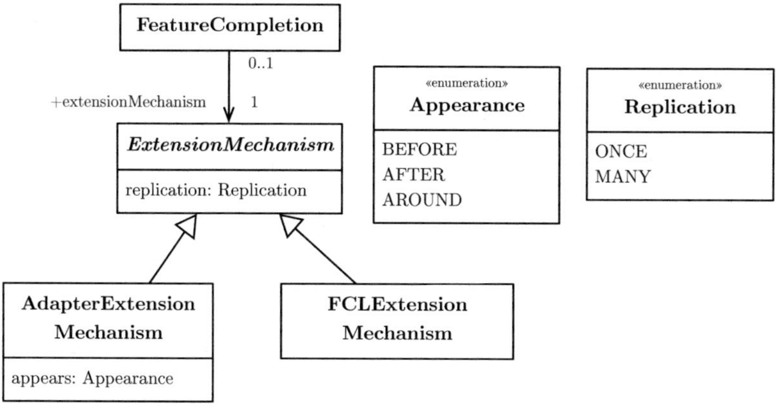

Figure 7.14.: View of the feature completion meta model from the perspective of the extension mechanisms (relevant part for the definition process). FCLExtension-Mechanism is omitted.

The adapter mechanism uses the following elements: The enum `Replication` of ExtensionMechanism defines whether the pair of adapters and components of the subsystem is instantiated once (ONCE) or several times (MANY). `AdapterExtensionMechanism` also has the enum `Appearance`, which models the corresponding call sequence. We can model the call sequences from section 7.2.6.1.

7.2.7. Feature Completion Solution

In this Section, we describe the feature completion solution model to design the solution specific part that is individual for every subsystem solution. We describe the application of the reference architecture to solutions of feature completions from the solution developer's perspective. To do this, we will first introduce several concepts that are necessary for the application. Several concepts are similar to the feature completion reuse profile described in Section 7.2.3.2, but differ in detail in their semantics. At the beginning, we introduce several model concepts and their rationale. Again we use UML profiles for non-intrusive extension of meta models. As before, this ensures meta model independence of the demonstrated approach. Pleas note that the feature completion solutions must be modelled using the same meta model than the later base architecture.

7.2.7.1. Model & Rationale

For the definition of the solution specific parts several concepts and entities can be reused from the previous sections. However, semantic differences and refinements arise from the perspective of use, which are described in the following.

The focus of the creation of the solution-specific part requires the annotations between corresponding elements of the reference architecture and the components of the subsystem solutions. This annotation steps are carried out by the solution developer. To model the relations between the reference architecture and the components of the solutions is distinct by two different types:

- Fulfils complementum visnetis annotation: Using the fulfils complementum visnetis, we relate abstract features to concrete entities of the subsystem solution. Interfaces of software components of the solution come in relation with the abstract features of feature completions. This allows the desired feature to be built into the base architecture automatically.
- Requires complementum annotation: The requires complementum annotations relates the abstract concept of required services of feature completions to the concrete entities of the subsystem solution that requires services from the base architecture. Such entities might be required interfaces of software components.

Both enable an extension of the following three model entities of component-based software architectures:

- Signature
- Interface
- Component

The semantics of the extension depends on the type of annotation: In the case of the fulfils complementum visnetis annotation, the three entities mentioned above are configured in the complementum visnetis: `Signature` means that the feature of the subsystem contained in the complementum visnetis is reused in the base system by integrating a single signature of an interface. In the case of `Interface`, the entire interface is responsible for realizing the particular feature. Similarly, `Component` defines that all provided interfaces of a subsystem are responsible to fulfil the feature. The distinction is necessary because some features are used by a single signature in an interface, others by an entire interface, and others by all interfaces of a component.

In the case of the requires complementum role, `Signature` defines a single signature of an interface is required in the base architecture. Similarly, `Interface` means an entire interface, with all its signatures, is required. If `Component` is modelled, all interfaces of a component is required to be included into the base architecture.

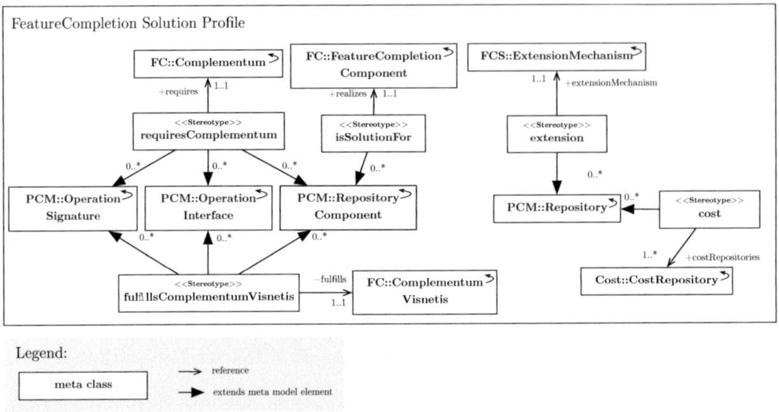

Figure 7.15.: Illustration of the feature completion solution profile: Stereotypes, entities, relations.

7.2.7.2. UML Profile

The solution profile extends component-based software architecture models with entities that creates relationships between the reference architecture elements of the feature completion and the concrete model elements of subsystems corresponding to these reference architecture elements. The reuse profile extends the base architecture model to include entities for the defined placement of the model elements of the subsystem. In other words, the model elements of the solution profile and reuse profile each form a pairwise counterpart to each other. Figure 7.15 show the stereotypes, entities and relations of the feature completion solution profile.

The feature completion solution profile defines five different stereotypes: The stereotype `extension` assigns the concrete extension mechanism to the repository containing the components of the subsystem solution. The stereotype `cost` assigns a cost model (a cost repository) to the repository containing the components of the subsystem solution. This is based on the assumption that each subsystem solution is stored in its own repository. If all subsystem solutions are in a common repository, only one annotation is required.

The stereotype `isSolutionFor` assigns the functional concerns of the reference architecture to components of the subsystem solutions. More concrete, by the stereotype, the solution developer assigns a feature completion component to a corresponding component of the subsystem architecture model. This step is necessary to enable a transparent exchange of different feature completion solutions when automatically including the features. In the PCM, component corresponds to the entity `PCM::RepositoryComponent`.

Using the `fulfillsComplementumVisnetis` stereotype, a solution developer uses the fulfilment role to assign a specific feature to concrete model elements that are instances of the three meta classes. In a subsequent step, the weaving mechanism uses the annotations to automatically resolve the relationship between the feature and the model element that actually implements the feature.

The stereotype `requiresComplementum` defines the model elements that a complementum visnetis requires from the base architecture to provide its service. The `requiresComplementum` stereotype attaches the entity `FC::Complementum` from the FeatureCompletion meta model to any referenced model elements of other meta models. In the case of the PCM, the appropriate model elements correspond to `PCM::OperationSignature`, `PCM::OperationInterface`, and `PCM::RepositoryComponent`. As before, the domain expert selects concrete signatures, interfaces or components of the model of the solution that require services or infrastructure of the base architecture.

7.3. Applying the Reference Architecture to Solutions

This section introduces how solution developers apply the reference architecture to solutions of a feature completion. Let us consider again the logging example with the concrete subsystem solution log4jv2. We assume, a reference architecture for the feature completion logger has already been developed (see example of section 7.2.5). Thus, suitable feature completion components and corresponding relationships, i.e. *requiredFeatureCompletionComponents*, have already been modelled. In addition, we assume the software architecture models of the subsystem architecture has already been analysed and suitable UML profiles have been created for the corresponding meta model.

The solution developer carries out three steps to apply a feature completion solution to the reference architecture:

1. *Identify features:* Identification and annotation of the features provided by the subsystem.
2. *Components annotation:* In this step, the reference architecture is aligned to the software architecture of the subsystem solution. Solution developers identify software components that correspond to the feature completion components. They using the stereotype `isSolutionFor` for the annotation.
3. *Annotate perimeter interfaces:* The solution developer uses the stereotype `fulfillsComplementumVisnetis` to annotate features to concrete elements of the subsystem solutions that fulfil the feature (provided perimeter interface). If a feature requires services of the base architecture, the corresponding requiring model elements of the subsystem solution are annotated by using the stereotype `requiresComplementum`. (required perimeter interface).

The steps are introduced and applied in the following sections.

7.3.1. Identify features

The solution developer analyses the features defined for the subsystem and aligns them to the features provided by the solution to be modelled. Features can be derived from different sources: Experienced domain experts can use their knowledge deriving features. Alternatively, documents or a review of the source code can be done.

To identify the features of log4jv2 we have reviewed both source code and documentation. Figure 7.3 shows the extracted features. Log4jv2 supports logging to console `LogToConsole`, SQL database logging `LogToSQL`, NoSQL database logging `LogToNoSQL`, file logging `LogToFile`, and message queue logging `LogToMessageQ`. For this application example, we concentrate on the SQL database logging feature.

Feature Completion Component	Subsystem Component
Collector	Logging
Appender	FileAppender, DatabaseAppender ConsoleAppender
Formatter	PatternFormatter, CSVFormatter

Table 7.1.: Feature completion component to log4jv2 software component relation.

7.3.2. Components annotation

The solution developer analyses the software architecture of the subsystem solution that should be applied to the reference architecture of the feature completion logger. To apply the meta model the solution developer can either review the source code or use the documentation of the subsystem solution.

For modelling the subsystem solution log4jv2 with its components and relationships, we mainly considered the documentation and the source code. The software architecture of the subsystem solution is described in Section 2.3.3. Figure 2.8 shows an overview of the components and the simplified system model of log4jv2. We have identified 6 components, that solution developers aligns to the FCCs of the FC `Logging`. They use the feature completion solution profile to connect components and their corresponding feature completion component using the `isSolutionFor` stereotype.

Table 7.1 shows an overview of the components of log4jv2 and the corresponding feature completion components. The feature completion component `Collector` is responsible for collecting the data from the base system for processing and logging. In log4jv2 the component `Logger` represents the feature completion component `Collector`. It performs all operations that collects the raw log data.

The feature completion component appender is realized by several components: `FileAppender` provides services for writing to a file. The `DatabaseAppender` provides services for logging to SQL databases. Finally, the `ConsoleAppender` writes the log data back to the console.

FCC	Software Interfaces provided	Software Interfaces required	FCC Perimeter Interfaces
Collector	ILogging	IAppend,	ILogging
Appender	IAppend	IFormat ISQL	ISQL
Formatter	IFormat		

Table 7.2.: Relation between software interfaces, FCC, and perimeter interfaces of *log4jv2* (simplified).

The feature completion component `Formatter` is realized by two components: The `PatternFormatter` and the `CSVFormatter`. Both provide several services for formatting the output to the required format that is suitable for the intended appender.

7.3.3. Annotate perimeter interfaces

7.3.3.1. Identification

The perimeter interfaces of the feature completion components can be identified by the use of the architecture model of the subsystem. Table 7.2 gives an overview of the interfaces of the log4jv2 components that make up the individual feature completion components. In addition, the corresponding perimeter interfaces are shown. The components of the `Collector` comprises the interface *ILogging* that provides operations for recording the raw data coming from the base system. ILogging provides the signature `logToSQL` to store the data to an SQL database. For the actual data recording, the collector components require additional services from the `Appender` via the interface `IAppending`. The `Appender` of log4jv2 is particularly versatile and therefore comparatively complex. To simplify the demonstration and simplify the example, we use a coarse-grain abstraction of the system.

The signature `console()` of `IAppender` is responsible for writing the data to the console. For writing the data to the database we use the signature `persistToSQLDB(Data)`.

The interface `IAppender` represents the provided services of the Appender. The Appender itself requires external services from the subsystem solution by the `IFormat` interface and from the base architecture. These services are required using the interfaces `IFormat` and `ISQL`. `ISQL` has the signature `persistToDB(Data)` for requiring services of an SQL database.

The Formatter finally processes the layout for the corresponding service of the Appender. To simplify the example, we only show an excerpt from the signatures of both interfaces. The responsibility of the provided interface `IFormat` is to change the format of the log data into text for processing the data to the console by using the signature `formatToText(Data)`. If the log data should be stored in a database system, the signature `formatToSQL(Data)` processes the log data to JDBC database instructions.

In total, two types of interfaces are important for using log4jv2:

- Interfaces that provide log4jv2 services (i.e. the provided system provides interfaces).
- Interfaces that log4jv2 requires from the base system in order to realize its own services.

7.3.3.2. Application

The aforementioned two types of interfaces represent the perimeter interfaces. Table 7.2 shows the perimeter interfaces for the individual feature completion components of log4jv2. As a result of the analysis of the log4jv2 architecture, `ILogging` represents the provided perimeter interface, while *ISQL* is the required perimeter interface. The complementum visnetis connects features of the feature objectives with the requires complementum, i.e. services required from the base architecture. The feature *LogToSQL* requires the database. Thus, the complementum visnetis connects the provided perimeter interface with the required complementum. The required complementum *database* includes the *ISQL* interface. The solution developer then assigns the complementum and complementum visnetis to the `requiring` and `providing` roles of the corresponding feature completion components. The perimeter providing including the feature LogToSQL is assigned to the providing role of *Collector*, while `Appender` gets the perimeter providing including the complementum `database`.

For annotating the complementum visnetis the solution developer uses the stereotype `fulfillsComplementumVisnetis`. For the requires complementum, the stereotype `requiresComplementum` is used. To do so, the stereotype `fulfillsComplementumVisnetis` is assigned to the signature `logToSQL(Data` of the `ILogging` interface. This fulfils the Feature `LogToSQL`. The stereotype `requiresComplementum` is assigned to the signature `persistToDB(Data)` of the `ISQL` interface. This fulfils the Complementum `database`.

7.4. Multi Type Hierarchy

In accordance with the component hierarchy (see Section 3.1.3), we define a multi type hierarchical model that we use for the classification of the feature completion model and process. The multi type hierarchy is designed to be in accordance with common roles of typical software engineering processes and is oriented at its phases. The multi type hierarchy has been already published in one of our publications Busch et al. [Bus+16]. The separation into different phases and roles helps in the following two considerations:

First, it clearly separates and structures responsibilities in the development process. A clear separation and structure helps the individuals involved to understand which phase of the development they are currently in and to undertake the necessary tasks at the right time. In the feature completion development process there are three roles involved namely the subsystem domain expert, the solution developer and the software architect. The subsystem domain expert defines the feature completions, the features provided and dependencies to the base architecture, as well as for the definition of the reference architecture of each feature completion. The solution developer is responsible for annotating the abstract feature completion model defined by the domain expert to the concrete subsystem comprising software components. Finally, the software architect is responsible for reuse and integration into the desired base architecture. The temporal aspect of the creation of the individual parts can be divided as follows: Subsystem

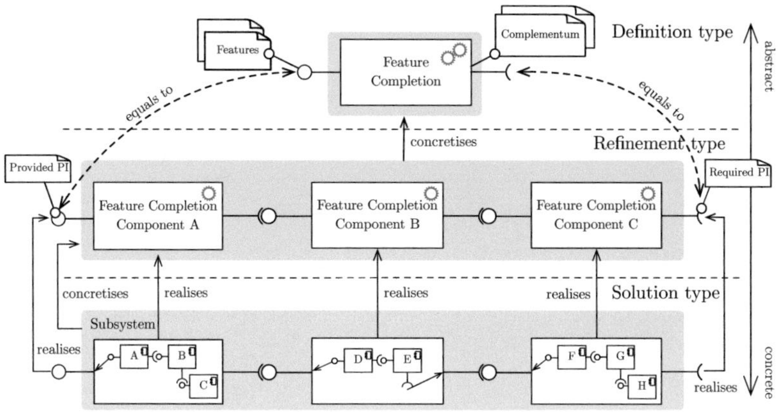

Figure 7.16.: Schema of the multi type model showing the types and how they are related to each other

domain experts start by defining possible features and reuse mechanisms. They model them in detail on the basis of the reference architecture. Based on the resulting model, solution developers can then apply the reference architecture to their subsystems. In parallel, already modelled solutions can be reused from software architects in their individual contexts.

Second, automatic processes need a representation of the entities and formalized instructions to be processed and analysed. A clear separation helps to clearly separate the formalized entities between design phase and reuse phase and thus to increase the comprehensibility of the meta model on the one hand and to improve the extensibility and maintainability on the other hand.

7.4.1. Types

The main structure of the feature completion model is defined by three types. A high level overview of the multi type hierarchy and its types is depicted in Figure 7.16.

7.4.1.1. Definition Type

The *Definition type* is the most abstract part of the hierarchy. This part in the previously introduced meta model is reflected in the features, feature objectives and required services of a subsystem. The definition itself is created by the solution domain expert who has specific knowledge from the feature completion domain. Features and Complementum represent the elements that are visible externally. They are especially necessary for the reuse of feature completions. The software architect who reuses the feature completion relies on this part in particular. Knowledge of deeper layers of the hierarchy is not necessary for reuse.

The features provided by the feature completion are particularly important for later reuse. The dependencies of feature completion to the base architecture are also of central importance since this are the dependencies to the base architecture.

The architecture of a particular solution as well as the solution specific parts are omitted on the definition type. Neither the particular solution developer nor solution-specific parts are necessary for the initial modelling of the features that are provided by the feature completion and the dependencies to the base architecture. This accidental complexity [Bro87] is hidden by abstracting from the reference architecture and the solution specific parts.

7.4.1.2. Refinement Type

The *Refinement type* extends the definition type with the coarse-grain reference architecture of a feature completion. This refinement is basically done by the subsystem domain expert who has defined the feature completion. This part mainly reflects in the previously introduced meta model in the feature completion, feature completion component and their relationships. The reference architecture of a feature completion comprises the feature completion components, their interfaces and relationships to each other. All model elements defined at this level are used to refine and enrich the elements of the definition type. The feature completion from the definition type is extended to have a reference architecture subsystem solutions (on the solution type) can be applied to.

The features of the feature completion are refined by the provided perimeter interfaces. The features required from the base architecture correspond to the required perimeter interfaces. The functionality of the features result from several logical concerns, i.e. the feature completion components and their interaction with each other. The feature completion components define the structure on which the solution developer must adhere when applying the reference architecture to solutions.

On this level no solution specific parts have to be modelled. We decided to abstract from the solution specific part to avoid the need of taking knowledge of particular solutions into account when defining the reference architecture. This process allows to model feature completions detached from solution specific considerations.

7.4.1.3. Solution type

The *Solution type* defines the solution specific parts. It is used to enrich the refinement type by solution-specific elements. This part is mainly reflected in the previously introduced meta model in the solution profile. Solution developers annotate the abstract feature completion components with the software components actually realising their features. In addition, they annotate the abstract perimeter interfaces with the component interfaces.

The solution type therefore addresses concrete components and their association to the abstract elements from the other types. The solution developer does not need to know the domain in detail to model the solution-specific parts, but can concentrate on the particular characteristics of the solution to be added to the reference architecture. As in the definition type, this reduces complexity and thus the number of possible errors.

7.5. Assumptions and Limitations

Architecture constraints: the current version of the meta model allows the definition of simple architecture constraints, such as together, isolation and separation constraints for software components. A concatenation of the constraints, as required by conditions such as

if CompA together with CompB then isolate CompC

is currently not possible. In principle, however, OCL constraints or a domain-specific language might be used to describe more complex architecture constraints.

Application of solutions: Only solutions that correspond to the reference architecture defined by the feature completion can be applied to the meta model. If solutions differ greatly in their architecture, i.e. no relation can be found between the abstract feature completion component together with its required feature completion components and the actual software architecture of the solution, it is not possible to apply the solutions to the feature completion reference architecture. Such solutions then cannot be used in the optimization process.

Component-based software architecture model: We assume the subsystem solutions base on a meta model providing entities to model the software components and their relationships. For now, the meta model requires concepts such as components, interfaces (required and provided), as well as their connection through an assembly connector. For the architecture constraints, additional entities for the deployment of the components to hardware resources is required. In principle, however, the use of our meta model would also be possible with fixed wiring (in contrast to loose coupling using interfaces of software components). The referenced meta model elements would have to be adapted accordingly to the concepts. This would be possible by using the UML profiles non-intrusively.

Restrictions for change operations: The meta model allows the definition of additive modifications on software architecture models. Modifying architecture models by reducing software components or make changes according to a given pattern is not possible. The meta model therefore does not support to enforce cross-architecture changes, such as required for architecture patterns or architecture styles. However, this restriction should be sound and sufficient for modelling and reusing of existing (implemented) subsystem solutions.

7.6. Summary

The main purpose of this chapter is the development of a meta model that allows modelling and lightweight reuse of subsystems and subsystem solutions. To achieve this, we have developed a meta model defining entities for modelling subsystems to realize requirements that can be used in different contexts. We have developed the meta model hierarchically, so that modelling the subsystems can be done step by step. The subsystem domain expert builds an abstract model that is refined by the solution developer and finally used by software architects. Furthermore, the models can be used in an automated process to evaluate solutions against each other due to their different degrees of abstraction. Degrees of freedom of software architectures coming from the new concepts can span a space for automatic exploration of different solutions of a subsystem and its configuration in the base architecture. For this purpose, in Section 8.7, we present different degrees of freedom, which model the different characteristics of the supported features, solutions and their configurations. Finally, in Chapter 8, we use the degrees of freedom instances to generate the architecture candidates to be evaluated and optimized.

8. Model Weaving using Feature-driven Degrees of Freedom

In this chapter, we describe how to include models by weaving mechanisms. We extend the base architecture models by subsystem solution models depending on the desired features. Our weaving mechanism combines the base software architecture model and the subsystem solution, its software components respectively when software architects annotate a certain feature to the system view-type of the base architecture. Several parts of the concepts have been published in one of our publications [SBK17]. Concepts to extend abstract control flow have been published in the Master's thesis from Eckert [Eck18], supervised by me.

To weave models, we consider two methods, namely the integration using adapters and the integration by changing the abstract control flow such as loops, and branches. Both inclusion mechanisms use the meta model presented in Chapter 7. The model instances of the meta models are used by the weaving mechanism as instructions to generate the necessary architecture elements and place the subsystem solutions at the desired positions in the software architecture model.

Automated model weaving reduces the modelling effort for the software architects. Especially with many modelling options, automatic generation of models is important to simplify the time-consuming and error-prone step. The quality attributes of generated models can then be evaluated, on this basis. These results of the evaluation can be used in the optimization step creating and evaluate new architecture candidates, with respect to the requirements. Finally, suggestions can be offered to the software architect to support the selection of the right candidate to be implemented. Automatic generation of the models therefore makes it easier to quickly evaluate many architecture models and find better candidates. This with less manual effort and all the possibilities offered by optimization approaches for software architectures.

The chapter is structured as follows: First, in Section 8.1, we present the process of weaving software architecture models. This includes the general process as well as the model extension by adapters and the abstract control flow. Section 8.2 abstracts the weaving process to a higher level, the level of meta meta models. We show the general extension of meta models based on triple graph grammars. Section 8.3 shows the weaving process when using adapter extension, while Section 8.4 introduces the process using the extension by the abstract control flow. Section 8.5 applies the weaving mechanism to the PCM. Section 8.6 introduces how we apply the architecture constraints. By the meta model, several new architecture degrees of freedom become applicable, that we introduce in Section 8.7. The chapter concludes with assumptions, limitations in Section 8.8 and finally the summary in Section 8.9.

8.1. Extending Software Architecture Models

Assembled software architecture models can only be extended with new functionality by interrupting existing control flows. When two components are connected by assembly connectors, this connection could be interrupted and extended by a certain service. We have shown the general extension process in Figure 8.1. The control flow of the base architecture model is interrupted to process the service of the subsystem. The integrated model interrupts the originally intended control flow of the base model by integrating the red marked component of the base model B and changes the control flow (red marked control flow). Afterwards, the previous control flow is continued.

In component-based software architectures, however, new functionality cannot be integrated at any position and requires architecture changes: usually, the interfaces (provided or required) for the service to be integrated are not compatible with the interfaces that are contained in the base architecture.

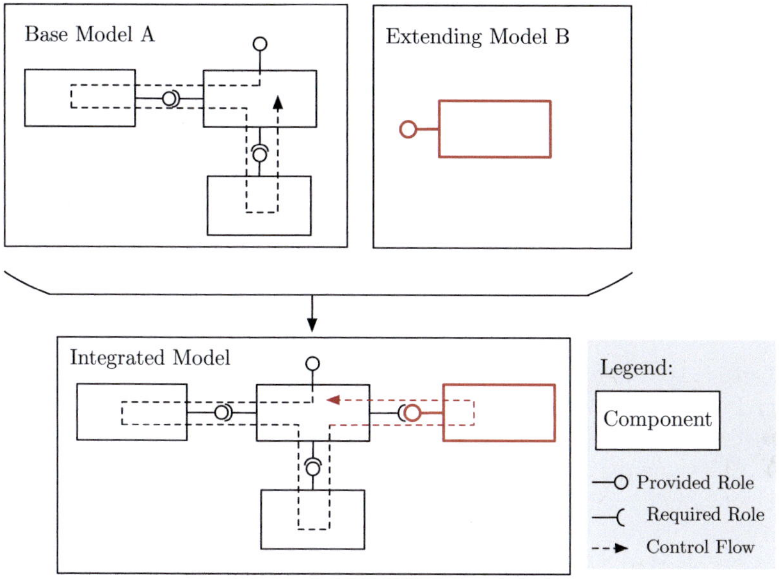

Figure 8.1.: General extension process of base model and extending model into one integrated model with changed control flow. The red marked component and control flow was added to the control flow of the base model A to integrate the functionality of the extending model B.

The extension of a base architecture by features can be carried out by two strategies: extension by adapters to make interfaces compatible and the invasive extension of the abstract control flow. The extension by adapters is a comparatively lightweight extension strategy and is based on manual annotation by the software architect of the desired features in the base architecture. This extension should be used whenever software architects want to evaluate the impact of features on a few positions in the base architecture. In addition, the extended positions in the base architecture are explicitly modelled by annotations and are therefore well comprehensible.

Software architects should use the extension by the abstract control flow when either elements of the abstract control flow should be extended or when whole classes of positions should be evaluated. By defining classes of positions software architects can determine to extend the system by features wherever a certain signature is called. In such cases, it may not be exactly clear which exact positions are relevant in the base architecture. The extension mechanism automatically finds all desired positions of such a class. This reduces the modelling effort. In contrast to extension using adapters, however, the positions that are extended are modelled implicitly.

8.2. Model Transformation using Triple-Graph-Grammars

Extending models requires operations for adding or deleting model elements and propagating these changes to affected model elements. The following sections therefore define concepts for additive model transformation based on TGGs and the propagation of changes to model elements affected by the transformation. TGGs are suitable for describing model transformations between models. The transformation itself consists of a set of rules. The basic concepts of TGGs have been introduced in Section 3.1.1.4.

8.2.1. Model Transformation

The model transformation considers the effects on model elements in the model that are influenced due to addition operations when applying rules. This model transformation starts from a central entry point that is used as the seed.

A model change of element $ME1$ can therefore have an effect on model element $ME2$. Consequently, the elements of $ME2$ are inconsistent relative to the meta model and its rules for consistency.

Let us consider the assembly context and the allocation context of the PCM. An additive operation considering the assembly contexts in the system model leads to inconsistencies of the allocation model. The allocation model is inconsistent since there are unallocated assembly contexts in the allocation context model. This also applies in the opposite case. If an allocation context is removed, the corresponding assembly context must also be removed. The analysis and correction of this inconsistency is fixed by the model transformation.

Let us consider the view-type VT_i that comprises the initial additive model modification. This modification could affect other view types $VT_{j \neq i}$.

More formally this can be expressed as follows: let us define M_{VT} as the set of all model elements of a given view type. Let $G_{mod} := (V, E, s, t)$ be an out-tree, while V are the vertices of a graph, E the edges of a graph. The function $s : E \longrightarrow V$ results the source vertex, while the function $t : E \longrightarrow V$ results in the target vertex given a specific edge. A path in a graph can be defined as a sequence, such as $(v_0, ..., v_i, v_{i+1}, ..., v_n)$. G_{mod} represents an out-tree containing the vertex v_0. v_0 represents the root of the tree. For all remaining vertices v_i there is exactly one path from v_0 to v_i. In the model transformation, the vertices $V \subseteq M_{VT}$ represent the meta model elements of the view type that are affected by a model change of the primary model element v_0. An edge $e \in E$ indicates that a change of a model element $s(e) \in V$ implies that another model element $t(e) \in V$ is affected, which must also be modified accordingly [SBK17].

8.2.2. Weaving component-based Software-Architecture Models

To weave two component-based software-architecture models, i.e. a base architecture model and an extending model, i.e. subsystem solution model, we require the components and the corresponding dependencies between the components (via their interfaces) to be included. We assume that the underlying software architecture model relies on concepts of interfaces, assembly contexts between interfaces and component allocation to hardware resources.

In the first step, the new components must be included into the system model. Further the corresponding assembly contexts between the components must be transformed. Several assembly contexts must be generated, others must be transformed due to new control flows introduced by the subsystem solution. Note that there is a dependency between assembly contexts and allocation contexts. Therefore, the model transformation must be analysed and applied based on the changed assembly contexts for the corresponding allocation contexts.

Based on TGGs and the concepts of model transformation, we define the problem in the context of the component-based software architecture model PCM.

In the following, we refer to G_{mod} as a transformation tree that specifies the model transformation according to a given view-type model element v_0. Given the out-tree G_{mod} with $V \subseteq M_{VT}$ and $v_0 := m_0 \in M_{VT}$. m_0 corresponds to the model elements that triggers the first model change. We assume the set $S_{G_{mod}}$ contains all paths of G_{mod}, starting with v_0 and ending with v_n. Here v_n denotes the vertex which is subject to $\nexists e \in E : s(e) = v_n$. Beginning with v_0 the model change propagates to v_n for all paths $p \in S_{G_{mod}}$. The corresponding operation for forward propagation must be applied to each pair (v_i, v_{i+1}) in the path. This results in the corresponding forward propagation operation $f_{v_i -> v_{i+1}}$. The forward propagation performs the model to preserve consistency between model $v_{i+1} = m_1 \in M_{VT}$ and $v_i = m_2 \in M_{VT}$. If the affected pair (v_i, v_{i+1}) has already been included in another path, it no longer needs to be transformed [SBK17].

To make models compatible, two strategies can be applied, namely the extension by adapting the relevant interfaces and the extension of the abstract control flow of the component intended for extension. Both strategies are presented in the following sections.

8.3. Adapter Extension

Extending a software architecture model using adapters essentially integrates two or several models. The adapter adapts the corresponding interfaces to make them compatible. In a meta model explicitly modelling provided and required interfaces, the adapter encapsulates all required and provided interfaces required for integration.

The extension by adapters provides the following advantages:

- **Non-intrusive extension:** Adapter extension is a non-intrusive extension strategy for component-based software architectures. Non-intrusive integration means that the involved models remain unchanged, but additional model elements are used in order integrate to them.

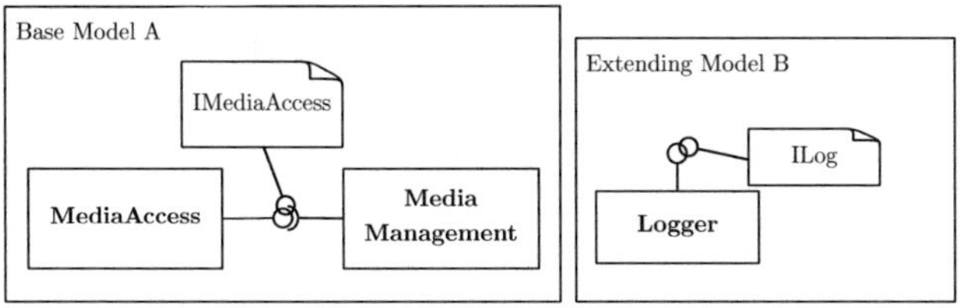

Figure 8.2.: Excerpt from initial architecture model Media Store: Incompatible interfaces `IMediaAccess` and `ILog`.

- **Lightweight assembly between models**: Models are lightweight coupled with each other. Only the caller sequence is changed, but no internal behaviour of the components.
- **Multiple delegation:** Once an adapter has been created and assembled, it can be used by the system as often as required by delegation.
- **Quality attributes through model integration:** By integrating subsystem by adapters allows analysing the quality attributes of the overall software architecture comprising base architecture and services of the subsystem.

Integration using adapters consists of two parts, namely the generation of the appropriate adapter and its connection to the base software architecture model.

8.3.1. Adapter Generation

8.3.1.1. Rationale

To make interfaces compatible by adapters, the adapter must include the interface(s) of the service to be included and the interface of the assembly connector to be extended. Figure 8.2 shows an excerpt from our running example (see Chapter 2) showing the initial condition at time t_0. The `UserManagement` component provides the `IMediaAccess` interface, which is also required by the `MediaManagement` component. At the same time, the `Logger` component provides the `ILog` interface. However, this interface is

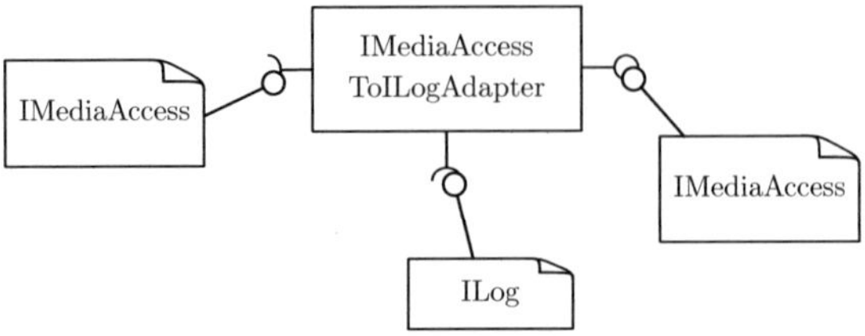

Figure 8.3.: Resulting adapter for IMediaAccess and ILog, with roles.

incompatible to `IMediaAccess`. If the control flow between `UserManagement` and `MediaManagement` should be monitored by a logging mechanism, the logger functionality must be included at the assembly connector between these two components. However, without an adapter the interface `IMediaAccess` and `ILog` are not compatible and therefore can not be assembled by an assembly connector. The first step is therefore to generate an adapter that makes these interfaces compatible to each other.

8.3.1.2. Adapter Construction

Two aspects are relevant when generating the adapter: First, the relevant interfaces the adapter requires is determined. Each of the interfaces needs its corresponding role. Second, we need to generate the appropriate control flow in the adapter. In addition to including adapters and new components of the subsystem solution in an architecture, they must be integrated in the control flow of the base architecture. This could be compared with using libraries when implementing software. Libraries have to be included in the workspace. Then they must be called on the desired positions in the source code.

The result of generating the suitable interfaces and roles for the adapter is shown in Figure 8.3. The adapter component `IMediaAccessToILogAdapter` combines the interfaces with the corresponding roles that are necessary to make the two interfaces `IMediaAccess` and `ILog` compatible.

The adapter provides the interface `IMediaAccess` in the providing role for later assembly of the corresponding requiring role of the `MediaManagement` and component. Further it comprises the same interface in the requiring role for assembly of the corresponding providing role of the `MediaAccess` component. Finally, the adapter requires the `ILog` interface for the assembly of the corresponding providing role of the Logger.

When assembling the control flow of the adapter, its construction is defined by the parameters that we have introduced in detail in Section 7.2.6.1. Accordingly, one of the three options *before*, *after* and *around* can be chosen. These options control whether the control flow first calls the service `ILog` (before), first the service of `IMediaAccess` (after) or first `ILog`, then `IMediaAccess` and again `ILog` (around).

8.3.2. Adapter Assembly

The adapter of the extending system B is integrated into a base system A as follows:

1. Remove the original assembly connector of the base system model A to be extended.
2. Create the assembly connector for the two previously assembled components from base model A to the adapter.
3. Create the assembly connector for the service to be included from the extending model B to the adapter.

Figure 8.4 shows the result of the assembly for an excerpt from our running example: The `IMediaAccessToILogAdapter` comprises the interface `IMediaAccess` to be connected with `MediaAccess` and `MediaManagement`. Further, it comprises `ILog` to connect to the `ILog` interface of Logger. To assemble base system and subsystem, we first, remove the assembly connector between `MediaAccess` and `MediaManagement`. Then, we use an assembly connector to connect the `IMediaAccess` (providing) of `MediaAccess` with `IMediaAccess` of the adapter (requiring). Second, we use an assembly connector to connect the `IMediaAccess` (requiring) of `MediaManagement` with `IMediaAccess` (providing) of the adapter. Finally, we connect `ILog` (requiring) of the adapter with `ILog` (providing) of Logger.

After making the interfaces compatible, we need to create the SEFF for the adapter to call the services accordingly. This is done by external call actions in the adapter's for the provided services of `IMediaAccess`. Depending on

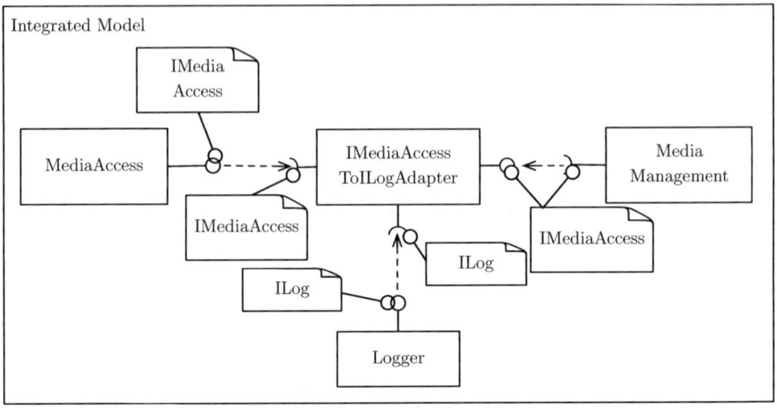

Figure 8.4.: Resulting integrated model using an adapter.

the selected options *before*, *after* and *around*, the external call actions are created accordingly. For each required signature an external call action is included in the control flow. If all signatures of an interface need to be included, for each signature an external call action is generated.

8.4. Abstract Behaviour Extension

Similar to the adapter extension, the abstract control flow extension integrates incompatible models. By extending the abstract control flow of the base system the services of subsystems can be integrated without the need of generating adapters. In contrast to the adapter extension, no interfaces have to be made compatible when the abstract control flow is extended. There is no need to make interfaces compatible, since the control flow of the base model is modified directly. Here, the SEFF of the base architecture is extended by external call actions to the subsystem's services. This results in the following advantages:

- **Simplicity:** the software architecture models do not contain any additional components for making models compatible. The models already contain all needed interfaces and components for implementing the functionality.

- **Granularity:** the extension can be implemented more fine-granularly by extending the control flow. We can extend the behaviour of base system's services on the level of statements and control flow elements, such as branches or loops.
- **Classes of extension points:** through more-fine granular modelling, whole classes of positions to be extended can be defined. By defining classes software architects can define many positions where features should apply in the base system without annotating all positions by hand. Such a fine-granular annotation would not be possible by using adapters.

For defining classes of positions, we use our DSL that we introduced in Section 7.2.6.2.

8.4.1. Extending the Control Flow

Three different abstract control flow elements can build a SEFF: Internal actions, external call actions, and control structures, such as loops, branches, or forks. All these elements can be extended by using the abstract behaviour extension. How to extend these elements is described in the following.

8.4.1.1. Internal Action Extension

Internal actions abstract from calculation operations such as sorting a list. Figure 8.5 shows how to include a service after am internal action of the SEFF. This strategy allows to extend all internal actions of a certain SEFF of a signature.

By this, the software architect does not need to have detailed knowledge of the internal control flow of a service or component to instrument at instruction level.

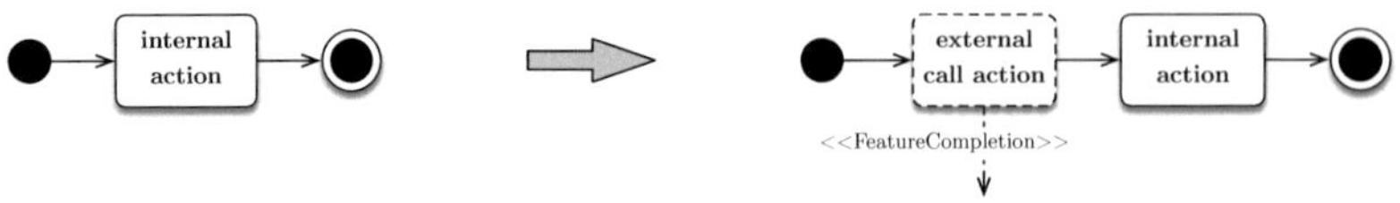

Figure 8.5.: Illustration of the extension on internal actions (according to the Master's thesis [Eck18], supervised by me).

Figure 8.6.: Illustration of the extension on external calls actions (according to [Eck18]).

8.4.1.2. External Call Extension

The external call extension is shown schematically in Figure 8.6. Software architects can use this strategy to extend all calls to a particular signature. This strategy can be used, if all external calls to a particular signature within an architecture should be extended.

External calls to a certain signature could potentially be distributed in many SEFFs of the base system. By using the external call extension, software architects can extend the base model black-box, i.e. software architects do not need to know SEFFs calling a signature that should be extended.

The new functionality is introduced by the additional use of external calls. According to the selected option, the external call action is extended before, after or around by the services of the subsystem.

8.4.1.3. Control Structure Extension

The control structure extension strategy is shown schematically in Figure 8.7. It extends all constructs that influence the behaviour of a component, such as loops, branches, and forks. The BEFORE and AFTER options refer to the insertion at the beginning or end of the behaviour of the control structure. With this extension strategy, it is possible to extend the internal

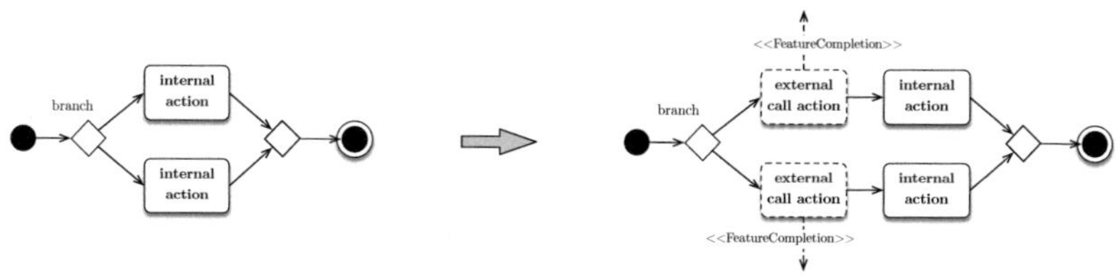

Figure 8.7.: Illustration of the extension on control structures (according to [Eck18]).

control flow, for example certain control structures such as loops, as before, without knowing the internal process in detail.

Similar to the other extension strategies, control structure elements of certain SEFFs can be extended by defining whole classes. Thus, software architects can extend black box.

An application example for the extension of loops would be the recording of user behaviour or the detection of performance problems in the system. A second example could be the detection of performance problems in certain branches by including loggers. A further application example would be the extension of loops by services of intrusion detection systems. Malicious behaviour or intentional overloading of the system by users could be detected by including sensors.

8.5. Formal Mechanism for PCM Transformation

This section describes the formal mechanisms for PCM model transformation for the extension of models. Section 8.5.1 describes the model transformation using the adapter extension method, while Section 8.5.2 describes the method for model transformation by the abstract control flow.

8.5.1. Adapter Extension

The transformation for the PCM adapter extension considers the four PCM view-types, repository, assembly, allocation and usage profile. In the following, we introduce the transformation of the models on the basis of the TGG model transformation introduced in Section 8.2.

The transformations are based on the following notation:

- Model Θ corresponds to a set of model elements $\theta \in \Theta$.
- Roles refer to interfaces that they either provide or require. The function $f_p : R \rightarrow \mathcal{P}(P)$ inputs a required role $r \in R$ of the set of all required roles R, and outputs a set of provided roles $p \in \mathcal{P}(P)$ in which each provided role provides exactly the interface r requires. P is the set of provided roles and $\mathcal{P}(P)$ denotes the power set of P.
- $\mathcal{T} : M \rightarrow M$ is an in place transformation, where M represents the set of all possible instances of a given meta model. The result is a model $m_2 \in M$, with $m_1 \in M \neq m_2 \in M$.
- Function $f_\phi : (AC \times AC) \rightarrow \mathcal{P}(\Phi)$ requires a tuple of assembly contexts as input parameters and outputs a set of connectors that connect the two assembly contexts. Φ is defined as the set of all available connectors. f_ϕ can result in a set of several connectors. AC is the set of all available assembly connectors.

Example: Let us assume we have the assembly contexts ac_1 and ac_2, which bind the required roles r_1 and r_2 in the context of component c_1. Additionally, we have component c_2, which binds the complementary provided roles p_1 and p_2, while applies: $p_1 \in f_p(r_1), p_2 \in f_p(r_2)$. Therefore: given ac_1 and ac_2, $|f_\phi(ac_1, ac_2)| = 2$.

8.5.1.1. Adapter Generation & Repository Transformation

The integration process of two models starts with adding the adapter to the repository model $R \in M_{VT}$ that is created by the graph morphism δ_R. The adapter is first generated and placed in the repository for later integration into the system model. The adapter requires the complementary roles of the interfaces that should be assembled. $c_{adapter}$ describes all roles the adapter requires for making compatible the relevant interfaces of the base architecture model and the extending architecture model:

$$c_{adapter} = \{c^{base}_{role_{required}}, c^{base}_{role_{provided}}, c^{subsystem}_{role_{provided}}\} \tag{8.1}$$

$c^{base}_{role_{required}}$ corresponds to the required role of the base system, while $c^{base}_{role_{provided}}$ corresponds to the provided role of the base system. $c^{subsystem}_{role_{provided}}$ corresponds to the provided role of the subsystem to be included. In addition to the roles of the interfaces, the abstract control flow must be modelled: the three options before, after and around can be used. The control flow for the options is defined as follows: The *before* option results in a control flow that first calls the services of the adapter and then the services of the base system. The *after* option passes the control flow to the base system components first. After returning, the control flow is passed to the subsystem components. The *around* option first passes the control flow to the components of the subsystem, then to the components of the base system and finally again to the components of the subsystem.

Together with the roles, interfaces, and the control flow, the adapter becomes part of the main component repository.

$$\mathcal{T}(R) = \{c_0, c_1, \ldots, c_{m-1}\}, \tag{8.2}$$

while C represents all components in the repository, $c_{adapter} \in C$, and $\{c_{subsystem_0}, c_{subsystem_1}, \ldots, c_{subsystem_{o-1}}\} \subset C$ and o is the number of components of the subsystem solution to be included.

8.5.1.2. Assembly Transformation

The assembly transformation again starts from the out-tree G_{mod} (see Section 3.1.1.4) after the initial model change δ_R has been carried out. To extend the base system by features of the subsystem, the assembly view-type must be adapted accordingly. In the following, we define the forward propagation operation $f_{R \to S}$:

The assembly view-type S contains several assembly contexts and assembly connectors. Given the already transformed repository model $\mathcal{T}(R)$, the sets with the assembly contexts AC and connectors Φ, which are already contained in the assembly model S to be transformed.

First, we create an assembly context $ac_{adapter}$ for the adapter and for each component of the subsystem. The corresponding interfaces, the corresponding roles of the interfaces (providing and requiring) are assembled by the adapter. Let ac_{c_0}, ac_{c_1} be the assembly contexts for both components that should be extended. The transformation results in the following notation, while AC' represents the set of assembly contexts after applying $T(S)$[1]:

$$\exists_{=1} ac_{adapter} \in AC' : |f_{\Phi}(ac_{c_0}, ac_{adapter})| = 1 \wedge |f_{\phi}(ac_{adapter}, ac_{c_1})| = 1$$

In addition to the adapter, all other components and connectors that are necessary for the service of the subsystem must now be assembled by the corresponding connectors.

8.5.1.3. Allocation Transformation

The forward propagation operation $f_{Ass \rightarrow All}$ transforms the allocation context. The assembly of the subsystem components and the adapter results in additional components that have to be allocated to the hardware. The transformation results in:

$$|All'| = |All| + |(AC' \setminus AC)|, All' = \mathcal{T}(All)$$

AC' corresponds to the previously created assembly contexts.

8.5.2. Abstract Behaviour Extension

The transformation of the PCM abstract control flow extension considers the PCM view-types, abstract control flow (SEFF), assembly and allocation.

8.5.2.1. Behaviour Transformation

The internal behaviour description is transformed so that the corresponding calls are delegated to the feature completion. First, the required positions are determined according to the placement strategies and then the corresponding calls are woven into the base software architecture model. According to the placement strategies, three possibilities to call the service representing the feature are conceivable: the strategy before (Appearance.BEFORE) the

[1] $\exists_{=1} a \in X$ means it exists exactly one element a in the set X

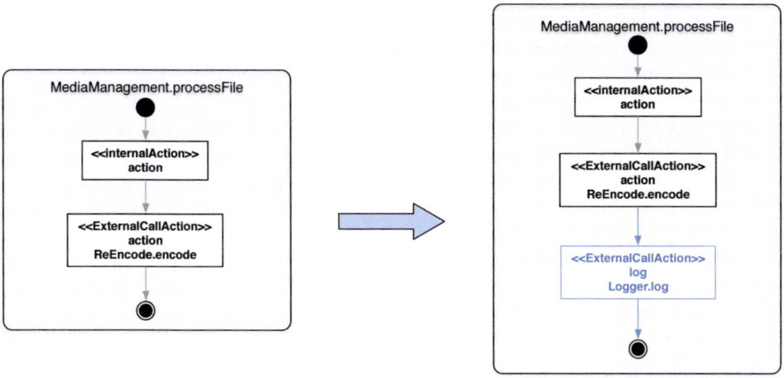

Figure 8.8.: Internal action weaving (AFTER appearance) on the example of Media-Management SEFF of Media Store and Logger (after [Eck18]).

base system control flow sequence is called, after (Appearance.AFTER) the base system control flow sequence, or before and after in combination (Appearance.AROUND). How the actual transformation looks like mainly depends on the chosen strategy.

Internal Action Placement

To extend internal actions, the transformation first searches for the relevant component in the base system. In this component, the SEFFs are then extended by external call actions to the service of the subsystem to be included. To do so, the transformation first identifies the appropriate SEFF. Within this SEFF, extensions are made to all internal actions. Depending on the placement policy before, after or around the internal action is extended accordingly. An extension of all internal actions is relevant for logging or IDS concerns, for example. Figure 8.8 shows an example of the internal action strategy.

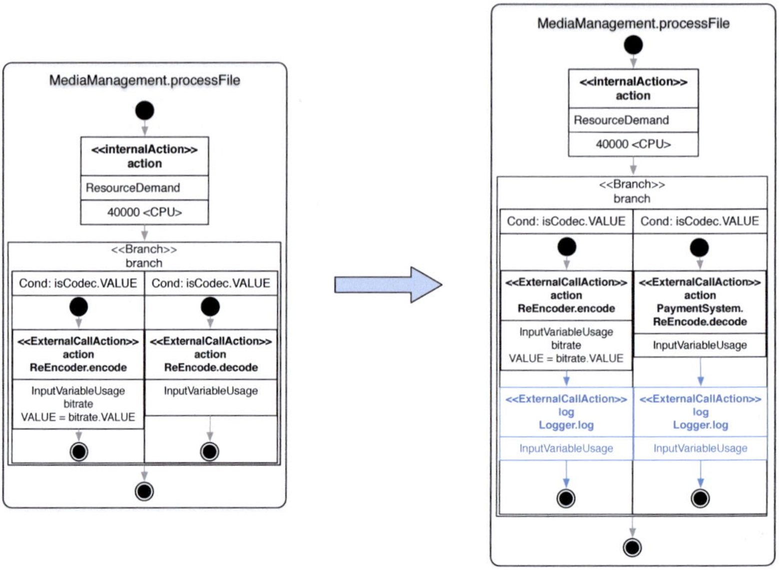

Figure 8.9.: Control flow weaving (AFTER appearance) on the example of MediaManagement SEFF of Media Store and Logger (after [Eck18]).

Control Structure Placement

For the extension of control structures, the transformation proceeds similar as for the extension of internal actions. First, the appropriate SEFF is determined and the control structure to be extended is determined. If branches are to be extended, then branches are searched and extended to the subsystem by external call actions according to the placement policy. This is done analogously for loops and forks. Figure 8.9 shows an example of the control structure strategy.

External Call Action Placement

Extending external call actions by external call actions to the subsystem works analogously to the two previously introduced strategies. The appropriate SEFF is determined. Its external call actions are extended by external

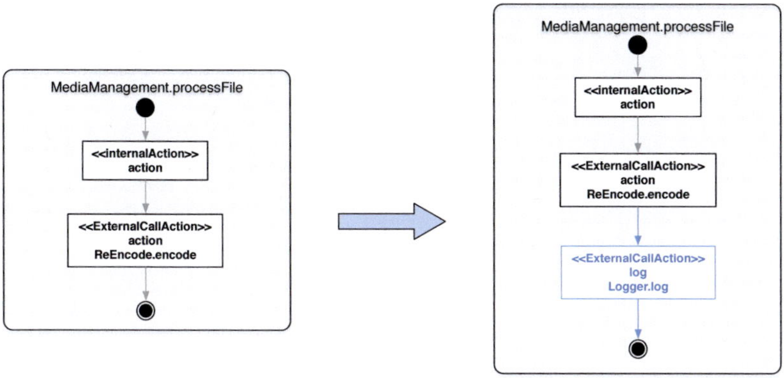

Figure 8.10.: External call action weaving (AFTER appearance) on the example of MediaManagement SEFF of Media Store and Logger (after [Eck18]).

call actions to the subsystem according to the placement policy. Figure 8.10 shows an example of the external call action strategy.

8.5.3. Weaving PCM Models

The actual transformation is realized by generating and applying the necessary weaving instructions. Various instructions determine the position in the model the functionality of the subsystem should be placed. Depending on the chosen weaving strategy, the actual weaving instructions are generated and placed. Each weaving instruction defines one of the previously defined abstract operations of the model transformation, which are then executed.

In terms of the adapter extension, the first weaving instruction depends on the annotations applied to the components in the system model, the complementum visnetis. Then the necessary changes are propagated through the model according to the model transformation. The complementum visnetis annotated by the software architect determines the assembly connectors of the system to be extended by a certain feature of the subsystem. To extend the system by adapters, the first step is to find the complementum visnetis annotated to assembly connectors by software architects. Then, the existing connection between the two existing assembly contexts must be resolved in order to include additional components, such as the corresponding adapter and components required for the new functionality.

After extracting the weaving locations, the necessary model elements can be created and woven. The necessary interfaces and the roles that the adapter must provide are analysed and the adapter is generated accordingly. The necessary assembly contexts can then be created, woven and the components required for the actual service are extracted from the feature completion component's structure. The necessary subsystem solution and its components are finally woven into the base architecture model to the desired positions.

For the abstract behaviour extension the later position(s) (i.e. weaving locations) of the feature must be deduced from the abstract control flow definition, modelled by the DSL introduced in Section 7.2.6.2. First, the defined advices are considered and the corresponding weaving locations are aggregated in the system model. The extracted weaving locations are then mapped to a corresponding weaving instruction. Therefore, we take the three different placement strategies into account. In addition, we determine the signatures relevant for realizing the selected features. We determine the relevant perimeter providing and requiring interfaces with the corresponding feature completion component.

To determine the components and interfaces of a subsystem solution to be included in the base software architecture model, the signature or interface to be included is the starting point. The signature or interface to be included is part of the perimeter interface of an FCC that is part of the subsystem's reference architecture. The reference architecture defines what other FCCs a certain FCC requires. By this, we can determine all FCCs that are required for realizing a certain perimeter interface and thus realizing a certain feature. Knowing all required FCCs allows us determining all software components of subsystem solutions required for realizing a certain feature. This is, because abstract FCCs and concrete software components are set in relation due to the `isSolutionFor` annotation of the reuse profile (see Section 7.2.7.2). As a result, we determined all interfaces and software components to be included into the base software architecture model for realizing a certain feature. Knowing the desired positions a feature should be included, the concrete software components and interfaces allows to determine the weaving instructions.

The determination of the weaving instructions is an upfront process which is necessary for the actual weaving process. The weaving instructions serve as rules used by the weaving engine to finally extend the models.

8.6. Architecture constraints

As already introduced in Section 7.2.4, architecture constraints can be used to enforce restrictions on the allocation of feature completion components in the base architecture model, and thus of the individual feature completions of a subsystem. This main concepts of the architecture constraints have been published in the Master's thesis from Scheerer [Sch17], supervised by me. Three configurations of constraints are supported, namely *together*, *isolated*, and *separated*. In this section, we focus on deployment constraints. Compliance with the constraints is automatically checked after the inclusion step has been performed.

The meta model for defining the constraints is shown in Figure 8.11. Its architecture makes it comparatively easy to add new constraints. The interface `IDesignSpaceConstraint` represents the main element that must be implemented to add a new type of constraint.

We distinguish between two different deployment constraints, namely constraints that are parametrized using the `featureTarget` annotations (`FeatureTargetConstraint`), namely together (`TogetherDeploymentConst-raint`) and separated (`SeparatedDeploymentConstraint`). The second group is directly bound to a feature completion component, namely the isolated constraint. Constraints can be checked for entities that implement the meta class `ConstrainableElement` (see Section 7.2.4).

The previously introduced weaving instructions are generated based on the results of the Design Space Exploration (DSE). The result of the DSE is a phenotype that represents the characteristics of a concrete architecture candidate, i.e. a concrete software architecture model. The software architecture is later generated from the phenotype (see Section 3.3.2.1). The actual constraint checking is performed on the phenotype.

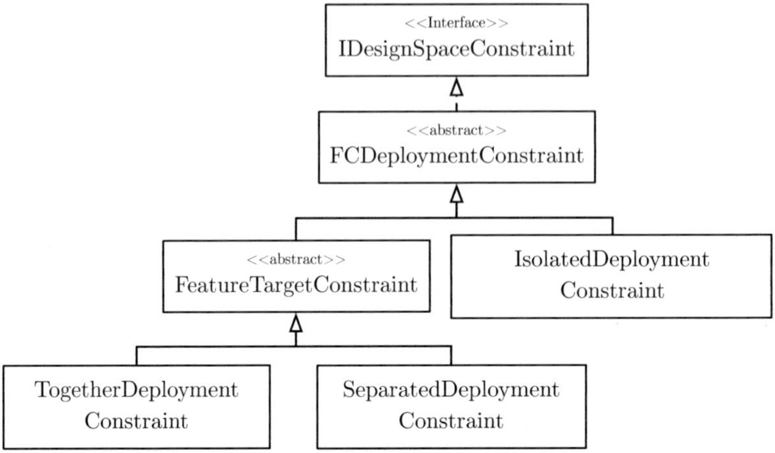

Figure 8.11.: Meta Model for the management and usage of architecture constraints (according to [Sch17])

To check the design decision, we denote DD_g the set of a design decision of a design decision genotype g with a certain configuration of selected design options. Let us assume a deployment constraint was defined for a given feature completion component *fcc* to be allocated in isolation. $DD_g^{alloc} \subseteq DD_g$ is a subset that contains only the design decision with the allocation degrees of freedom. $choice : DD_g^{alloc} \rightarrow RS$ returns the selected resource container of a design decision $d \in DD_g^{alloc}$. RS represents the set of all resource containers. The given configuration is only valid if the following applies:

$$\nexists d \in (DD_g^{alloc} / d_{fcc}) : choice(d) = choice(d_{fcc}) \tag{8.3}$$

Equation (8.3) is true if the selected resource container of the degree of freedom $d_{fcc} \in DD_g^{alloc}$ does not appear more than once.

The verification of the two remaining constraints, together and separated, is carried out similarly. The basis is the actual selected allocation. The selected allocation is then compared to the existing constraints for verification. If there are two or more FCCs with *together* constraints, but are not deployed at the same resource container, the architecture is marked as invalid. If two or more feature completion components allocated on the same resource container are allocated and a *separate* constraint exists at the same time, the architecture is marked as invalid. Invalid candidates are discarded and not used for later analysis.

An alternative to invalidating and subsequently regenerating architecture candidates is to try healing the candidate. In the case of a violated *together* constraint, one of the FCCs can be selected as the primary FCC. As a result, all remaining FCCs defined in the constraint are regarded as secondary FCCs. The allocation of all secondary FCCs is then changed so that all secondary FCCs are allocated to the resource container of the primary FCC. Thus, the architecture candidate would be healed and would not have to be discarded.

When the constraint *separate* is violated, the following procedure can be used for healing the candidate: if two or more FCCs violate the same separate constraint, one of these candidates is marked as the primary FCC. The remaining secondary FCCs are then re-allocated. Note: for many constraints, such a simple procedure could result in an infinite loop. For example, if not enough resource containers are available to implement the constraint.

8.7. Feature-driven Architecture Degrees of Freedom

Subsystems, their reference architecture, subsystem solutions that implement the reference architecture, different features and options for including them into base architecture models allow spanning new degrees of freedom in software architecture models. These degrees of freedom can be used for an automatic model generation and optimization of software architectures. The following new degrees of freedom become possible:

- **Implementation-specific subsystem configuration:** Feature completions represent abstract elements with the purpose of uniform structuring of subsystem solutions. The purpose of uniform structuring is that a weaving mechanism can also exchange non-uniform architecture models of different solutions of the feature completion and in particular without manual effort by the software architect. Thus the exchange mechanisms from Koziolek [Koz11] introduced in Section 3.3 for software components are extended. By extending the exchange of complex structures, subsystems with an internal complex structure can now be automatically exchanged.

- **Multiple inclusion configuration:** If subsystems should be included several times in the base architecture with simultaneous multiple instantiation of software components, this degree of freedom offers to integrate components of the subsystem solutions several times. The underlying components are not included in the base architecture by multiple delegation, but by multiple instantiation and assembly.
- **Optional configuration:** Software architects can defines features as optional. This means that the optimization instantiates and evaluates both possibilities, namely a software architecture with included feature and without the inclusion of the feature. The software architect can directly observe the effects of the presence of the feature (without additional modelling effort).
- **Feature configuration:** Features linked by XOR can be exchanged to evaluate the impact of different features on quality attributes in the base architecture against each other.

Figure 8.12 shows our meta model showing the degrees of freedom.

8.7.1. Subsystem Selection Degree

8.7.1.1. Rationale

As already outlined in the previous chapters, a feature can be realized by different implementations. Each of these different realizations, however, fulfils the same function. Each realization fulfils a feature in a very similarly (functional equivalent) way, while the quality requirements can differ greatly due to differences in architecture and implementation. Without model-based analyses and simulations, however, effects on the quality attributes cannot be observed at design time. To determine at design time whether a particular solution meets the quality requirements is hard without any model-based, automated analysis. Therefore, the degree of freedom

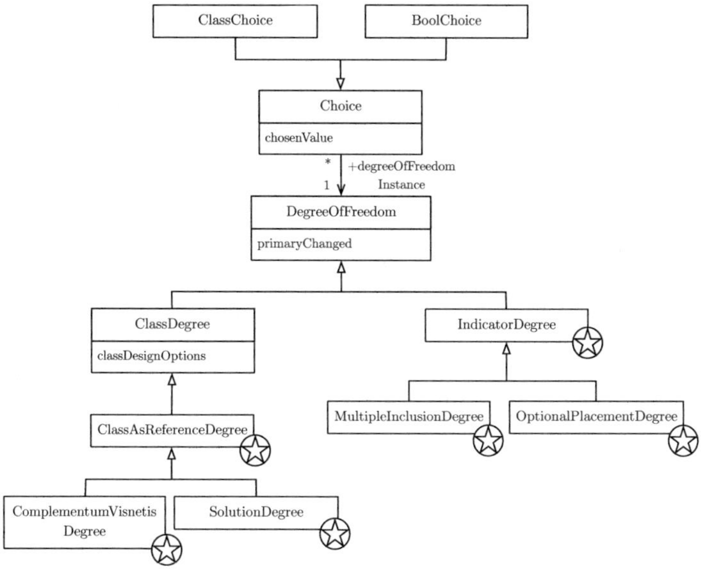

Figure 8.12.: Meta model for the definition of the newly introduced architecture degrees of freedom (derived from [Eck18]). Entities marked with asterisk are newly introduced.

to subsystem selection automatically exchanges different solutions, creates the corresponding model and prepares the model for analytical quality attribute analysis or quality attribute simulations. In addition, the black box principle is adhered to, which means that the software architect does not need to know about the internal structures of the individual solutions. On the basis of the results of the analyses, design decisions can be analysed, the best ones selected and finally implemented.

8.7.1.2. Realization

The selection of the actual subsystem is represented by the `SolutionsDegree` (fig. 8.12). The design alternatives (ClassChoices) of the degree of freedom contain all components required for the implementation of the selected feature by all subsystem solutions implementing the feature. A subsystem selection degree determines a certain subsystem solution fulfilling the desired feature to be included into the base architecture model. This step is required, because there might be features that are not realized by every subsystem solution (see core features and optional features in Section 7.2.2).

8.7.2. Feature Selection Degree

8.7.2.1. Rationale

Features can be linked by XOR to be modelled as alternative features. Features modelled as alternatives can be exchanged to each other. These features usually fulfil very similar functionalities, but are not completely equivalent to each other. In addition, they cannot be integrated together into the base architecture. Using our running example, the logging system, we could compare two alternative features to each other, namely the sql database logging and file logging features. However, if software architects want to evaluate both (technical) realizations against each other, this degree of freedom can be used.

8.7.2.2. Realization

The feature selection degree is created by using the entity `ComplementumVisnetisDegree`, whose value range (ClassChoice) corresponds exactly to the set of alternatively available features (see Algorithm 2).

The algorithm first iterates over the available alternative features and creates a complementum visnetis degree. The new complementum visnetis degree is then added to the list of design options *D*.

Algorithm 2 Generating the Complementum Visnetis Degree (according to [Eck18]). FeatureSelection and FeatureList have been defined by using the DSL introduced in Section 7.2.6.2.

function ADDCVDEGREE(featureSelection)
  for all featureList **in** featureSelection.featureLists **do**
    $D_{CV} \leftarrow$ **new** ComplementumVisnetisDegree(featureList)
    for all cv **in** featureList.features **do**
      D_{CV}.classDesignOptions $\leftarrow$ D_{CV}.classDesignOptions $\cup$ cv
    end for
    D $\leftarrow$ D $\cup$ D_{CV}
  end for
end function

It is required to check which of the available solutions (defined via the SolutionDegree) actually support the currently selected features, since not every solution realizes the features of the subsystem. If a feature is not supported by a specific subsystem solution, the generated instance is discarded [2].

8.7.3. Multiple Inclusion Degree

8.7.3.1. Rationale

The software architect selects the degree of freedom *multiple inclusion* whenever is unclear whether a feature should be implemented once and used with the help of multiple delegation or whether it should be instantiated separately for each call and addressed by delegation.

Whether a feature is instantiated once or several times can influence the resulting costs (e.g. due to licence costs) or other attributes such as the reliability of the base system.

[2] Another solution might to heal the model. Healing the model would be particularly relevant if very often randomly invalid models were generated (for example, if there are many features that are implemented by only a few solutions).

8.7.3.2. Realization

To define the `MultipleInclusionDegree`, we use the corresponding entity of the meta model (fig. 8.12). The corresponding *Choice* is the `BoolChoice`, which determines whether a feature completion is instantiated and included once or multiple instantiated and included. The attribute multiple = false causes an initial lookup for adapters and/or feature implementing components that are already included in the software architecture model, and then to use them again by delegation. The attribute multiple = true again creates adapters, assembly connectors and allocates components and finally delegates the call to the newly created instances. Once again, weaving instructions are generated from phenotype, which is converted by the weaving mechanism into the architecture candidates.

8.7.4. Optional Choice Degree

8.7.4.1. Rationale

Using the degree of freedom feature selection the software architect can determine a certain feature to be optionally included in the base software architecture. If features are marked as optional, for each of the optional features a degree of freedom is spanned, which allows creating the generated software architectures both with the feature and without the feature included. Which of the both options is selected is determined by the DSE. Thus, for all cases (and all combinations of these cases) the quality properties of the resulting architecture candidates can be determined and optimized.

8.7.4.2. Realization

To define the degree of freedom for the optional selection of features, the software architect uses the entity `OptionalPlacementDegree` (shown in Figure 8.12). The possible value range lies within the BoolChoice, i.e. if a feature is included optionally, the BoolChoice is selected with the value true, or as false in the opposite case. During candidate generation, the optimization for BoolChoice = true selects between presence and non-presence of the feature, while BoolChoice = false selects mandatory presence for the feature.

8.8. Assumptions and Limitations

The previously presented weaving mechanism realizes its function within the following assumptions and has the following limitations:

- **Cohesion of meta model elements:** We assume that all model elements are defined or referenced within a meta model so that all necessary model elements are accessible by traversing. If necessary model elements cannot be achieved by model traversing, the meta model of base model and subsystem solution models must be adapted.
- **Additive operations:** the weaving mechanism defined operations for model transformation for the additive transformation of models. Operations for removing model elements are not supported. This means that operations that require the removal of model elements, such as components, cannot be performed.
- **Architecture re-modelling:** The model weaving mechanism does not support extensive changes in the software architecture. For example, the described operations cannot be used to implement layering if, for example, a rich client is present.
- **Changes to the call sequence:** The model weaving focuses on the change of the call sequence of services between component boundaries. Other call sequences or changes are not supported.

8.9. Summary

In this chapter, we have shown how models can be assembled automatically. With the help of two extension mechanisms, we have shown how features can be extended on desired positions in software architecture models automatically. The desired positions can be defined either by annotations or a domain-specific language for defining desired positions in a base architecture. On the basis of the meta model presented in the previous chapter, new degrees of freedom can be spanned. Using the degrees of freedom as a basis architecture candidates can be generated. The architecture candidates can finally be instantiated to software architecture models by the model weaver. The automatically generated models include the desired features at different positions in the software architecture and can be used for further automatic analysis such as quality attribute analysis. The weaving mechanism is used by *CompARE* to instantiate the architecture models by using the relevant degrees of freedom and to evaluate them according to the quality attributes relevant for the requirements of the software system.

9. Modelling and Analysis of Architecture Knowledge

Most methods for evaluating quality attributes can either quantify the resulting properties or determine them in a qualitative manor. Both approaches have their respective advantages: quantified objective functions are usually more precise and return their results based on a mathematical basis. They represent knowledge about correlations concerning a quality attribute, for example in simulations or mathematical constructs such as Petri nets.

Qualitative determining approaches have their strength in evaluating quality attributes difficult to quantify. Quality attributes are considered difficult to quantify or unquantifiable if their evaluation causes too high cost or if there is no suitable objective function or the objective function has not been sufficiently well researched.

The *usability* quality attribute is an example for quality attributes difficult to quantify. For the quantitative determination of usability, user studies must usually be carried out, which are considered costly and therefore cost-intensive. An example of a non-quantifiable quality attribute is determining security properties in component-based software architectures. By now, there is no sufficiently evaluated function or simulation for determining the quality properties of safety or security, on the level of the quality attribute performance. The method we have proposed in Chapter 5 has many limitations and requires a high modelling effort.

Nevertheless, when designing their individual components or system, software architects often have an idea of the usability of individual software components or of the expected security level. However, this knowledge cannot yet be used in methods for the quantitative determination of quality properties and thus remains an unused resource. Especially in the selection and optimization of quality-supporting requirements, i.e. reuse of subsystems, it is often necessary to consider quality attributes that are difficult to quantify or not quantifiable at all.

In this chapter, we therefore present our quality effect specification, based on *qualitative reasoning* to enrich approaches for the quantitative determination of quality attributes with qualitatively modelled architecture knowledge. Thus, we can jointly evaluate and optimize them and, as a result, improve architecture decisions by using a broader knowledge base. The extension enables the software architect to answer previously unevaluated questions, such as determining the costs with regard to (quantifiable) quality attributes, as performance or monetary costs resulting from an improvement of a not-quantified, i.e. qualitatively-valued quality attribute, such as security. Questions arising from conflicting quality attributes can also be considered.

The chapter is structured as follows: In Section 9.1, we extend the evaluation space of quality properties, which was previously intended for quantitative evaluation procedures. We introduce elements necessary for qualitative evaluation and describe a method for attaching and evaluating these values to components. In Section 9.2, we describe how to carry out quality analyses for component-based software architectures using qualitative reasoning. To this end, we first introduce a model and describe how the knowledge contained in the models can be evaluated. In Section 9.3, we explain how architecture candidates can be evaluated on the basis of these models, describe in Section 9.4 assumptions and limitations, and close the chapter in Section 9.5 with a summary.

9.1. Extending the Quality Evaluation Space

Section 3.2.3 describes the Quality Modelling Language (QML), which, among other things, makes it possible to model dimensions and their possible characteristics. The QML is essentially designed to model dimensions and their characteristics with regard to quantifiable values. It is also possible to define any elements as values within dimensions, but very limited and not sufficient for more complex expressions. We therefore extended the QML to include a model for declaring not-quantified quality attributes and the qualitative knowledge annotation model for extending software components to include qualitatively modelled quality properties. As a result quantitative and qualitative determined values can be defined, evaluated and optimized together. Main conceptional parts have already published in our paper Busch et al. [BK16]. We define two different models:

- **Qualitative Knowledge Declaration Model:** The qualitative knowledge declaration model specifies dimensions of quality attributes and their possible characteristics. It is used to model quality attributes by using qualitative representations in arbitrary dimensions.
- **Qualitative Knowledge Annotation Model:** The qualitative knowledge annotation model annotates quality attributes and their properties or a qualitative reasoning-based model to describe the quality attributes and their properties on software components.

9.1.1. Qualitatively-valued Quality Attributes

In contrast to quantified quality attributes, qualitatively-valued quality attributes do not base on objective functions evaluated by simulations. Rather, the quality properties can be derived from informally available architecture knowledge. Although different, even nominal scale levels are generally possible, the more frequent modelling variant is the ordinal scale level. Between the individual possible values of the dimension, the absolute values are less important than their order relation. The values, on the other hand, have a subordinate role or play no role for the calculation itself, but are used for the actual modelling process by the software architect or solution developer. Thus, no evaluation in the sense of *Solution A is twice as powerful as solution B* is possible, but the natural considerations by experts can be modelled, automatically evaluated and made more comprehensive. This also can be used for the documentation of informally available architecture knowledge. The knowledge can be reused, automatically evaluated and automatically optimized, together with quantitatively available knowledge.

The decision whether quality attributes should be modelled quantified or qualitatively-valued depends on several reasons:

- **Significance:** Each quality attribute has to be evaluated for its importance. The importance must be high enough to justify the costs to apply a quantitative method. However, it may make sense to model the quality attribute qualitatively. This might be useful if the quality attribute fulfils a secondary purpose: secondary purpose fulfils the quality attribute when quality-supporting activities lead to side effects on the quality attribute, the reduction in its property might be not critical, but should be kept in mind.
- **Effort:** A method or metric may be available, but the expected benefit of evaluation and analysis of the quality attribute is dominated by the time and cost involved in carrying out the quantified analysis and would therefore not be taken into account. This is consistent to the previously mentioned quality attribute usability: A user study could be performed and would return quantitative results, but would be very time-consuming and cost-intensive and would possibly not sufficiently fulfil the expected benefit. Note: this is of course particularly dependent on the project requirements and must be decided on a case-by-case basis.
- **Missing metric:** No method or metric exists for the quality attribute to be evaluated to quantify or method and metric are not applicable to the underlying scenario. For example, safety or security is often a particularly important requirement, but is not taken into account due to a lack of applicable methods for quantifying the quality attribute.

9.1.2. Modelling Dimensions for Not-quantified Quality Attributes

QML as a language for specifying quality requirements and quality attributes already offers many entities for modelling not-quantified quality attributes and their dimensions. However, QML lacks in entities for typed instantiation of elements within a dimension and the possibility of modelling the values at different scale levels. Therefore, we extend QML's `Dimensions` meta model and the `Contract` meta model with entities to express these constructs.

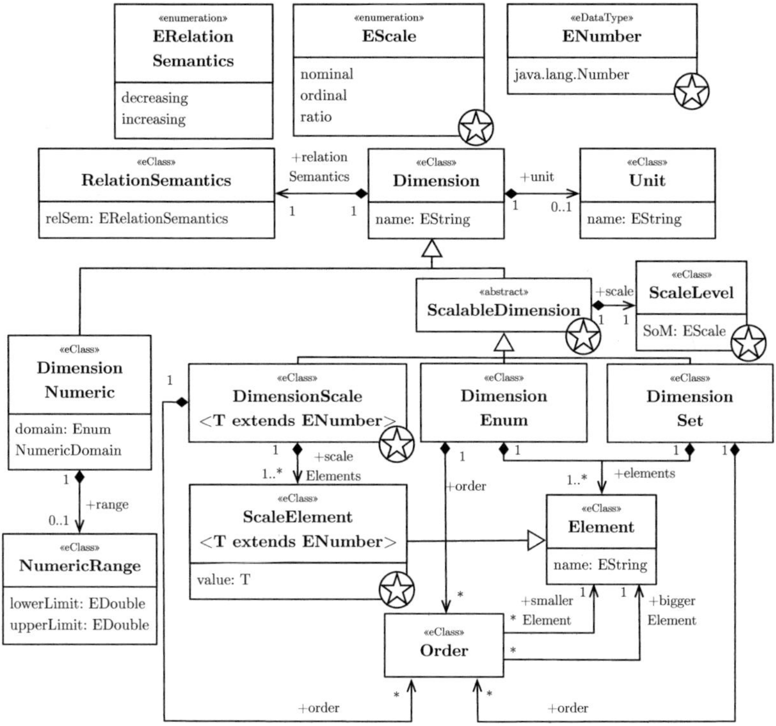

Figure 9.1.: Extension of the quality evaluation space on the basis of QML. Own extensions are marked with asterisk (based on [NMR10]).

9.1.2.1. Dimension

Figure 9.1 shows our extension of the QML dimensions meta model. QML has been introduced in Section 3.2.3. A quality attribute can consist of several quality dimensions. Several dimensions could be defined for the quality attribute *monetary costs*: *Initial costs*, *maintenance costs* and *operation costs* would be three examples. Each of them could model a common unit, namely the unit *monetary units*.

Within the dimension, its possible values that can be used by a property, the unit, and the semantics of larger or smaller values must be modelled.

In the original QML there are concepts to express values of dimensions. However, these focus on numerical values with the usual semantic such as two is twice as good as one, or four is twice as good as two, as would be suitable for the quality attribute costs. However, to model qualitatively-valued quality attributes, a numerical dimension is less suitable. More suitable are dimensions that can be individually defined. To do so, we introduced a new dimension, the `DimensionScale`. This type of dimension allows either to model any element of type `String` within the dimension or to assume typed values based on numerical elements. All types of Enum `ENumber` can be instantiated, namely integer, short, double, float or byte. The chosen type depends on the quality attribute. Each of the possible values is represented by the `ScaleElement`. In contrast to numerical dimensions, each individual element must be defined upfront. Then an order can be assigned to the elements of the dimension. This makes it possible to distinguish between smaller and larger, i.e. better or less good properties.

The scale level of the dimension can be modelled using the `ScaleLevel` entity. Ordinal, nominal or ratio scale levels are possible. When modelling qualitatively-valued quality attributes, for example, an ordinal scale level might be appropriate. The `ScaleLevel` can also be used by the `DimensionEnum` and the `DimensionSet` that allow defining enums or sets of values. `Dimension-Numeric` is implicitly on ratio scale level.

9.1.2.2. Contract

The contract and our extensions are shown in Figure 9.2. The contract specifies quality requirements or quality constraints of valid architectures based on the dimensions using the `Criterion`. `Constraints` can be defined by defining upper and lower limits for a dimension. All valid architecture candidates must meet these restrictions, i.e. the quality properties are within the defined range. When no constraints should be determined in advance, software architects model the dimensions as objective. Thus, according to the considered quality attributes, the best possible candidate would result without taking constraints into account. In other words, an objective improves the dimension as good as possible.

One or more evaluation aspects can be defined by the `Criterion` entity. The criterion can be used to determine possible valid values of the evaluation result. We extend the existing `ValueLiteral` of the evaluation aspect `StochasticEvaluationAspect` by the `ScaleLiteral`, which defines a set of possible `ScaleElements` previously defined in the dimension. This allows determining valid values from the set of `ScaleElements` for the given requirements.

9.1.2.3. Example

With the aforementioned extensions, quantified and qualitatively-valued quality attributes can be modelled. Dimensions can be specified in the suitable kind and can then be applied to software architectures, evaluated and finally optimized.

As an example, we consider performance as a quantified quality attribute and usability and security as a qualitatively-valued quality attribute. Figure 9.3 shows an example of the three quality attributes. We model one dimension for each of the quality attributes. We model the system's response time as a dimension representing the quality attribute performance. Response time is represented as a numerical dimension with the unit milliseconds and a descending relation semantic, i.e. smaller values are preferred in favour of larger values. The contract belonging to the performance can be modelled either as constraint or objective within the optimization. For performance, we use a constraint, namely an average response time of less than 500 ms for a particular service.

For the qualitatively-valued quality attribute `Usability` we define the dimension *UserSatisfaction*. Let us consider the subsystem Logger from our running example. The user satisfaction of different logging systems result in different quality properties of the software architecture's quality attributes. For example, each system has its strength and weaknesses in processing or displaying the recorded data. This results in differences in user satisfaction. The dimension user satisfaction may have the values $\{\{low\}, \{medium\}, \{high\}\}$. This defines the dimension space. In addition, we define an order relation. We define the order relation $\{low\} < \{medium\} < \{high\}$ (not shown in Figure 9.3). We define the relation semantics as increasing in order to express greater values of user satisfaction to be better values. Furthermore, we model the dimension user satisfaction as an objective. We model the scale level as ordinal, since we are not familiar

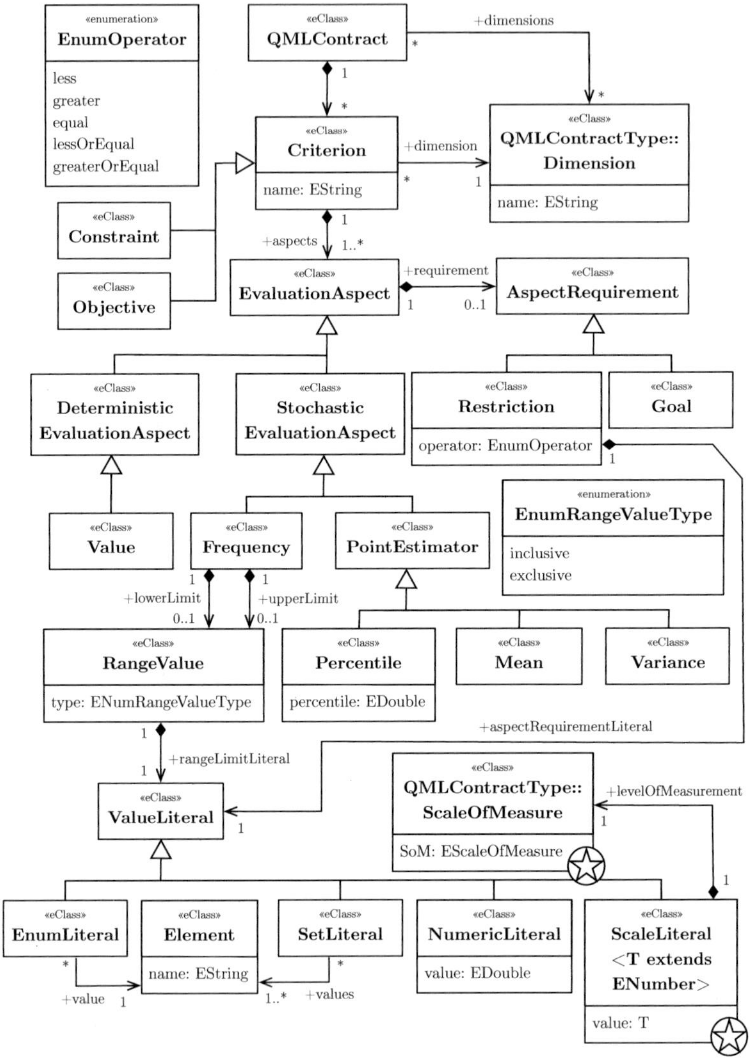

Figure 9.2.: Extensions of the contract on the basis of QML. Own extensions are marked with asterisk (based on [NMR10]).

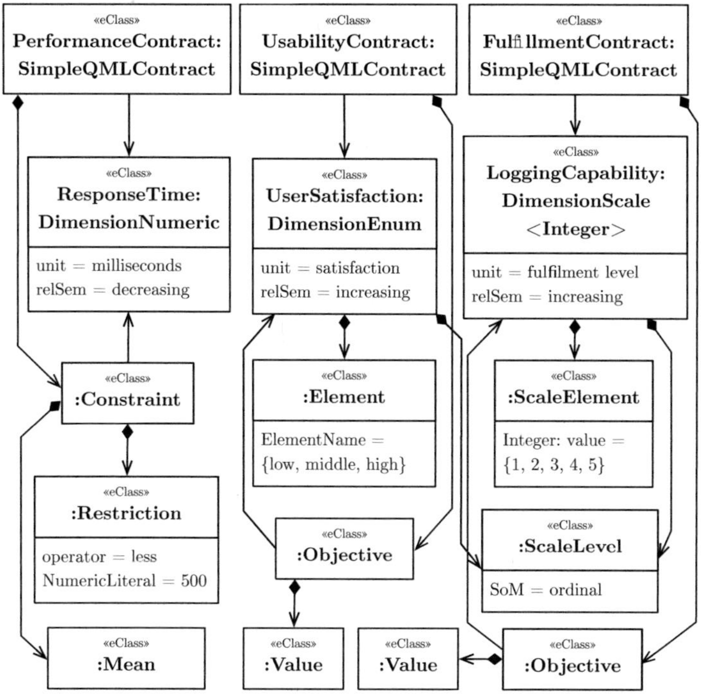

Figure 9.3.: Instance of extended QML dimensions and contract by using performance, usability, and security as quality attributes each with appropriate dimensions. Each element *low, middle, high,* and *1, 2, 3, 4, 5* would be represented in its own class. For space reasons, we have represented this in a set notation.

with the improvement of the value *medium* in comparison to *low* or *high* in comparison to *medium* in terms of user satisfaction. As measurement unit we have chosen the unit *satisfaction*. However, the unit is not crucial for the optimization, but rather for the final review by software architects.

The quality attribute *FunctionalFulfillment* describes how well a system fulfils its actual task. In *FunctionalFulfillment* several quality dimensions are combined. However, it should express the informal reasoning of software architects. A suitable dimension for the quality attribute *FunctionalFulfillment* is *LoggingCapability*. This dimension should define the utility of the subsystem's main function *logging*. The definition of such a dimension is necessary, since without its consideration the use of such a system would not bring any additional benefit for the optimization, but might lead to additional performance effort. The dimension *LoggingCapability* is difficult to quantify. Thus, we have decided to define it as qualitatively-valued. We define the following numerical values for the dimension: $\{1, 2, 3, 4, 5\}$. As before, we use an increasing relation, and the scale level ordinal. As with user satisfaction, the dimension should be optimized as good as possible. Thus, we select *objective*. The unit is defined as *fulfilment level*.

9.1.3. Quality Annotation Model

The quality annotation model (QAM) assigns the quality specification to components of software architectures. Let us consider the *Logger* system from our running example. The user satisfaction of the `CSVLogging` component might be moderate, which is why we choose the value *medium*. The `Logging` component can be assigned the value *4* to the quality attribute with the dimension logging capability. Alternatively, more complex constructs, such as instances of the quality definition language are possible, as presented in the following sections.

Figure 9.4 shows the meta model of our quality annotation model. The `QARepository` serves as a container for the quality annotations (QA). The relation of a quality annotation always contains several elements:

- the component to be annotated, the `PCM::RepositoryComponent`.
- the dimension in which the value ranges, the `QMLContractType::Dimension`
- the quality specification.

The quality specification is either the `QualitySpecification` that can be a single value by using the `QMLContract::ValueLiteral` or an instance of the Quality Rule Specification that we introduce in the next section.

A simplified instance of such an annotation of two dimensions on two components with different values is shown in Figure 9.5. The quality repository contains two quality annotations, each annotating a value of a specific dimension to a software component of the Logger subsystem.

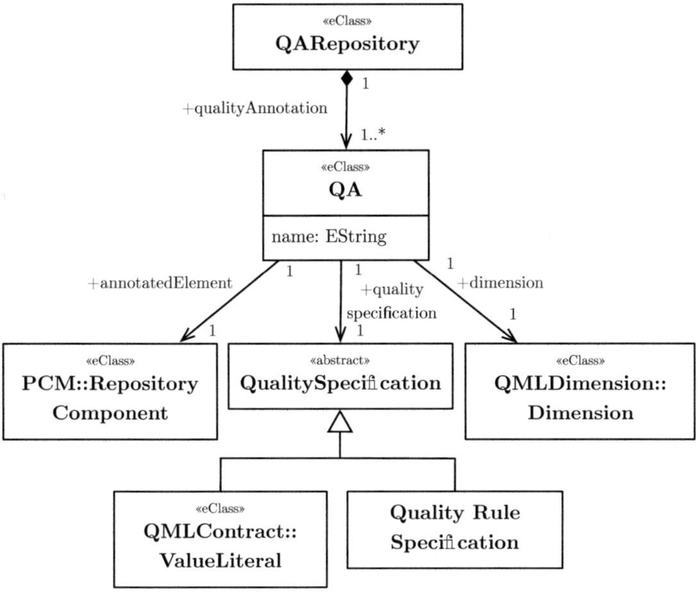

Figure 9.4.: Quality annotations meta model for the reference between software components, quality dimensions, and quality specifications. *QMLDimension::* refers to the QML dimensions. *QMLContract::* refers to the QML contract.

Simplified, we assume the logging component is solely responsible for fulfilling the logging functionality. The `EnumLiteral` *4* is assigned to the `Logging` component as a value from the dimension *LoggingCapability*. The second annotation assigns the `ScaleLiteral` *middle* from the dimension space of *UserSatisfaction* to the component `CSVLogging`, which represents the quality attribute *usability*.

These two annotations can be used in a later step, the candidate evaluation, together with quantified quality attributes to jointly evaluate the specified qualitatively-valued quality attributes. The evaluation allows making design decisions regarding the software architecture based on the Pareto-optimal results.

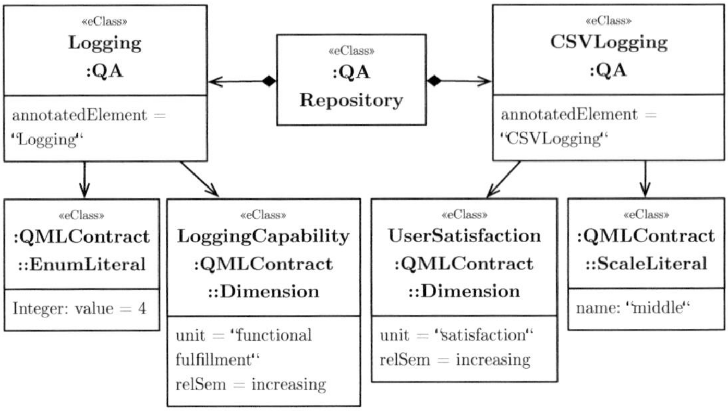

Figure 9.5.: Example instance of quality annotations with two dimensions and corresponding values.

9.2. Quality Analysis using Qualitative Reasoning

The quality analysis using qualitative reasoning can be used to evaluate informal modelled architecture knowledge. Such informal knowledge could be based on experience by software architects or other experts. Another source for informal knowledge may be knowledge bases or other documents. For representing informal knowledge, we use the previously defined qualitatively-valued quality dimensions. We combine them with qualitative reasoning from the field of artificial intelligence. This enables analysis of more complex dependencies between informal modelled quality attributes than annotating values to components (as shown in the previous section). The concepts of the quality analysis using qualitative reasoning have already been published in one of our publications in Schneider et al. [SBK18].

The quality knowledge specification and analysis is divided into three parts: i) entities for modelling knowledge (that was already introduced in Section 9.1.2), ii) rules encapsulating more complex relationships between the knowledge, and iii) an analysis engine considering the knowledge and rules for evaluating the quality attributes of the software architecture. The rules for evaluating the knowledge will be introduced in Section 9.2.1 in more detail. Afterwards, in Section 9.2.2, we introduce the knowledge analysis on the basis of the rules.

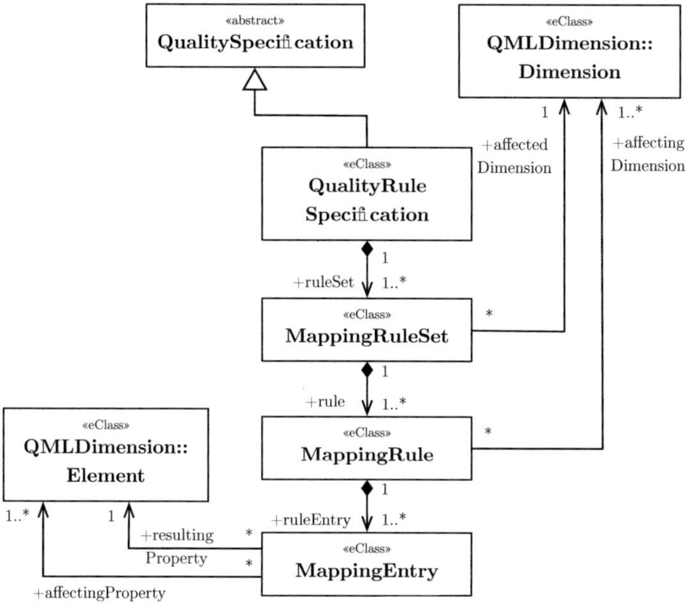

Figure 9.6.: Schematic representation of the quality rule meta model with its meta classes and references between meta classes. *QMLDimension::* refers to the QML meta model.

9.2.1. Quality Rule Specification

A service of a system is realized by several components, which are connected with each other by connectors. Together, they realize services. The quality property of a certain service depends on these components and their properties. This characteristic is used by the qualitative rule specification and the analysis. The analysis determines the relevant components for the service, calculates their dependencies and the resulting quality properties.

Figure 9.6 shows a schematic representation of our meta model of the quality rule specification. The specification of the rules consists of three parts, namely the mapping entries (ME), the mapping rules (MR) and the mapping rule set (MRS). The mapping rule set consists of mapping rules, while a mapping rule consists of mapping entries. A mapping entry can be compared to a set with key(s) and value elements. The mapping entry defines two kinds of quality properties, namely the quality property that is affecting (affectingProperty) and quality attributes that are affected (resultingProperty). A mapping entry can be seen as mapping specification from an affecting property to an affected property.

As introduced before, the quality property of a certain service depends on the quality properties of all components that are part of the service. When analysing the resulting quality property for a certain component of the service, we need to consider the quality properties of the components connected to that component. Thus, the connected components can have influence on the quality attributes of the component whose quality attributes are calculated. To evaluate the quality attribute of a component that depends on another component, we need the mapping rule. The mapping rule defines the mapping entries for a certain quality dimension. In other words it describes what value results if a quality property of another component needs to be taken into account. A quality dimension can also be influenced by other quality dimensions. Thus, there can be several affecting properties resulting in one value. The mapping rule set in combination with the mapping rule describes how a quality dimension of a component is influenced by several other quality dimensions of connected components.

The result always corresponds to a particular component that is currently calculated. At the end the results of all components of the service are reduced to a single value, representing the quality property of the service.

The interrelationships and semantics of the entities are introduced in the following in more detail.

9.2.1.1. Mapping Entry

Model

A mapping entry E represents the pair $E := ((k_n)_{n \in o}, v)$, while n is the number of input values mapping to one v, $o \subset \mathbb{N}_+$, and o is a finite set. (k_n)

represents the sequence of all input elements, i.e. `QMLDimension:Element`, used for the mapping and v represents the resulting quality property of a quality dimension considered. A mapping entry contains a sequence of input elements, because several quality attributes, i.e. the first element of the pair E, can affect the resulting quality property (the result) of another quality attribute. More precisely, on the basis of the mapping entry E the resulting quality property v of another dimension based on the sequence of elements of several input dimensions (k_n), i.e. $E\colon\ (k_n) \rightarrow v$ is calculated. All elements k_n and v of a mapping entry must be defined within the same dimension space D, i.e. $(k_n), v \in D$. D contains all valid elements defined in `ScaleLiteral`. If only one dimension, e.g. privacy is considered, there is only one input sequence. If several dimensions, e.g. privacy and accessibility should be considered there are two input sequences mapping on one resulting value v. The size and order of the sequences must agree to each other, so that a mapping can be calculated. Therefore, consistency defined when two input sequences are equally in length and order: $\left(k_n^1\right) = \left(k_m^2\right) \Leftrightarrow n = m \wedge \forall \left(i\right)_{i=1}^{n} \left(k_i^1 = k_i^2\right)$.

It makes sure that two sequences are equal in length n, m, and equally in the dimension space.

Example

A mapping entry first requires a dimension to model the values of the dimension space used as input and output values. Let us assume the dimension `Privacy` may have the dimension space $\{--, -, 0, +, ++\}$.

Let as assume the mapping entry $((a, b), c)$, while the input value a and b is mapped to the output value c. An example mapping maps the input value $++$ of the quality attribute privacy to the output value $+$ (cf. second column of Table 9.1). Semantically the property of privacy with the value $++$ leads to the resulting value $+$ (what in turn could mean very high security anywhere in the system can not improve the security strength since there is a weak link in the system).

9.2.1.2. Mapping Rule

Model

A mapping rule R results in a quality property of a quality dimension

MR: Privacy				
IN:	++	+	0	-
OUT:	+	0	-	--

Table 9.1.: One-dimensional mapping rule with a sequence of mapping entries using the example dimension privacy (according to [SBK18]). The mapping rule specifies the influence of privacy on another dimension to be determined.

MR	Accessibility				
	IN	++	+	-	--
Privacy	++	++	++	+	0
	+	+	+	-	0
	0	0	+	-	-
	-	-	0	--	--
	--	-	-	--	--

Table 9.2.: Multi-dimensional mapping rule with sequences of mapping entries using the example dimension privacy and accessibility (according to [SBK18]). The mapping rule specifies the influence of privacy and accessibility on another dimension to be determined.

by a given quality property of another quality dimension. A mapping rule consists of quality dimensions q_n and a set of mapping entries $\{e_m\}$, i.e. $R := (q_n, \{((k_n), v)_m\})$, while n is the number of quality dimensions, and m is the number of mapping entries. Each mapping entry $e_m \in R$ of a mapping rule must be uniquely assigned to a resulting output value of the dimension. The mapping rule can only process defined input values. Undefined pairs between input element and output value do not have any effect on the resulting result. This reduces the initial modelling effort, because rules can be defined coarse-grain first and can then refined as needed.

Example

A mapping rule comprises the mapping entries defined above. Table 9.1 shows a mapping rule for the one-dimensional case of the privacy dimension.

The two lines correspond to the sequence of the mapping entries, whereby one mapping entry corresponds to one column. Semantically, the map-

MRS: Reliability					
MR: Fault tolerance					
IN:	++	+	-	--	
OUT:	++	+	--	--	
MR: Recoverability					
IN:	++	+	0	-	--
OUT:	++	+	-	-	--

Table 9.3.: Mapping rule set showing the influence of the mapping rules for fault tolerance and recoverability on the reliability of the currently analysed component (according to [SBK18]).

ping rule is based on the previously introduced example for the mapping entries.

Table 9.2 shows a mapping rule for the multi-dimensional case. First, a further dimension, accessibility, is defined. For a better understanding, we have assigned the same dimension space of privacy to accessibility. However, the two spaces may differ as long as the conditions defined in the previous section are satisfied.

In the multi-dimensional cases, for example, several values from different dimensions can be mapped to a result value of another dimension considered. The approach is designed to analyse the resulting quality of a certain system or service. Thus, the quality attribute privacy is influenced by the privacy and accessibility of another component in the system. The mapping entry for this relationship might be modelled as follows: Privacy = ++, Accessibility = + leads to Privacy = ++. Semantically, this mapping entry expresses that the privacy of another component with the value ++ in combination with the accessibility + at the end results in the value ++. The dimension of the value ++ gets semantic in combination with the mapping rule set.

Similarly, this can be extended to any number of dimensions. It should be noted that the modelling effort per dimension increases accordingly.

9.2.1.3. Mapping Rule Set

Model

The MRS comprises the mapping rules defining the influence between different quality attributes. Further, it defines how a particular quality attribute of a component is influenced by quality attributes of another component. The MRS comprises several mapping rules r_n and a quality

Algorithm 3 Function for the quality knowledge analysis of a software architecture (according to [SBK18]).

function KNOWLEDGEEVALUATION(*softwareArchitecture*, *QARepository*)
  qualityValues ← [ ]
  ($components_n$) ← TOPOLOGICALSORT(*softwareArchitecture*)
  for all *component* **in** ($components_n$) **do**
    qualityValues ⊕ QUALITATIVEREASONING(*component*, *QARepository*)
  end for
  return AGGREGATE(*qualityValue*)
end function

dimension d that is affected by the rules, i.e. $MRS := (d, r_n)$. Values that are included in the rules and values that are derived from the result of the rules must always correspond to the values that occur within the dimension.

Example

Table 9.3 shows an example of a mapping rule set for the quality dimension reliability. In addition, we define the two dimensions of fault tolerance and recoverability with the dimension space that we have already used in the previous examples. The mapping rule set results in the output value that defines the influence of the mapping rules for the dimension fault tolerance and recoverability of influencing components on the reliability of the component under consideration. According to Table 9.3, Recoverability = 0 of a component if the service results in Reliability = −. If values of several dimensions have to be aggregated to one value, mean or a mapping rule can be used for aggregating the values.

In practice, usually several components influence the quality of the components under consideration. Details of the evaluation are introduced in the following section.

9.2.2. Quality Knowledge Analysis

The quality knowledge analysis evaluates the quality properties of a software architecture. The software architecture, the modelled architecture knowledge and the rules modelling the influences are required as inputs. The process of knowledge analysis is represented by four algorithms that are introduced in the following. The $\leftarrow$ symbol describes the assignment of a value to a variable. The $\oplus$ symbol describes the operation of adding an element to a list.

The evaluation of informally modelled architecture knowledge of a software architecture essentially consists of three parts:

- **Topological sorting:** Topological sorting arranges all components of a system hierarchically so that calculations that are dependent on other components of the system can be analysed linearly, i.e. no returns or recursions are necessary for the analysis.
- **Qualitative reasoning:** Qualitative reasoning evaluates the architecture knowledge annotated to software components of a system and the rules that relate this knowledge and results in one or more result values.
- **Value aggregation:** In value aggregation, several result values are combined to one total result, which can then be processed or optimized in further steps.

Algorithm 3 defines the main function of the quality knowledge analysis. The function `KnowledgeEvaluation` requires the software architecture and the QARepository that contains the quality attribute annotation of the software components as input parameters. The software architecture includes the architecture of the system, with interfaces and connectors, as well as dependencies between the services. This information is necessary for the topological sort and qualitative reasoning analysis.

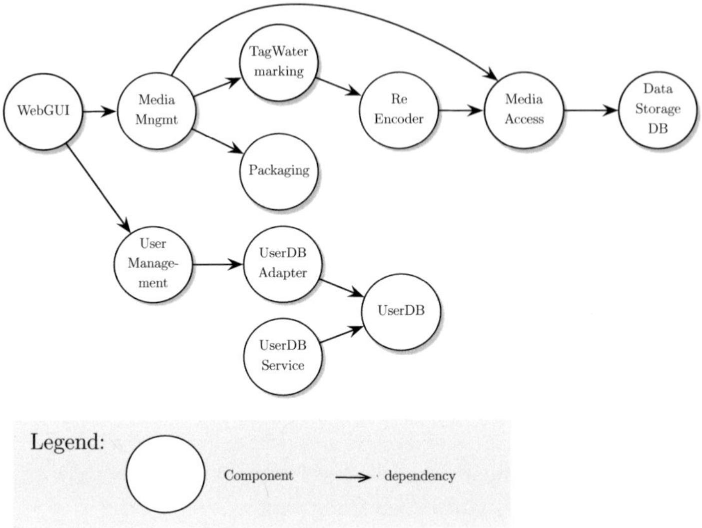

Figure 9.7.: Acyclic graph of Media Store's system view-type.

Algorithm 3 first generates a list containing all results of the qualitative reasoning function. All evaluated values belonging to the software architecture model are subsequently added to this list. In the second step, all components of the software architecture model are topologically sorted. Subsequently, the qualitative reasoning function evaluates the quality properties of the given components. In the last step, if there are several values, these values are aggregated and finally returned.

9.2.2.1. Topological Sorting

To evaluate the quality properties of software architectures, all other components that influence the component under consideration must be included in the analysis in addition to the component that is examined. Each of these components can also depend on other components. This requires all components from which a considered component is dependent have already been evaluated. However, dependency can nest itself theoretically arbitrarily deep. Based on the assumption that a software architecture does not contain cycle dependencies, we use an acyclic graph from the components and their connectors, which in turn fulfils the assumption that all nodes in a dependency have already been evaluated.

With the help of topological sorting, we generate a linear order of a directed acyclic graph. For topological sorting we take the nodes of a graph as components and its edges as connectors between the required and provided services of two components. When all components of a system are topologically sorted, an evaluation of the quality attributes can be performed linearly.

Let us consider our running example from Chapter 2, the Media Store system. The acyclic graph of the system view-type is shown in Figure 9.7. Let us calculate the resulting quality property of a dimension of the `MediaManagement` component. Thanks to the topological sorting the dependencies can be derived: Media management depends on `TagWaterMarking`, `Packaging` and `MediaAccess`. `TagWatermarking` in turn depends on `ReEncoder`. `ReEncoder` depends on `MediaAccess` and `MediaAccess` on `DataStorageDB`. If the `MediaManagement` quality properties should be calculated, the quality property of `MediaAccess` is calculated first. Once this has been calculated, the `ReEncoder` quality property can be calculated. The quality property of `TagWatermarking` can be calculated next. `Packaging` has no dependencies, so all `MediaManagement` dependencies are already calculated. On this basis, the resulting quality property of `MediaManagement` can now be calculated.

9.2.2.2. Qualitative Reasoning

The qualitative reasoning function evaluates the given component and returns the resulting quality property. The function uses the mapping rule set of a particular component to calculate the influences of other components on the quality attributes of the component under consideration. Algorithm 4 shows the procedure of qualitative reasoning for one component of the system.

First, the algorithm determines all components that influence the considered component. To do this, the `Required` function returns all components that provide the services the considered component requires by its required

Algorithm 4 Function for quality reasoning on one component (according to [SBK18]).

```
function QualitativeReasoning(component, QARepository)
    qualityValues ← [ ]
    (components_n) ← Required(component)
    for all c in (components_n) do
        qualityValues ⊕ GetQualVals(c)
    end for
    req ← Aggregate(qualityValues)
    for all mrs in GetMRSs(component, QARepository) do
        qualityValues ⊕ CalculateQP(mrs, req)
    end for
    qualityValues ⊕ GetQualVals(comp)
    qualityValues ← Aggregate(qualityValues)
    UpdateQualityValues(component, qualityValues, QARepository)
    return qualityValues
end function
```

interfaces from other components. These required components then influence the resulting quality properties of the quality attributes through their provided services. The topological sorting ensures that every required mapping rule set of the components fulfilling the required services has already been evaluated and its results can be used for the evaluation of the component under consideration. The `GetQualVals` is a getter function for the values of a component previously calculated. In the case of multi-value results, i.e. when the function returns several values as a result, the algorithm aggregates the values for each quality dimension to a single value result. This result is then included in the evaluation on the basis of the mapping rule set. The `GetMRS` function returns the mapping rule set of the component under consideration. The actual evaluation of the mapping rule set takes place in the `CalculateQP` function that is shown in Algorithm 5 in detail. The `CalculateQP` function returns the resulting quality property on the basis of the mapping rule set and the quality property. This result can be comprised of multiple values and must therefore be aggregated. Before the quality properties, i.e. *qualityValues* are finally returned, the mapping rule set matching the component is updated with the newly calculated values (ready to be used in the next calculation step). `UpdateQualityValues` assigns the calculated `qualityValues` to the corresponding component.

Algorithm 5 shows the `CalculateQP` function in detail. Using a mapping rule set, which contains the influenced quality dimensions and mapping rules as well as the quality properties resulting the qualitative reasoning, the algorithm calculates the influence of the rules on these quality properties.

In lines 3 – 18 the relevant rules to be applied are determined. To do so, every rule is analysed for relevant quality dimensions. The `Dimensions` helper function extracts all dimensions of a mapping rule. `Dimension` extracts the dimension of `qualityVal`. If the dimension of `qualityVal` matches in the process relevant quality dimension, the value of the dimension is added to the set evaluatedVals.

In lines 13 – 17 the resulting properties of a dimension on the basis of mapping rules are calculated. Several mapping rules and mapping rule sets can result in several resulting quality properties, the *evaluatedVals*. `GetKey` is a helper function to get the sequence of a mapping entry, The function `GetME` is a helper function to get the resulting quality property of a mapping entry *me*. *keyElement* is a temporary variable that is used to store values relevant for the calculation of the resulting quality attributes.

Depending on the scale level, we calculate the arithmetic mean or the median using the `Average` function. Alternatively, another mapping rule could be applied. The resulting quality property can then be used as result or can be stored to be used for calculating the quality property of the next component in the topology.

9.2.2.3. Value Aggregation

The `Aggregate` function combines several quality property values into one result value. The function therefore inputs a list of values and combines them to one result value. The values that belong to the same dimension can be aggregated to one value for further processing or serve as final result.

Algorithm 6 shows the process of the aggregation function. In lines 3 – 5, the quality properties are grouped by dimension. In the next step, lines 7 – 10, depending on the scale level, the mean value (by the `Average` function)

Algorithm 5 Calculation of the quality property for a dimension using a mapping rule set (according to [SBK18]).

```
function CalculateQP(mrs, qualityValues)
    evaluatedVals ← [ ]
    for all mr in mrs do
        keyElement ← [ ]
        (q_n) ← Dimensions(mr)
        for all q in (q_n) do
            for all qualityVal in qualityValues do
                if Dimension(qualityVal) == q then
                    keyElement ⊕ qualityVal
                end if
            end for
        end for
        for all me in mr do
            if GetKey(me) == keyElement then
                evaluatedVals ⊕ GetME(me)
            end if
        end for
    end for
    resultingVal ← Average(evaluatedVals)
    return (Dimension(mrs), resultingVal)
end function
```

is determined either by arithmetic mean or median, the dimensions are summarized and finally returned so that they can be further processed in the calling function. The `valueForDimension` function returns the valueLiteral from the qualityValue.

9.3. Candidate Evaluation

Using the aforementioned models, namely the simple assignment of values from the QML to software components or the quality specification model based on qualitative reasoning, quality dimensions of qualitatively-valued quality attributes can be annotated on components of software architectures.

Algorithm 6 Function to the aggregation of multiple quality results.

function AGGREGATE(*qualityValues*)
    dimToValue ← [ ][ ]
    for all *qualityValue* **in** *qualityValues* **do**
        dimToValue[DIMENSION(*qualityValue*)] ⊕ VALUEFORDIMENSION(qualityValue)
    end for
    aggregatedQualityValPerDim ← [ ]
    for all *dimension* **in** *dimToValue* **do**
        aggregatedQualityVal ← AVERAGE(*dimToValue*[*dimension*])
        aggregatedQualityValPerDim ⊕ (*dimension*, *aggregatedQualityVal*)
    end for
    return *aggregatedQualityValPerDimension*
end function

Quality properties for a specific service of the software architecture can then be calculated. This section has already been described in one of our publications Busch et al. [BK16].

Let d be a quality dimension (such as user satisfaction) and let $v_d(m)$ be the quality value resulting from the qualitative reasoning analysis or an annotated value to a software component (such as the value 4 in Figure 9.5) in a candidate model m. Further, let us define a simple objective function Φ_d from the set of valid PCM instances M to the set of possible values $\mathcal{V}_d$ of the quality dimension d (from the QML dimensions model in Figure 9.1) as $\Phi_d : M \rightarrow \mathcal{V}_d$. $\Phi_d(m)$ is the resulting quality property for a particular service of the software architecture for a candidate model m: $\Phi_d(m) = v_d(m)$.

We can now use the objective function Φ_d to include the corresponding dimension as objective in the design space exploration process to optimize quality attributes for specific services. This also enables a joint consideration of quantified and not-quantified quality attributes with their respective dimensions [BK16].

9.4. Assumptions and Limitations

- **Annotation of values (from the QML) to software components:** When software architects annotate values directly to software components without using the quality specification model, only exactly one value can be assigned to one software component per system for each dimension. This restriction results from the lack of a function for composing several values of the same dimension that are annotated to individual components.
- **Order on values of dimensions:** Without an order on the values within qualitatively-valued dimensions with nominal scale level, the objective based automated analysis and optimization is no longer possible. However, it can be used to define constraints or goals that should be achieved by the architecture candidates.
- **Cyclic Software Architectures:** Software architectures in which components are assembled that require each other are not supported. Topological sorting is based on a graph structure that requires a directional and acyclic graph. However, the definition of cyclic dependencies is an anti-pattern for good modelling of software architectures according to [Pag88]. Nevertheless, such architectures can always be converted into a flat structure by combining cyclic components into one and can be computed with this method after the transformation.

9.5. Summary

This chapter introduces the quality effect specification. The modelling concepts can be used to qualitatively model informal knowledge, applied to component-based software architecture models, and (automatically) evaluated by using qualitative reasoning mechanisms. The models and analyses can be combined with quantitative objective functions. The combined models and analyses can be used in automated processes such as *CompARE* to analyze and optimize software architectures. The focus can be extended from quality attributes with quantitatively determinable quality attributes to the analysis of qualitatively modelled knowledge.

Part III.

Evaluation and Conclusion

10. Evaluation & Case Study Systems

This chapter describes the evaluation of *CompARE*. As described in Chapter 6, *CompARE* can be integrated in the existing component-based software engineering process (CBSE). One of the goals of the evaluation is to show possible benefits when using *CompARE* in CBSE.

Software architects should have a tool-supported approach to make better and well-informed design decisions that affect the software architecture and its quality attributes. The two main goals can be formulated as follows: (1) *CompARE* should support software architects in reusing complex subsystems to support software requirements by features, systematically making better architecture decisions and at the same time reducing the manual analysis effort. (2) In addition to quantified quality attributes, the analysis should allow expressing informally available architecture knowledge to include additional aspects not previously specified in quantitative terms for improving the optimization.

For the evaluation of the two main goals, we consider different validation levels suggested by Böhme and Reussner [BR08] covered by a goal-question-metric (GQM) plan ([Sol+02]). To do so, we incorporate new features intro three base systems. We model two subsystems as reusable systems realizing features. They are represented by two different feature completions, each with two different real-world subsystem solutions. Each system is either used in real application contexts or is based on real applications. All systems and their models should therefore represent realistic settings and should support relevant business requirements.

The remainder of the evaluation is as follows: In Section 10.1, we introduce the validation questions and apply them to the levels of validations. Section 10.2 shows our evaluation concept and the GQM plan. Section 10.3

describes the implementation of *CompARE* in the automated design space optimization framework *PerOpteryx*[1]. In Section 10.4, we introduce the systems we use as our extending systems, namely the subsystem solutions. Section 10.5 introduces the feature completions for the subsystem solutions. The base systems, used for including the features are explained in detail in Section 10.6.

Chapter 11 introduces the first part of the evaluation. We demonstrate how features can be included into a base architecture using real-word systems and introduce the questions to be answered by using *CompARE* in typical design decision scenarios regarding the introduction of new features. Chapter 12 demonstrates how qualitatively modelled knowledge can be used to answer evaluation questions in the context of different real-word systems. We demonstrate how qualitative knowledge can be combined with quantitative objective functions and discuss possible evaluation questions on software architecture design. Finally, Chapter 13 introduces an additional scenario demonstrating how annotation positions of features and different solutions can be evaluated automatically to support the product selection. We use a base system that is loosely based on a real system and two real-world subsystem solutions to be included in the base system.

In our three part evaluation, we apply 11 scenarios and several sub scenarios to demonstrate the use and possible benefits of *CompARE*.

10.1. Levels of Validation for the CompARE Approach

CompARE is a model-based approach for reuse and analysis of features in software architecture models. Reuse allows automatic model generation with subsequent evaluation and optimization of different degrees of freedom. The three validation levels of Böhme and Reussner have been adapted according to the validation requirements.

[1] https://sdqweb.ipd.kit.edu/wiki/PerOpteryx

10.1.1. Level I: Validation of Accuracy

Level I considers the accuracy of predictions. The accuracy of predictions is concerned with the comparison of predicted values and real values actually determined at the systems to be evaluated. First of all, metrics are required to evaluate the accuracy. Then values are collected, for example by measurements, interviews or plausible derivation (comparison to the gold standard), then represented using the metrics and finally the predicted values are compared with the collected values. Two types are relevant:

1. The accuracy of predictions based on simulations or analytical models compared to observed (measured) values of the actual system represented by the model.
2. The accuracy of qualitatively valued quality attributes represented by modelling informal architecture knowledge using qualitative reasoning.

Prediction Accuracy: The prediction model must output accurate predictions for typical quantified quality attributes, such as performance. *CompARE* must also provide accurate results after the variation of the models when applying feature completions and their degrees of freedom.

Qualitative Analysis Accuracy: The results of the estimation of qualitatively valued quality attributes must result in the same orientation as the actual value of the system. This means if a design decision influences the quality attributes of the actually implemented system positively, the positive influences must also be visible in the estimation and vice versa. We discussed the validation of accuracy in the appropriate sections.

10.1.2. Level II: Validation of Applicability

Level II is considered with the applicability of *CompARE*. Model-driven approaches require information derived from the actual system and its artefacts, such as documentation, source code, and specified requirements. On the basis of this data, analyses can be carried out which estimates quality attributes, without the presence of source code or the necessity of its execution.

For automatic analysis and processing, however, data must not only be collected, but must also be able to be represented by a model. By using models the analysis and optimization can be processed automatically. Automated optimization and result derivation allows finding better architecture candidates that have been unknown to software architects.

CompARE focuses in particular on the feature-driven integration of new functionalities in existing base systems (or systems under development), as well as the modelling of informally available architecture knowledge for the joint evaluation and optimization of quality attributes. The modelling and reuse of the subsystems has the following advantages:

Subsystems should be easier reusable by software architects, at the same time hiding the architecture complexity of complex subsystems, so that the effort for reusing the models should remain low. Several subsystem solutions should be automatically exchanged to find the optimal solutions and make the product selection easier.

A further relevant aspect, besides reuse and automatic usage in automatic processes, is the role-separated modelling of the necessary data. In contrast to the classical CBSE process, new roles are necessary especially for modelling and reuse of subsystems.

In summary, the level II validation of applicability is considered with the ability to apply models to real systems within the CBSE process taking into account different roles, i.e. to create models for automatic weaving, evaluation and optimization. In addition to modelling of subsystems, the reuse of models is particularly relevant to enable software architects to configure previously generated models for the time-efficient evaluation of design decisions of certain base systems.

10.1.3. Level III: Validation of Benefits

Validation level III is concerned with the benefits of the approach. Applied to *CompARE*, the original CBSE process could be compared with the extended CBSE process. The comparison includes both the additional models required by *CompARE* and their modelling effort as well as new insights that cannot be derived without *CompARE* or can only be derived with great effort.

Level III validation could be carried out by comparing the results in terms of cost, time, and compliance with quality requirements to other processes. Such a comparison, however, causes high costs. Comparing two processes has a lot of threats to validity: The project success is dependant to several factors. Due to differences in the experiences of the participants, challenges regarding the complexity of the project and the willingness of the involved stakeholders to cooperate, the outcome is highly influenced.

Due to the high effort and costs involved in level III validation, we do not carry out this level, but extend level II in order to have a look on potential benefits by using *CompARE*.

10.2. Evaluation Concept

This section describes the evaluation concept for the *CompARE* approach. The concept is based on challenges described in Section 1.2. We are guided by a Goal Question Metric (GQM) plan as suggested by Basili and Weiss [Sol+02]. The goal is to validate the hypotheses and thus validate the concepts of the *CompARE* approach. First, evaluation questions are defined that support the hypotheses. Then we describe metrics in the form of scenarios and their meaning, which should explain and demonstrate the questions and benefits.

10.2.1. Hypothesis I: Automated model weaving

Hypothesis I states that "by using *CompARE*, automatic model generation in software architecture design enables reuse of subsystems." The hypothesis is divided into two sub-hypotheses. The associated contributions of the respective sub-hypotheses are interrelated that the hypothesis above is fulfilled. Two parts are required for automatic model generation using model weaving, namely the reuse model and the ability to reuse models in a feature-driven way. Sub-hypothesis I.I considers the reuse model, while sub-hypothesis I.II considers reuse by features.

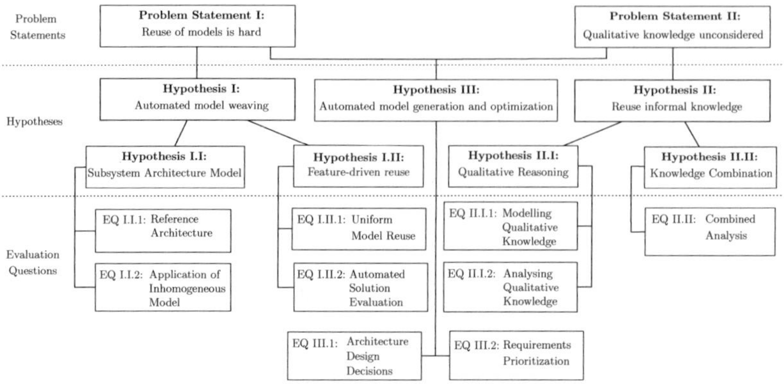

Figure 10.1.: Overview of the evaluation structure.

10.2.1.1. Hypothesis I.I: Subsystem architecture model

Hypothesis I.I proposes "a reference architecture can be applied to a set of (functionally) similar software architecture models, so that they have a common structure and can be reused by automatic model generation." For the hypothesis, two evaluation questions must be answered: First, we must clarify whether a reference architecture can be found for different software architecture models that implement similar features. Secondly, it must be clarified whether inhomogeneous software architecture models can be applied to this reference architecture so that they can be automatically included into base software architecture models. These evaluation goals are refined into two evaluation questions:

> **Evaluation Question I.I.1: Reference Architecture**
> Can a reference architecture be found for a class of reusable subsystem solutions that reflects the internal architecture of different solutions?
>
> **Evaluation Question I.I.2: Application of Inhomogeneous Models**
> Can inhomogeneous software architecture models, i.e. subsystem solutions, corresponding to the same subsystem be applied to the reference architecture to enable automatic model weaving?

10.2.1.2. Hypothesis I.II: Feature-driven reuse

Hypothesis I.II states "a subsystem modelled with the reference architecture and several subsystem solutions can be reused by annotating features and can be automatically included by using *CompARE* in a software architecture model." In addition, the software architect reusing the subsystem should receive suggestions on the product selection. Both evaluation goals are answered by two evaluation questions:

> **Evaluation Question I.II.1: Uniform Model Reuse**
> Can software architecture models that are structured using the reference architecture be reused in another software architecture model by the annotation of features?

> **Evaluation Question I.II.2: Automated Solution Evaluation**
> Can models of subsystem solutions that are structured using the reference architecture be automatically included in a base architecture model and optimized, so that software architects get suggestions on the optimal product selection?

10.2.2. Hypothesis II: Reuse informal knowledge for architecture optimization

Hypothesis II states that we can "reuse informal architecture knowledge in automated design space exploration approaches". Even informally available architecture knowledge can be analysed without quantitative measures. Informally modelled knowledge can be used together with quantitatively modelled knowledge. The combination of these two knowledge representations can then be used to automatically optimize software architecture models according to quality attributes. The hypothesis is divided into two sub-hypotheses, namely sub-hypothesis II.I, which considers qualitative reasoning that can be used to represent qualitative knowledge. Sub-hypothesis II.II refers to the combination of both modelling types of representation and proposes how to analyse them in combination.

10.2.2.1. Hypothesis II.I: Qualitative Reasoning

Hypothesis II.I considers modelling and analysis of informal architecture knowledge. This type of architecture knowledge is either based on expert experience or refers to documented knowledge that can also be available in natural language. We model this knowledge, so that it can be used for analyses or optimizations. Informal architecture knowledge can be modelled and automatically analysed by qualitative reasoning techniques. The following two evaluation questions refine the two evaluation goals:

> **Evaluation Question II.I.1: Modelling Qualitative Knowledge**
> Can informal knowledge such as expert knowledge or knowledge from documents be modelled so that it can be used for automatic analyses?

> **Evaluation Question II.I.2: Analysing Qualitative Knowledge**
> Can qualitatively modelled knowledge be analysed so that complex relationships between quality attributes can be observed in component-based software architecture models?

10.2.2.2. Hypothesis II.II: Knowledge Combination

Hypothesis II.II considers the combination of two types of knowledge representation. The hypothesis considers qualitatively modelled knowledge can be combined with quantitatively modelled knowledge to support new trade-off decisions. The following evaluation question analyse the hypothesis:

> **Evaluation Question II.II: Combined Analysis**
> Can qualitatively represented and quantitatively represented architecture knowledge be combined to derive meaningful results from the analysis?

10.2.3. Hypothesis III: Automated model generation and optimization

Hypothesis III is based on the two previous hypotheses and considers additional value of the models and analyses in combination. Hypothesis III proposes by "defining a reference architecture for structuring subsystems and their different solutions, new architecture decisions, such as feature-driven use can be evaluated and requirements can be prioritized according to both qualitatively modelled and quantitatively modelled quality attributes." The hypothesis is examined by the following two evaluation questions:

> **Evaluation Question III.1: Architecture Design Decisions**
> Which architecture design decisions considering quality attributes can be evaluated when reusing subsystem solutions which are applied to the subsystem's reference architecture?
>
> **Evaluation Question III.2: Requirements Prioritization**
> Can requirements be prioritized on the basis of the results of the proposed method?

10.2.4. Achieved Levels of Validation

On the basis of the aforementioned levels of validation of Böhme and Reussner, we classify the implemented contributions. We implemented *CompARE* in PerOpteryx to validate the results of automatic model weaving and the qualitatively modelled quality attributes, as well as their combination with quantitative objective functions. We base on the optimization of models that was proposed by A. Koziolek [KH06b] and evaluated in various case studies such as in Gooijer et al. [Goo+12]. On this basis, we discuss the accuracy in Section 11.10 and Section 12.4 (level 1).

Using different case study systems, comprising real existing systems and scientific systems, we applied different real world scenarios and showed which scenarios and questions can be answered by using *CompARE* (level 2). We were not able to conduct a study on the economic benefits of the overall approach. This was not possible due to the lack of available scenarios in real industry context and the absence of a realistic, accessible setups. Nevertheless, one of *CompARE*'s main goals is reducing the manual effort

No.	Evaluation Question	Section	Lvl
EQ I.I.1	Uniform Software Architecture	10.5	2
EQ I.I.2	Inhomogeneous Model Application		
EQ I.II.1	Uniform Model Reuse	11, 13	2
EQ I.II.2	Automated Solution Evaluation	11.3, 13	2
EQ II.I.1	Modelling Qualitative Knowledge	12.2, 12.3	2
EQ II.I.2	Analysing Qualitative Knowledge		
EQ II.II	Combined Analysis	12.2, 12.3	3
EQ III.1	Architecture Design Decisions	11.4, 11.5, 11.7 11.8, 11.9, 13	3
EQ III.2	Requirements Prioritization	11.5, 11.7, 12.2.1, 12.3.2, 13	3

Table 10.1.: Evaluation questions, section where to find the in-depth description and achieved evaluation levels. Several sections are cross cutting, and several questions are considered in several sections. The overview shows the main sections evaluating the questions.

required for modelling, simulating and evaluating results. The reduction of effort can therefore serve as estimation of economic benefits (level 3). An overview of the achieved levels and the corresponding evaluation scenarios is shown in Table 10.1.

10.3. CompARE Implementation

CompARE extends PerOpteryx by two units, namely the weaving engine and the evaluation of qualitatively modelled knowledge. The weaving engine integrates the subsystems and its solutions that include the selected features in the base architecture. The evaluation of qualitatively modelled knowledge evaluates quality attributes on the basis of qualitative reasoning.

10.3.1. Weaving Engine

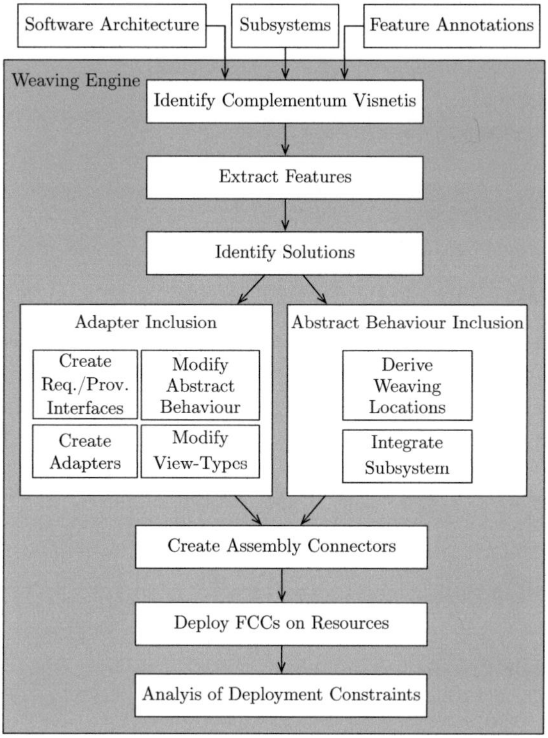

Figure 10.2.: Conceptual overview on *CompARE*'s weaving engine.

Figure 10.2 shows an overview of the concepts of the *CompARE* weaving engine. The weaving engine consists of seven steps. Three input models are used, namely the base software architecture, the feature annotations and the reference architecture of the subsystem, together with the software architecture of the subsystem solutions.

In the first step, the *Identify Complementum Visnetis* step, the selected positions are determined to apply the features. the these positions, the desired features are included later and connected to the base architecture.

The desired features are extracted in the second step, the *Extract Features* step. The features annotated in the software architecture are then compared with the selected features.

In the third step, the *Identify Solutions* step, all solution alternatives are identified that support the previously selected features. Depending on the selected inclusion mechanism (adapter or extension of the abstract behaviour), the corresponding mechanism is selected.

For the *Adapter Inclusion*, all necessary interfaces (required and provided) must first be determined, generated and assigned to the adapter component. Depending on the selected appearance (i.e. before, after, around), the required abstract behaviour of the adapter is generated. In addition, influenced view-types are modified.

For the extension of the *Abstract Behaviour*, we first derive all affected weaving locations. On the basis of the abstract control flow definition language, the weaving locations are not explicitly modelled, but must be derived first. In the second step, call sequences to the subsystem are generated at the corresponding derived locations. Similar to the extension using adapters, the appearance must be considered and the call sequences generated accordingly.

In the next step, the *Create Assembly Connectors*, the components must be assembled. The new assembly connectors affects both subsystem software components and generated adapters.

In the sixth step, the *Deployment of FCCs on Resources*, *CompARE* deploys the components of the FCCs to hardware resources. Finally, in the last step, the *Analysis of Deployment Constraints*, *CompARE* analysis whether the deployment fulfils the defined architecture constraints.

10.3.2. Qualitative Knowledge Analysis

The qualitative knowledge analysis consists of two parts, namely the topological sorting of the software components of the system and the qualitative reasoning analysis for the qualitative evaluation of quality attributes.

Topological sorting sorts the software components of a system sequentially. The correct order can be derived by analysing all outgoing external calls or required interfaces from each component. These external calls reference interfaces arranged in the component repository. There, each interface is assigned to a corresponding software component. This assignment can be derived from the system model. If all externally called interfaces are assigned to a component and their call sequences are determined, the determined dependencies and their sequence are stored. Subsequently, the next component in the sequence is then considered. This analysis process is continued until there are no more required interfaces (from the view of the component currently being considered). For the analysis of the topological sorting we use the Java implementation of the algorithm from Keith Schwarz [Sch10] as basis.

Based on the typologically sorted sequence of the software components of the system, we can apply the qualitative reasoning analysis. For the analysis of the topologically sorted software architecture, *CompARE* requires quality annotations. The quality annotations are technically implemented as ecore-based models.

First, the quality annotations model is used and the corresponding static quality properties for each modelled quality attribute is assigned to the software components. In the next step, the quality effects from the components involved in realizing the service considered are evaluated. The first considered component is corresponding to the first component of the called service in the topological sorted software components sequence. When all effects on quality attributes have been analysed, the next component is evaluated. The analysis is performed until the effects on quality attributes of all dependent components have been evaluated .

10.3.3. Integration in PerOpteryx

The process steps described in the previous section have been integrated into the PerOpteryx software architecture optimization process as follows. We have extended both the input models and the optimization process. An overview of the refined process is shown in Figure 10.3. Our extended version PerOpteryx has been presented in [BFK19].

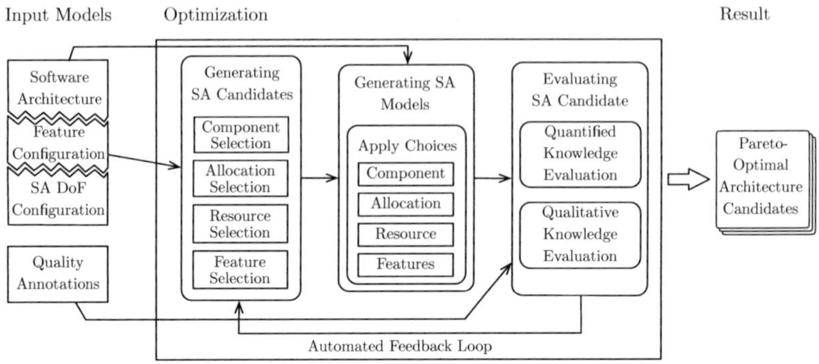

Figure 10.3.: PerOpteryx with extended SA model generation and qualitative knowledge analysis (derived from [BFK19]).

10.3.3.1. Input Models

The previous version of PerOpteryx requires three types of input models, namely the software architecture, the degrees of freedom configuration, describing the component selection, component allocation, and resource configuration. To annotate cost information, PerOpteryx requires the cost annotation model, which annotates costs to components and resource containers. We extend the input models by a feature configuration that extends the software architecture model and additional degrees of freedom in the degrees of freedom configuration. To evaluate more complex qualitative modelled quality attributes with qualitative reasoning, we extend the quality annotation model (originally consisting only of cost annotations) with our description language for arbitrary quality attributes.

10.3.3.2. Optimization

The optimization consists of three parts, namely generating the software architecture candidates, generating the models from the candidate description, as well as the evaluation of the generated software architecture candidate regarding its quality attributes.

In the first step, the generation of the software architecture candidate, an architecture candidate is generated from the degree of freedom space. If certain features should be included into the architecture, the desired positions for the feature completion components of the features are added to the model. These are then allocated to hardware.

In the next step, the generation of the concrete software architecture model, the PCM model instance is generated from the previously generated architecture candidate. In this step, components are assembled, allocated and resource configurations adapted. If features are required, an additional step is necessary. From the component repository, the concrete components matching the feature, the FCCs and the software components of the selected solution must be determined. Once all the necessary components have been determined, the interfaces required for functionality must be made compatible. In case of selecting the adapter extension as strategy, adapters are generated and the corresponding assembly connectors are generated. The components required for feature implementation are then allocated according to the architecture candidate.

In the final step of the optimization, the evaluation of the software architecture candidate model, the two modules, quantitative evaluation and qualitative evaluation, are carried out. After the quantitative evaluation, the qualitative reasoning mechanisms are executed on the software architecture model.

The results of both evaluation procedures are then combined and reused in a feedback loop to generate new, improved architecture candidates. This loop is continued until a scheduling criterion is met. The end of the optimization run finally results in a set of Pareto-optimal architecture candidates regarding the modelled degree of freedom configuration.

10.4. Subsystem Case Study Systems

This section describes the architecture, models of several subsystems, subsystem solutions and shows how they can be applied in the context of *CompARE*. First, several subsystems are introduced, their architectures described and modelled, and finally applied to the feature completion meta model. As a result, we obtain models that can be used for the integration into base systems to evaluate different design decisions at design time. Overall, we have examined four subsystem solutions applied on two subsystems: Logging systems log4j version 1 and log4j version 2 in Section 10.4.1. In Section 10.4.2, we introduce features of the logging subsystem. Further, we consider the intrusion detection systems AppSensor and OSSEC HIDS in Section 10.4.3. In Section 10.4.4, we introduce features of the intrusion detection subsystems.

10.4.1. Apache's log4j

Apache's log4j was developed out of the fact that every major application has had its own logging or tracing API. This increased the need to develop a reusable framework to allow lightweight reuse of the logging functionality without having to rethink and properly make all the design decisions of this subsystem.

Log4j was originally developed for Java, but later ported to many other programming languages, such as C, C++, C#, Perl, and several others. By acquiring logging statements in program code, low-level logging is possible. Thus, logging calls can be used for debugging or for measuring local performance bottlenecks. These functionalities are also supported by debugger and performance tracing frameworks. However, Brian W. Kernighan and Rob Pike describes the following in [KP99, p. 119]: "As personal choice, we tend not to use debuggers beyond getting a stack trace or the value of a variable or two. One reason is that it is easy to get lost in details of complicated data structures and control flow; we find stepping through a program less productive than thinking harder and adding output statements and self-checking code at critical places. Clicking over statements takes longer than scanning the output of judiciously-placed displays. It takes less time to decide where to put print statements than to single-step to the critical section of code, even assuming we know where that is. More important, debugging statements stay with the program; debugging sessions are transient."

In addition, logging can be integrated into the base architecture with comparatively low effort. In contrast to debugger outputs, logging can also be used in parallel to long-term recording in real operation of the application

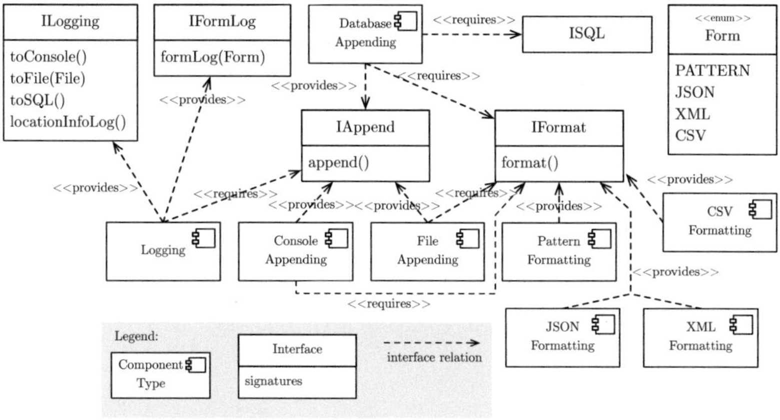

Figure 10.4.: Extended repository model of Apache log4j version 1.

to obtain context information about the application or to identify errors that are difficult to observe.

10.4.1.1. log4j Version 1

A detailed documentation about architecture and functionality of log4j version 1 (in the following called log4jv1) was described by Ceki Gülcü in [Gül03].

The main functional concerns of log4jv1 can essentially be divided into several parts. The first part contains the external interfaces, providing all services that can be demanded by the base system. Further several modes for logging can be selected, such as `error`, `warn`, `info`, `debug`, to use different log levels. The collected data is then processed in the next part.

The next part forwards the recorded data to the configured output medium. Possible output targets are console, files, graphical components, remote sockets and NT event logger. This output can then be processed to different formats. Pattern layout formats the output according to a certain pattern. The pattern is based on the formatting pattern of the `Printf` function, which is known from the C language. Beyond pattern layouting, we can format

Component	Internal Action	Resource Demand	Init. cost
Logging	log internal	$2.4 \cdot 10^{-3}$	100.0
Console Appending	append internal	$2.2 \cdot 10^{-3}$	100.0
FileAppending	append internal write to file	$2.3 \cdot 10^{-3}$ $5 \cdot 10^{-8} \cdot \mathit{DoublePMF}[(8025; 0.99996)$ $(3210000; 0.00003)(6420000; 0.00001)]$	100.0
Database Appending	append internal db write overhead	$2.4 \cdot 10^{-3}$ $5 \cdot 10^{-8} \cdot \mathit{DoubPMF}[$ $(2210000.0; 0.56551)(5420000.0; 0.40035)$ $(8630000.0; 0.01181)[..]]$	500.0

Table 10.2.: Excerpt of RD-SEFFs and costs of log4jv1 services/components.

the data into a CSV format, a JSON layout or a customizable XML layout. The repository of log4jv1 that was previously used in the running example has been extended and is shown in Figure 10.4. The repository diagram represents an abstraction of the software architecture.

The main functionality of log4jv1 is addressed via the `ILogging` interface and implemented by the `Logging` component. The recorded raw data is then processed further by calling the services of the `IAppend` interface. `IAppend` is implemented either by the components `ConsoleAppending`, `FileAppending` or `DatabaseAppending`, depending on the output medium selected. All three components require the `IFormat` interface to apply to the correct output format. The `IFormat` interface is converted accordingly by the four formatting implementations, namely `CSVFormatting`, `PatternFormatting`, `JSONFormatting` and `XMLFormatting`. The `DatabaseAppending` component also requires an SQL interface `ISQL` to write the data to the database. Whether the formatter is used depends on whether the interface `IFormLog` is called with parameters of the enum `Form`.

For performance analysis we have modelled the abstract behaviour and RD-SEFFs for the processor resource demand of the components implementing the features console logging, file logging, SQL logging and pattern formatting. Further, we derived a cost model that describes the initial costs of the components. An overview of the RD-SEFFs with focus on internal actions and initial costs of several components are shown in Table 10.2. External calls are not shown in the table and can be derived from the architecture description.

10.4.1.2. Apache's log4j Version 2

Apache's log4j version 2 (called log4jv2 in the following) is the next generation of log4jv1 and comes with several new appendings and layouts. This also results in new features. The internal architecture differs from the previous version as a result from new features. In addition, new log levels are supported such as `all`, `trace`, `warn`, `fatal`. The architecture of log4jv2 is shown in Figure 10.5. The repository diagram represents an abstraction of the software architecture.

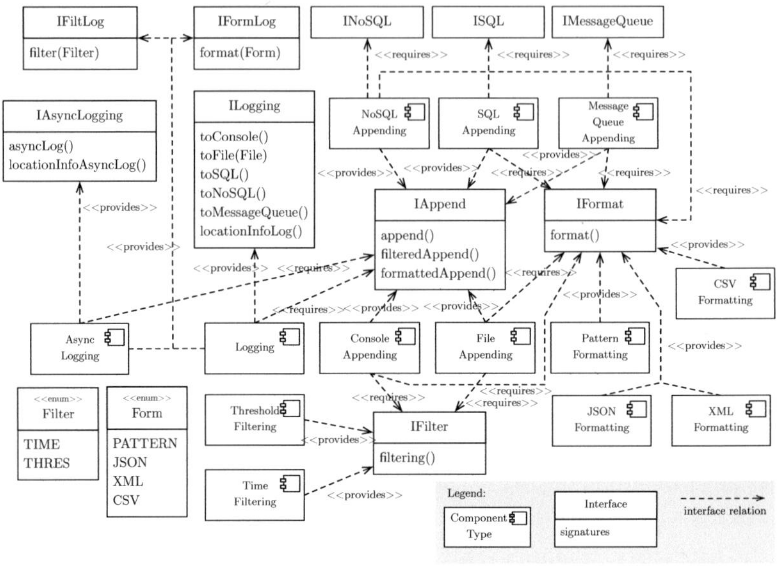

Figure 10.5.: Repository model of Apache log4j version 2.

Data can now be captured and written asynchronously, i.e. it is not necessary to wait for the commit of the respective output medium and the user workload can be continued before write process on the medium is finished.

Appending now allows extended write operations to different database systems, such as SQL, but also NoSQL databases (such as MongoDB in different versions and CouchDB) or to transfer data to the Java Persistence API (JPA). In addition to extended connections to databases, extended network functions such as writing to streams, sockets, SSL encrypted connections, writing to the distributed streaming platform Apache Kafka, or the Java Messaging Service (JMS) are available.

In appending, various logging events can be filtered to evaluate the recorded data later in a more focused manner and not to oversee essential information due to the excessive amount of data that is actually not relevant.

Further, there are filter options included, such as filtering over certain threshold values or filtering over certain points in time.

Layouts known from log4jv1 like Pattern, CSV, JSON and XML are also available in log4jv2. The described appendings, filterings and layoutings are only a small part of the possibilities offered by log4jv2. Altogether log4jv2 supports 29 appendings, 11 filterings, and 11 layouting options.

The services of log4jv2 are accessed via its interfaces. The interface provides logging using `ILogging` that can be optionally set as asynchronous logging by using `IAsyncLogging`. In addition, the filters for the selection of the actually written data can be addressed via the `IFiltLog` interface. Synchronous logging is implemented by the `Logging` components and asynchronous logging via the `AsyncLogging` component. As log4jv1, writing to the output medium is carried out via the `IAppend` interface and the associated components, `ConsoleAppending`, `FileAppending`, `SQLAppending`, `NoSQLAppending`, and `MessageQueueAppending` for using the respective appenders. All appender components can filter log data and therefore require the `IFilter` interface. Filtering is realized via the two components `ThresholdFiltering` and `TimeFiltering` (not all components are shown in the figure). The interfaces `ISQL`, `INoSQL`, and `IMessageQueue` are required from the base system by log4jv2 if the corresponding appender should be used. Whether the formatter is used depends on whether the interface `IFormLog` is called with parameters of the enum `Form`. Additionally, two filtering options can be selected by using the `Filter` enum.

For the performance analysis of log4jv2 we have modelled the abstract behaviour of the components and thus the services of the framework. In addition, we have determined the RD-SEFFs and can perform performance analyses based on both. We also added cost annotations for the initial cost of components to the model. Table 10.3 shows a summary. For the following features, which are implemented by components, we have modelled the abstract behaviour with associated RD-SEFFs: console logging, file logging, NoSQL logging, SQL logging, pattern layouting, XML layouting, CSV layouting and JSON layouting.

Component	Internal Action	Resource Demand	Initial cost
Logger	log internal	$1.6 \cdot 10^{-3}$	50
Console Appending	append internal write to console	$6.4 \cdot 10^{-3}$ $5E{-}8 \cdot DoublePMF[(28890; 0.999964)$ $(321E4; 3, 5E{-}5)(642E3; E{-}6)]$	50
File Appending	append internal write to file	$2.4 \cdot 10^{-3}$ $5 \cdot 10^{-8} \cdot DoublePMF[(28890; 0.999952)$ $(321E4; 0.000032)(642E4; 0.000015)(963E4; E{-}6)]$	50
NoSQLAppend	append internal	$6.4 \cdot 10^{-3}$	500
SQL Appending	append internal db write overhead	$6.4 \cdot 10^{-3}$ $5 \cdot 10^{-8} \cdot DoubPMF[[(2210000.0; 0.1476)$ $(5420000.0; 0.7765)(8630000.0; 0.0281)[..]]$	500
Pattern Formatting	format pattern layout	$5 \cdot 10^{-8} \cdot DoublePMF[(205440; 0.999769)$ $(321E4; 0.000213)(642E4; 12E{-}6)(963E4; 3E{-}5)[..]$	50
XML Formatting	format XML layout	$5 \cdot 10^{-8} \cdot DoublePMF[(385200.0; 0.999959)$ $(963E4; 0.00003)(1.605E7; 0.000008)(2.568E7; 0.000002)]$	50
CSVFormatting Formatting	format CSV layout	$5 \cdot 10^{-8} \cdot DoublePMF[(5136E2; 0.9983)(1605E3; 0.0011)$ $(321E4; 0.00044)(642E4; 0.00013)(963E4; 0.00002)[..]$	50
JSONFormatting Formatting	format JSON layout	$5 \cdot 10^{-8} \cdot DoublePMF[(353100.0; 0.999939)$ $(642E4; 0.000047)(1.605E7; 0.000011)(2.247E7; 0.000002)[..]$	50

Table 10.3.: Excerpt of RD-SEFFs and costs of log4jv2 services/components.

10.4.2. Features of the Logging Systems

Several features can be derived from the previous two sections, which describe the architecture of the two subsystem solution systems. The modelled features correspond to a meaningful subset of the features that can be derived from the architecture and that are actually provided by the two logging solutions.

Table 10.4 shows an overview of the features provided by both logging solutions. Basing on this, we derive a set of core features and a set of optional features. Core features correspond to the features with numbers 1-3 and 9-12 in Table 10.4. Optional features correspond to features 4-8. However, not all combinations of features can be configured at the same time. For example, it is not possible to use SQL database logging and NoSQL database logging at the same time. Further, only one formatting option and one filtering option can be selected at the same time. Furthermore, either synchronous or asynchronous logging can be used.

Configurable options and limitations of features are shown in the feature model in Figure 10.6. All features are grouped by feature groups on which restrictions can be defined. A total of three main groups and two subgroups can be derived. The main groups define features regarding the categories appending, formatting and filtering.

With appending, the four appending options *File*, *Database*, *MessageQueue*, and *Console* are available as alternatives. One subgroup considers synchronous and asynchronous file logging, while the other subgroup defines alternatives for the selected database technology. Synchronous file logging and asynchronous file logging as features can only be selected alternatively. Database appending can be used as a subgroup in which we can alternatively select (XOR) *SQL* or *NoSQL* database appending. The appending group has the special feature that at least one of its features must be selected and that several (OR) can be selected.

The second group is optionally selectable and contains the four formatting features, namely *Pattern*, *CSV*, *XML* and *JSON*. All four features are alternatives (XOR).

The fourth group concerns filtering. Their features are optionally selectable. *Threshold value* and *filtering by time* is possible.

No.	Feature	Solution log4jv1	Solution log4jv2	Core Feature	Optional Feature
(1)	ConsoleLogging	✓	✓	✓	✗
(2)	FileLogging	✓	✓	✓	✗
(3)	SQLDatabaseLogging	✓	✓	✓	✗
(4)	NoSQLDatabase Logging	✗	✓	✗	✓
(5)	MessageQueue Logging	✗	✓	✗	✓
(6)	AsyncFileLogging	✗	✓	✗	✓
(7)	ThresholdFiltering	✗	✓	✗	✓
(8)	TimeFiltering	✗	✓	✗	✓
(9)	PatternFormatting	(✓)	✓	✓	✗
(10)	JSONFormatting	✓	✓	✓	✗
(11)	XMLFormatting	✓	✓	✓	✗
(12)	CSVFormatting	✓	✓	✓	✗

Table 10.4.: Features of Apache log4jv1 and log4jv2. Features in brackets mean that features are partially implemented.

10.4.3. Intrusion Detection Systems

Logging can be used as a passive instrument for attacker detection and is particularly useful for the subsequent detection of attacks in computer forensics. However, if attacks have already been successfully carried out, they can only be detected retrospectively. In this case, company assets such as personal customer data, credit card information or strategic material such as company secrets, patents or technology information have already been stolen. At best, data loss can lead to customer loss or, at worst, to criminal investigation and threat to a company's existence. Facebook suffered a slowdown in growth, presumably due to the consequences of the Cambridge

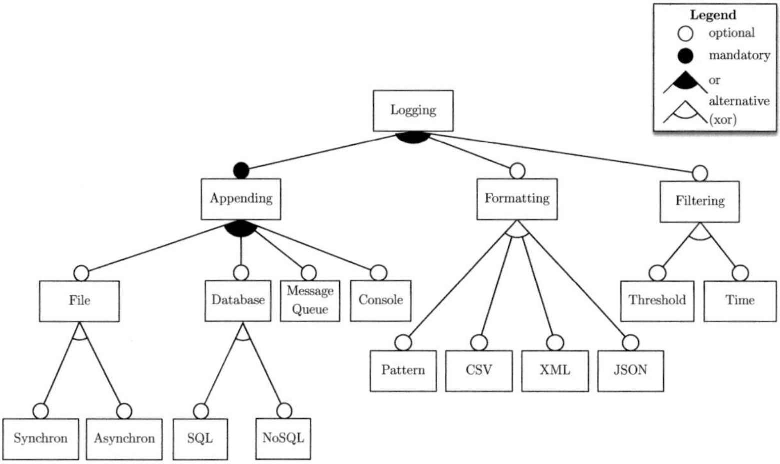

Figure 10.6.: Feature model of the Logging systems.

Analytica (cf. [Theb]) data scandal. This slowdown cost Facebook a market capitalization of $ 119 billion (the total market capitalization of McDonald's at the time) [Thea].

It therefore makes sense to intervene even before the loss of data and to detect attacks that are actively in progress and take countermeasures. Intrusion detection and prevention systems provide functions and measures for the preventive detection of attacks and the application of countermeasures to prevent them.

The actions mentioned concern the detection (and possibly prevention) of external attackers. A distinction is made between different groups of attackers. Less skilled attackers usually carry out direct, obvious and less planned pre-emptive attacks, while advanced attackers or professional groups carry out attacks with large financial capacity targeted and planned in advance. Intrusion detection systems focus on attacks that are carried out by less skilled attackers. High skilled attacks are usually not detected by intrusion detection systems.

If software architects wants to use such a system, they must be aware that this type of system cannot detect hidden attacks, but only react to rule-based modelled patterns that have been specified beforehand. These rules can, for example, be created by the security engineer specifically for the system to be used and pre-configured actions. However, such systems usually offer a number of pre-configured rules that can be used as a basis for customization. A certain degree of reuse of knowledge is therefore nevertheless given [WJ15].

From a technological point of view, there are two types of systems: the first class analyses log files generated by Linux daemons such as sshs, imapd, etc. (OSSEC) while the second class considers network traffic (Snort) and application behaviour (AppSensor).

For the evaluation of *CompARE*, we use two systems, namely AppSensor and OSSEC. AppSensor analyses network traffic and analyses application behaviour, while OSSEC works on the basis of log file analysis.

10.4.3.1. AppSensor

AppSensor version 2 is an implementation of an IDS from OWASP. The OWASP offers a detailed architecture documentation and feature description in the AppSensor reference manual [WJ15], which we use together with the source code creating the following architecture models. Figure 10.7 shows an abstraction of the AppSensor's repository with its components and interfaces. The architecture of AppSensor was initially created automatically using the reverse engineering tool SoMoX [Kro12] to automatically generate the software architecture model. The initial design derived by SoMoX was used as a basis and refined having a more detailed model of the software architecture.

The architecture of AppSensor contains 14 components and a total of 17 interfaces. The functionality itself is provided via the interfaces `IDetect`, `IAction`, `IStaticAnalysis` and `IEvent`. The interfaces are implemented by the `DetectionPoint` component. Starting here, the collected data is propagated through the architecture of the subsystem. First the `EventManager` processes the collected raw data. In the `RequestHandler`, the request to be analysed is first stored for analysis by the `EventStore` and analysed in the `EventAnalysisEngine`. If an attack is detected, it is first analysed in `AttackAnalysisEngine` and stored by `AttackStore`. The `AccessController`

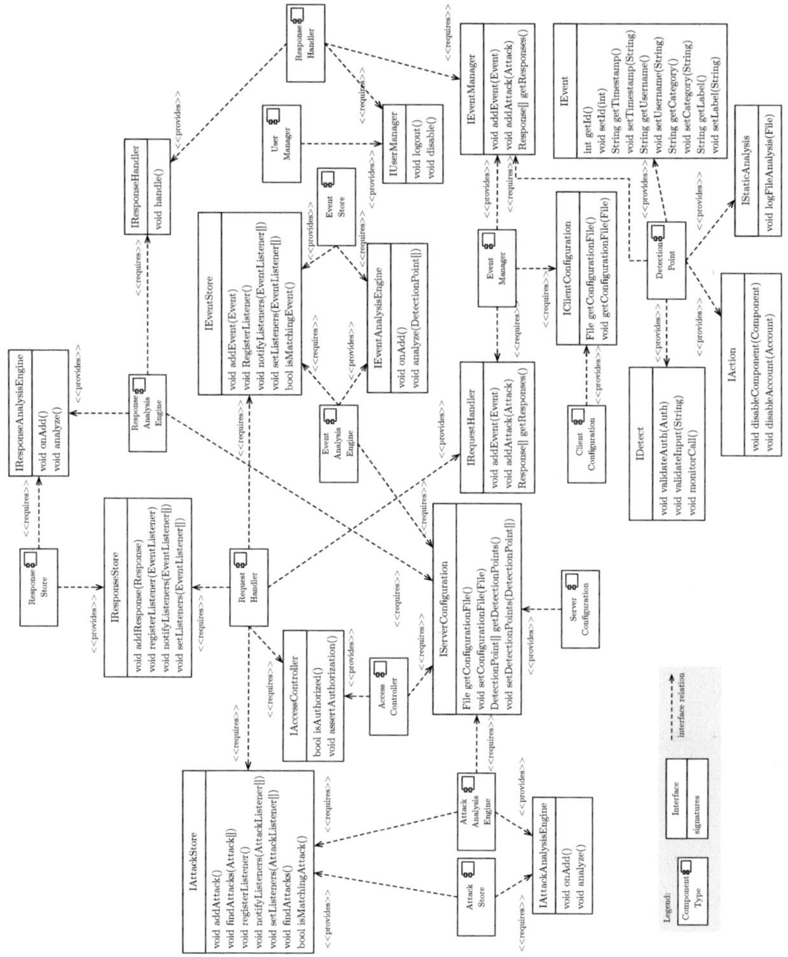

Figure 10.7.: Repository model of the OWASP AppSensor intrusion detection system.

checks the validity of the evaluation. If a reaction to the attack is available, the countermeasure is processed by the `ResponseHandler`. Possible countermeasures are first processed in `ResponseAnalysisEngine`, initiated and stored by `ResponseStore`. Countermeasures are additionally implemented by the `UserManager`. Transverse components are `ServerConfiguration` and `ClientConfiguration`, which manage user-specific configurations.

The attributes `DetectionPoint`, `Event`[2], `Attack`, `EventListener` and `Response` are data types within the system. They each manage information about the type of request, attack or response to the attack and are passed between the analysis and response components. In addition, `EventListeners` can be registered, which in turn are used to trigger specific responses. `DetectionPoint` defines the entry point of the analysis request in the base system. The attributes themselves are not central to the architecture and are not included in the overview.

Using profilers, we have carried out measurements, to determine response time distributions of the services of the AppSensor components and modelled them as RD-SEFFs. This allows us to simulate the response times of the overall system's services when we include AppSensor in base systems. We have also created and annotated cost annotations.

10.4.3.2. OSSEC

Open Source HIDS SECurity (OSSEC) is a free open source host-based attacker detection system that analyses log files generated by Linux services, integrity checks of system files, Windows registry integrity, rootkit detection, and process surveillance. In addition, OSSEC can take active countermeasures to defend against the attack. For our evaluation we use OSSEC version 2. OSSEC in version 2 was developed in the programming language C and can be compiled and used on a number of operating systems, such as Windows, Linux, MacOS and various virtualization solutions. The software component repository model is shown in Figure 10.8 and has been reverse engineered based on a source code analysis.

OSSEC consists of seven components and seven interfaces. The system communicates event-based, thus the system has three event messages used for message passing. These are either emitted or handled by the components. The interaction between the subsystem and the base system is event-based

[2] Events from AppSensor should not be confused with the concept of event-based communication. AppSensor uses call and response semantics.

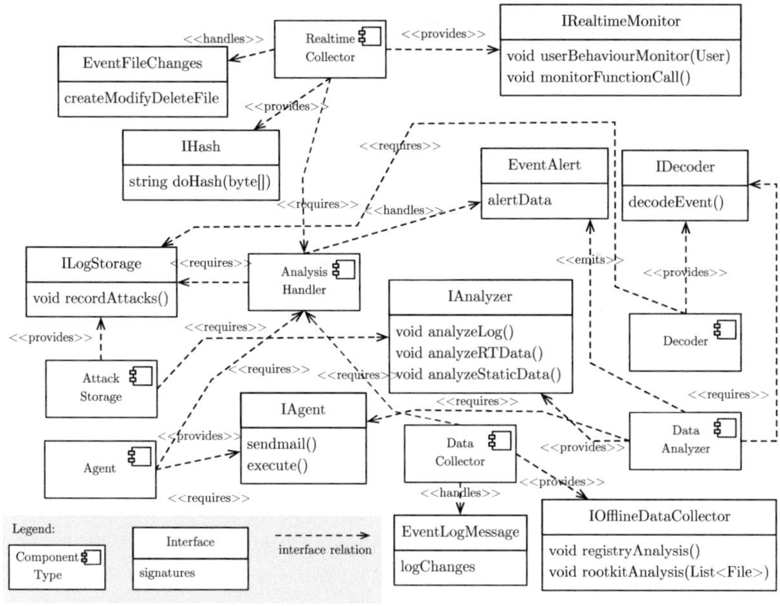

Figure 10.8.: Repository model of the OSSEC intrusion detection system.

as well. The base system emits either an `EventLogMessage` or an `EventFileChanges`. The `DataCollector` component handles the first, while the `RealtimeCollector` component handles the latter. Real time data, such as data on the behaviour of users in the system or monitoring of function calls is monitored by the `RealtimeCollector` by using the `IRealtimeMonitor` interface. If log files change and should be analysed, the `DataCollector` processes the log message event. Static offline analysis data, such as Windows registry analysis data and file-level rootkit analysis data, are also collected by the `DataCollector` using the `IOfflineDataCollector` interface. Real-time analysis of file changes is also captured by handling the `EventFileChanges` event. Both `RealtimeCollector` and `DataCollector` require the `IAnalyzer` interface, which is implemented by the `DataAnalyzer` component. `LogAnalyzer` decodes the collected data using the `Decoder` component (by accessing via the interface `IDecoder`) and emits an `EventAlert` in case of an attack. The emitted alarm events are handled by the `Analysis-`

`Handler` component. For handling, several signatures of the `IAgent` interface can be used, which, implemented via the `Agent` component, either carries out notifications or executes commands as resulting actions. In addition, the `AnalysisHandler` processes sensor data and can store alarms in the `AttackStorage` component, which service is provided by the `ILogStorage` interface.

As already for the AppSensor model, we have enriched the OSSEC architecture model with performance annotations. We modelled the abstract behaviour of several services and added resource demands that we have collected by performance measurements by profilers. For the purpose of cost estimation, we have added additional cost annotations.

10.4.4. Features of the Intrusion Detection Systems

Several features can be derived from the architecture description, the documentation and the source code of the two previously introduced intrusion detection and prevention systems. As with the logging systems, we have presented a subset of the features supported by the systems, which should represent meaningful features of the systems and contribute significantly to influencing the quality attributes of the overall system.

We have identified a total of nine features, that we have classified into three core features and six optional features. We present a summary of the features in Table 10.5. The first core feature is an analyser observing inadmissible frequently calls of services (3). This can occur whenever attackers attempt to increase the load by massively using certain services of the base system to such an extent that the processing of requests from legitimate users is no longer possible. Another core feature is the deactivation of accounts (4), for example, when an attack is previously detected using a particular account. Log file analysis (6) is another core feature. Different rules could be used to process log files.

AppSensor supports three additional optional features. User data can be verified (1). We can also check whether a user is allowed to execute certain commands. Another optional feature is the validation of input data (2). This can be used, for example, to search queries for control commands. With another optional feature, components can be deactivated (5) in the event of an attack, for example to ensure the operation of other core functions of the base system or to protect sensitive data.

OSSEC supports three additional optional features. On Windows systems, the registry (7) can be analysed. Abnormal modifications on the windows registry can be detected. Another feature is the static integrity analysis of files (8) in the file system. In addition, critical system files can be checked for rootkits (9).

No.	Feature	Solution		Core	Optional
		AppSensor	OSSEC	Feature	
(1)	Authorization check	✓	✗	✗	✓
(2)	Input validation	✓	✗	✗	✓
(3)	Functional abuse	✓	✓	✓	✗
(4)	Disable account	✓	✓	✓	✗
(5)	Disable components	✓	✗	✗	✓
(6)	Log file analysis	✓	✓	✓	✗
(7)	Registry analysis	✗	✓	✗	✓
(8)	File integrity	✗	✓	✗	✓
(9)	Rootkit check	✗	✓	✗	✓

Table 10.5.: Features supported by OWASP AppSensor and OSSEC.

10.5. Modelling the Feature Completions

The subsystems introduced in the previous sections can be modelled by two feature completions, namely the *Logging* feature completion and the *IDS* feature completion. In Section 10.5.1 we describe the *Logging* feature completion, while Section 10.5.2 describes the *IDS* feature completion. Each section introduces the reference architecture and their application to the subsystem solutions. Finnaly, in Section 10.5.3 we provide a final discussion.

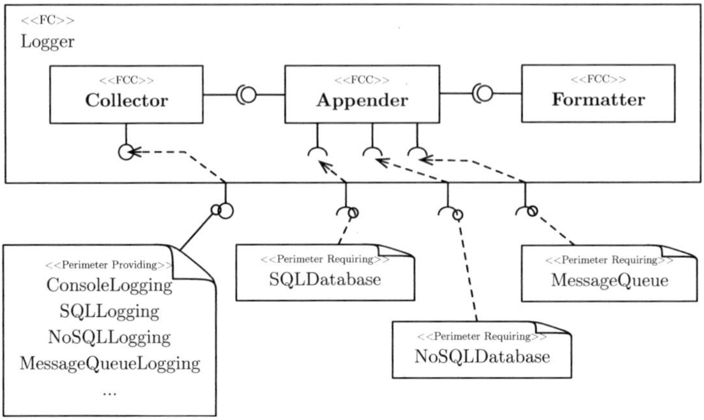

Figure 10.9.: Refinement type of the feature completion *Logger.*

10.5.1. Logging Feature Completion

The definition type of the *Logging* feature completion models the provided features [Kie+16a] and the required complementum. Provided features correspond to the mandatory and optional features from Table 10.4. Required complementum uses essential services from the base architecture that are required by certain features. Figure 10.9 shows the refinement type of the logging feature completion. The feature completion is divided into the appropriate feature completion components and their dependencies, i.e. the reference architecture of the subsystem. The logging feature completion consists of three FCCs, namely *Collector, Appender,* and *Formatter* (see Section 7.2.5). *Appender* is dependent on *Formatter,* while *Collector* is dependent on *Appender. Appender* requires additional services from the base architecture, namely an SQL interface for database access, and the message queue service [Bus+16].

The solution type aligns the abstract FCCs to software components of the subsystem solutions. Table 10.6 shows the alignment of log4jv1 and log4jv2 to the logger feature completion components, while Table 10.7 shows the perimeter interfaces to concrete interfaces and signatures mapping. In the case of log4jv1, the FCC *Collector* consists of one compo-

FCC	log4jv1	log4jv2
Collector	Logging	AsyncLogging Logging
Appender	ConsoleAppending FileAppending DatabaseAppending	ConsoleAppending FileAppending NoSQLAppending SQLAppending MessageQueueAppending ThresholdFiltering TimeFiltering
Formatter	PatternFormatting JSONFormatting XMLFormatting CSVFormatting	PatternFormatting JSONFormatting XMLFormatting CSVFormatting

Table 10.6.: Alignment of abstract refinement type to concrete solution type of the Logging feature completion.

nent, namely the `Logging` component. In the case of log4jv2, the *Collector* consists of the components `AsyncLogging` and `Logging`. The *Appender* is responsible for writing the data to an output medium. In the case of log4jv1, this consists of three components, namely `ConsoleAppending`, `FileAppending`, and `DatabaseAppending`. log4jv2 consists of 6 components, namely `ConsoleAppending`, `FileAppending`, `NoSQLAppending`, `SQLAppending`, `ThresholdFiltering`, and `TimeFiltering`. Finally, in the case of log4jv1, the *Formatter* consists of the four components `PatternFormatting`, `JSONFormatting`, `XMLFormatting`, and `CSVFormatting`, while in the case of log4jv2, four components are responsible, namely `PatternFormatting`, `JSONFormatting`, `XMLFormatting`, and `CSVFormatting`.

In Table 10.7 features correspond to the provided perimeter interfaces. Therefore, the table shows the relations between feature, provided perimeter interface and realizing component (consisting of the set of all provided interfaces), interface or signature. Both log4jv1 and log4jv2 provide their services by calling individual signatures in corresponding interfaces.

Perimeter (prov)	log4jv1	log4jv2
ConsoleLogging	ILogging(toConsole())	ILogging(toConsole())
FileLogging	ILogging(toFile(File))	ILogging(toFile(File))
SQLDBLogging	ILogging(toSQL())	ILogging(toSQL())
NoSQLDBLogging	-	ILogging(toNoSQL())
MessageQueueLogging	-	ILogging(toMessageQueue())
AsyncLogging	-	IAsyncLogging(asyncLog())
ThresholdFiltering	-	IFiltLog(filter(THRES))
TimeFiltering	-	IFiltLog(filter(TIME))
PatternFormatting	IFormLog(formLog(PATTERN))	IFormLog(format(PATTERN))
JSONFormatting	IFormLog(formLog(JSON))	IFormLog(format(JSON))
XMLFormatting	IFormLog(formLog(XML))	IFormLog(format(JSON))
CSVFormatting	IFormLog(formLog(CSV))	IFormLog(format(CSV))

Table 10.7.: Provided perimeter interfaces of the Logger feature completion to concrete interfaces and signatures of log4jv1 and log4jv2.

In addition to the FCC *Formatter*, the *Appender* requires up to three other services from the base system, namely an *SQL database*, a *NoSQL database*, and a *MessageQueue*. However, only log4jv2 supports NoSQL logging and MessageQueue logging, which is why these two required perimeter interfaces are only relevant for log4jv2 and only SQL database logging is relevant for version 1. Both log4jv1 and log4jv2 require an SQL interface for SQL database logging, while log4jv2 requires a NoSQL interface for NoSQL logging and a message queue from the base system for MesseQueue logging.

10.5.2. IDS Feature Completion

From the analysis of the two intrusion detection systems AppSensor and OSSEC, the *IDS* feature completion results as follows: on the definition type, the feature completion provides a total of 9 features. No additional services are required of the base system by required complementum. The refinement type is shown graphically in Figure 10.10. The refinement type is defined by a set of five feature completion components. This consists of a `Sensor`, a `Manager`, the `Analysis`, `Response` and `Store`. The sensor is responsible for recording the required data as a basis for attacker detection. The sensor is in a requiring relation to the manager, which handles the management and distribution of data. The manager triggers an analysis step (requiring relation to *Analysis*), whose result may require a response (requiring relation to response). Analysis requires response in case of countermeasures against the attack should be carried out. Both *Analysis* and *Response* can require data to be stored. This storage step is performed by *Store*. *Store* may require additional data from the *Analysis* (requiring relation to *Analysis*). As before the perimeter providing interface provides the features as introduced in Section 10.4.4.

The relation between FCC and components of AppSensor considered on the solution type is shown in Figure 10.11 graphically. One component is assigned to the FCC `Sensor`, while two components are assigned to `Response`. Three components are responsible for FCC `Analyzer`, while `Store` is realized by two components. The remaining five components are assigned to the FCC `Manager`.

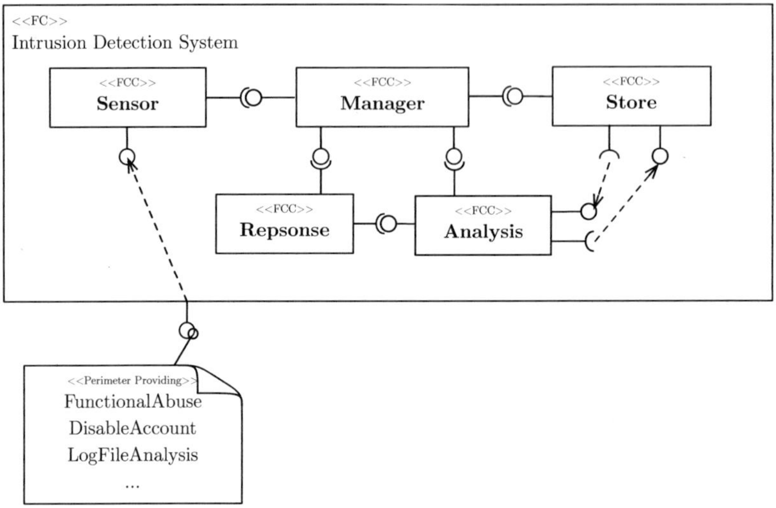

Figure 10.10.: Refinement type of the feature completion *Intrusion Detection System.*

Figure 10.12 shows the relation of the FCCs and software components of the OSSEC system's solution type. Sensor consists of two components, the `RealtimeCollector` and the `DataCollector` with the respective provided interfaces and processed events. *Response* consists of the component `Agent` and the provided interface `IAgent`. *Analyzer* consists of the components `DataAnalyzer` and `Decoder`, with the two corresponding provided interfaces. *Store* consists of the `AttackStorage` component, while *Manager* consists of the `AnalysisHandler` component. Both components provide their corresponding interfaces respectively process the corresponding events.

Table 10.8 provides an overview of the relations between the perimeter interfaces and the component interfaces. AppSensor implements the AuthorizationCheck using the `IDetect` interface and the `validateAuth(Auth)` signature. `IDetect` is also responsible for *InputValidation*. The signature `validateInput(String)` is responsible. *FunctionalAbuse* is also implemented by `IDetect` with the signature `monitorCall`. *DisableAccount* belongs to the *Response*. This is implemented by the interface `IAction` with the signature `disableAccount(Account)`. *DisableComponents*, also a *Response*, and used by the signature `disableComponent(Component)`. *Log-*

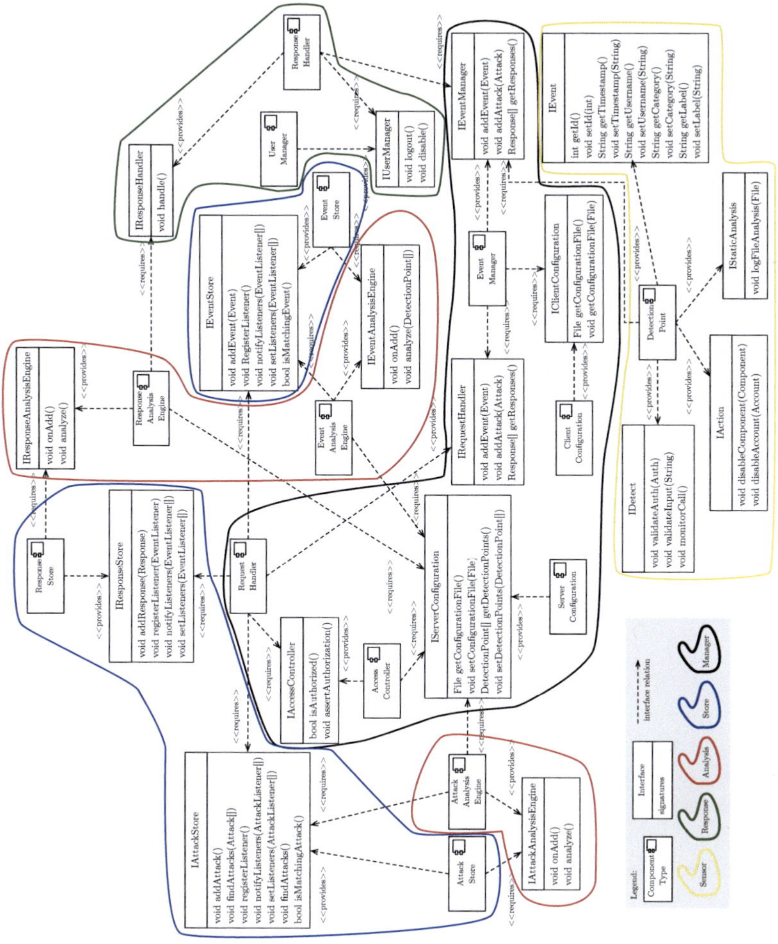

Figure 10.11.: Alignment of the IDS feature completion components to AppSensor software components.

FileAnalysis is implemented via the `IStaticAnalysis` interface and the associated `logFile(File)` signature.

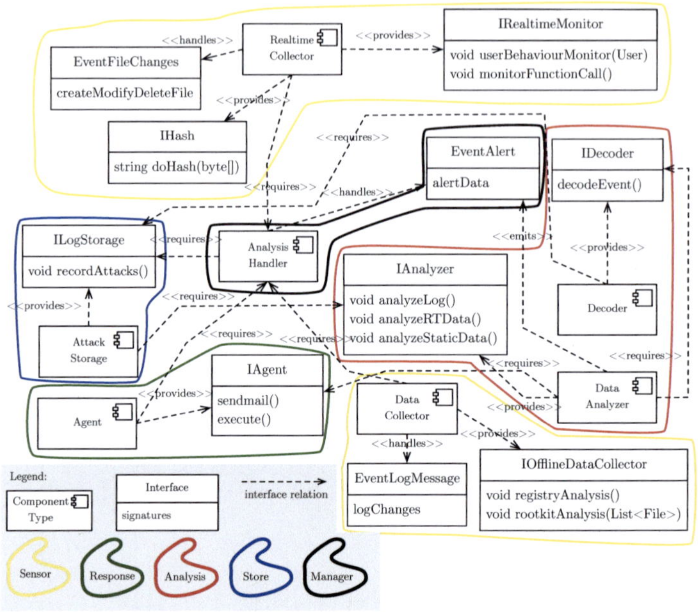

Figure 10.12.: Alignment of the IDS FC's components to concrete OSSEC software components

OSSEC implements *FunctionalAbuse* using the `IRealtimeMonitor` interface. The associated signature for implementing the feature is `monitorFunctionCall`. *DisableAccount* is implemented by using `IRealtimeMonitor`. The associated signature for this is `userBehaviourMonitor(User)`. *LogFileAnalysis* is implemented by the `EventLogMessage` event. *RegistryAnalysis* and *RootkitAnalysis* are implemented by the `IOfflineDataCollector` interface. The corresponding interface is called `registryAnalysis`, respectively `rootkitAnalysis(List<File>)`. *FileIntegrity* is also implemented by an event, namely `EventFileChanges`.

Perimeter (prov)	AppSensor	OSSEC
AuthhorizationCheck	IDetect(validateAuth(Auth))	-
InputValidation	IDetect(validateInput(String))	-
FunctionalAbuse	IDetect(monitorCall())	IRealtimeMonitor(monitorFunctionCall())
DisableAccount	IAction(disable Account(Account))	IRealtimeMonitor(user BehaviourMonitor(User))
DisableComponents	IAction(disable Component(Component))	-
LogFileAnalysis	IStaticAnalysis(log File(File))	EventLogMessage(logChanges)
RegistryAnalysis	-	IOfflineAnalysis(registryAnalysis())
FileIntegrity	-	EventFileChanges(createModifyDeleteFile)
RootkitAnalysis	-	IOfflineAnalysis(rootkitAnalysis(List<File>))

Table 10.8.: Provided perimeter interfaces of the IDS feature completion to interfaces and signatures of AppSensor and OSSEC.

10.5.3. Discussion

In the previous sections, we answered the evaluation questions EQ I.I.1 and EQ I.I.2 from Section 10.2. We showed how subsystems can be modelled using the feature completion meta model and how subsystem solutions can be applied to the subsystem's reference architecture. We have demonstrated how such models can be created and applied to real-world systems. We showed how to model very different solutions, such as AppSensor and OSSEC, in the architecture as well as similar solutions, such as log4jv1 and log4jv2. We annotated these models to the reference architecture of the respective subsystem. For each subsystem, we modelled several features and annotated them according to the subsystem solutions.

10.6. Base System Case Study Systems

This section describes the base systems which the previously modelled feature completions could be integrated to include new functionality by features. Altogether we consider three base systems: Business Reporting System in Section 10.6.1, Remote Diagnostic Solution in Section 10.6.2 and mRUBiS in Section 10.6.3.

10.6.1. Business Reporting System

This section introduces context information, functionality, architecture, and PCM model of the first example system, the Business Reporting System (BRS). The BRS and the associated PCM model have already been used in several publications [Koz11; BSK15; BK16]. Typical scenarios for optimizing the software architecture have been shown. In these studies it has been shown the PCM model of the BRS shows promising results for the applied scenarios and that the optimization provides plausible candidates.

10.6.1.1. System Architecture

The Business Reporting System (BRS) allows users to generate business reports and derive statistically evaluated data on current business processes

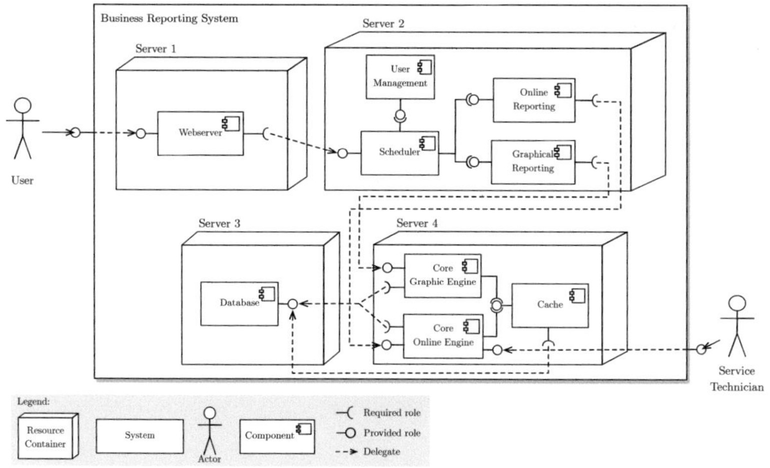

Figure 10.13.: System model of the Business Reporting System [BK16].

from the dataset. We show the system architecture of the BRS in Figure 10.13. The architecture is loosely based on a real system, introduced by Wu and Woodside [WW04].

The system is a four-tier system consisting of nine software components. In total, there are two different interfaces that can be accessed from outside. The first interface addresses services within the `Webserver` component, which is intended for processing user requests to generate reports or retrieve raw data from the system. Here, the `UserManagement` component is used to check the authorization of the request. The requests received from the user are then forwarded to the `Scheduler` component, which is delegated either to the `OnlineReporting` component or to the `GraphicalReporting` component, depending on the request. These in turn requires data from the appropriate components for data aggregation, namely the `CoreGraphicalEngine` or the `CoreOnlineEngine`. Both data aggregation components can either access the `Database` or alternatively, for faster access, via a `Cache` component. This component also loads data from the database in case of cache misses. As an alternative to user access via the `Webserver` component, a service technician can directly access the `CoreOnlineEngine` component for maintenance purposes.

To analyse the performance properties and the expected costs, the model has annotations for simulating the performance and costs. Performance annotations are modelled as abstract behaviour using Palladio's RD-SEFF mechanism. In addition to the behaviour, the performance of the four hardware nodes is specified with a CPU clock rate of 1500 processing units. In addition, there is a usage scenario that reflects the usage of the system.

Cost annotations consist of costs for hardware, such as the selected CPU, as well as initial acquisition costs or development costs for the software components. The underlying PCM models for simulating performance and costs were adopted from [Koz11].

10.6.1.2. Architecture Degrees of Freedom

The PCM model of the BRS has three degrees of freedom, namely component selection, component allocation, and resource selection such as adjustment of the CPU clock rate. Feature inclusion is added as a new degree of freedom. This degree of freedom itself in turn opens up new degrees of freedom, namely the optional integration of features, the product selection, i.e. subsystem solution and an optional multiple instantiation of subsystem-specific components.

Component selection is realized by replacing individual standard components already allocated in the system with functionally equivalent components. The difference between these components is that they differ in their quality properties. For this purpose, the repository contains several components that provide and require the same interfaces. This is the case, for example, for the `Webserver` component.

In **component allocation**, each individual placement of standard components on the individual hardware nodes can be modified. The system has nine servers (four of which are initially in use). Component allocation in particular is an interesting degree of freedom for adding new functionality through new components. If additional components are assembled and allocated, nodes could be overloaded. This can significantly reduce the average response time of the system service. Thus, this degree of freedom has to be taken in mind especially when adding new software components.

When **adjusting the CPU clock rate**, the standard clock frequency of 1500 processing units can be adjusted with the product from the interval [0.5;2]. A higher clock rate has a correspondingly positive effect on the response time of the system service. The cost function serves as a counter movement, which is negatively influenced by a higher clock frequency (higher costs). Using the example of the BRS, all nine servers can be adjusted in their clock rate.

Feature inclusion is used by the software architect by extending assembly connectors with feature annotations in the system (see Section 7.2.6.1). Alternatively, the language described in Section 7.2.6.2 can be used to extend different positions in the architecture simultaneously with features. Once the position is modelled, the degree of freedom is determined whether the modelled feature extension should actually be applied or remain unchanged (*optional degree*).

Within the BRS system, for example, it would be conceivable to extend the connector between `Webserver` and `Scheduler` by the feature *SQLDatabaseLogging*. If the feature should be included optionally, a degree of freedom containing two elements $\{true, false\}$ is spanned. The feature SQLDatabaseLogging is supported according to Table 10.4 by log4jv1 and log4jv2.

If the feature in the dimension optional degree is selected, then another degree of freedom is spanned optimizing **solution alternatives**. If the feature is supposed to be included to several positions than between `Webserver` and `Scheduler`, but for example additionally between `Scheduler` and `UserManagement`, there arise two further options: it can be additionally selected whether the subsystem is to be integrated several times and delegated once in each case or integrated once and delegated several times (**multiple instantiation**). This degree can have a significant effect especially in the case of quality attributes that are influenced by the number of deployed components such as reliability or costs (for example in case of purchasing costs for components). This could have also positive effects on the performance such as for load balancing purposes.

For the feature inclusion degree of freedom, additional opportunities for realization are possible: Several other features could be selected, such as features shown in Table 10.4. In addition, features of other feature completions, can be integrated to include several subsystems in one base system. However, each feature must be manually marked for use or optional

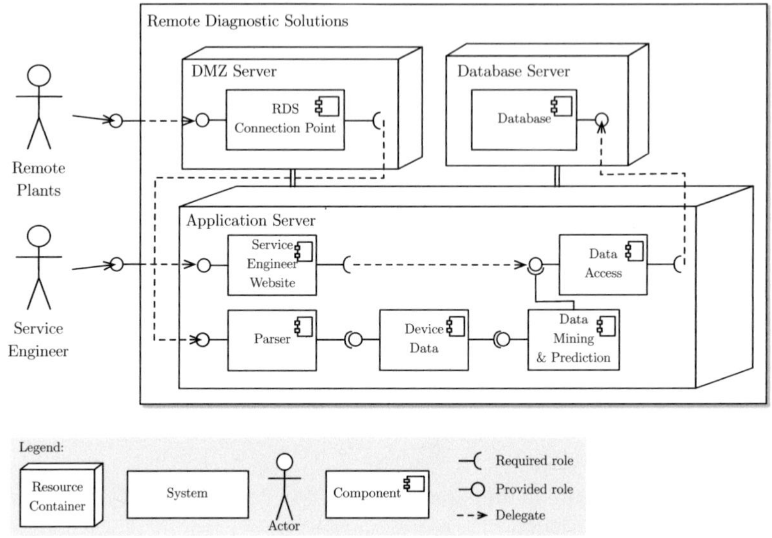

Figure 10.14.: System model of the Remote Diagnostic Solutions (after [BK16]).

use. The process remains semi-automatic, because the semantics of features are not modelled formally, but only represented in natural language.

10.6.2. Remote Diagnostic Solution

Remote Diagnostic Solutions (RDS) system represents a real-world system applied in real-world applications. We show how *CompARE* could be applied in real-world systems widely used in industry. The RDS system, developed by ABB, is used to collect, aggregate, and report status data of power plants and industrial plants.

The RDS periodically records status data of industrial plants and generates service reports for the early detection of sensors or other components that may soon fail. These data are visualized and can be reviewed by the service engineer. In addition to querying status reports, service engineers can also remotely control and configure various parts of the connected systems.

In addition to actions controlled by human actors, the RDS can carry out predefined actions independently.

The server-side system of the RDS consists of several million lines of C++ code. The source code itself is not publicly accessible, which is why the evaluation presented here is based on the PCM model from [Koz11; Goo+12] that abstracts from code. We show the system architecture of the RDS in Figure 10.14.

10.6.2.1. System Architecture

The abstraction of the RDS model for the case study described here comprises seven software components distributed on a 3-tier system. The 3-tier system is a classic division of frontend (DMZ server), application server and back end (database server). For reasons of isolation, the component that provides the access point for the connected remote plants is distributed on the DMZ server. From here, the collected sensor data is send to the `Database` component that is isolated on the database server via the processing units on the application server. Once the data has been received at the `RDSConnectionPoint` component, it is converted into a suitable data format for further processing in the `Parser`. The appropriately processed data is then separated in `DeviceData` according to connected systems, preprocessed and evaluated in the `DataMining&Prediction` component. In this component, predictions for possible imminent failures are also created. The processed data is then forwarded to the database system via the `DataAccess` component and stored using the `Database` component. In addition to the public interface for connecting to remote plants, the service engineer can also access the data that has already been saved using the interface of the `ServiceEngineerWebsite` component. Data access to the database is performed via the `DataAccess` component.

In addition to the static architecture, the model has performance annotations to describe the abstract behaviour. In addition, cost annotations are modelled, which are used, as with the BRS system, to analyse cost. We reuse the cost model from the BRS system for calculating the processor costs. Each server system has a CPU clock rate of 2000 processing units.

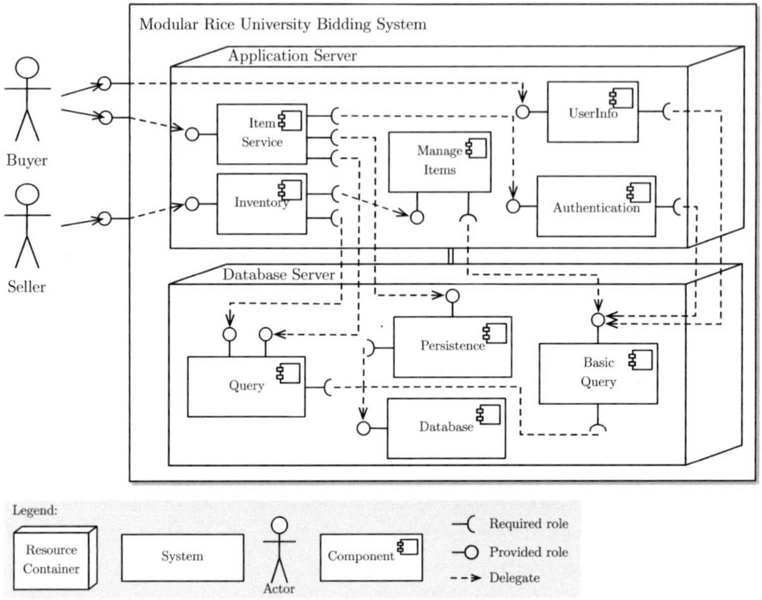

Figure 10.15.: System model of the Modular Rice University Bidding System (mRUBiS).

10.6.2.2. Architecture Candidates

As with the previous model, the BRS model, different degrees of freedom are possible: the components shown in section 10.6.2.1 can again be distributed differently among hardware resources. A total of five server systems are available. For each server the CPU clock rate can be adjusted again. The interval [0.5; 2] as factor is possible. In addition, the feature inclusion degree of freedom can be selected with the aforementioned sub degrees. Once again, any features of the two feature completions can be applied to different parts of the system.

10.6.3. Modular Rice University Bidding System

Modular Rice University Bidding System (mRUBiS) is a community case study [Vog18; AM] of HU-Berlin and implements an auction platform based on eBay.com. The case study was originally developed to evaluate design patterns of applications and the performance scalability of application servers. mRUBiS is a component-based system and realized with Enterprise Java Beans 3 (EJB3). Internally mRUBiS uses data entities modelled in EMF. The GlassFish Application Server is used as execution environment.

mRUBiS implements a marketplace where traders can sell goods or offer them at auction. The system supports several shops which can offer their own goods for sale.

The system provides numerous external services for user access: Sellers can post new items on the platform and check their inventory. Buyers can register on the platform, as well as log in, browse items in different categories, bid on items and submit reviews.

For our evaluation, we use as usage scenario a mix of get seller info, place bids and get bid history.

10.6.3.1. Software Architecture

mRUBiS internally consists of 16 components and 16 interfaces. In our model, we have chosen a two servers hardware configuration to deploy the components. The system comprises an application server and a database server. The mRUBiS repository model comprises nine software components. Figure 10.15 depicts the system architecture of mRUBiS.

Buyers use the `ItemService` component to search for items or place bids. This first authenticates the users by the `Authentication` components and then forwards requests to the `Database` components via the `Query` component according to the desired service. If the user submits a bid, the bid is finally stored in the database using the `Persistence` component. In addition, the buyer can edit user information using the `UserInfo` component. For this purpose, `UserInfo` accesses `BasicQuery` and persists the changes in `Database`. The `Authentication` component collects the necessary data using the `BasicQuery` component.

Sellers can use the `Inventory` component to add new items and check their inventory. New items are forwarded to and processed in the database using the `Query` component. If the inventory should be checked, this is done using the `ManageItems` component. This performs a pre-processing of the requests, forwards the requests to the `BasicQuery` component and finally forwards it to the `Database`.

The architecture model of mRUBiS has performance annotations and cost annotations. For the performance evaluation, we modelled the usage scenario *perform bid* as follows: If a bid should be submitted, seller information is first retrieved using operation `getUserInfo` of the component `UserInfo`. This request is delegated to the operation `findUserById` of the component `BasicQuery`. Subsequently, operation `getItemBidHistory` of the component `BidServiceBean` retrieves the bids already submitted (history). The operation `findItemBidHistory` of the component `Query` performs an extended request. Before the bid is submitted, the identity of the user is first checked with the operation `authenticate` of the component `Authentication`. This accesses the `BasicQuery` component and retrieves the user data with the operation `findUserByNickname`. Then the availability of the item is checked using operations `checkAvailabilityOfItem` and `retrieveAvailabilityOfItem`. Finally the bid is placed by calling `persistBid` of component `Persistence` and saved in the `Database`.

The mRUBiS cost model again models the cost function for processors, as previously described in Section 10.6.1. In addition, the software components are annotated with initial costs.

10.6.3.2. Architecture Candidates

Our mRUBiS architecture model supports several degrees of freedom: Five server systems are available on which components can be distributed to distribute the load. Each server system has a CPU clock rate of 200 processing units. This clock rate can be adjusted during optimization using the [0.5; 2] interval as a factor. As with the previous case study systems, mRUBiS can be extended with different features of the feature completions. Furthermore, the feature inclusion degree of freedom is applicable together with its sub-degrees of freedom.

11. Evaluation Part I: Including Features into Software Architectures

This chapter describes scenarios for the evaluation of the research questions described in Section 10.2.1. All evaluation scenarios use the models described in the previous sections, namely the models of the subsystems and the related feature completions (see Section 10.4). These features are included into the models of the base systems (see Section 10.6). The scenarios are used to demonstrate how *CompARE* can be used to evaluate design decisions such as including features on desired positions in a base system and support software architects at product selection and requirements prioritization. In the scenarios, we use the degrees of freedom we introduced in the previous part for the respective base system in addition. We use the systematic process *CompARE* and its implementation in the PerOpteryx tool chain (see Section 10.3) to evaluate our research questions. Several scenarios of this chapter and models are based on the Master's thesis of Maximilian Eckert [Eck18], supervised by me.

11.1. Preliminaries

The scenarios are part of the development process of the mRUBiS software system, in which several software components have already been implemented to fulfil several (functional) requirements. For each scenario we have carried out 100 iterations with 20 candidates each. More than 1000 valid architecture candidates have been evaluated for most of the scenarios. For all the following scenarios we have used Franks' LQN Solver [Fra+09] to calculate the response time. The convergence value is 0.001 and the iteration limit is 20.

11.1.1. Requirements

All scenarios are within the following main requirements:

- Statistical data shall be systematically recorded for the submission of bids on the trading platform.
- Statistical data shall be systematically recorded for all actions carried out regarding requests when searching for items in the stores.
- Statistical data shall be systematically recorded on all database enquiries arising from the management of offered items on the trading platform.
- The existing SQL database shall be used to log data.
- The storage of the data shall take place in a given pattern-based format.

The requirements mentioned serve as basic requirements. Their feasibility and how to achieve them is to be evaluated in the scenarios. If the evaluated quality attributes lie outside these requirement limits, requirements may have to be prioritized.

We use the previously modelled degrees of freedom regarding the placement of components and hardware configuration from Section 10.6.3.1. The use of our feature completion Logging is the best suitable for the aforementioned requirements.

Two necessary features can be derived from these requirements, namely *SQLDatabaseLogging* and *PatternFormatting*. We choose the abstract control flow extension mechanism for extending the mRUBiS base architecture model.

Listing 11.1: PointCut definition for the scenarios

```
pointCut {
  PointCut allPersistBidCalls {
    placementStrategy ExternalCallPlacementStrategy {
      matchingSignature persistBid
    }
  },
  PointCut allActionsInQuery {
    placementStrategy InternalActionPlacementStrategy {
      forAllInternalActionsIn Query
    }
  },
  PointCut allActionsInBasicQuery {
    placementStrategy InternalActionPlacementStrategy {
      forAllInternalActionsIn BasicQuery
    }
  },
  PointCut allControlFlowsInBasicQuery {
    placementStrategy ControlFlowPlacementStrategy {
      forAllControlFlowsIn BasicQuery
    }
  }
}
```

11.1.2. Pointcuts

As the aforementioned requirements as a basis, we use the pointcut definitions from [Eck18] to define the scenario. The pointcuts are shown in Listing 11.1.

In summary, the four pointcuts describe which entities of the abstract behaviour of our components (covering the requirements) should be extended. The extended feature itself will be defined later. Furthermore, the placement strategy (see Section 7.2.3 and Section 8.1) is determined, as well as whether the placement should be performed on a signature or on a control structure. The pointcut *allPersistBidCalls* extends the signature *persistBid* by features (still to be defined). The pointcut *allActionsInQuery* extends all internal actions in the `Query` component by (still to be defined) features. The pointcut *allActionsInBasicQuery* extends all internal actions of the `BasicQuery` component. The fourth pointcut, *allControlFlowsInBasicQuery*, extends all control flows contained in the `BasicQuery` component with a (still to be defined) feature.

11.1.3. Models

For all following scenarios, we use the following models and mechanisms:

As base architecture model we use the mRUBiS software architecture model from Section 10.6.3.1. Additionally, we use the feature completion models Logging and the related subsystem solution models of both log4j variants from Section 10.4.1.1 and 10.4.1.2. For the definition of the weaving positions, we use the method of the abstract control flow extension. We use the extension by the abstract control flow, since internal actions and control flow elements within components must be extended to evaluate the requirements.

11.2. Preliminary Scenario: Effects on quality attributes

Using additional functionality usually influences the resulting quality attributes of the overall system. When we add new source code, the system load usually increases, potential new security flaws being created, or potential new errors arise that affect the reliability of the system. However, it is often unclear at design time how positive or negative a certain feature affects the relevant quality attributes. If the effect of the negative impact remains within acceptable limits, stakeholders could adhere to the implementation of the feature.

This scenario should show how design decisions regarding feature selection can in general affect the quality attribute's response time and cost.

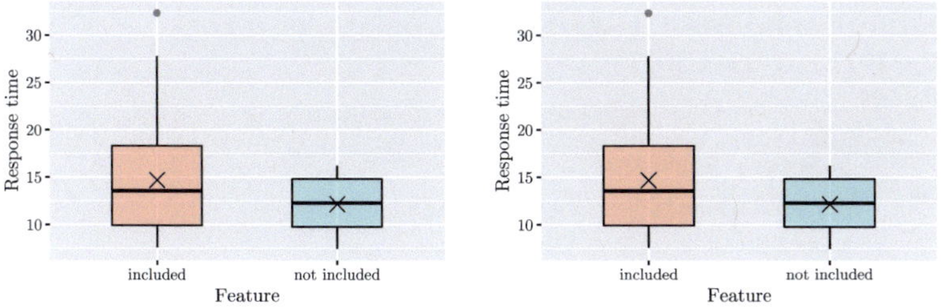

(a) Box plot showing the response times of all evaluated candidates

(b) Box plot showing the response times of the Pareto-optimal candidates

Figure 11.1.: Box plots showing the relationship between including SQL database logging and pattern formatting in mRUBiS and the resulting response time for the service of the overall system. Cross mark indicates the arithmetic mean.

Design questions

This evaluation scenario considers whether the integration of additional functionality by features can influence quality attributes of the overall system, such as response time or system costs. Therefore, the following design question can be derived:

- What costs in terms of response time must stakeholders expect if they want to record data to an SQL database and with pattern formatting of all internal actions of the `Query` component, both before and after the actual internal actions?
- What are the Pareto-optimal candidates considering response time and costs for recording to an SQL database and with pattern formatting of all internal actions of the `Query` component, both before and after the actual internal actions?

Models

The model presented in Listing 11.2 refines the previously defined pointcut. From Logging, the *SQLDatabaseLogging* and *PatternFormatting* features

Listing 11.2: Advice for the preliminary scenario.

```
featureCompletion Logging({SQLDatabaseLogging},
{PatternFormatting})
advice {
    Advice {
        appears AROUND
        pointCut allActionsInQuery
        placementPolicy OPTIONAL
    }
}
```

should be integrated into all internal actions of the `Query` component (pointcut *allActionsInQuery*). Data should always be written before and after the call of the internal actions (appears AROUND). In addition, both the presence of the feature and the absence of the feature in the base architecture are evaluated (placementPolicy OPTIONAL).

Evaluation results & Discussion

For the evaluation of the scenario, PerOpteryx automatically generates a total of 1010 architecture candidates. The evaluation results in a total of 102 Pareto-optimal architecture candidates.

Figure 11.1 shows box plots of the response time behaviour of the overall system, both results with and without the feature. When considering all candidates and the Pareto-optimal candidates, we can conclude the following: If features are included, the response time of the overall system increases. For all evaluated candidates, the median is 13.25 ms for candidates with included features versus 12.64 ms to the candidates without additional features. The arithmetic mean is 14.60 ms versus 13.32 ms. For the Pareto-optimal candidates, the median is 13.56 ms and 12.28 ms respectively. The arithmetic mean is 14.68 ms versus 12.15[1] ms. Overall, analyzing the evaluated Pareto-optimal candidates we can see 20.82 % higher response

[1] We have normalized the arithmetic mean and median of candidates without features to the cost values of candidates with included features so that value pairs are better comparable. If there are value gaps, these were approximated linearly.

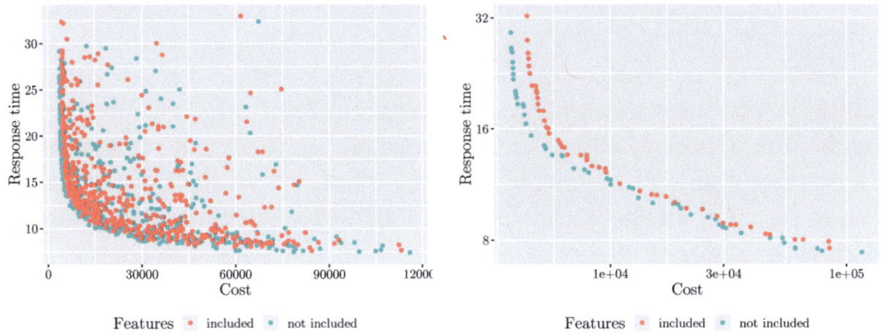

(a) All evaluated and valid candidates (#1010) **(b)** Pareto-optimal candidates (#102)

Figure 11.2.: All evaluated, valid, and Pareto-optimal candidates (preliminary scenario) of the response time and cost evaluation of presence and absence of features.

times for the candidates including the additional features. This value should not be understood as that generally solutions with integrated features increase the response time for 20.82 %. Rather, the results are only valid for our evaluated candidates and should only give an idea for higher response times when including features considering our scenario.

Figure 11.2 shows the plots of all evaluated candidates, each with presence and absence of features, as well as the Pareto-optimal candidates of both options. In the case of candidates with lower costs, we can see the response time is higher at constant costs. With increasing costs, the two curves approach each other. If features are included, the response time and costs are higher compared to candidates without additional features.

As a result of the evaluation, we deduced that if additional features are included in the base architecture, stakeholders can either expect higher monetary costs or higher response times. Furthermore, the lower cost barrier for architecture candidates with included features is 16.81 % higher compared to architecture candidates without additional features. If the cost barrier becomes too high, requirements may need to be re-prioritized or a different set of features may need to be selected and re-evaluated.

11.3. Scenario I: Evaluation of different realizations

In the first scenario, we evaluate the different realizations of the requirements. The required features remain constant, i.e. there is no prioritization of requirements with regard to features. Thus, we do not limit the selection of possible solutions. According to Table 10.4, both solutions log4jv1 and log4jv2 support all required features, which is why both solutions are considered in the optimization.

log4jv2 comes with a re-engineered code structure, therefore it tends to be better maintainable, provides more features, which can be easier adapted and replaces log4jv1, which should have a positive effect on the life cycle of the system.

The scenario shows how the mentioned properties can be set in relation to the resulting quality attributes if required.

Design questions

In this evaluation scenario, we focus on the evaluation of both solutions of the logging FC. In addition, we secondarily evaluate the placement of the components and the resource configuration. The main design questions of the scenario can be formulated as follows:

- Which of the available solutions is optimal for the selected placements in terms of the quality attributes performance and cost?
- How do both solutions differ in terms of the quality attributes response time and costs of the overall system?

Models

To complete the previously defined pointcuts, we complement them by the advices shown in Listing 11.3. In summary, the three advices define that the two features *SQLDatabaseLogging*, in combination with *PatternFormatting*. They are mandatory to be included (placementPolicy MANDATORY) to

Listing 11.3: Advices for scenario I.

```
featureCompletion Logging({SQLDatabaseLogging},
{PatternFormatting})
advice {
    Advice {
        appears BEFORE
        pointCut allPersistBidCalls
        placementPolicy MANDATORY
    },
    Advice {
        appears BEFORE
        pointCut allActionsInQuery
        placementPolicy MANDATORY
    },
    Advice {
        appears BEFORE
        pointCut allControlFlowsInBasicQuery
        placementPolicy MANDATORY
    }
}
```

the three of the four already defined pointcuts, namely *allPersistBidCalls*, *allActionsInQuery* and *allControlFlowsInBasicQuery*. Logging must be performed before (appears BEFORE) the calls of the services of the configured positions.

Evaluation results & Discussion

For the evaluation of the scenario, PerOpteryx automatically generates a total of 1010 architecture candidates. Figure 11.3a shows the scatter diagram of all evaluated architecture candidates, divided into response time, costs and evaluated solution, namely log4jv1 and log4jv2. The evaluation results in a total of 43 Pareto-optimal architecture candidates. All Pareto-optimal architecture candidates are shown graphically in Figure 11.3b.

The analysis of the Pareto-optimal candidates shows log4jv2, compared to log4jv1, seems to be cheaper in monetary costs. A cheaper price is bought by

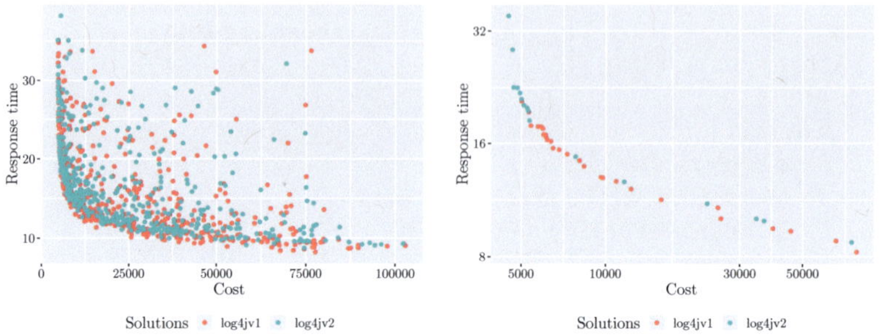

(a) All evaluated and valid candidates (#1010) **(b)** Pareto-optimal candidates (#43)

Figure 11.3.: All evaluated, valid, and Pareto-optimal candidates (scenario I) of the response time and cost evaluation of both logging solutions, namely log4jv1 and log4jv2.

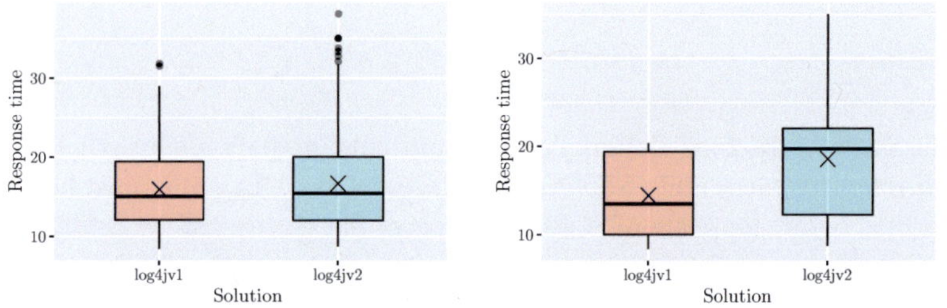

(a) Box plot showing the response times of all evaluated candidates **(b)** Box plot showing the response times of the Pareto-optimal candidates

Figure 11.4.: Box plots showing the relationship between the solution used in mRUBiS and the resulting response time for the service of the overall system. Cross mark indicates the arithmetic mean.

higher response times. This also becomes clear by reviewing all evaluated candidates. Candidates using log4jv2 tend to be more expensive and lead to weaker response times of the overall system. The box plots in Figure 11.4 also illustrates the overall higher level of response times to be expected when using log4jv2. For all evaluated candidates the median and arithmetic mean for mRUBiS with log4jv1 is at 15.03 ms, and 15.91 ms respective, while using log4jv2 results in 15.42 ms for the median and 16.64 for the arithmetic mean. The difference for the Pareto-optimal results is even higher. For log4jv1 the median is at 13.48 ms, while the arithmetic mean is at 14.42 ms. For log4jv2 the median is at 19.71 ms, while the arithmetic mean is at 18.56 ms.

The number of architecture candidates evaluated, however, is only an excerpt from all possible configurations, so that the analysed result cannot be generalized to all possible architecture candidates. Furthermore, additional architecture decisions (which have not been considered) could influence the results. However, the result can serve as an assessment of the tendency if the evaluated question should be used as a basis for further evaluation questions. For example, log4jv2 provides additional features that may be desirable in a later evaluation scenario. It might be useful to consider whether the increased response time later would be worth features that become important, or whether the older version with lower response times should later be used. If log4jv1 is used, architects should remark that technical debts may arise, which would later necessitate a refactoring leading to additional costs. This additional costs are not reflected in this analysis.

11.4. Scenario II: Using multiple inclusion

Usually, in component-based software architectures components are deployed once and can then be used by any parts of the system by delegating. If the degree of distribution of the individual components of the software system to many hardware resources increases, network connection runtimes can have negative effects on the response time of the services. In addition to the network load, bottlenecks of hardware on which this component was deployed can decrease the performance of the overall system. For these reasons, replication through multiple deployment can improve the response time of the system. On the other hand, additional deployments are usually associated with higher costs due to licence models.

The scenario presented here therefore examines when and to what extent multiple deployment of logging can help to improve the software quality.

Listing 11.4: Excerpt from behaviour description for scenario II.

```
multiple BehaviourInclusion behaviourIncl _ZZ {
    ...
}
```

Design questions

Replication of components can provide better load balancing across hardware resources [TT85]. If components are deployed and allocated multiple times, the load can potentially be better distributed across multiple systems. We therefore set the following new requirement for the base system:

> In the mRUBiS base system, the data logging requirements should be implemented such that the necessary functionalities can be used and deployed for each call exclusively.

From this new requirement we can derive the following design question for evaluation:

> How does multiple inclusion of Logging features influence the quality attributes response time and costs?

Models

For the evaluation of multiple inclusion, we use the same advices as in scenario 1. To use multiple inclusion, the placement description must be extended as shown in Listing 11.4. The keyword *multiple* before the corresponding behaviour description instructs the weaving mechanism to multiply the component instance of the components to be included and allocate them to resource containers.

Evaluation results & Discussion

For the evaluation of the scenario, PerOpteryx automatically generates a total of 1010 architecture candidates. Figure 11.5 shows the scatter diagram

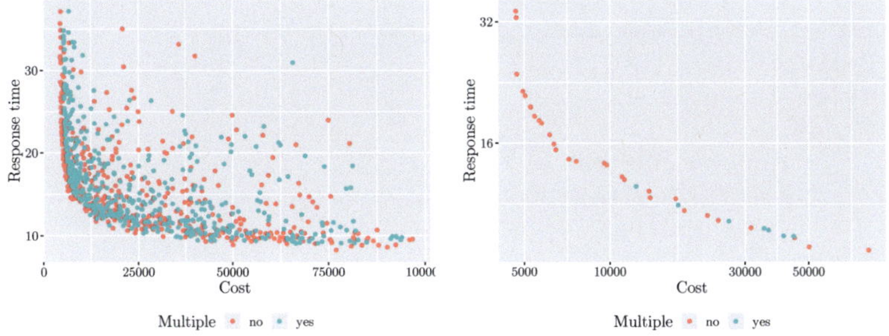

(a) All evaluated and valid candidates (#1010) **(b)** Pareto-optimal candidates (#36)

Figure 11.5.: All evaluated, valid, and Pareto-optimal candidates (scenario II) of the response time and cost evaluation of including a subsystem one time, while delegating all caller locations to the same components versus including a subsystem multiple time, having for each caller location an own subsystem instance.

of all evaluated architecture candidates, divided into response time, costs and evaluated solution, namely log4jv1 and log4jv2. The evaluation results in a total of 36 Pareto-optimal architecture candidates. The tendency of the resulting response times for the two options can be derived from the overview of all evaluated candidates: Cheaper candidates are more frequent in multiple delegation, while candidates with lower response times result in candidates with multiple inclusion. From the results we can conclude that architecture candidates with multiple inclusion result in higher costs than architecture candidates with multiple delegation. This finding is supported by the scatter plot of the Pareto-optimal architecture candidates. Using multiple, better response times can be expected. One reason might be the placement of the components to be better optimized, i.e. heavily loaded hardware can be disburdened by a lower load due to fewer amounts of calls, or overloaded network connections can be discharged by local deployment. This reduces the overall response time.

By this results, we can find if the architecture design focuses on the costs of the system, multiple *delegation* would be preferable. If resources are to be used more evenly and shorter response times of the service are required, multiple *instantiation* is the better choice.

Listing 11.5: Advice for scenario III.a.

```
featureCompletion Logging({SQLDatabaseLogging},
{PatternFormatting})
advice {
    Advice {
        appears AROUND
        pointCut allActionsInBasicQuery
        placementPolicy OPTIONAL
    },
    Advice {
        appears AROUND
        pointCut allPersistBidCalls
        placementPolicy OPTIONAL
    },
    Advice {
        appears AROUND
        pointCut allActionsInQuery
        placementPolicy OPTIONAL
    }
}
```

11.5. Scenario III.a: Annotating features at different components

Logging solutions, in particular, implement a cross-cutting concern that can be applied anywhere in the system (e.g. to record data). The decision whether data of a component should be recorded results from the requirements. However, the resulting quality attributes can have retroactive effects on the requirement. This is relevant, for example, if the specification of a functional requirement describes to record data from a particular component, but the implementation of these requirements would have negative effects on certain quality attributes, so that both requirements cannot be implemented at the same time. In this case, requirements must be prioritized. If a certain limit of the quality attribute response time, for example, must not be exceeded, either the functional requirement must be changed or the solution of the requirement must be changed, for example by a solution with less performance overhead.

This scenario shows how to analyse the impact on the response time and cost quality attributes when features are added to different components.

Design questions

Different partial functionalities of systems are called with different frequency. The reason is these partial functionalities are called by the system with varying frequency, for instance due to loops. If, for example, data should be filtered, how often the filter function is called depends on the routine that calls the filter. In contrast, a sort function, for example, can return the sorted result in one single run. The difference in this complexity has effects when extending these functions with additional features, such as with features from the Logging subsystem. If a particularly frequently called functionality is annotated, the new functionality is also called correspondingly often. To demonstrate effects coming from the weaving positions in the base architecture, we annotate features to three different annotation positions in mRUBiS. The positions are defined by the pointcuts *allActionsInBasicQuery*, *allPersistBidCalls*, and *allActionsInQuery*. The following design questions can therefore be defined:

- Which architecture candidate are Pareto-optimal with regard to the quality attributes response time and costs when extending the internal actions of the `BasicQuery` component in the base system before and after executing its internal actions?
- Which of the architecture candidates are Pareto-optimal with regard to the quality attributes response time and costs when extending *persisting bids* in the base system before and after executing the bid?
- Which of the architecture candidates are Pareto-optimal with regard to the quality attributes response time and costs when extending the internal actions of the `Query` component in the base system before and after executing the internal action?

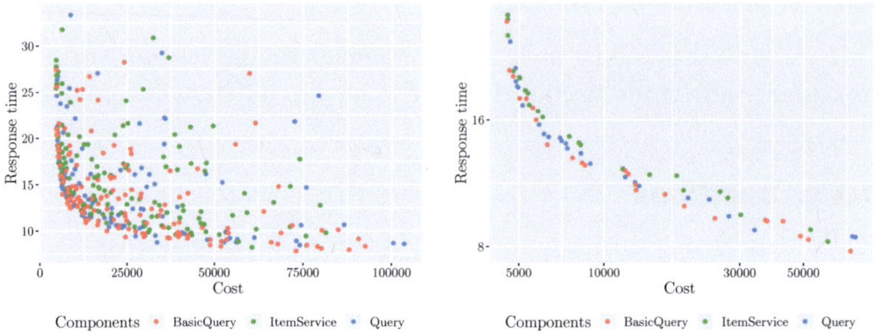

(a) All evaluated and valid candidates (#388) **(b)** Pareto-optimal candidates (#72)

Figure 11.6.: All evaluated, valid, and Pareto-optimal candidates (scenario III.a) of the response time and cost evaluation of different components as inclusion targets for the selected features.

- Which architecture candidates are globally Pareto-optimal with regard to the quality attributes response time and costs across all three positions in the base system?

Models

The advices shown in Listing 11.5 complete the pointcut definition for evaluating the design questions. Both features are used to extend the three pointcuts *allActionsInBasicQuery*, *allPersistBidCalls*, and *allActionsInQuery*, each enclosing the construct (appears AROUND) and each with optional placement policy (placementPolicy OPTIONAL).

Evaluation results & Discussion

For the evaluation of the scenario, PerOpteryx automatically generates 388 valid architecture candidates. Figure 11.6 shows the scatter diagram of all evaluated architecture candidates, divided into response time, costs and evaluated solution, namely log4jv1 and log4jv2. The evaluation results in a total of 72 Pareto-optimal architecture candidates.

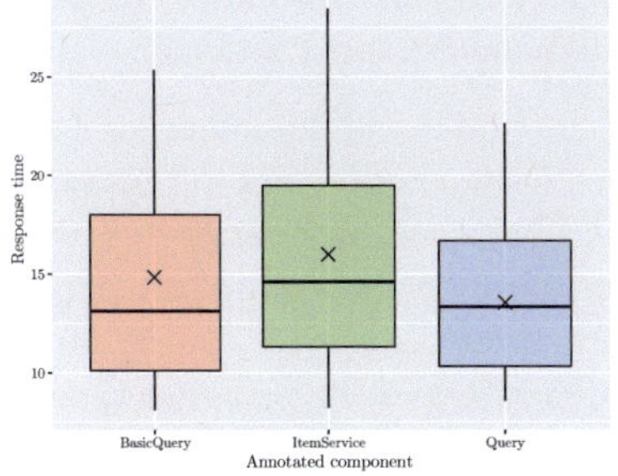

(a) Box plot showing response times of the three annotation positions in mRUBiS

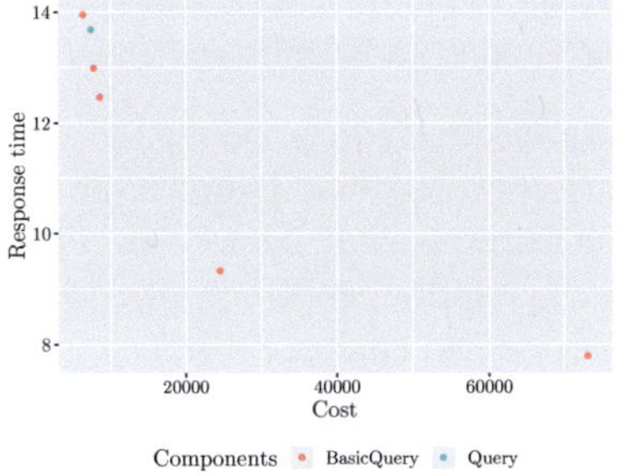

(b) Scatter plot showing the quality attributes response time and cost of Pareto-optimal architecture candidates across all annotation positions.

Figure 11.7.: Box plot and scatter plot for scenario III.a. Cross mark in the box blot indicates the arithmetic mean.

The scatter diagram in Figure 11.6 shows the three groups resulting from the annotation at the three positions in the mRUBiS architecture. The highest overall response times result from the annotation of the `ItemService` component, which executes the bids of the users. This is followed by the annotation of the internal actions of the `Query` component, while the extension of the `BasicQuery` component results in the lowest response times. This result is also supported by the box plots of the response times in Figure 11.7a. Annotating `BasicQuery` results in an response time of 13.13 ms (median), while annotating `ItemService` results in 14.61 ms), and annotating `Query` results in 13.34 ms. Again, we approximated missing values for `BasicQuery`, and `Query`, while `ItemService` was used as the base line. The results can be explained by the internal complexity of the individual services of the components. While `ItemService` is internally composed of several internal actions, the `BasicQuery` component (which implements the simplest logic) contains only one single internal action. The response times of `Query` is between annotating and `ItemService`.

Considering the Pareto-optimal results across all positions, it results that the use of `ItemService` does not result in Pareto-optimal architecture candidate. The findings are shown graphically in Figure 11.7b. The results are dominated by `BasicQuery`, followed by the annotation of the `Query` component (with only one Pareto-optimal architecture candidate).

As a result, it can be derived that, depending on the requirement for necessary recorded data that must be collected from components, differences in the response time behaviour of the overall system can be expected. Once again, requirements may have to be prioritized if response time is a particularly critical attribute that is more important for the project than recording data at a certain position in the software system. If the response time behaviour is relevant at most, an annotation of the `BasicQuery` component should be preferred. However, it should be noted that the trade-off between relevance of the collected data and effects on response time should be considered separately.

11.6. Scenario III.b: Increasing the number of annotated components

Similar to the previous scenario of analysing the impact of features on individual components on the quality attributes of the system, this scenario considers the impact of the number of components annotated with features. If stakeholders want to collect as many data as possible, functional requirements can specify data should be recorded on as many positions in the system as possible. As before, such a requirement may violate the limits of acceptable quality properties. In particular, if, for example, data should be recorded to a central database system, this can overload hardware and thus slow down the overall system.

The scenario presented here therefore shows how the influence can be evaluated of the collection of data with varying number of annotated positions in the system.

Design questions

In the previous scenario, we evaluated different annotation positions in the mRUBiS system. If as many data as possible should be collected, the relevant question is how many components can be annotated so that the quality attribute requirements can still be met. Therefore, we can define the following design questions:

- How does the annotation of several positions at the same time influence the quality attributes response time and costs?
- Which architecture candidates are Pareto-optimal in terms of quality attributes response time and cost for annotating one position, two positions, and three positions in the mRUBiS system?

Models

For this scenario, we use the models from scenario III.a again.

Evaluation results & Discussion

For the evaluation of the scenario, PerOpteryx automatically generates a total of 622 architecture candidates. Figure 11.8a shows the scatter diagram of all evaluated architecture candidates, divided into response time, costs and evaluated solution, namely log4jv1 and log4jv2. The evaluation results in a total of 199 Pareto-optimal architecture candidates. Figure 11.8 shows the Pareto-optimal results of the three groups. We can identify three corridors approximated using the LOESS[2] method: while a single annotation usually produces slightly cheaper and more efficient candidates in terms of response time, the candidates with three annotations rank behind for both quality attributes. As expected, annotating two services in mRUBiS results in values in between 1 and 3 annotations at the same time.

Annotating three times compared to one time results in 16.92 % on average (22.16 % median) higher response times compared to one time annotation[3]. Annotating two times results in 4.96 % higher response times on average (7.27 % median). If the focus is on better response times and lower costs,

[2] a non-parametric, local regression method

[3] We have normalized the arithmetic mean and median of candidates with different numbers of annotations to the cost values of candidates with 1x annotations so that value pairs are better comparable. If there are value gaps, these were approximated linearly.

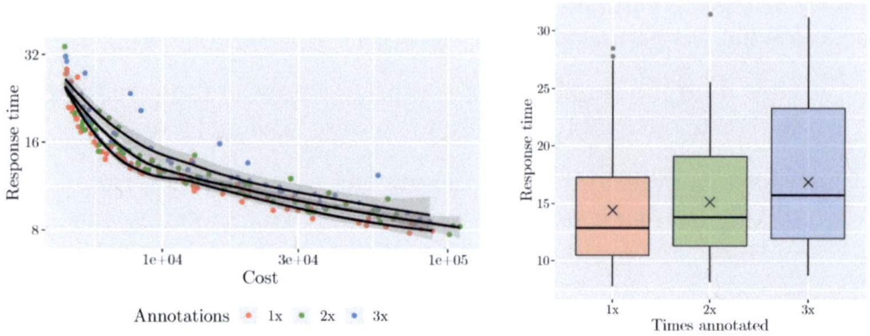

(a) Pareto-optimal candidates (#199) showing response time and costs (scenario III.b) when annotating different numbers of components.

(b) Box plots showing the distributions of the differences in response times when annotating components

Figure 11.8.: Scatter plot and box plot showing the results of scenario III.b

then stakeholders would have to lower the requirements for amount of data collection.

11.7. Scenario IV: Annotating the abstract control flow

As described in Section 8.5.2, internal actions or control structures such as branches or loops can be extended by *CompARE*. This can be useful, for example, to record data when calling a certain branch or for all iterations of a loop call. Especially when annotating loops, results in many logging calls. This can result in negative effects on quality attributes such as performance.

This evaluation scenario shows how the effects of feature annotations on different elements of the abstract behaviour of components can affect quality attributes and how these effects can be analysed.

Design questions

PerOpteryx can annotate different parts of the (abstract) control flow. However, the annotation within a loop has a different complexity compared to the annotation of an internal action, since a loop usually results in many calls. For recording data, for example, this means that increased response times are to be expected when annotating loops. To evaluate this in advance, we define the following design questions:

- What effects on the quality attributes response time and costs are to be expected if, in addition to recording the data of the call when bidding, data on all internal actions of the `BasicQuery` component should be recorded (appearance before)?
- What effects can be expected on the quality attributes response time and costs if, in addition to recording the data of the call at bidding, data on all control flow elements of the `BasicQuery` component should be recorded (appearance around)?

Models

Listing 11.6 shows the advices required for scenario IV. Before (appears BEFORE) the actual call of the bid submission (i.e. the pointcut *allPersistBidCalls*) the two features are included mandatory (placementPolicy MANDATORY). Both features are later contained in every architecture candidates. The two features are included according to the model at the two pointcuts *allActionsInBasicQuery* and *allControlFlowsInBasicQuery*, each enclosing the statement (appears AROUND). It should be included optionally (placementPolicy OPTIONAL).

Evaluation results & Discussion

For the evaluation of the scenario, PerOpteryx automatically generates 758 valid architecture candidates. Figure 11.9 shows the scatter diagram of all evaluated architecture candidates, divided into response time, costs and evaluated solution, namely log4jv1 and log4jv2. The evaluation results in a total of 112 Pareto-optimal architecture candidates.

Listing 11.6: Advices for scenario IV.

```
featureCompletion Logging({SQLDatabaseLogging},
{PatternFormatting})
advice {
    Advice {
        appears BEFORE
        pointCut allPersistBidCalls
        placementPolicy MANDATORY
    },
    Advice {
        appears AROUND
        pointCut allActionsInBasicQuery
        placementPolicy OPTIONAL
    },
    Advice {
        appears AROUND
        pointCut allControlFlowsInBasicQuery
        placementPolicy OPTIONAL
    }
}
```

The evaluation of all evaluated architecture candidates already shows the trend for the highest response times when recording data on bids in combination with recording at all control structures to be considered in the scenario. As expected, recording only the bids is in the lead in terms of low response times and costs. The Pareto-optimal results also show a similar picture. While the annotation of internal actions has only small additional performance and cost overhead, the annotation of all control structures can be expected to be considerably more complex. Here, the trade-off to be taken becomes particularly clear: if all control structures should be annotated to receive the largest amount of data, higher response times must be accepted compared to the annotations of bids and internal actions only.

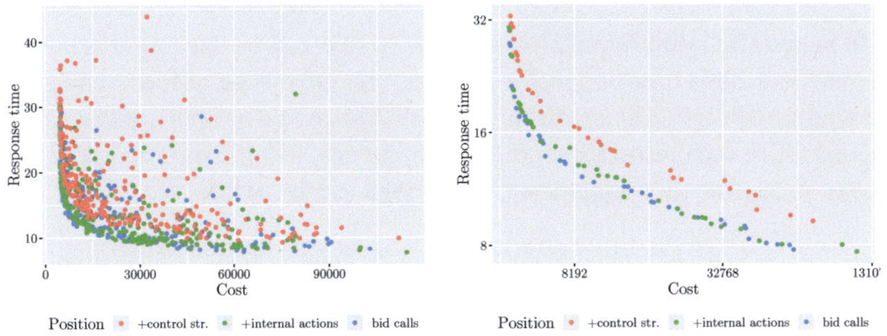

(a) All evaluated and valid candidates (#758)

(b) Pareto-optimal candidates (#112)

Figure 11.9.: All evaluated, valid, and Pareto-optimal candidates (scenario IV) of the response time and cost evaluation of different placement strategies in the abstract control flow of software components, namely bid calls only, bid calls and control structures on basic query in addition, and bid calls and internal actions of basic query in addition.

11.8. Scenario V: Evaluation of feature alternatives with fixed features set

The Logging subsystem provides different options for formatting the output. For example, the output can be formatted according to a certain pattern or the output can be formatted as XML or JSON. Processing data and output into the respective output format is realized by different source code, thus differs in complexity and reliability and therefore leads to differences in the resulting quality attributes of the overall system, as for example the response time of the service. One of the selected features must always be supported by the evaluated architecture candidates. Thus, it can be chosen afterwards which feature from the selected alternatives in the software system would be optimal with regard to the relevant quality attributes.

This scenario shows the analysis of the effects of different features on the quality attributes response time and cost of the overall system, which are still to be understood as alternatives to each other at design time.

Design questions

There are often different features available that can be used as alternatives because of their functional similarity, such as the type of formatting. For example, formatting as a pattern, JSON, or XML could be open for discussion. The quality attributes, for example, can be decisive for the final selection. From these, the following design questions can be defined:

- Which of the three alternative features *PatternFormatting*, *JSONFormatting*, and *XMLFormatting* result in Pareto-optimal software architectures in terms of response time and cost of recording data at bidding (before), at all internal actions in query (appearance before), at all internal actions in `Query` (appearance around), and at all control flow elements in `BasicQuery` (appearance around) in the mRUBiS system?
- How do the feature alternatives differ in response time and cost at the before defined positions in mBUBiS?

Models

The advices from Listing 11.7 define the modelled requirements for the design questions. The *FileLogging* feature will be included mandatory, while the feature group will have freedom to choose between the formatting features, namely *PatternFormatting*, *XMLFormatting*, and *JSONFormatting*. However, one of the three formatting options must always be selected.

The advice definition for the four pointcuts is to be included mandatory (placementPolicy MANDATORY) for all feature groups (although there are still variation options for formatting within the three options). Pointcuts *allPersistBidCalls* and *allActionsInQuery* each extend before the call (appears BEFORE), while *allActionsInBasicQuery* and *allControlFlowsInBasicQuery* each enclose the call (appears AROUND).

Listing 11.7: Placement description for scenario V.

```
featureCompletion Logging({FileLogging},
   {PatternFormatting ,XMLFormatting ,JSONFormatting}
)
advice {
   Advice {
      appears BEFORE
      pointCut allPersistBidCalls
      placementPolicy MANDATORY
   },
   Advice {
      appears BEFORE
      pointCut allActionsInQuery
      placementPolicy MANDATORY
   },
   Advice {
      appears AROUND
      pointCut allActionsInBasicQuery
      placementPolicy MANDATORY
   },
   Advice {
      appears AROUND
      pointCut allControlFlowsInBasicQuery
      placementPolicy MANDATORY
   }
}
```

Evaluation results & Discussion

For the evaluation of the scenario, PerOpteryx automatically generates 986 valid architecture candidates. Figure 11.10 shows the scatter diagram of all evaluated architecture candidates, divided into response time, costs and evaluated solution, namely log4jv1 and log4jv2. The evaluation results in a total of 159 Pareto-optimal architecture candidates.

When comparing the quality attributes by using the different features in mRUBiS, we find response times and costs slightly differ from each other. This result is supported by the estimation of the three result corridors using

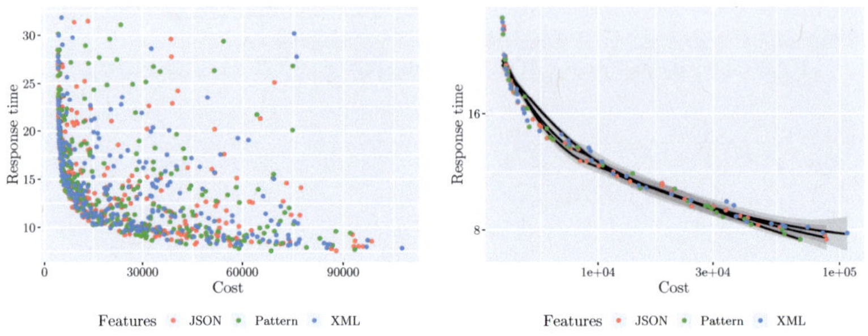

(a) All evaluated and valid candidates (#986)

(b) Pareto-optimal candidates (#159)

Figure 11.10.: All evaluated, valid, and Pareto-optimal candidates (scenario V) of the response time and cost evaluation of different layouting formats of the logging solutions regarding JSON, Pattern, and XML formatting.

the LOESS method. Only the architecture candidates with lower response times show the trend *PatternFormatting* works slightly faster than JSON, followed by XML formatting. Architecture candidates with lower costs and higher response times show low differences. This can be explained because formatting data cause comparatively low effort in comparison to the overall logging process. In general, however, the procedure can be used to evaluate different features that are available as alternatives against each other. Further evaluation examples could be sorting of data such as bubble sort, insertions sort or quick sort implementations. Depending on the application and pre-sorting of data, different results in terms of response time could be expected.

11.9. Scenario VI: Evaluation of feature alternatives considering optional features

Design decisions could open for discussion in early stages of the design process. For example, the decision to use a particular feature of the Logging subsystem may depend on further factors. Further factors may include the resulting quality attributes using one or more features. For example, if a feature reduces a certain quality attribute too much, requirements might be re-prioritized. Analysis with optional features is therefore important because not all products implement all features (if desired features are not contained in the set of core features). The more design decisions have not yet been defined in advance (like configuring features to be optional), the better solutions can be found.

This scenario therefore shows the analysis of optional design decisions to find trade-off decisions between features.

Design questions

Different solution support different features. In the case of Logger, log4jv2 supports writing to a NoSQL database, while log4jv1 does not support this feature. However, if software architects decide in advance NoSQL should be supported, they exclude all architecture candidates using log4jv1. An exclusion of this solution also excludes a lot of potentially better candidates (we remember that log4jv1 can have potentially lower resource requirements). Thus, if the design decision is not fixed yet, it may be useful to select certain features as optional, so that more solutions can be evaluated even if they do not support several features. Then, depending on the results of the quality features and requirements can be re-prioritized. Basing on this, the following design questions can be defined:

- Which of the three features *FileLogging*, *SQLDatabaseLogging* and *NoSQLDatabaseLogging* provides globally Pareto-optimal architecture candidates regarding the quality attributes response time and costs for recording data at bidding (appearance before), recording data at all internal actions in `Query` (appearance before), recording data at all internal actions in `Query` (appearance around), and recording data at all control flow elements in `BasicQuery` (appearance around) in the mRUBiS system?
- Which architecture candidates are Pareto-optimal according to the use of the feature alternatives with regard to the quality attributes response time and cost?

Listing 11.8: Placement description and advices for scenario VI.

```
featureCompletion Logging(
{FileAppending ,SQLAppending ,
optional NoSQLAppending}, {PatternFormatting}
)
```

- Which subsystem solution is Pareto-optimal within one of the three features when using them at the 4 locations in the mRUBiS system?

Models

Listing 11.8 shows the models for the evaluation of the design questions. Scenario VI is related to scenario V. However, here, one of the features is configured as optional feature. *FileAppending*, *SQLAppending*, and *Pattern-Formatting* are mandatory features, while *NoSQLAppending* is an optional feature. The advice definitions remain the same and are reused from scenario V.

Evaluation results & Discussion

For the evaluation of the scenario, PerOpteryx automatically generates 1009 valid architecture candidates. Figure 11.11 shows the scatter diagram of all evaluated architecture candidates, divided into response time, costs and evaluated solution, namely log4jv1 and log4jv2. The evaluation results in a total of 114 Pareto-optimal architecture candidates.

In the context of the four inclusion positions in the mRUBiS architecture, write operations of the recorded log data to a file can be performed with the lowest response times. Writing to a NoSQL database is slightly faster than writing to an SQL database system. The slowest configuration in our simulation is writing data into an SQL database system. When writing to the database systems, we assume the standard configuration of the NoSQL database system MongoDB (version 3.4.10) and the standard configuration of the MySQL (version 5.7.20) database system. If the hardware and configuration of the file system and the database systems is different, the expected

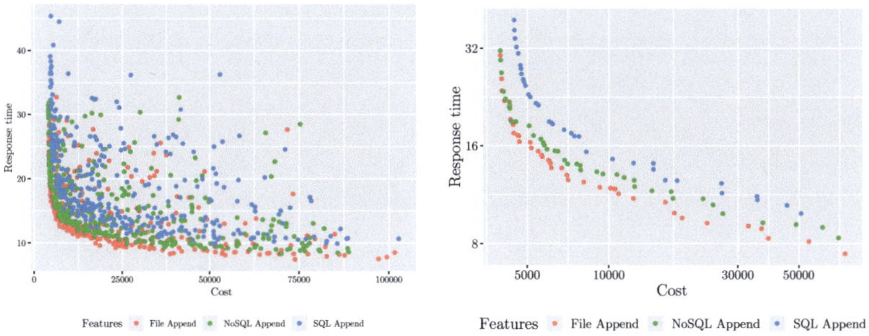

(a) All evaluated and valid candidates (#1009) **(b)** Pareto-optimal candidates (#114)

Figure 11.11.: All evaluated, valid, and Pareto-optimal candidates (scenario VI) of the response time and cost evaluation of different layouting formats of the logging solutions regarding the features FileAppending, NoSQLAppending, and SQLAppending. NoSQLAppending was set to be an optional feature.

values may differ from the values shown here. However, the evaluation shows different features of Logging can result in different results of quality attributes of the overall system.

Figure 11.12 shows a comparison of the response times and costs of the Pareto-optimal architecture candidates when using the *FileAppending* and *SQLAppending* features as alternatives. The Pareto-optimal architecture candidates of the two features are grouped according to the two subsystem solutions log4jv1 and log4jv2. While *FileAppending* can be implemented from both systems with similar response times and costs, there are significant differences in *SQLAppending*. If log4jv1 is used, lower response times can be achieved in the overall system. *NoSQLAppending* is only implemented from log4jv2. If *NoSQLAppending* must be used, the trade-off between using the feature, to response times and costs has to be made.

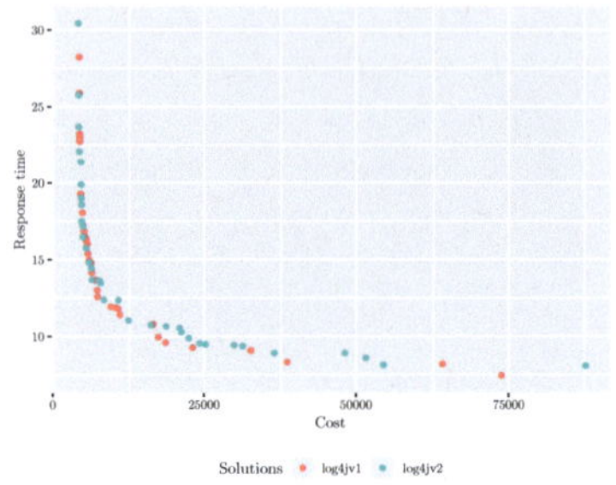

(a) Pareto-optimal candidates comparing response times and cost of file appending using different solutions

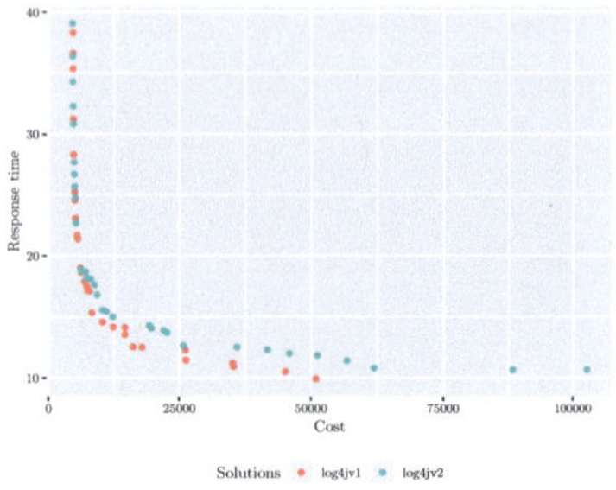

(b) Pareto-optimal candidates comparing response times and cost of sql appending using different solutions

Figure 11.12.: Comparison of both features *FileAppending* and *SQLAppending* grouped by both logging solutions log4jv1 and log4jv2.

11.10. Accuracy of the Optimization

At model level, including features at desired positions in the software architecture model by weaving means including software components into the base system. For the simulation of performance properties and costs, we exclusively use PCM concepts. The simulation engine of the performance properties was not adapted or extended in the presented work. All newly introduced elements such as subsystems, subsystem solutions and features are no longer included in the transformed model. The performance evaluation and optimization of the scenarios shown in these scenarios therefore rely on already evaluated concepts. [Hap09] and [Reu+16] have shown Palladio's performance analysis can provide accurate results. Koziolek [Koz11] has shown that optimizing PCM models provide accurate results for the quality attributes performance and costs along the three degrees of freedom: component selection, hardware selection, and component allocation. The new degrees of freedom introduced in this dissertation are reduced to these three degrees of freedom using transformations. Therefore, the accuracy of analyses of quality attributes and the optimization of software architectures shown in this dissertation is based on the results of these studies.

11.11. Discussion

Scenarios 1 – 6 demonstrate in detail evaluation questions EQ I.II.1, EQ I.II.2, EQ III.1, and EQ III.2 from Section 10.2. We show how the models of subsystems and subsystem solutions can be reused to extend existing base software architectures by features. We show how different solutions can be automatically evaluated with regard to the quality attributes of the overall system. In addition, we show the evaluation of new architecture design decisions such as considering feature selection and different feature positions can influence quality attributes. Based on these results, we discuss how requirements can be prioritized and how the results can be used as a basis for discussions with stakeholders.

12. Evaluation Part II: Qualitative Modelled Knowledge

This chapter evaluates the research questions from Section 10.2.2. We evaluate the combination of the two knowledge models using two systems, namely *Business Reporting System* (cf. Section 10.6.1) and *Remote Diagnostic Solutions* (cf. Section 10.6.2), together with the IDS subsystem (cf. Section 10.5.2), with the solutions AppSensor (cf. Section 10.4.3.1) and OSSEC HIDS (cf. Section 10.4.3.2) to show the applicability and benefits of our approach.

When evaluating the combination of quantified quality attributes in combination with qualitatively modelled quality attributes, we show how trade-off decisions can be made between several quality attributes of different types regarding the software architecture.

12.1. Evaluation process

Figure 12.1 shows the evaluation process schematically. We perform the evaluation in three steps, namely model creation, model annotation and model exploration that we have already used in one of our publications [BK16].

- *Model creation:* We use the QML model extended in Section 9.1 to define dimensions to be evaluated and optimized during the evaluation. In addition, we determine which dimensions should be considered as quantified dimensions and which dimensions should be considered as qualitatively valued dimensions.

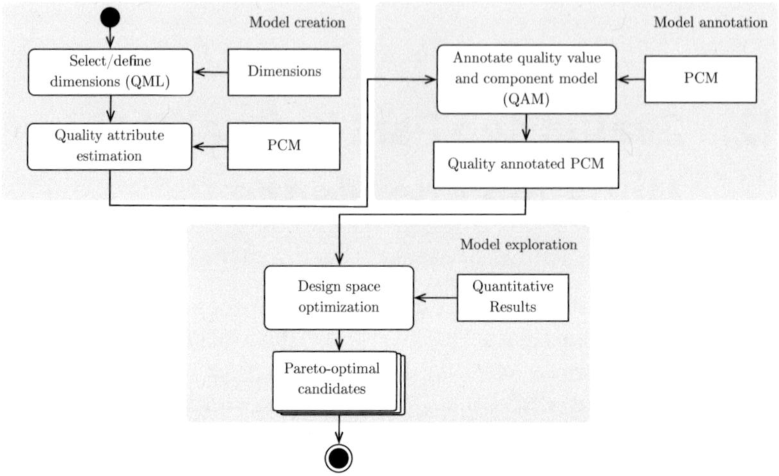

Figure 12.1.: Schematic overview of the evaluation process of part II of the evaluation (according to [BK16]).

- *Model annotation:* Using the quality annotations model, the defined quality dimensions are annotated to the affected components together with the corresponding values of this dimension.
- *Model exploration:* We use PerOpteryx to carry out the design space exploration to calculate the Pareto-optimal architecture candidates. For this purpose, quantitative and qualitative modelled quality attributes are considered together.

12.2. Combining both types of knowledge

This section shows how software architects can combine two qualitatively modelled quality attributes, namely usability and security with the two quantified quality attributes, performance and cost in order to make trade-off decisions between them.

12.2.1. Scenario VII: Combination of usability and security

This scenario considers the evaluation of design alternatives for quality attributes when no quantitative objective function is available or might be too costly for the project to carry out quantitative analysis. Further, improving several quality attributes often means reducing others at the same time. This scenario therefore demonstrates how such trade-off decisions can be modelled and analysed. Two new requirements for the Business Reporting System consider the improvement of usability and the improvement of security quality attributes:

- The graphic representation of the business reports shall be improved in terms of illustration of business areas and the corresponding business values to improve the understanding by the user.
- The user management of the business reporting system shall be improved so that the probability of successful attacks is reduced and the business data is better protected.

12.2.1.1. Design questions

The previously introduced requirements could be implemented by four components of which two each represent alternatives in pairs.

The Business Reporting System has a component for showing the business reports generated by the system, namely the `GraphicalReporting'` component. The `GraphicalReporting'` component provides a graphical representation using a list of several individual business figures from different areas of the company. The alternative component `GraphicalReporting"` could have the following appearance and properties: `GraphicalReporting"` groups the business figures by business areas, sorts them according to importance, and displays selected, particularly relevant data by scatter plots. This might increase the user satisfaction when using `GraphicalReporting"` [MS; Nie97]. `GraphicalReporting'` requires less resources than component `GraphicalReporting"` due to the simple graphical representation. We therefore assume the fourfold resource requirement due to the increased need for the graphical representation for `GraphicalReporting"`. Both components implement the functionality in a very similar manner, provide and require the same interfaces. They only differ in the representation of the data.

The second requirement concerns the user management of the BRS. While the original component `UserManagement'` in the system could be a proprietary development, the alternative component `UserManagement"` could implement a more extensively tested and widely used third-party component, for example an OAUTH2 implementation. The OAuth 2.0 authorization framework [IET12] "is the industry-standard protocol for authorization" [Gro]. It can be used in mobile or desktop devices and is widely used in practice [Par17; RS16; Bih15; Nas17]. Thus, it can be classified as more secure in terms of restricting access for unauthorized users than a less tested proprietary development. Due to more complex algorithms to guarantee the security properties, we assume a double resource requirement for `UserManagement"`.

On the basis of the two pairwise alternative components, the following design questions can be derived which are to be evaluated:

- What are the Pareto-optimal architecture candidates for all combinations of all possible properties of the dimensions of security and usability, such as security = low, usability = low or security = high, usability = low?
- To what extent does the improvement of the user experience influence the response time and the costs of the overall system?
- To what extent does the improvement of the access restriction capabilities influence the response time and the costs of the overall system?

12.2.1.2. Models

For the evaluation we require several models that we have taken from our evaluation in [BK16]. First, we model the dimensions of the quality attributes and their possible properties using QML. We show an excerpt of the model in Figure 12.2. Then properties must be annotated from the set of possible properties of a dimension to the corresponding component using the QAM.

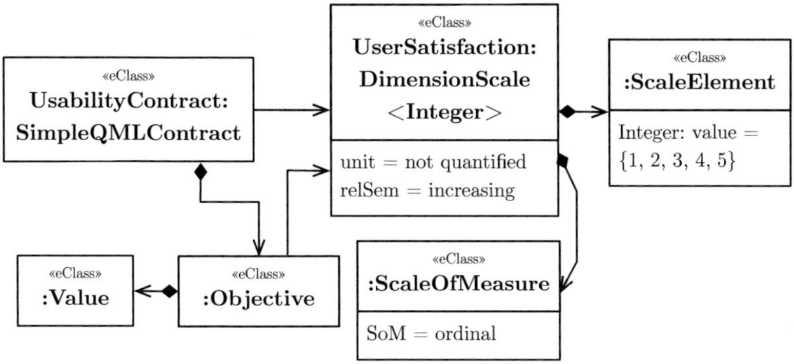

Figure 12.2.: Excerpt from the QML dimension *UserSatisfaction*. Each Element *1, 2, 3, 4, 5* would be represented in its own class. For space reasons, we have represented them in a set notation.

We assign the dimension *UserSatisfaction* to the quality attribute usability. For user satisfaction, we model five possible quality attributes, defined as set and consisting the attributes {1,2,3,4,5} that represent the levels of user satisfaction. Higher values mean higher quality. The quality attribute security defines the dimension *AccessRestriction*. For the dimension we model three possible values that a component can have, namely {low, medium, high}. In this dimension, high means better security. All values estimate the quality of a component with respect to the corresponding dimension. Among themselves and within a dimension, the properties follow an order relation on ordinal scale level. Both dimensions are defined as objectives, while their value shall be optimized.

According to Section 12.2.1.1, we assign from the dimension user satisfaction the value 2 to the component `GraphicalReporting'`, while the alternative implementation `GraphicalReporting"` has the value 4. Further, we assign from the dimension access restriction the property *low* to the component `UserManagement'`, while the alternative component `UserManagement"` has the value `high`. For the annotations, we use the QAM.

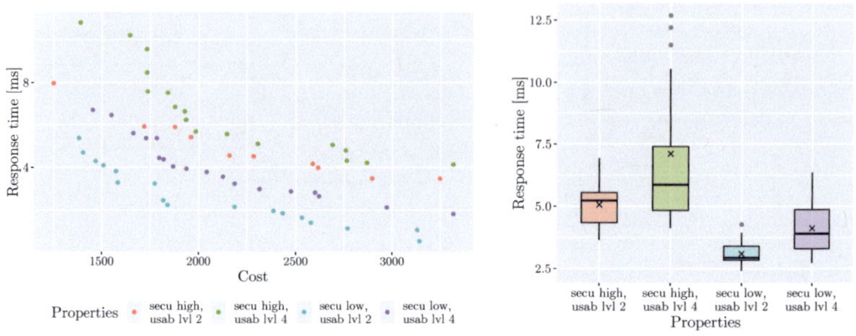

(a) Scatter plot showing the Pareto-optimal architecture candidates grouped by security and usability dimension

(b) Box plot showing the response times for the architecture candidate grouped by security and usability dimension

Figure 12.3.: Scatter plot and box plot for scenario VII. Cross mark in the box blot indicates the arithmetic mean.

Evaluation results & Discussion

For the evaluation we have carried out 200 iterations 20 candidates each, with a total of 2586 architecture candidates. PerOpteryx calculated 63 Pareto-optimal architecture candidates out of these. The Pareto-optimal architecture candidates are shown in Figure 12.3a.

Altogether we can identify four corridors, grouped according to the individual levels of usability, represented by the dimension *UserExperience* and security, represented by the dimension *AccessRestriction.* As expected, the architecture candidates with the lowest quality properties are most cost-efficient to be used and also result in the lowest response times. The architecture candidates with one of the higher quality property and one of the lower quality property from the respective dimensions are in the middle field. We find the architecture candidates with a lower level of security are cheaper and faster than those with high usability. As expected, the architecture candidates with high security and high usability level are the most expensive candidates and have the highest response times.

These results are supported by the box plots in Figure 12.3b. The box plot shows the response times for the four groups of combinations of the

Arithmetic mean	Security low	Security high
Usability low	100 %	164 %
Usability high	133 %	229 %

Table 12.1.: Overview of the average additional effort in terms of response time considering the two quality attributes security and usability within their respective dimensions.

respective possible characteristics of the properties for each dimension. The values for the response times of each group are approximated on the basis of the costs of the group *security low, usability level 4.* On the basis of this data, predictions about the additional costs (in terms of response time) can be calculated caused by improving a certain quality attribute. Table 12.1 summarizes the findings of the evaluation.

The difference between the lowest security and the lowest usability, to the highest security and the highest usability is 129.34% arithmetic mean (99.59 % median) additional costs regarding response time (green area). On this basis, software architects can decide whether the highest level of the respective dimension justifies the increase in response time or whether a requirement prioritization in favour of one of the dimensions becomes necessary (red, purple area). If response time is even the most critical factor, response time must be prioritized at the highest level, which would lead to an architecture candidate from the blue area.

12.2.2. Scenario VIII: Security

This scenario extends the model of a real-world system, the RDS (see Section 10.6.2), by annotations of qualitatively modelled quality attributes. The focus of this scenario is on showing how quality requirements on security, namely better protection against data loss and improved protection against unauthorized access, could be evaluated and how trade-off decisions could be analysed. Two new requirements can be defined for improving the RDS in terms of security:

- The input processing of data should become more secure so that the effort for attackers increases to inject malicious code.
- The database, which stores the recorded values and aggregated status data, should be better protected against data loss.

The models and evaluation results are based on models used in the evaluation in [BK16].

Design questions

In the base system of the RDS, the functionality of the input processing of data and storage of the measurement data is implemented by the components `Parser` and `Database` respectively. Two alternative components with different quality properties could be used to improve the quality attributes mentioned above.

The alternative input processing component `Parser"` could have a higher quality regarding the dimension intrusion prevention, but requires the double CPU resources than `Parser`. `Database"` has improved data loss prevention capabilities, where we assume a fourfold resource requirement for CPU resources. Both components can be used as pairwise alternatives because they provide and require the same component interfaces.

The following design questions can be derived from the pairwise alternative components:

- Which architecture candidates are Pareto-optimal when the quality attribute security should be improved?
- Which security improvements is Pareto-optimal in terms of costs and response time?

Models

Again, we use QML to model the quality attribute, dimensions, and possible properties for the dimensions. For the annotation of properties to components, we use QAM again.

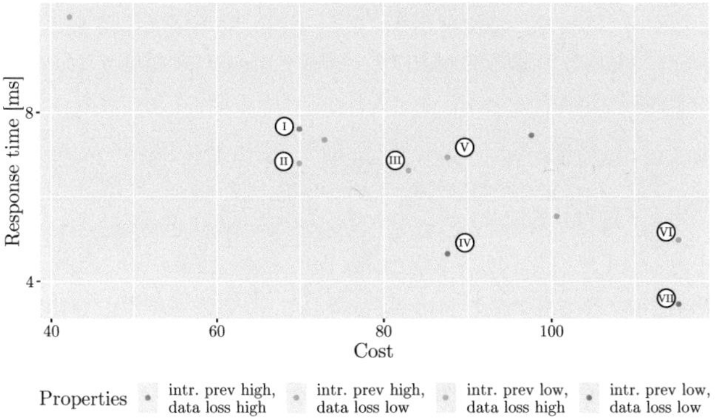

Figure 12.4.: Scatter plot showing the Pareto-optimal architecture candidates of the RDS system grouped by the security dimensions data loss prevention and intrusion prevention. Annotated results are further explained in the results and discussion section.

For both dimensions intrusion prevention and data loss prevention, we use the three values {low, medium, high}. From the dimension intrusion prevention, we assign the value *low* to `Parser`, while we annotate the value *high* to `Parser"`. We annotate the `Database` component with the value *low* from the dimension data loss prevention, while we use *high* for `Database"`.

Evaluation results & Discussion

PerOpteryx automatically evaluated 814 valid architecture candidates. The optimization resulted in 11 architecture candidates as Pareto-optimal candidates. In Figure 12.4 the candidates are numbered consecutively by I - VII for better clarity of the following findings.

With the small number of Pareto-optimal candidates, the candidates can be examined in pairs: Candidate I and candidate II have identical costs and the identical level of data loss prevention. Candidate II, however, achieves a lower level of intrusion prevention and has lower response times. If stakeholders could accept lower intrusion prevention, the architecture would achieve 0.99 ms lower response time at the same monetary cost. Alternatively, performance could be reduced by 0.99 ms in favour of better intrusion prevention.

Candidates II and III reveal a sweet spot within the Pareto-optimal results: With the same quality regarding intrusion prevention and data loss prevention, an improvement of only 0.19 ms would increase the cost of the software system by 18.6 %. Stakeholders must decide whether the 0.19 ms improvement in response time justifies the 18.6 % cost increase.

The pairs consisting of candidates IV and V, as well as VI and VII show interesting findings comparing them to each other. On the cost axis, the candidates within each pair are at the same value. Interesting findings are shown by the analysis of the axis over the response time. While the difference at cost value 87 between candidates with low intrusion prevention and low data loss prevention to high intrusion prevention and low data loss prevention is 2.16 ms higher (48.3 % higher), the difference at cost value 115 is reduced to 1.01 ms (30.3 %). With increasing financial resources, the negative influence on the response time of the better intrusion prevention can therefore be reduced. The difference results from a resource contention that can be reduced by better hardware resources. However, more hardware resources are more expensive. With a small budget, the use of components with the better intrusion prevention security features cause 96.5 % higher response times, while with 31.6 % higher budget worsening the response time is reduced to 30.3 % by using better security features. A further finding is that when using components with better intrusion prevention, and increasing the budget by 36 % might achieve almost the same response time as for candidates with lower intrusion prevention. If the decision is made in favour of better quality properties, it might be promising to evaluate further architecture candidates in which the quality attributes are analysed with a further increase in budget. This could improve the response time even more.

12.3. Using qualitative reasoning

In this section we show scenarios demonstrating the purpose of qualitative reasoning for the evaluation of qualitatively modelled knowledge. Qualitative reasoning allows modelling effects between different quality attributes and to combine them with quantitative methods. In the following two scenarios, we consider the BRS and RDS systems.

12.3.1. Scenario IX: Effects between quality dimensions when using different implementations

This scenario evaluates how quality dimensions can influence the quality dimensions of other quality attributes. More concrete, the *ability for backups* can have an influence on the quality attribute *recoverability* and thus on the quality attribute usability in the dimension *ease of data recovery.* When considering further quality dimensions together, a manual examination quickly becomes tedious and an analysis prone to error. We therefore focus on the automatic analysis of effects to make trade-off decisions between the different quality dimensions of different quality attributes. We would like to analyse the following requirement for the BRS:

> The data recovery process of the overall system shall be improved.

The models and evaluation results have already been shown in one of our publications [SBK18].

Design questions

Each implementation has different quality properties, such as the quality of the backup process, which in turn affects the recoverability and thus the quality of the recovery process in the event of data loss. For the investigation and implementation of the requirements from the previous section, three components have to be considered with regard to the BRS: `Database`, `CoreOnlineEngine` and the `WebServer` component. For each component, there is an alternative component, which differs in quality attributes as for instance the quality properties of the ability for backups with regard to the quality of the database backup process, recoverability with regard to fault tolerance and the quality of the backup process. Thus, this has an indirect effect on usability with regard to the ease of the data recoverability dimension. In addition, they differ in terms of resource demand and costs. This results in the following design questions:

- How does the quality attributes recoverability and ability for backups of individual components influence the quality attribute usability, in the dimension ease of data recovery of the overall system?
- How does the quality of the data recovery process influence the overall response time of the services and costs of the software system?

Models

In the first step, we define the attributes for the quality dimension. This is the basis of the models and thus possible characteristics that define the properties of a quality dimension. In other words, the characteristics correspond to possible values that a property of a quality attribute can have. We use $DS = \{--, -, 0, +, ++\}$ for our quality dimensions. The value *++* corresponds to the highest quality property within the dimension and -- to the lowest. The intermediate values correspond to gradations at ordinal scale level. *0* corresponds to a neutral quality property.

For the evaluation of the design questions, we annotate the pairwise alternatives of the three components `Database`, `CoreOnlineEngine` and `WebServer` with the corresponding values from the respective quality dimension: In practice, software architects often have the choice between different database management systems (DBMS), such as those available from different vendors. Known examples for DBMS are be the Oracle Database 12c and the IBM DB2 10.5. Both DBMS have similar features and functionalities, but differ in their quality attributes. However, quality attributes, such as the ability for backups are difficult to quantify. In such cases, however, qualitative comparison of the alternative systems within the same quality dimension is possible. Such a qualitative comparison can be based on the

MRS: Recoverability					
MR: Ability for backups					
IN:	++	+	0	-	--
OUT:	++	++	+	0	-

MRS: Usability					
MR: Recoverability					
IN:	++	+	0	-	--
OUT:	++	++	+	0	-

Table 12.2.: MRS modelling the influence of ability for backups to recoverability (left) and recoverability to usability (right).

personal experience of software architects or on reviews of technical reports such as the Oracle Technical Comparison report [Ora13]. This report proposes that the quality of the backup process of the Oracle Database 12c can be ranked higher than the backup process of the alternative system. We annotate this information to the corresponding database components in the component repository using QAM. To be conformed to the technical report, we annotate the quality of the backup process of the IBM DBMS with the value *0*. The Oracle database, with slightly better quality, we annotate with *+* and assume that measurements regarding CPU resource demands of the Oracle DBMS observe on average 1.5 times the amount of the IBM database, as well as double the initial costs.

We define a similar model for `CoreOnlineEngine`. For one of the two `CoreOnlineEngine` components, the `CoreOnlineEngine"` we assume a 20 % lower CPU resource demand and 80 % lower costs. The 2nd component has a lower fault tolerance.

Microsoft's TechNet report [Mic09b] describes a correlation between the quality of the backup process and the recoverability. We model this correlation in the MRS shown in Table 12.2 (left). Using QAM, we annotate the MRS model to both components. The MRS models that if any required component (in the system) defines a certain quality of the backup process (ability for backups), this has a direct effect on the recoverability of the `CoreOnlineEngine` component. The ease of the data recovery process after a system failure depends, among other factors, on the availability of data backups.

We model usability as additional quality attribute. Web server components that are more user-friendly than others would intuitively improve the overall usability of the entire software system. We assume `WebServer"` is more

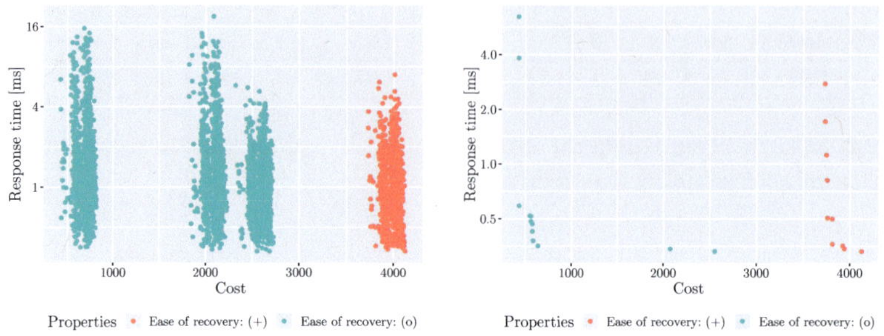

(a) Scatter plot showing all evaluated and valid candidates of scenario IX

(b) Scatter plot showing all Pareto-optimal architecture candidates of scenario IX

Figure 12.5.: Scatter plots showing the four fields of architecture candidates and the Pareto-optimal architecture candidates regarding response time, costs, and ease of recovery.

user-friendly and requires the double CPU resource demand. Nielsen describes in [Nie12], that usability of user interfaces depends on how easily users can recover the system from errors that have occurred. Basing on this, we conclude that the quality attribute usability of individual components is positively influenced by an improvement of recoverability of the components of the service. Therefore, we annotate the two alternative web server components with the MRS from Table 12.2 (right).

Evaluation results & Discussion

PerOpteryx evaluates in 400 iterations, with 20 candidates each a total of 6015 valid architecture candidates, of which 22 result as Pareto-optimal candidates. Again, we used Franks' LQN Solver [Fra+09] to calculate the response time. The convergence value is 0.001 and the iteration limit is set to 20. All evaluated architecture candidates are shown in Figure 12.5a, while the Pareto-optimal candidates are shown in Figure 12.5b.

The scatter plot of all architecture candidates shows four fields of candidates. These four fields represent the combinations of components, with their different quality attributes, with regard to usability, recoverability and ability for backups. Gaps between the candidate groups occur due to different initial costs of the software components and differences in resource demands, which affect the costs for hardware.

When analysing the components used in the four areas, we can find each area uses a different set of software components: Area one includes `Webserver'`, `CoreOnlineEngine'`, or `CoreOnlineEngine"`, and the `IBM database` component. Area two includes `Webserver"`, `CoreOnlineEngine'` or `CoreOnlineEngine"`, and the `IBM database` component. Area three includes `Webserver'`, `CoreOnlineEngine'` or `CoreOnlineEngine"`, and the `Oracle database` component. The last area contains `Webserver"`, `CoreOnlineEngine'` or `CoreOnlineEngine"`, and the `Oracle database` component. We find only candidates using `Webserver"` and the *Oracle database* components can achieve an overall improvement in the ease of recovery dimension. According to our qualitative reasoning model, the selection of the `CoreOnlineEngine` has no influence on the overall quality property of the dimension ease of recovery.

A closer analysis of the results considering the Pareto-optimal results shows a lower cost barrier of 424 cost units for candidates with a lower ease of recovery. The lower cost barrier for architecture candidates with better ease of recovery is 3728 cost units. Similar response times can be achieved with both lower and higher ease of recovery. However, better ease of recovery requires higher budgets. On the basis of the results, software architects and other stakeholders can now decide if the additional costs justify the higher ease of recovery. In cases where backup recovery is critical for the business scenario, stakeholders may accept the significantly higher costs. In applications where ease of recovery is less critical to the business model, the costs might be too high and the decision would be in favour of the less expensive architecture candidates.

12.3.2. Scenario X: Effects between quality dimensions when using different features

In scenario 10, we consider different configuration options of the same software component. This scenario evaluates different features to be selected, as for example the use of another algorithm due to another configuration of the software component. For example, the DBMS Microsoft SQL Server recovers data in *simple* and *full* modes in case of data loss. To assess differences between features, we use the RDS as base system with a focus on storing the measurement data. The models and evaluation results have already been presented in our publication [SBK18].

Design questions

Software architects often need to know at design time what effects the individual features have on the overall quality of the software system (in which the database system is used). With this knowledge, software architects can analyse at design time whether requirements can be met by using individual features. Again it is interesting how differences in recoverability influence the usability dimension ease of recovery. On this basis, the scenario evaluates the following design question:

> How does the selection of features and the resulting quality property of the dimension ease of recovery affect the response time and costs of the overall system?

Models

To model the relevant quality dimensions, we use Microsoft's technical report *Microsoft recovery model report* [Mic16] as basis for the architecture knowledge. The report describes the differences between the two recovery modes. According to the report, recoverability is better fulfilled in full mode, but has a negative effect on system performance.

Thus, we model the full mode's *ability for backup* of the database with positive influence *(+)* and the simple mode with negative influence *(-)*. We reuse the *DS* from the previous scenario. Due to the higher resource demands, we assume the *full* mode requires four times the CPU resource demands compared to the *simple* mode. In addition, we extend the model with the two MRS models from Table 12.3 to model the influence of ability for

MRS: Recoverability					
MR: Ability for backups					
IN:	++	+	0	-	--
OUT:	++	+	0	-	--

MRS: Usability					
MR: Recoverability					
IN:	++	+	0	-	--
OUT:	++	+	0	-	--

Table 12.3.: MRS modelling the influence of ability for backups to recoverability (left) and recoverability to usability (right).

backups on recoverability and recoverability on usability (of the dimension ease of recovery).

Evaluation results & Discussion

PerOpteryx evaluated 2030 valid architecture candidates, in 200 iterations with 20 candidates each. 9 of these candidates were resulted as Pareto-optimal. Again, we used the LQN solver [Fra+09] to calculate the response time. The convergence value is 0.001 and the iteration limit is 20.

The Pareto-optimal architecture candidates are shown in Figure 12.6. Again, the candidates are grouped according to the usability dimension *ease of recovery*, *response time* and *cost*. Overall, we find a higher ease of recovery leads to higher response times. If lower response times are required, the architecture candidates result in significantly higher costs. The lower limit for response time is 5.24 ms for candidates with ease of recovery (++), while the highest response time is 4.57 ms for candidates with ease of recovery (+). Looking at the candidates that represent the barriers, the candidate with ease of recovery (++) results in 62.83 % higher cost (whereby the candidates are not directly comparable due to the differences in response times).

If either response time or costs are in the focus of the optimization, decision makers should select architecture candidates with lower ease of recovery. On the other hand, it is clear that better recovery of data in the event of an error results in higher response times or costs. On the basis of the results, however, this trade-off decision can be discussed with a data basis and requirements can be prioritized with the stakeholders.

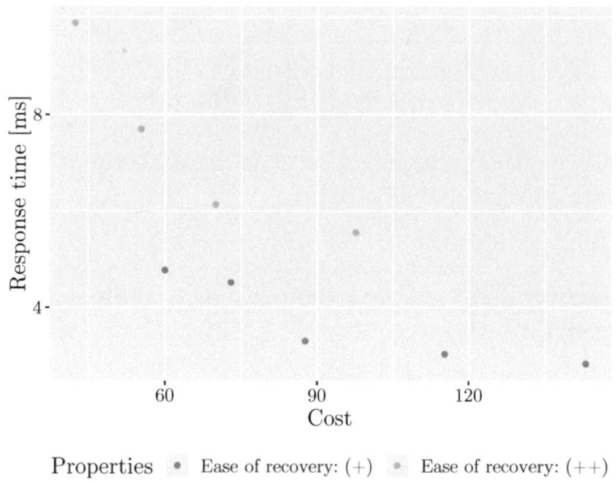

Figure 12.6.: Scatter plot showing the Pareto-optimal architecture candidates of the RDS system grouped by ease of recovery, response time, and costs.

12.4. Accuracy of Evaluating Qualitative Modelled Knowledge

The accuracy of the evaluation of qualitatively modelled knowledge depends on the level of detail and accuracy of the knowledge itself. Due to the lack of real setups and the possibility to model knowledge from experienced software architects, we relied on documents from system vendors themselves. However, documents from vendors are not necessarily a reliable knowledge source. They usually contain information about positive properties of the described systems, as well as negative properties of the systems from competitors. However, the evaluation of the knowledge itself has shown that the modelled knowledge when combining with quantitatively modelled knowledge results plausible values. Without the modelling of qualitative knowledge, optimization as shown would not have been possible. Systems with better quality properties such as recoverability would not have been included in the set of Pareto-optimal results due to higher resource demand. Accordingly, these candidates would not have been visible in the results and would not have been considered as promising candidates.

12.5. Discussion

In scenarios 7 – 10 we demonstrate in detail evaluation questions EQ II.I.1, EQ II.I.2, EQ II.II, and EQ III.2 from Section 10.2. The scenarios show how qualitatively-valued quality attributes can be modelled and analysed. We show how a combined analysis of both types of knowledge representation could be carried out and which results could be expected. Based on these results, requirements could be prioritized and discussed with stakeholders.

13. Evaluation Part III: Optimizing Annotation Positions and Solution Selection

By reusing 3rd party systems for the implementation of features, well-considered design decisions and often a well-tested code base of these systems are reused. Security is one of the big topics in modern software systems and one of the enablers of modern business models. Implementing security features is hard and there are many pitfalls. Even popular open source cryptography libraries, such as OpenSSL has been shown to be prone to common security pitfalls, such as the *Heartbleed* vulnerability [Dur+14]. Implementing such security critical systems from scratch could lead even more to unsecure systems. Thus, crypto libraries, access control systems or other security critical systems, such as intrusion detection systems, should not be written from scratch, but established 3rd party systems should be used.

Even if software architects have decided reusing libraries and even if the type of security feature to be implemented has already been defined, the solution selection and its possible placement in the base architecture is unclear. Each change in selected product and placement in the base architecture changes the resulting quality attributes, such as performance and costs. Possible questions in detail are demonstrated in this scenario.

Let us assume the stakeholders want to improve the quality attribute security with regard to the quality dimension *recognition of external attacks*. Features of the IDS subsystem implement such requirements. The BRS (Section 10.6.1) could be attacked on several positions in its architecture, where attacker detection could be applied to detect and prevent attacks. We use the two subsystem solutions AppSensor (Section 10.4.3.1) and OSSEC (Section 10.4.3.2) as alternative solutions. To implement the requirements, they are alternative implementations of the IDS subsystem. As a constraint for this scenario, a lightweight and non-intrusive model extension mechanism should be used.

13.1. Design questions

Let us review the software architecture of BRS. We show the system architecture of BRS in Figure 10.13.

The particularly critical positions in the BRS software architecture with regard to possible functional abuse are mainly components handling user interactions, such as user management and generation of reports. Two positions are liable for this type of attack and use case: First, we focus on the assembly connector between `UserManagement` and `Scheduler` performing user logins and user logoffs. Second, we focus on the assembly connector between `GraphicalReport` and `CoreGraphicEngine`. These components focus on the user interaction between user and system while generating reports. To detect functional abuse, we use the feature *FunctionalAbuse* to ensure a function that is used for realizing a business use case cannot be abused for attacking the system. The following three design questions can be derived:

- What influence does the use of the feature *FunctionalAbuse* have on the performance and costs of the overall system at the two aforementioned assembly connectors of the BRS?
- What are the differences in performance and cost based on the number of inclusion positions?
- Which of the two subsystem solutions is optimal with regard to the feature *FunctionalAbuse* at the two architecture positions and taking into account the environmental parameters (such as usage scenario, resource setup) of the BRS?

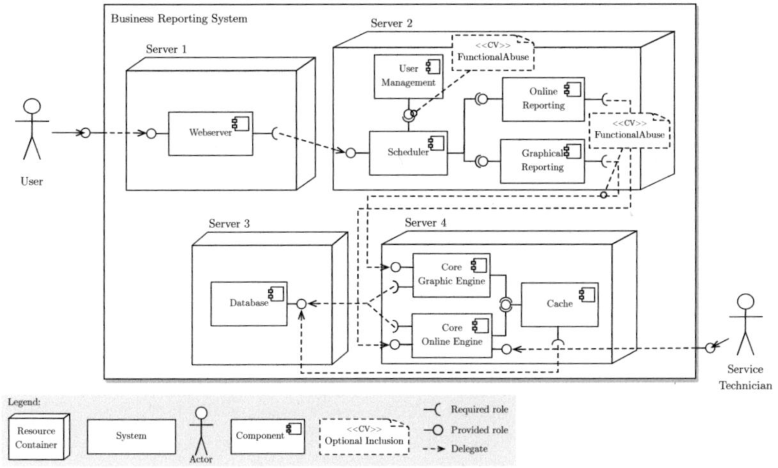

Figure 13.1.: Feature annotated BRS system view-type.

13.2. Scenario Application

Figure 13.1 shows the extension of the system view-type of the BRS architecture model schematically. Software architects can evaluate the design questions by annotating the assembly connectors with the complementum visnetis annotation, which connects the *FunctionalAbuse* to the desired components of the system. As annotation positions, we select the assembly connector between the components `UserManagement` and `Scheduler`, and `GraphicalReporting` and `CoreGraphicEngine`. Both annotation positions are configured as optional and are therefore considered in the design space exploration as optional inclusion positions. This creates a design space spanning from zero weaving positions to two weaving positions. Within this range there is scope for exploration and optimization. Further, the applied subsystem solution can be varied for each candidate architecture model. The design space further considers the allocation of the remaining components, software components of the feature completion components, implementing functional abuse, as well as resource scaling of the processing resources of the 4-tier system. The CPU resources of each of the four server systems can be selected in the range of 1000 to 4000 MHz during de-

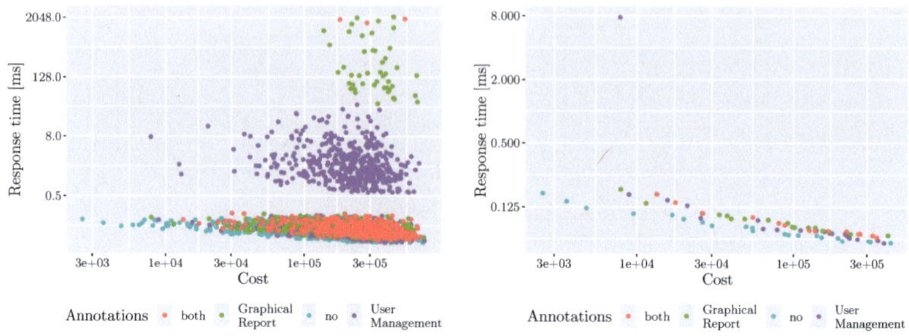

(a) All evaluated and valid candidates (#3053) **(b)** Pareto-optimal candidates (#74)

Figure 13.2.: All evaluated, valid, and Pareto-optimal candidates (scenario part III) of the response time and cost evaluation of different annotation positions of features.

sign space exploration. Further annotation positions would be conceivable, such as the entry points between actors and `Webserver` component, and `CoreGraphicEngine` component. In this scenario, however, we concentrate on the assembly connectors mentioned above.

For model weaving, we consider three component repositories: the repository with the components of the BRS system, the repository with the components of AppSensor and the repository with OSSEC components. We also use the feature completion model of the IDS, as well as the feature model, which models the feature objectives of the IDS feature completion. We extend the system view-type of the BRS model with our reuse profile and annotate the stereotype `featureTarget` to the assembly connectors. As feature, we configure *FunctionalAbuse* as optional desired. We also define a QML contract type, contract and profile that models the quality attribute performance with the dimension response time and cost as quality attributes to be evaluated. Both quality attributes are defined as objectives. This models can then be used for the evaluation of the design questions mentioned.

13.3. Evaluation results & Discussion

The first two design questions from Section 13.1 can be analysed by the plots shown in Figure 13.2. Altogether, PerOpteryx analysed 3053 valid architecture candidates. Out of these, 74 candidates are Pareto-optimal. Several areas can be identified in which the architecture candidates can be grouped. The largest field of architecture candidates, in which also the Pareto-optimal architecture candidates are located, shows relatively small effects on quality attributes performance and costs when including *FunctionalAbuse*. The annotation of the assembly connector between `GraphicalReport` and `CoreGraphicEngine` has higher effects on performance and costs, than the annotation of the assembly connector between `UserManagement` and `Scheduler`. Annotating both connectors results in even more cost-expensive and resource demanding candidates. However, the results of annotating both positions of the architecture, are slightly distorted: 957 architecture candidates could not be evaluated because the system was overloaded due to the high calculation effort. Annotating both components tend to result in higher response times. Nevertheless, PerOpteryx evaluated architecture candidates having both annotations with comparatively low response times. However, these candidates tend to be more expensive. Allowing the DSE to increase the processing resources further, the high demanding candidates could probably be evaluated. This would probably result in higher costs.

Figure 13.3 shows the automatically evaluated architecture candidates for analysing design question three. All 1535 evaluated candidates as well as the 57 Pareto-optimal candidates show a division into four fields: The first area (red) shows the feature of AppSensor on the assembly connector between `GraphicalReport` and `CoreGraphicEngine`. The second area (green) shows AppSensor at the connector between the `Scheduler` and `UserManagement` connector. The third area (blue) shows the solution OSSEC, at the connector between `GraphicalReport` and `CoreGraphicEngine`. Finally, the last area (purple) shows the solution OSSEC, at the connector between `Scheduler` and `UserManagement`. The results show for both positions OSSEC is the faster and cheaper solution than AppSensor. All architecture candidates including OSSEC result in an average response time of far less than 0.5 ms, while the use of AppSensor extends the average response time to at least 0.5 ms up to more than 2 s. The results show OSSEC is the faster and

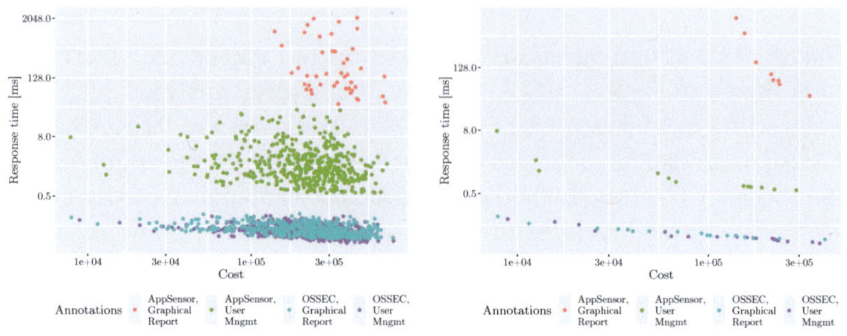

(a) All evaluated and valid candidates (#1535) **(b)** Pareto-optimal candidates (#57)

Figure 13.3.: All evaluated, valid, and Pareto-optimal candidates (scenario part III) of the response time and cost evaluation comparing both IDS solutions, namely AppSensor and OSSEC. Further, the plots show two different positions of the feature *FunctionalAbuse*.

cheaper solution for both positions. If the feature positions for a particular solution are analyzed, there is another interesting finding: while using OSSEC there is almost no influence on performance and costs annotating the connector between `GraphicalReport` and `CoreGraphicEngine` or the connector between `Scheduler` and `UserManagement` component. Annotating the first is slightly cheaper than annotating the latter. In contrast, when using AppSensor, annotating the connector between `GraphicalReport` and `CoreGraphicEngine` results in a much higher response time than annotating the other connector.

Another interesting result can be derived from the following analysis: If, for example, AppSensor is mandatory to be used, the `Scheduler` to `UserManagement` connector could be extended by the feature with smaller performance and cost overhead compared to extending the other. This decision may be necessary, for example, if further features need to be included and are not supported by OSSEC. Annotating as many components as possible with *FunctionalAbuse* and simultaneously implement a feature not supported by OSSEC, the following trade-off decision could be made: Use of AppSensor, annotation of the *FunctionalAbuse* feature on the `Scheduler` to `UserManagement` component, with simultaneous integration of the *InputVal-*

idation feature at a further position in the BRS that needs to be evaluated in a subsequent step. Use of OSSEC would not be possible in this scenario, because *InputValidation* is no supported feature. By this decision the possibility to implement further features would be prioritized higher than to achieve the lowest response times and costs.

The analysis evaluates the evaluation questions EQ I.II.1, EQ I.II.2, EQ III.1 and EQ III.2 from Section 10.2. We show how the adapter extension mechanism can be used to reuse models uniformly and how different subsystem solutions can be evaluated automatically. We discuss and show how different desired positions of the system can be extended by features by using annotations. We show how to evaluate the effects on quality attributes of the overall system due to different architecture decisions such as the position of features and the selected subsystem solutions. On this basis, requirements can be prioritized and used as a basis for discussions with stakeholders.

14. Concluding Discussion

14.1. Threats to validity

The following sections describe possible threats to validity:

Scenario selection: The performance of the approach and the possible questions to be evaluated were carried out scenario-based. Thus, the results for the scenarios mentioned and the derived results can only be applied to these scenarios. Nevertheless, the scenarios demonstrate relevant questions in the software architecture design process.

Modelling informal knowledge: In the study on evaluating informal knowledge through qualitative modelling methods, the evaluation relies on document-based on knowledge sources. Some knowledge sources originate from the manufacturers itself, which might have limits in their objectivity. The evaluation is based on the assumption these sources have provided truthful information about the performance and other quality attributes of their products. The results of the analyses at least follow our expectations.

Quality evaluation: To evaluate the quality attribute performance, we rely on the Palladio approach and the LQN solver. The accuracy of the LQN solver is difficult to verify. However, both tools are widely used by the community such as used in [Goo+12].

Argumentative validation: Several evaluation questions or sub-questions could only be answered argumentatively. Examples, measurements or even empirical experiments would have been preferred, but were not possible due to a lack of realistic setups and resources.

14.2. Evaluation results

The first part of the validation considers modelling feature completions and the application of real-world systems as subsystem solutions to the subsystem's reference architecture. EQ I.I.1 considers whether a reference architecture can be found for subsystems. Using the two feature complications *Logging* and *IDS*, we showed we can define a reference architecture that can be applied to multiple subsystem solutions. EQ I.I.2 considers whether several inhomogeneous software architecture models of subsystem solutions can be applied to the subsystem's reference architecture. We answered this question by modelling 2×2 subsystem solutions and applying them to two subsystems, namely *Logging* (log4jv1 and log4jv2) and *IDS* (AppSensor and OSSEC).

The previously modelled subsystems can be used to automatically evaluate design decisions regarding software architectures when reusing complex subsystems. EQ I.II.1 and EQ I.II.2 consider the questions on reuse and automatic evaluation of such design decisions. EQ I.II.1 examines whether models can be reused uniformly. How they can be uniformly reused is described in detail in scenarios I - VI and in scenario of part III. Features are included in base systems to reuse the functionality of several subsystem solutions uniformly (and without having internal knowledge of these solutions).

EQ I.II.2 focuses mainly on the automatic evaluation of different subsystem solutions. In scenario I, we show in detail how alternatives can be automatically evaluated with regard to subsystem solutions and how suitable decisions or architecture candidates can be selected. Evaluation part III shows another scenario on how subsystem solution alternatives can be evaluated against each other.

The evaluation questions regarding informal knowledge for the optimization of software architectures are considered by EQ II.I.1 and EQ II.I.2. Scenarios VII - X show in detail how informal knowledge can be qualitatively modelled and how the models can be automatically analysed. We showed how qualitatively modelled knowledge can be modelled and which analysis and trade-off decisions become possible.

How to combine qualitatively modelled knowledge and quantitative modelled knowledge is considered by EQ II.II. Scenarios VII - X describe in detail which design decisions are supported when combining and analysing both types of knowledge. We showed how trade-off decisions can be supported by including architecture knowledge in the decision support process.

Questions regarding automatic model generation and model optimization are considered by the research questions EQ III.1 and EQ III.2. The new possibilities of *CompARE* regarding modelling and analysis, as well as model generation methods, allow further architecture decisions to be evaluated automatically. EQ III.1 considers which architecture decisions can be supported automatically and how they influence the software architecture design. We answer this questions in detail in scenarios I to VI, and the scenario in part III of the evaluation. Finally, EQ III.2 examines the possibility of requirements prioritization by combining the presented contributions. We explain the prioritization of requirements in detail by scenarios III.a, IV, VII, X, and the scenario in part III. We discuss how the results of *CompARE* can be used for prioritizing requirements and use the results as basis for discussions with stakeholders.

14.3. Summary

The previous three parts evaluate the research questions from Section 10.2. Part one of the evaluation shows scenarios improving reuse and evaluation process of subsystems during the design of the software architecture regarding reuse of features, as well as their configuration by using *CompARE*. We show how these different scenarios can be modelled, analysed, evaluated, and we describe our findings basing on these results. Finally, we discussed which conclusions for the software architecture design and the requirements can be drawn from the results.

Part two of the evaluation shows how qualitative knowledge can be modelled, combined with quantitative knowledge and finally evaluated. We show how qualitatively valued knowledge can be used together with quantitative models and how qualitative reasoning mechanisms can be used to evaluate complex effects between quality attributes. We demonstrate how transitive effects between quality attributes can be modelled and evaluated.

Further, we discussed what findings can be derived for the requirements and design process.

Finally, in part three of the evaluation we show another scenario with a different set of models and design questions. Using these models and design questions, we show how the mechanisms of *CompARE* can support software architects and stakeholders at software architecture design. We find also surprising results can be observed by evaluating subsystem solutions and different positions of features in a base architecture model.

To support software architects in the component-based software architecture process, we show that

- Subsystem models can be automatically integrated into base models to integrate new features automatically. This automatic integration of features can be used to support decisions on software architectures regarding these features without having to create all models manually.
- Knowledge can be qualitatively modelled and optimized with quantitatively modelled knowledge. Thus, trade-off decisions can be made regarding the qualitatively valued quality attributes and quantitative quality attributes. On this basis, requirements can be prioritized.

Another conclusion considers future work regarding the evaluation: when comparing software architectures with presence and absence of features it can be useful to make certain parameters constant when selecting architecture candidates. For example, architecture candidates can be better compared if the feature selection is evaluated with constant resource configuration. To decide whether a particular feature should be used or not, tactics to evaluate the feature selection with constant resource environment might be useful. Such a setup would be interesting to get more findings on the quality attributes influenced by several subsystem solutions and several positions of features in the base architecture model.

15. Future Work & Conclusion

15.1. Future Work

This section describes the outlook for future work based on the contribution of this dissertation.

15.1.1. Change operations for modifying software architectures

CompARE currently supports operations to add new functionality, e.g. by software components or other model entities. However, no further operations are supported yet. For example, the approach does not support substitution of entities, which can be used to replace a standard component with a subsystem. Further, components cannot be removed. Substitution operations or subtraction operations would enable new degrees of freedom, such as replacing previous implementations with new, complex subsystems and would allow analysing their effects on quality attributes. However, the supported operations are sufficient to perform changes regarding reuse of subsystems.

15.1.2. Reference Architecture

CompARE requires for the weaving of subsystems into a base architecture correspondence between the architectures of all subsystem solutions and the subsystem reference architecture. All subsystem solutions that cannot be applied to the subsystem reference architecture, cannot be integrated automatically into base systems to the current state of the art of the approach. A further abstraction of the reference architecture could solve this limitation. Thus, the allocation between the individual feature completion components and the subsystem solution software architecture components could be carried out more fine-granularly. An expressive correspondence model could enable a fine-granular mapping between the abstract model and the software architecture model of the subsystem solution. Such a flexible correspondence model would support experts to use potentially arbitrary software architecture models as subsystem solutions.

15.1.3. Architecture constraints

CompARE supports architecture constraint validation, but only three conditions can be validated: Namely, whether elements are together, separated, or allocated in isolation on resource containers. Thus, *CompARE* can only validate the correct allocation of entities in component-based software architecture models. However, no functional constraint checking can be performed. A promising constraint would be whether certain components or services in the software architecture are placed in the system correctly. Such a check could exclude or at least avoid errors regarding the placement of functionalities already in the design phase. It would also be useful to replace the validation with constraints in the object constraints language[1] or a similar language.

15.1.4. Architecture patterns and styles

CompARE enables subsystems with complex internal architecture to be automatically woven into a base architecture. However, it does not offer the possibility to apply architecture patterns or styles. For example, it is not possible to model the architecture of a model view controller, pipe-lining, or other architecture patterns and automatically apply them to the existing architecture. To enable this, the reuse meta model could be further extended and the weaving mechanism could be extended for applying large-scale changes. In addition, a specification for sequential processing of operations and the definition of the operation itself would be required (similar to the rule-based approaches or the architecture templates from Lehrig et al. [LHB18]).

[1] https://www.omg.org/spec/OCL/About-OCL/

15.1.5. Empirical validation

We have shown in detail possible benefits of *CompARE* in the three-part validation by discussing several scenarios. According to the validation results, relevant design questions can be answered occurring in the software development process regarding software architecture and its quality attributes. An empirical validation based on real requirements and real stakeholders would be helpful to validate the relevance of the benefits for practice. It would be interesting to learn to what extent different subsystems can be modelled and reused as intended. In this context, it would also be interesting to calculate a cost/benefit calculation that results from the additional modelling effort and possible cost savings that result from new findings from the early analysis.

15.1.6. Usability study

During the design of *CompARE*, we focussed on a simple reuse of already modelled feature completions. Only a few adjustments are required to automatically include features in the base software architecture. However, a controlled user study would provide insight in the *CompARE*'s usage process. We could examine how the process could be simplified or whether the already designed usage process can be well-used by study participants. In such a study different requirements could be made, which could be applied to base architectures. In this case, the control group would model by standard CBSE processes, while the second group would use *CompARE*. The process of modelling subsystems and the application of the reference architecture to subsystem solutions could be evaluated similarly. Different solutions could be applied to a given subsystem and appropriate feature completion, as well as reference architecture. Finally, a questionnaire could be used to get information on improvements of the process.

15.2. Conclusion

This section is a summary of this dissertation. We start with summarizing the topic and the motivation to work on this dissertation. Then, we discuss the research questions and the resulting contribution of the *CompARE* approach. Finally, we discuss insights that we can derive from the evaluation.

Topic and motivation

The presented dissertation considers the reuse of complex subsystems in component-based software architectures based on models for the purpose of automatic optimization regarding quality attributes. It should enable software architects to reuse models without deeper knowledge of the internal software architecture of libraries, frameworks or other 3rd party systems during software architecture design. Further, software architects should be automatically supported by software architecture design decisions. The optimization of several new degrees of freedom considering feature selection, product selection of several subsystem solutions, and positions of features in the base architecture complements previous component-based software architecture optimization approaches. The quality attributes considered by *CompARE* exceeds the set of quality attributes regarded in similar optimization procedures by qualitatively valued quality attribute modelling. As a result of the optimization, software architects can review the Pareto-optimal architecture candidates and make trade-off decisions according to the relevant quality attributes and the requirements of the system. This should help to make the software architecture design process more efficient and reduce the risk of designing systems that do not fit the actual software requirements.

Research topics

The research topics address three parts: a meta model for reusing complex subsystems, the automatic model weaving to extend component-based base software architecture models with subsystems on the desired positions, and the modelling of informal knowledge in a qualitative representation and its automatic analysis using qualitative reasoning.

Contributions of the CompARE approach

CompARE automatically supports software architects in making trade-off decisions regarding reuse of subsystems and resulting quality attributes. The approach supports automatic reuse of subsystems, design decision support for feature selection, product selection and feature positions in the base software architecture regarding the quality attributes of the overall system. To support the contributions, we propose a meta model for modelling subsystems, its reference architecture, and model entities to apply component-based software architecture models of subsystem solution to the reference architecture. Using the subsystem model, our weaving engine automatically includes the subsystem models in the base architecture model. Our extension for combining qualitatively valued architecture models and quantitative objective functions then uses the generated models to evaluate the quality attributes of the overall software architecture model. We also show how *CompARE* can be classified into the component-based software engineering process defined by Cheesman and Daniels [CD00], as well as H. Koziolek and Happe [KH06b] and A. Koziolek [Koz11].

Evaluation

For the evaluation of *CompARE*, we show 11 scenarios and several sub scenarios in which we use three base systems to include features of four real-world subsystem solutions. The evaluation shows how design decisions in the software architecture design process can be automatically evaluated using *CompARE*. Further, we show how these results can be used as a basis for requirements prioritization and for the optimal selection and placement of 3rd party subsystems.

By scenarios for the analysis of informal knowledge in combination with quantitative modelled knowledge, we show how trade-off decisions regarding quality attributes and software architecture design can be made and which results can be derived from such analysis.

A. Approach

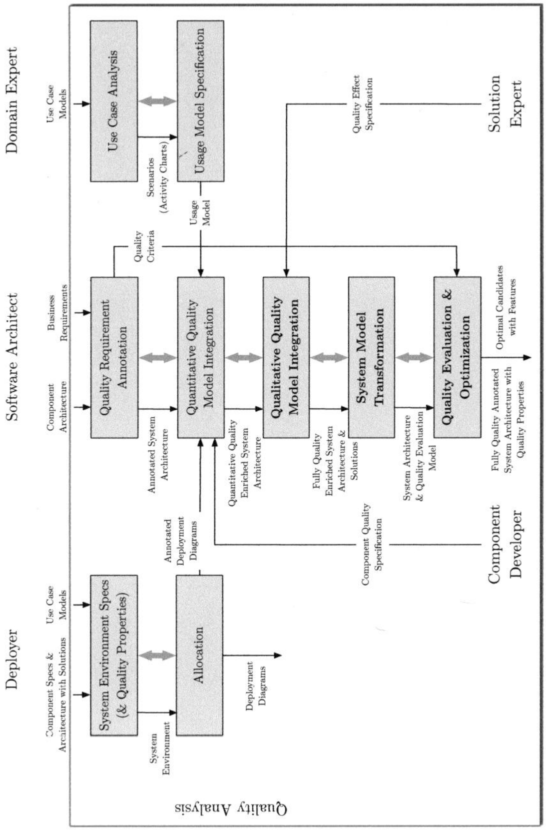

Figure A.1.: Quality Analysis Workflow of the extended CBSE process (based on [KH06b]).

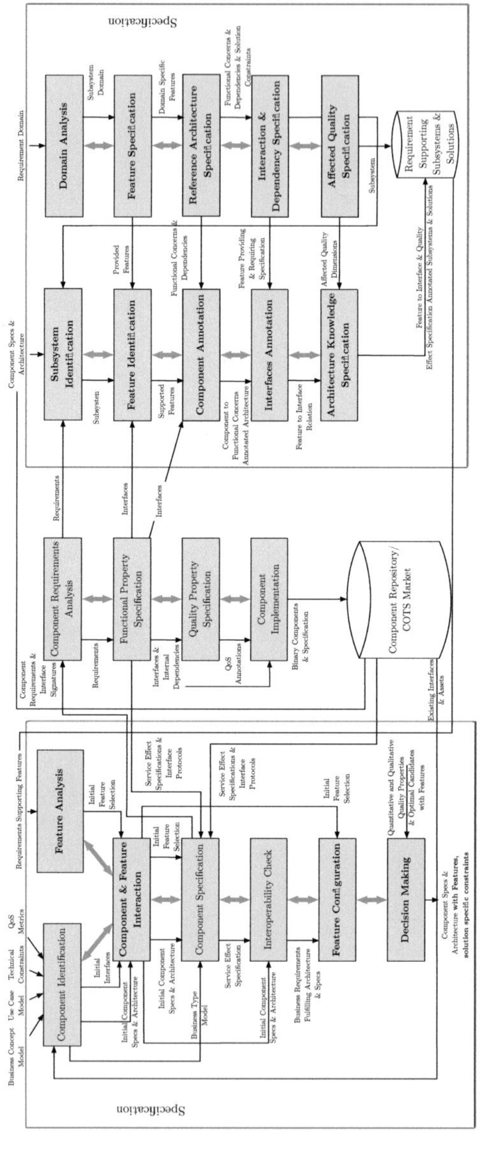

Figure A.2.: Specification Workflow of the extended CBSE process (based on [KH06b]).

B. Meta Models & Profiles Overview

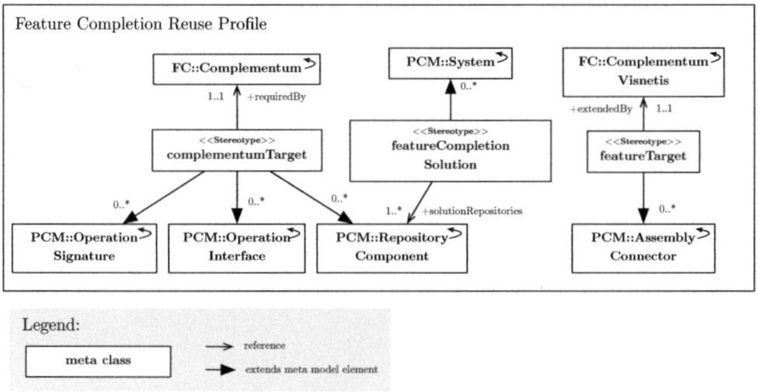

Figure B.1.: FeatureCompletion Reuse Profile

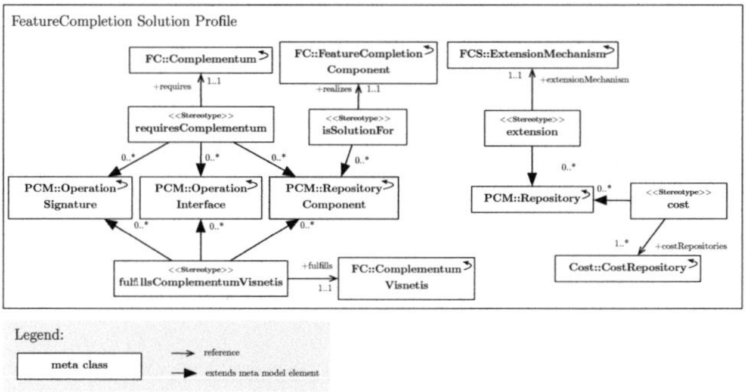

Figure B.2.: FeatureCompletion Solution Profile

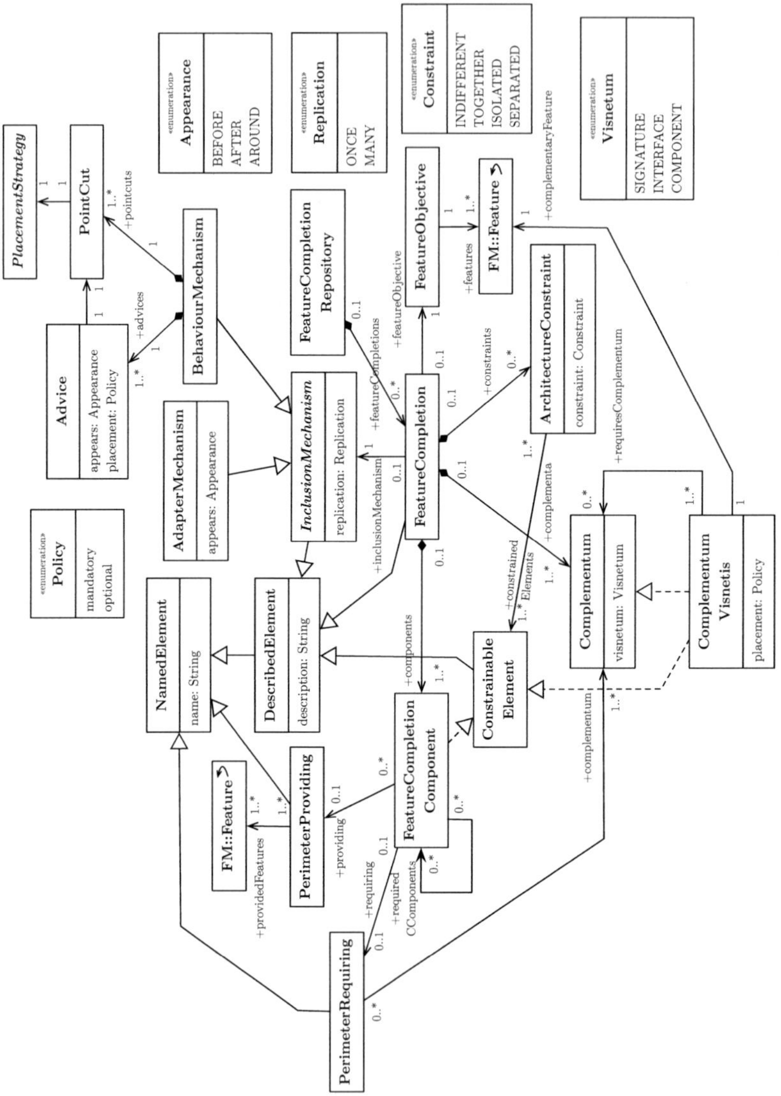

Figure B.3.: Feature Completion (meta model)

C. Publications that dissertation bases on

ICSA'19	Axel Busch, Dominik Fuchß, and Anne Koziolek. *PerOpteryx: Automated Improvement of Software Architectures.* In Proceedings of the IEEE International Conference on Software Architecture (ICSA2019): Tool Demo Track, Hamburg, Germany, 2019, ICSA'19. IEEE, Hamburg, Germany. 2019
SE'18	Axel Busch and Anne Koziolek. *Considering Not–quantified Quality Attributes in an Automated Design Space Exploration.* In Software Engineering 2018, Fachtagung des GI–Fachbereichs Softwaretechnik, 06.–09. March 2018, Ulm, Deutschland, 2018.
ECSA'18	Yves Schneider, Axel Busch, and Anne Koziolek. *Using Informal Knowledge for Improving Software Quality Trade–off Decisions.* In Proceedings of the 12th European Conference on Software Architecture, Madrid, Spain, ECSA'18. Springer, Berlin, DE. 2018.
MEMOCODE'17	Max Scheerer, Axel Busch, and Anne Koziolek. *Automatic Evaluation of Complex Design Decisions in Component–based Software Architectures.* In Proceedings of the 15th ACM–IEEE Intern. Conference on Formal Methods and Models for System Design, Vienna, Austria, MEMOCODE'17, pages 67–76. ACM, New York, NY, USA. 2017.

QoSA'16	Axel Busch and Anne Koziolek. *Considering Not-quantified Quality Attributes in an Automated Design Space Exploration.* In Proceedings of the 12th International ACM SIGSOFT Conference on the Quality of Software Architectures, Venice, Italy, QoSA'16, pages 50–59. IEEE. 2016.
CloudSPD'16	Axel Busch, Yves Schneider, Anne Koziolek, Kiana Rostami, and Jörg Kienzle. *Modelling the Structure of Reusable Solutions for Architecture-based Quality Evaluation.* In Proceedings of the 2nd Workshop on Cloud Security and Data Privacy by Design co-located with the 8th IEEE International Conference on Cloud Computing Technology and Science (CloudCom 2016), Luxembourg, CloudSPD'16, pages 521–526. IEEE. 2016.
ModComp'16	Jörg Kienzle, Anne Koziolek, Axel Busch, and Ralf Reussner. *Towards concern-oriented design of component-based systems.* In 3rd International Workshop on Interplay of Model-Driven and Component-Based Software Engineering, CEUR. 2016.
QRS'15	Axel Busch, Misha Strittmatter, and Anne Koziolek. *Assessing Security to Compare Architecture Alternatives of Component-Based Systems.* In Proceedings of the IEEE International Conference on Software Quality, Reliability & Security, Vancouver, British Columbia, Canada, QRS '15, pages 99–108. IEEE Computer Society. 2015, Acceptance Rate (Full Paper): 20/91 = 22%.
SE'15	Axel Busch. *Automated decision support for recurring design decisions considering non-functional requirements.* In Software Engineering 2015 — Workshopband, 2015, GI Lecture Notes in Informatics. Doctoral Symposium.

Bibliography

[Abd+14] Hani Abdeen et al. "Multi-objective Optimization in Rule-based Design Space Exploration". In: *Proceedings of the 29th ACM/IEEE International Conference on Automated Software Engineering*. ASE '14. Vasteras, Sweden: ACM, 2014, pp. 289–300. ISBN: 978-1-4503-3013-8. DOI: 10.1145/2642937.2643005. URL: http://doi.acm.org/10.1145/2642937.2643005.

[AKM13] Omar Alam, Jörg Kienzle, and Gunter Mussbacher. "Concern-oriented software design". In: *International Conference on Model Driven Engineering Languages and Systems*. Springer. Berlin, Heidelberg, 2013, pp. 604–621.

[Ale+09] A. Aleti, S. Bjornander, L. Grunske, and I. Meedeniya. "ArcheOpterix: An extendable tool for architecture optimization of AADL models". In: *2009 ICSE Workshop on Model-Based Methodologies for Pervasive and Embedded Software*. May 2009, pp. 61–71. DOI: 10.1109/MOMPES.2009.5069138.

[AM] System Analysis and Germany Modeling Group at the HPI/University of Potsdam. *Modular Rice University Bidding System (mRUBiS)*. URL: https://www.hpi.uni-potsdam.de/giese/public/mdelab/mdelab-projects/case-studies/mrubis/ (visited on 02/21/2019).

[BA96] Shawn A. Bohner and Robert S. Arnold. *Software change impact analysis*. IEEE Computer Society Press, 1996.

[Bac+05] F. Bachmann, L. Bass, M. Klein, and C. Shelton. "Designing software architectures to achieve quality attribute requirements". In: *SW Proceedings* 152.4 (Aug. 2005), pp. 153–165. ISSN: 1462-5970. DOI: 10.1049/ip-sen:20045037.

[BB01] Barry W. Boehm and Victor R. Basili. "Software Defect Reduction Top 10 List". In: *IEEE Computer* 34.1 (2001), pp. 135–137. DOI: 10.1109/2.962984. URL: https://doi.org/10.1109/2.962984.

[BCW12] Marco Brambilla, Jordi Cabot, and Manuel Wimmer. *Model-Driven Software Engineering in Practice.* Synthesis Lectures on Software Engineering. San Rafael, California: Morgan & Claypool, 2012. URL: http://www.morganclaypool.com/doi/abs/10.2200/S00441ED1V01Y201208SWE001.

[Bec08] Steffen Becker. *Coupled Model Transformations for QoS Enabled Component-Based Software Design.* Vol. 1. Karlsruhe Series on Software Quality. Universitätsverlag Karlsruhe, Jan. 2008.

[Bec15] Kristian Beckers. *Pattern and Security Requirements: Engineering-Based Establishment of Security Standards.* Springer Publishing Company, Incorporated, 2015. ISBN: 3319166638, 9783319166636.

[BFK19] Axel Busch, Dominik Fuchß, and Anne Koziolek. "PerOpteryx: Automated Improvement of Software Architectures". In: *Proceedings of the IEEE International Conference on Software Architecture (ICSA2019): Tool Demo Track.* ICSA'19. to appear. Hamburg, Germany: IEEE, 2019.

[Bih15] C. Bihis. *Mastering OAuth 2.0.* Packt Publishing, 2015. ISBN: 9781784392307.

[Bin+96] Pam Binns, Matt Englehart, Mike Jackson, and Steve Vestal. "Domain-Specific Software Architectures for Guidance, Navigation and Control". In: *International Journal of Software Engineering and Knowledge Engineering* 6 (1996), pp. 201–227.

[BK16] Axel Busch and Anne Koziolek. "Considering Not-quantified Quality Attributes in an Automated Design Space Exploration". In: *Proceedings of the 12th International ACM SIGSOFT Conference on the Quality of Software Architectures.* QoSA'16. Venice, Italy: IEEE, 2016, pp. 50–59. DOI: 10.1109/QoSA.2016.10.

[Bos00] Jan Bosch. *Design and Use of Software Architectures: Adopting and Evolving a Product-line Approach.* New York, NY, USA: ACM Press/Addison-Wesley Publishing Co., 2000. ISBN: 0-201-67494-7.

[BPS04] Danilo Beuche, Holger Papajewski, and Wolfgang Schröder-Preikschat. "Variability management with feature models". In: *Science of Computer Programming* 53.3 (2004). Software Variability Management, pp. 333–352. ISSN: 0167-6423. DOI: https://doi.org/10.1016/j.scico.2003.04.005. URL: http://www.sciencedirect.com/science/article/pii/S0167642304000954.

[BR08] Rainer Böhme and Ralf Reussner. "Validation of Predictions with Measurements". In: *Dependability Metrics.* Vol. 4909. Lecture Notes in Computer Science. Springer-Verlag Berlin Heidelberg, 2008. Chap. 3, pp. 14–18. URL: http://www.springerlink.com/content/662rn13014r46269/fulltext.pdf.

[Bra+08] Jürgen Branke, Kalyanmoy Deb, Kaisa Miettinen, and Roman Slowinski, eds. *Multiobjective Optimization. Interactive and Evolutionary Approaches.* Berlin, Germany: Springer. Lecture Notes in Computer Science Vol. 5252, 2008.

[Bre+09] Bert Bredeweg et al. "Garp3—Workbench for qualitative modelling and simulation". In: *Ecological informatics* 4.5 (2009).

[Bro87] Frederick P. Brooks Jr. "No Silver Bullet Essence and Accidents of Software Engineering". In: *Computer* 20.4 (Apr. 1987), pp. 10–19. ISSN: 0018-9162. DOI: 10.1109/MC.1987.1663532. URL: https://doi.org/10.1109/MC.1987.1663532.

[BSK15] Axel Busch, Misha Strittmatter, and Anne Koziolek. "Assessing Security to Compare Architecture Alternatives of Component-Based Systems". In: *Proceedings of the IEEE International Conference on Software Quality, Reliability & Security.* QRS '15. Acceptance Rate (Full Paper): 20/91 = 22%. Vancouver, British Columbia, Canada: IEEE Computer Society, 2015, pp. 99–108. DOI: 10.1109/QRS.2015.24.

[Bus+16] Axel Busch, Yves Schneider, Anne Koziolek, Kiana Rostami, and Jörg Kienzle. "Modelling the Structure of Reusable Solutions for Architecture-based Quality Evaluation". In: *Proceedings of the 2nd Workshop on Cloud Security and Data Privacy by Design co-located with the 8th IEEE International Conference on Cloud Computing Technology and Science (CloudCom 2016).* CloudSPD'16. Luxembourg: IEEE, 2016, pp. 521–526. DOI:

10.1109/CloudCom.2016.0091. URL: http://ieeexplore.ieee.org/document/7830732/.

[CD00] John Cheesman and John Daniels. *UML Components: A Simple Process for Specifying Component-based Software.* 2000. ISBN: 0201708515.

[CE00] Krzysztof Czarnecki and Ulrich W. Eisenecker. *Generative Programming: Methods, Tools, and Applications.* New York, NY, USA: ACM Press/Addison-Wesley Publishing Co., 2000. ISBN: 0-201-30977-7.

[CH15] Yulia Cherdantseva and Jeremy Hilton. "Information security and information assurance: discussion about the meaning, scope, and goals". In: *Standards and Standardization: Concepts, Methodologies, Tools, and Applications.* IGI Global, 2015, pp. 1204–1235.

[Chu+12] Lawrence Chung, Brian A Nixon, Eric Yu, and John Mylopoulos. *Non-functional requirements in software engineering.* Vol. 5. Springer Science & Business Media, 2012.

[Com+02] Santiago Comella-Dorda, John C. Dean, Edwin Morris, and Patricia Oberndorf. "A Process for COTS Software Product Evaluation". In: *COTS-Based Software Systems.* Ed. by John Dean and Andrée Gravel. Berlin, Heidelberg: Springer Berlin Heidelberg, 2002, pp. 86–96. ISBN: 978-3-540-45588-2.

[Con68] Melvin E Conway. "How do committees invent". In: *Datamation* 14.4 (1968), pp. 28–31.

[DDK02] Marc Dacier, Yves Deswarte, and Mohamed Kaaniche. "Models and tools for quantitat. assessment of operat. security." In: ed. by Sokratis K. Katsikas and Dimitris Gritzalis. IFIP Conference Procs. Chapman & Hall, Jan. 3, 2002, pp. 177–186. ISBN: 0-412-78120-4.

[Deb+02] K. Deb, A. Pratap, S. Agarwal, and T. Meyarivan. "A fast and elitist multiobjective genetic algorithm: NSGA-II". In: *IEEE Transactions on Evolutionary Computation* 6.2 (Apr. 2002), pp. 182–197. ISSN: 1089-778X. DOI: 10.1109/4235.996017.

[DK01] Arie van Deursen and Paul Klint. "Domain-Specific Language Design Requires Feature Descriptions". In: *Journal of Computing and Information Technology* 10 (2001), p. 2002.

[Dur+14] Zakir Durumeric et al. "The Matter of Heartbleed". In: *Proceedings of the 2014 Conference on Internet Measurement Conference.* IMC '14. Vancouver, BC, Canada: ACM, 2014, pp. 475–488. ISBN: 978-1-4503-3213-2. DOI: 10.1145/2663716.2663755. URL: http://doi.acm.org/10.1145/2663716.2663755.

[Eck18] Maximilian Eckert. "Conditional placement of architectural elements to optimize software architectures". 2018.

[Ecl19a] Eclipse Foundation. *Eclipse Modeling Framework (EMF).* https://www.eclipse.org/modeling/emf/. [Online; accessed 25-Mar-2019]. 2019.

[Ecl19b] Eclipse Foundation. *EMF Feature Model (archived project).* http://archive.eclipse.org/archived_projects/featuremodel.tgz. [Online; accessed 25-Mar-2019]. 2019.

[Ecl19c] Eclipse Foundation. *Xtext.* https://www.eclipse.org/Xtext/. [Online; accessed 25-Mar-2019]. 2019.

[Fal+11] Davide Falessi et al. "Decision-making techniques for software architecture design: A comparative survey". In: *ACM Computing Surveys (CSUR)* (2011).

[FK98] Svend Frølund and Jari Koistinen. *Qml: A language for quality of service specification.* Hewlett-Packard Laboratories, 1998.

[Fow02] Martin Fowler. *Patterns of Enterprise Application Architecture.* Boston, MA, USA: Addison-Wesley Longman Publishing Co., Inc., 2002. ISBN: 0321127420.

[Fra+09] Greg Franks, Tariq Omari, C. Murray Woodside, Olivia Das, and Salem Derisavi. "Enhanced Modeling and Solution of Layered Queueing Networks". In: *IEEE Trans. on Software Engineering* 35.2 (2009), pp. 148–161. URL: http://dx.doi.org/10.1109/TSE.2008.74.

[GKN15] Ian Gorton, John Klein, and Albert Nurgaliev. "Architecture Knowledge for Evaluating Scalable Databases". In: *12th Working IEEE/IFIP Conference on Software Architecture, WICSA 2015, Montreal, QC, Canada, May 4-8, 2015.* 2015, pp. 95–104. DOI: 10.1109/WICSA.2015.26. URL: https://doi.org/10.1109/WICSA.2015.26.

[Gli08] Martin Glinz. "A risk-based, value-oriented approach to quality requirements". In: *IEEE Software* 2 (2008), pp. 34–41.

[GMT05] C. Griffin, B. Madan, and T. Trivedi. "State space approach to sec. quant." In: *Computer Software and Applications Conference, 2005. COMPSAC 2005. 29th Annual International.* Vol. 2. COMPSAC, July 2005, 83–88 Vol. 1. DOI: 10.1109/COMPSAC.2005.145.

[Goo+12] Thijmen de Gooijer, Anton Jansen, Heiko Koziolek, and Anne Koziolek. "An Industrial Case Study of Performance and Cost Design Space Explorat." In: *Proceedings of the 3rd ACM/SPEC International Conference on Performance Engineering.* Ed. by Lizy Kurian John and Diwakar Krishnamurthy. ICPE. ICPE Best Industry-Related Paper Award. Boston, Massachusetts, USA: ACM, 2012, pp. 205–216. ISBN: 978-1-4503-1202-8. DOI: 10.1145/2188286.2188319. URL: http://icpe2012.ipd.kit.edu.

[Gre06] Greg Linden. *Marissa Mayer at Web 2.0.* http://glinden.blogspot.com/2006/11/marissa-mayer-at-web-20.html. [Online; accessed 04-Feb-2019]. 2006.

[Gro] Internet Engineering Task Force (IETF) OAuth Working Group. *OAuth 2.0.* https://oauth.net/2/. URL: https://oauth.net/2/.

[Gül03] C. Gülcü. *The Complete Log4j Manual.* QOS.ch, 2003. ISBN: 9782970036906.

[Hap09] Jens Happe. "Predicting software performance in symmetric multi-core and multiprocessor Environments". PhD thesis. 2009. 291 pp. ISBN: 978-3-86644-381-5. DOI: 10.5445/KSP/1000011806.

[Hap11] Lucia Happe. "Configurable Software Performance Completions through Higher-Order Model Transformations". PhD thesis. 2011.

[Her+11] Frank Hermann et al. "Correctness of model synchronization based on triple graph grammars". In: *MoDELS*. Springer. 2011.

[Hol92] John H Holland. "Adaptation in natural and artificial systems. 1975". In: *Ann Arbor, MI: University of Michigan Press and* (1992).

[IET12] Internet Engineering Task Force (IETF). *The OAuth 2.0 Authorization Framework*. https://tools.ietf.org/html/rfc6749. Oct. 2012. URL: https://tools.ietf.org/html/rfc6749.

[Int07] International Organization for Standardization. *ISO/IEC 25030: 2007: Software engineering – Software product Quality Requirements and Evaluation (SQuaRE) – Quality requirements*. Geneva, Switzerland. 2007.

[JBR99] Ivar Jacobson, Grady Booch, and James Rumbaugh. *The Unified Software Development Process*. Boston, MA, USA: Addison-Wesley Longman Publishing Co., Inc., 1999. ISBN: 0-201-57169-2.

[Jef] Jeff Sauro. *How much does a usability test cost?* https://measuringu.com/usability-cost/, year = 2018, note = "[Online; accessed 04-Mar-2019]".

[JO97] Erland Jonsson and Tomas Olovsson. "A Quantitat. Model of the Security Intrusion Proc. Based on Attacker Behavior." In: *IEEE Trans. Software Eng.* 23.4 (1997), pp. 235–245. URL: http://dblp.uni-trier.de/db/journals/tse/tse23.html#JonssonO97.

[KAK09] Jörg Kienzle, Wisam Al Abed, and Jacques Klein. "Aspect-oriented multi-view modeling". In: *Proceedings of the 8th ACM international conference on Aspect-oriented software development*. ACM. New York, NY, USA, 2009, pp. 87–98.

[Kan+90] K. C. Kang, S. G. Cohen, J. A. Hess, W. E. Novak, and A. S. Peterson. *Feature-Oriented Domain Analysis (FODA) Feasibility Study*. Tech. rep. Carnegie-Mellon University Software Engineering Institute, Nov. 1990.

[Kaz+96] R. Kazman, G. Abowd, L. Bass, and P. Clements. "Scenario-based analysis of software architecture". In: *IEEE Software* 13.6 (Nov. 1996), pp. 47–55. ISSN: 0740-7459. DOI: 10.1109/52.542294.

[Kaz+98] Rick Kazman et al. "The architecture tradeoff analysis method". In: *ICECCS*. IEEE. 1998.

[KH06a] Heiko Koziolek and Jens Happe. "A QoS-Driven Development Process Model for Component-Based Software Systems". In: *Proc. 9th International Symposium on Component-Based Software Engineering (CBSE'06)*. Ed. by Ian Gorton et al. Vol. 4063. LNCS. Springer, June 2006, pp. 336–343. ISBN: 3-540-35628-2. URL: http://dx.doi.org/10.1007/11783565_25.

[KH06b] Heiko Koziolek and Jens Happe. "A Quality of Service Driven Development Process Model for Component-basedSoftware Systems". In: *Component-Based Software Engineering*. Ed. by Ian Gorton et al. Vol. 4063. Lecture Notes in Computer Science. July 2006, pp. 336–343. ISBN: 3-540-35628-2. URL: http://dx.doi.org/10.1007/11783565%5C_25.

[Kie+16a] Jörg Kienzle, Anne Koziolek, Axel Busch, and Ralf Reussner. "Towards Concern-Oriented Design of Component-Based Systems". In: *3rd International Workshop on Interplay of Model-Driven and Component-Based Software Engineering* (Saint Malo, France). CEUR, Oct. 2016. URL: http://ceur-ws.org/Vol-1723/.

[Kie+16b] Jörg Kienzle, Anne Koziolek, Axel Busch, and Ralf H Reussner. "Towards Concern-Oriented Design of Component-Based Systems." In: *3rd International Workshop on Interplay of Model-Driven and Component-Based Software Engineering, ModComp 2016*. Ed. by F. Ciccozzi. 2016, pp. 31–36.

[Kie+16c] Jörg Kienzle et al. "VCU: the three dimensions of reuse". In: *International Conference on Software Reuse*. Springer. Berlin, Heidelberg, 2016, pp. 122–137.

[Kla14] Benjamin Klatt. "Consolidation of Customized Product Copies into Software Product Lines". PhD thesis. Karlsruhe Institute of Technology, Germany, 2014. ISBN: 978-3-7315-0368-2. URL:

http://digbib.ubka.uni-karlsruhe.de/volltexte/1000043687.

[Kle+93] M. H. Klein et al. *A Practitioners Handbook for Real-Time Analysis: Guide to Rate Monotonic Analysis for Real Time Systems.* Kluwer Academic Publishers, 1993. ISBN: 0-7923-9361-9.

[KLV06] Philippe Kruchten, Patricia Lago, and Hans van Vliet. "Building Up and Reasoning About Architectural Knowledge". In: *Quality of Software Architectures.* Ed. by Christine Hofmeister, Ivica Crnkovic, and Ralf Reussner. Berlin, Heidelberg: Springer Berlin Heidelberg, 2006, pp. 43–58. ISBN: 978-3-540-48820-0.

[Koz11] Anne Koziolek. "Automated Improvement of Software Architecture Models for Performance and Other Quality Attributes". PhD thesis. Karlsruhe, Germany: Institut für Programmstrukturen und Datenorganisation (IPD), Karlsruher Institut für Technologie, 2011. URL: http://digbib.ubka.uni-karlsruhe.de/volltexte/1000024955.

[KP99] Brian W. Kernighan and Rob Pike. *The Practice of Programming.* Boston, MA, USA: Addison-Wesley Longman Publishing Co., Inc., 1999. ISBN: 0-201-61586-X.

[Kro12] Klaus Krogmann. *Reconstruction of Software Component Architectures and Behaviour Models using Static and Dynamic Analysis.* Vol. 4. The Karlsruhe Series on Software Design and Quality. KIT Scientific Publishing, 2012.

[Kru02] Charles W. Krueger. "Variation Management for Software Production Lines". In: *Software Product Lines.* Ed. by Gary J. Chastek. Berlin, Heidelberg: Springer Berlin Heidelberg, 2002, pp. 37–48. ISBN: 978-3-540-45652-0.

[Kru08] C. W. Krueger. "The BigLever Software Gears Unified Software Product Line Engineering Framework". In: *2008 12th International Software Product Line Conference.* Sept. 2008, pp. 353–353. DOI: 10.1109/SPLC.2008.33.

[LG03] Anna Liu and Ian Gorton. "Accelerating COTS Middleware Acquisition: The i-Mate Process". In: *IEEE Softw.* 20.2 (Mar. 2003), pp. 72–79. ISSN: 0740-7459. DOI: 10.1109/MS.2003.1184171. URL: https://doi.org/10.1109/MS.2003.1184171.

[LHB18] Sebastian Lehrig, Marcus Hilbrich, and Steffen Becker. "The architectural template method: templating architectural knowledge to efficiently conduct quality-of-service analyses". In: *Softw., Pract. Exper.* 48.2 (2018), pp. 268–299. DOI: 10.1002/spe.2517. URL: https://doi.org/10.1002/spe.2517.

[LW13] J. Lenhard and G. Wirtz. "Measuring the Portability of Executable Service-Oriented Processes". In: *2013 17th IEEE International Enterprise Distributed Object Computing Conference.* Sept. 2013, pp. 117–126. DOI: 10.1109/EDOC.2013.21.

[Mad+02] Bharat B. Madan, Katerina Goseva-Popstojanova, Kalyanaraman Vaidyanathan, and Kishor S. Trivedi. "Modeling and Quantification of Security Attributes of Software Systems". In: *2002 International Conference on Dependable Systems and Networks (DSN 2002), 23-26 June 2002, Bethesda, MD, USA, Proceedings.* DSN'02, 2002, pp. 505–514. DOI: 10.1109/DSN.2002.1028941. URL: http://doi.ieeecomputersociety.org/10.1109/DSN.2002.1028941.

[Mad+04] Bharat B. Madan, Katerina Goševa-Popstojanova, Kalyanaraman Vaidyanathan, and Kishor S. Trivedi. "A Method for Modeling and Quantifying the Security Attributes of Intrusion Tolerant Systems". In: *Perform. Eval.* 56.1-4 (Mar. 2004), pp. 167–186. ISSN: 0166-5316. DOI: 10.1016/j.peva.2003.07.008. URL: http://dx.doi.org/10.1016/j.peva.2003.07.008.

[Man17] Object Management Group. *OMG Meta Object Facility Core – Version 2.5.1.* www.omg.org/spec/UML/2.5.1/. Dec. 2017. URL: https://www.omg.org/spec/UML/2.5.1/.

[Mar06] Marissa Mayer. *Google Speed Research.* https://www.youtube.com/watch?v=BQwAKsFmK_8. [Online; accessed 04-Feb-2019]. 2006.

[MCN92] John Mylopoulos, Lawrence Chung, and Brian Nixon. "Representing and using nonfunctional requirements: A process-oriented approach". In: *IEEE Transactions on SE* 18.6 (1992).

[McQ+06] Miles McQueen, Wayne. Boyer, Mark Flynn, and George Beitel. "Time-to-Compromise Model for Cyber Risk Reduction Est." In: *Quality of Protection.* Ed. by Dieter Gollmann, Fabio Massacci, and Artsiom Yautsiukhin. Vol. 23. Advances in Inform. Security.

Springer, 2006, pp. 49–64. ISBN: 978-0-387-29016-4. URL: http://dblp.uni-trier.de/db/series/ais/ais23.html#McQueenBFB06.

[Mel15] John Melton. “AppSensor: Real-Time Event Detection and Response”. In: *AppSec USA 2015*. San Fransisco, CA, USA, 2015.

[Mic09a] Microsoft. *Perimeter Firewall Design*. https://docs.microsoft.com/en-us/previous-versions/tn-archive/cc700828(v=technet.10). [Online; accessed 28-Feb-2019]. 2009.

[Mic09b] Microsoft TechNet. *Recoverability*. https://technet.microsoft.com/en-us/library/bb418967.aspx. [Online; accessed 31-Jan-2019]. 2009.

[Mic16] Microsoft Docs. *Recovery Models*. https://docs.microsoft.com/en-us/sql/relational-databases/backup-restore/recovery-models-sql-server. 2016.

[MS] Sepeedeh Margono and Ben Shneiderman. “A Study of File Manipulation by Novices Using Commands vs. Direct Manipulation”. In: ().

[Nas17] A.E. Nascimento. *OAuth 2.0 Cookbook: Protect your web applications using Spring Security*. Packt Publishing, 2017. ISBN: 9781788290630.

[Nat19] Nati Shalom and Yoav Einav. *Insights into In-Memory Computing and Real-time Analytics*. https://blog.gigaspaces.com/amazon-found-every-100ms-of-latency-cost-them-1-in-sales/. [Online; accessed 04-Feb-2019]. 2019.

[Nie12] Jakob Nielsen. *Usability 101: Introduction to Usability*. https://www.nngroup.com/articles/usability-101-introduction-to-usability/. [Online; accessed 31-Jan-2019]. 2012.

[Nie97] Jakob Nielsen. “Usability Engineering”. In: *The Computer Science and Engineering Handbook*. 1997, pp. 1440–1460.

[NMR10] Qais Noorshams, Anne Martens, and Ralf Reussner. “Using Quality of Service Bounds for Effective Multi-objective Software Architecture Optimization”. In: *Proceedings of the 2nd International Workshop on the Quality of Service-Oriented Software Systems (QUASOSS ’10), Oslo, Norway, October 4, 2010*.

ACM, New York, NY, USA, 2010, 1:1–1:6. ISBN: 978-1-4503-0239-5. DOI: 10.1145/1858263.1858265. URL: http://sdq.ipd.kit.edu/conferences_and_events/quasoss2010/.

[Ora13] Oracle HA Product Managemet. *Technical Comparison Oracle Database 12c vs. IBM DB2 10.5: Focus on High Availability.* Tech. rep. Oracle Corporation, 2013.

[Pag88] Meilir Page-Jones. *The Practical Guide to Structured Systems Design: 2Nd Edition.* Upper Saddle River, NJ, USA: Yourdon Press, 1988. ISBN: 0-13-690769-5.

[Par17] Aaron Parecki. *OAuth 2.0 Simplified.* Lulu.com, 2017. ISBN: 1387130102, 9781387130108.

[Reu+16] Ralf H. Reussner et al. *Modeling and Simulating Software Architectures – The Palladio Approach.* Cambridge, MA: MIT Press, Oct. 2016. 408 pp. ISBN: 9780262034760. URL: http://mitpress.mit.edu/books/modeling-and-simulating-software-architectures.

[RS16] Justin Richer and Antonio Sanso. *Oauth 2 in Action.* Manning Pubns Co, Aug. 2016. ISBN: 9781617293276.

[RSO08] Björn Regnell, Richard Berntsson Svensson, and Thomas Olsson. "Supporting roadmapping of quality requirements". In: *Ieee software* 25.2 (2008).

[SBK17] Max Scheerer, Axel Busch, and Anne Koziolek. "Automatic Evaluation of Complex Design Decisions in Component-based Software Architectures". In: *Proceedings of the 15th ACM-IEEE International Conference on Formal Methods and Models for System Design.* MEMOCODE'17. Vienna, Austria: ACM, 2017, pp. 67–76. ISBN: 978-1-4503-5093-8. DOI: 10.1145/3127041.3127059. URL: http://doi.acm.org/10.1145/3127041.3127059.

[SBK18] Yves Schneider, Axel Busch, and Anne Koziolek. "Using Informal Knowledge for Improving Software Quality Trade-off Decisions". In: *Proceedings of the 12th European Conference on Software Architecture.* ECSA'18. Madrid, Spain: Springer, 2018.

[SC12] Sam Supakkul and Lawrence Chung. "The RE-Tools: A multi-notational requirements modeling toolkit". In: *RE.* IEEE. 2012.

[Sch02] Stuart Schechter. "Quantitatively Differentiating System Security". In: *Workshop on Economics and Information Security.* 2002, pp. 16–17.

[Sch10] Keith Schwarz. *Topological sort algorithm for linear-time sorting of directed acyclic graphs.* `http://www.keithschwarz.com/interesting/code/?dir=topological-sort`. [Online; accessed 14-Dec-2018]. 2010.

[Sch16] Yves Schneider. "Modellierung der Struktureigenschaften von Subsystemen bei architekturellen Entwurfsentscheidungen in komponentenbasierten Systemen". 2016.

[Sch17] Max Scheerer. "Using Concern Weaving to Extend Component-based System Architectures". 2017.

[SGB05] Mikael Svahnberg, Jilles van Gurp, and Jan Bosch. "A Taxonomy of Variability Realization Techniques: Research Articles". In: *Softw. Pract. Exper.* 35.8 (July 2005), pp. 705–754. ISSN: 0038-0644. DOI: `10.1002/spe.v35:8`. URL: `http://dx.doi.org/10.1002/spe.v35:8`.

[SK16] Misha Strittmatter and Amine Kechaou. *The Media Store 3 Case Study System.* Tech. rep. 2016,1. Faculty of Informatics, Karlsruhe Institute of Technology, 2016. URL: `http://digbib.ubka.uni-karlsruhe.de/volltexte/documents/3792054`.

[Sol+02] Rini van Solingen, Vic Basili, Gianluigi Caldiera, and H. Dieter Rombach. "Goal Question Metric (GQM) Approach". In: *Encyclopedia of Software Engineering.* American Cancer Society, 2002. ISBN: 9780471028956.

[ST07] Vibhu Saujanya Sharma and Kishor S. Trivedi. "Quantifying software perf., rel. and sec.: An architecture-based approach." In: *Journal of Syst. and Softw.* 80.4 (Mar. 1, 2007), pp. 493–509. URL: `http://dblp.uni-trier.de/db/journals/jss/jss80.html#SharmaT07`.

[Sta73] Herbert Stachowiak. *Allgemeine Modelltheorie.* Wien: Springer Verlag, 1973. ISBN: 3-211-81106-0.

[SV06] Thomas Stahl and Markus Völter. *Model-Driven Software Development.* John Wiley & Sons, 2006.

[SV12] Thomas L Saaty and Luis G Vargas. *Models, methods, concepts & applications of the analytic hierarchy process.* Vol. 175. Springer Science & Business Media, 2012.

[Sva+03] Mikael Svahnberg, Claes Wohlin, Lars Lundberg, and Michael Mattsson. "A Quality-Driven Decision-Support Method for Identifying Software Architecture Candidates". In: *International Journal of Software Engineering and Knowledge Engineering* 13.5 (2003), pp. 547–573. DOI: 10.1142/S0218194003001421. URL: https://doi.org/10.1142/S0218194003001421.

[SW05] Mikael Svahnberg and Claes Wohlin. "An investigation of a method for identifying a software architecture candidate with respect to quality attributes". In: *Empirical SE* 10.2 (2005).

[Thea] The Guardian. *Over $119bn wiped off Facebook's market cap after growth shock.* https://www.theguardian.com/technology/2018/jul/26/facebook-market-cap-falls-109bn-dollars-after-growth-shock, year = 2018, note = "[Online; accessed 05-Mar-2019]".

[Theb] The Guardian. *The Cambridge Analytica Files.* https://www.theguardian.com/news/series/cambridge-analytica-files, year = 2018, note = "[Online; accessed 05-Mar-2019]".

[TMD09] Richard N. Taylor, Nenad Medvidovic, and Eric M. Dashofy. *Software Architecture: Foundations, Theory, and Practice.* Wiley, 2009. ISBN: 0470167742, 9780470167748.

[TT85] Asser N. Tantawi and Don Towsley. "Optimal Static Load Balancing in Distributed Computer Systems". In: *J. ACM* 32.2 (Apr. 1985), pp. 445–465. ISSN: 0004-5411. DOI: 10.1145/3149.3156. URL: http://doi.acm.org/10.1145/3149.3156.

[Ver13] Verizon. *Data Breach Investigations Report.* 2013.

[VL00] David A. van Veldhuizen and Gary B. Lamont. "Multiobjective Evolutionary Algorithms: Analyzing the State-of-the-Art". In: *Evolutionary Computation* 8.2 (2000), pp. 125–147.

[Vog18] Thomas Vogel. "mRUBiS: An Exemplar for Model-based Architectural Self-healing and Self-optimization". In: *Proceedings of the 13th International Conference on Software Engineering for Adaptive and Self-Managing Systems.* SEAMS '18. Gothenburg, Sweden: ACM, 2018, pp. 101–107. ISBN: 978-1-4503-5715-9. DOI: 10.1145/3194133.3194161. URL: http://doi.acm.org/10.1145/3194133.3194161.

[Wal+13] Martin Walker et al. "Automatic optimisation of system architectures using EAST-ADL". In: *Journal of Systems and Software* 86.10 (2013), pp. 2467–2487. ISSN: 0164-1212. DOI: https://doi.org/10.1016/j.jss.2013.04.001.

[WJ15] Groves Dennis Watson Colin and Melton John. *AppSensor Guide - Application-Specific Real Time Attack Detection & Response.* OWASP Foundation, 2015.

[WSJ07] Lingyu Wang, Anoop Singhal, and Sushil Jajodia. "Toward Measuring Network Security Using Attack Graphs". In: *Proceedings of the 2007 ACM Workshop on Quality of Protection.* QoP. Alexandria, Virginia, USA: ACM, 2007, pp. 49–54. ISBN: 978-1-59593-885-5. DOI: 10.1145/1314257.1314273. URL: http://doi.acm.org/10.1145/1314257.1314273.

[WW04] Xiuping Wu and Murray Woodside. "Performance Modeling from Software Components". In: *Proceedings of the 4th International Workshop on Software and Performance.* WOSP '04. Redwood Shores, California: ACM, 2004, pp. 290–301. ISBN: 1-58113-673-0. DOI: 10.1145/974044.974089. URL: http://doi.acm.org/10.1145/974044.974089.

[Xu08] Jing Xu. "Rule-based automatic software performance diagnosis and design improvement". PhD thesis. Carleton University, 2008.

[Xu12] Jing Xu. "Rule-based automatic software performance diagnosis and improvement". In: *Performance Evaluation* 69.11 (2012), pp. 525–550. ISSN: 0166-5316. DOI: https://doi.org/10.1016/j.peva.2009.11.003.

The Karlsruhe Series on Software Design and Quality

Edited by Prof. Dr. Ralf Reussner // ISSN 1867-0067

Band 1 **Steffen Becker**
Coupled Model Transformations for QoS Enabled Component-Based Software Design.
ISBN 978-3-86644-271-9

Band 2 **Heiko Koziolek**
Parameter Dependencies for Reusable Performance Specifications of Software Components.
ISBN 978-3-86644-272-6

Band 3 **Jens Happe**
Predicting Software Performance in Symmetric Multi-core and Multiprocessor Environments.
ISBN 978-3-86644-381-5

Band 4 **Klaus Krogmann**
Reconstruction of Software Component Architectures and Behaviour Models using Static and Dynamic Analysis.
ISBN 978-3-86644-804-9

Band 5 **Michael Kuperberg**
Quantifying and Predicting the Influence of Execution Platform on Software Component Performance.
ISBN 978-3-86644-741-7

Band 6 **Thomas Goldschmidt**
View-Based Textual Modelling.
ISBN 978-3-86644-642-7

Band 7 **Anne Koziolek**
Automated Improvement of Software Architecture Models for Performance and Other Quality Attributes.
ISBN 978-3-86644-973-2

Band 8 **Lucia Happe**
Configurable Software Performance Completions through Higher-Order Model Transformations.
ISBN 978-3-86644-990-9

Band 9 **Franz Brosch**
Integrated Software Architecture-Based Reliability Prediction for IT Systems.
ISBN 978-3-86644-859-9

Band 10 **Christoph Rathfelder**
Modelling Event-Based Interactions in Component-Based Architectures for Quantitative System Evaluation.
ISBN 978-3-86644-969-5

Band 11 **Henning Groenda**
Certifying Software Component Performance Specifications.
ISBN 978-3-7315-0080-3

Band 12 **Dennis Westermann**
Deriving Goal-oriented Performance Models by Systematic Experimentation.
ISBN 978-3-7315-0165-7

Band 13 **Michael Hauck**
Automated Experiments for Deriving Performance-relevant Properties of Software Execution Environments.
ISBN 978-3-7315-0138-1

Band 14 **Zoya Durdik**
Architectural Design Decision Documentation through Reuse of Design Patterns.
ISBN 978-3-7315-0292-0

Band 15 **Erik Burger**
Flexible Views for View-based Model-driven Development.
ISBN 978-3-7315-0276-0

Die Bände sind unter www.ksp.kit.edu als PDF frei verfügbar oder als Druckausgabe bestellbar.

Band 16 **Benjamin Klatt**
Consolidation of Customized Product Copies into Software Product Lines.
ISBN 978-3-7315-0368-2

Band 17 **Andreas Rentschler**
Model Transformation Languages with Modular Information Hiding.
ISBN 978-3-7315-0346-0

Band 18 **Omar-Qais Noorshams**
Modeling and Prediction of I/O Performance in Virtualized Environments.
ISBN 978-3-7315-0359-0

Band 19 **Johannes Josef Stammel**
Architekturbasierte Bewertung und Planung von Änderungsanfragen.
ISBN 978-3-7315-0524-2

Band 20 **Alexander Wert**
Performance Problem Diagnostics by Systematic Experimentation.
ISBN 978-3-7315-0677-5

Band 21 **Christoph Heger**
An Approach for Guiding Developers to Performance and Scalability Solutions.
ISBN 978-3-7315-0698-0

Band 22 **Fouad ben Nasr Omri**
Weighted Statistical Testing based on Active Learning and Formal Verification Techniques for Software Reliability Assessment.
ISBN 978-3-7315-0472-6

Band 23 **Michael Langhammer**
Automated Coevolution of Source Code and Software Architecture Models.
ISBN 978-3-7315-0783-3

Band 24 **Max Emanuel Kramer**
Specification Languages for Preserving Consistency between Models of Different Languages.
ISBN 978-3-7315-0784-0

Band 25 **Sebastian Michael Lehrig**
Efficiently Conducting Quality-of-Service Analyses by Templating Architectural Knowledge.
ISBN 978-3-7315-0756-7

Band 26 **Georg Hinkel**
Implicit Incremental Model Analyses and Transformations.
ISBN 978-3-7315-0763-5

Band 27 **Christian Stier**
Adaptation-Aware Architecture Modeling and Analysis of Energy Efficiency for Software Systems.
ISBN 978-3-7315-0851-9

Band 28 **Lukas Märtin**
Entwurfsoptimierung von selbst-adaptiven Wartungsmechanismen für software-intensive technische Systeme.
ISBN 978-3-7315-0852-6

Band 29 **Axel Busch**
Quality-driven Reuse of Model-based Software Architecture Elements.
ISBN 978-3-7315-0951-6
